Roberts' Ultimate Encyclopedia Of Hull Pottery

by
Brenda Roberts

"When the blue clay glints through the rusty hillside,
It is not the eye of Man that it beckons,
Nor to his itching fingers;
But to his world-old instinct of obedience
That bids him carry on the trade and tradition of his Father,
Who wrought beauty
From the willing earth."

"The Potteries," by Jean Starr Untermeyer; childhood memories of her native city, Zanesville, Ohio.

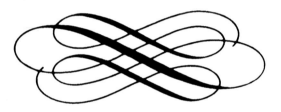

Printed in the United States of America
ISBN: 0-9632136-0-1

Additional copies of this book may be ordered from:

Brenda Roberts
Route 2, Highway 65 South
Marshall, Missouri 65340

$41.95 plus $4.00 postage and handling.

Published by:
Walsworth Publishing Company
306 North Kansas Avenue
Marceline, Missouri 64658

This book is dedicated to my sons,
Jason and Justin

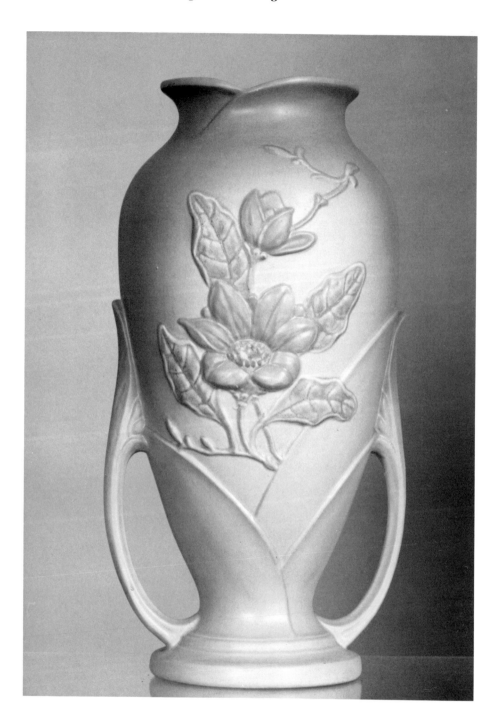

"pottery in its finest sense must have qualities of velvet-like feel to produce an emotional stir and justify a place among your finest possessions. This is a dominant characteristic. . . a balance of subdued color and style seldom obtained but always sought. See and feel the actual piece of ware to become as keenly enthused as were the inspired craftsmen."

Original Hull Promotional Materials, 1946.

Acknowledgments

How do I even begin to tell others just how important this work has been to me, and how do I thank those very special people who have contributed in so many, many ways.

The most valuable contributions have been in the form of spirit and support. My family has certainly been behind me in this effort and they are first on my list of many to whom I am appreciative.

My endless love and respect to my mother and dad who have taught me a personal pride and a belief that anything is possible. To my husband and best friend, Jim, and my sons, Jason and Justin, my love for their patience and forgiving natures during the hours I've spent away from home-life while traveling and researching. For the love and support of an entire family, thanks is merely a word, but it comes truly from the heart.

I must next pay special tribute to the Hull family which made their pottery tradition monumental for over eighty years. Many are now gone, but the memories remain, as does the respect of a nation. I am most grateful for the remembrances of visits granted, personal correspondence, guided tours through the Hull plant, and more. I have always been made to feel welcome in the heart of Ohio's Pottery Valley. And not by the Hulls exclusively, but by the warm local people and the pottery craftsmen within the Hull and other potteries that I have had the pleasure to visit.

Thanks to Larry Taylor, who was always anxious to offer his time and assistance in providing historical facts and information.

A special note of gratitude to Gene Whitlatch, a very special lady, who like myself, is committed to a truthful accounting of the Ohio area's pottery history.

To longtime friend Bob Lloyd, thanks for the years of collector's enthusiasm, the correspondence, the visits, and for sharing your collection. To new friends Jackie Bush, Don and Kari Collett, Duke and Nina Frash, Jerry and Sheri Potmesil, Joe and Betty Yonis, Juan and Bonita Klinehoffer and Larry and Sharon Skillman, who have assisted by sharing special items from their collections, sincere, heartfelt thanks for your caring and your sharing.

Sincere appreciation is noted to Lee Bearden and Casey Kotowicz, Lee's Studio, Marshall, Missouri, and Ted Wright of Zanesville, Ohio, for the wonderful photographs.

Table Of Contents

About The Author

An avid American art pottery collector and dealer of general line antiques since 1974, Brenda Roberts was commissioned by Collector Books, Paducah, Kentucky, for publication of, *The Collectors Encyclopedia of Hull Pottery,* in 1980. Collector interest for Hull Pottery has remained constant and has enabled this volume to be reprinted a number of times, the most current edition being reprinted in 1991, as well as five editions of companion price guides for this volume.

Since 1983, Brenda has been a member of the Advisory Board for, and a regular contributor to *Schroeder's Antiques Price Guide,* published annually by Collector Books. Roberts has also been a contributor to *Wallace-Homestead Flea Market/Collectibles Price Guide* and has written feature materials for publication in, *The Antique Trader Weekly, The National Journal of Glass, Pottery & Collectables, Tri-State Trader, Antique Week, American Clay Exchange, The Collector, The Glaze, American Collector,* and *The Daze, Inc.*

Roberts' continuing interest in The Hull Pottery and attention to detail, coupled with the new spirit of collector interest in Hull has brought about the publication, *Roberts' Ultimate Encyclopedia of Hull Pottery,* as well as, *The Companion Guide To Roberts' Ultimate Encyclopedia of Hull Pottery,* each with accompanying price guides.

She has owned and operated an antiques and appraisal business in Marshall, Missouri, called *Countryside Antiques,* and currently maintains a mail order antiques business of the same name. She is continuing research on American art potteries and has other research projects in progress.

About The Book

While the reasons for collecting are many, Brenda Roberts fell in love with Hull's lovely pastels at age 12, when she was elected to become custodian of a Magnolia ewer purchased by her mother at an estate sale. What began as a single, cherished family momento, escalated to the immense accumulation which allows her to share with you this historical account and pictorial essay of the rise and fall of the Hull Pottery.

The beginning of the gathering of the Roberts' prize trove, later on, in 1974, is not so unlike other rationales for assembling such a collection. Since the introduction of her first Hull publication, the justification for her continuation of the Hull collection has been founded almost entirely on the historical aspects of the company. The quest to bring together a full accounting of the history of the Hull firm has been paramount.

Roberts' Ultimate Encyclopedia Of Hull Pottery, entails the most comprehensive and authoritative work available on the subject of Hull Pottery, containing over 4500 examples from the author's collection of wares, company information, ads and original company brochure pages, as well as a thorough and complete history of the Hull Pottery Company from it's inception to demise, a descriptive listing of lines with dates of manufacture, a separate listing of cookie jars and canisters and over eighty illustrated trademarks.

Also available is an accompanying volume, *The Companion Guide To Roberts' Ultimate Encyclopedia Of Hull Pottery,* which is an indexed chronological guide of original company brochures identifying over 4000 Hull items, entailing Hull's earliest years of stoneware and semi-porcelain production, to lines of the 1950's. Additional brochures illustrate House 'n Garden, Ridge, Heartland and Blue-Belle dinnerware lines. This guide will assist in identification of many Hull items which are rarely found marked.

It is hoped the volumes will not only better acquaint the public of the superior excellence and predominant features of the products of the Hull Pottery, but also to coalesce the history of a respected company in a manner of which it is deserving.

Introduction

The Hull Pottery journey takes place in the small Village of Crooksville, Ohio, where pottery was a way of life, the industrial existence of which gave way to the region's being named "Pottery Center of the World." Beginning in 1905, with a single plant, Hull soon advanced to a second factory in 1907, both which operated until 1930. The first years of pottery production were devoted to common stoneware and stoneware specialties. Soon afterward, semi-porcelain dinnerware lines appeared, as did artwares and decorative tile. By the 1940's, additional classic lines of pastel matte artware emerged. The 1950's were satiated by a multitude of high quality art designs which were absolutely unequalled by others, in style, content and glaze treatments. Hull's final twenty-five years of pottery production centered on casual servingware, suitable for the kitchen or patio, and the vast Imperial floristware line.

Hull's days of reign and rule of the wholesale and retail pottery market have ended ... or have they? After eighty extremely eventful and productive years, the Hull Pottery is at rest ... or is it? While the tradition of operations have ended, the memories subsist, in lovely and serviceable wares which grace today's homes. During the Company's near century of pottery production, Hull wares were known to the trade to be exceptional in quality and value. Hull's popularity then, as now, can only be termed as monumental. The lines are quite diversified, all useful and decorative.

In 1950, the disastrous flood and fire earned Hull a local audience that took notice of lines that were never again to be produced. There were those who contemplated market speculation, however, when the company was reconstructed, the ware basically remained uncollected even though the public was acutely aware that many designs and glaze formulas were lost forever.

Hull's popularity was apparent in the early 1970's when a group of collectors ventured from better known potteries, to build the massive Hull collections that exist today. Although there were people "in the know," Hull remained rather unobtrusive for nearly another decade, while it remained on dealer's lowest shelves, taking a back seat to formidable rivals. The early Hull harbingers with powerful judgment and direction guided, while others observed and eventually supervened, and by the late 1970's, collector interest was profound and observable throughout the United States and Canada. Currently armed with knowledge of the final closing of the plant in 1985, Hull enthusiasts are noticeably prominent in all segments of the collecting market.

There are Hull collectors that specialize in specific art designs; items such as wall pockets, ewers, baskets and cookie jars; specific time frames such as pre or post 1950; and specific clay bodies such as stoneware, yellowware or tile; along with collectors of Hull's famous House 'n Garden dinnerwares, and more. The diversified lines of Hull Pottery offer limitless collecting potential. And, yes, there are collectors who collect all eras, bodies, styles and glazes of Hull Pottery, a phenomena which has made this publication a reality.

Ohio: The Pottery Center Of The World

In the late 1800's, Ohio was noted for clay products ranging from brick and drain tile to excellent ornamental wares. The Southern Muskingum and Northern Perry Counties of Ohio were booming in the stoneware industry at the turn of the Century. With the exception of farming, clay digging and wood chopping, potting was the only livelihood for men of this community. Ohio soon produced virtually every pottery style known, and in many cases, improved upon prior techniques used in the quality of clay and glazes. Local clays, an abundance of wood, coal as well as natural gas to fire the kilns, and a multitude of skilled craftsmen of the area has named the Crooksville and surrounding area, "Pottery Center of the World."

Pioneers found superior local clay veins fourteen feet thick, and clay working, a fact of life in this region, grew out of the farmer's need for inexpensive containers and tableware. Practically every farm had a small pottery. The part-time early pottery operations, worked by farmers between Fall and Spring, were named "Bluebird," because their production resumed when the bluebirds returned from the South and the clay could be mined.

Farmers were soon selling the utility wares needed for canning and the like, to others by way of door-to-door sales. There was a development of the industry on a larger scale after flatboats began transporting cargoes from Zanesville to New Orleans. Country potters hauled their wares to the Putnam boat landing where they unloaded and "stored" on the river bank until the buyers could carry wares onto the flatboats and pack for the shipment south.

In 1888, the effort to expedite stoneware manufacture prompted some potters to produce wares at the foot of Zanesville's Pierce Street, right on the river bank. The area potters were unable to produce adequate numbers when the demand for stoneware products rose to the thousands. However, the potters soon discovered they were able to increase their production by turning their wheels by steam power rather than foot power. Soon full production output was machine-made.

When railroads began operation in Zanesville and surrounding communities, making the shipments of stoneware more practical, it guaranteed nation-wide sales. The locals who had earlier sold wares by knocking on doors now billed the railroad car to some distant point with stop-over privileges at intervening points. Here they sold wares and further accommodated the merchant by delivering to the shop keeper's door.

The Legacy Begins: Addis Emmet Hull

Born in Ireland in 1809, Henry M. Hull, immigrated to the United States as a young man, and made his home in Ohio. Hull, who lived his entire life in the Ohio Valley was a farmer by trade, his death occurring in 1884. Hull and his wife, Vila, had eleven children, six being named in the United States Census of 1850: Jane, 10; Frances, 9; Mary, 7; Henrietta, 5; Robert, 2; and Elizabeth, 1.

One of the eleven, a son, Addis Emmet Hull, born at Todd's Post Office, Morgan County, Ohio, in 1862, was to create a family pottery tradition which not only would carry the Hull name through nearly a century of American manufacturing history, but also would leave the Hull name in the memories and in the hearts of countless historians, as well as stoneware and art pottery enthusiasts, years beyond the pottery's demise.

Hull Enters Manufacturing With Globe Pottery

The proven sales of stoneware, along with new-found marketing availability, could not be ignored by a determined businessmen by the name of Addis Hull. Hull had wide-gained experience in the pottery trade which led to the future organization and management of the A.E. Hull Pottery Company in Crooksville, Ohio.

Crooksville was rapidly becoming the center of the stoneware industry in this section of the State of Ohio, and Hull was acutely aware of this growing market. After finishing country schools, he attended Parsons Business College in Zanesville, Ohio. Addis Hull soon became a traveling salesman for his brother, J.J. Hull, who operated the Star Stonery Company. Hull's business training and personality traits made him a successful salesman, and during his travels for Star he recognized the continually increasing demand for stoneware items.

Other potters' success had given Hull the confidence he needed to join the pottery movement. Promoting himself from sales, Hull entered the field of stoneware manufacturing in 1901, by his association with the initial organizers of The Globe Stoneware Company. Hull was awarded much success, for in Globe's first year of production, the company reportedly had a grade of stoneware that was far superior to any which was being produced in the Valley. William A. Watts, Jeptha Darby Young, and Chester Tatman were Globe's initial organizers and Globe's board of directors elected W.B. Cosgrave, President; Addis E. Hull, General Manager; W.A. Watts, Secretary; S.H. Brown, Treasurer; and Jeptha Darby Young, Superintendent.

Workers of The Globe Stoneware Company are identified as Addis Hull, William Watts, J.D. Young, Ruben Dailey, Albert Aichele, John Wilson, Fred Young, George Aichele, Pat Spring, Frank Watts, Howard Spring, Walter Brown, George Watts, and Frank Wilson.

Hull Leaves Globe to Form A.E. Hull Pottery Company

Addis Emmet Hull, company founder

Although The Globe Stoneware Company had been successful from its inception, conflicts between company officials were ever present. The differences of opinion concerned nearly every facet of the company's operation. Hull continued as Manager of The Globe Pottery until 1904. At that time, major differences arose which could not be resolved and Hull, Watts and Young, Globe's Manager, Secretary, and Superintendent, resigned. Hull sold his interest in Globe, and in July, 1905, organized the A.E. Hull Pottery Company. William Watts and J.D. Young now served the A.E. Hull Pottery Company as Secretary-Treasurer and Superintendent, respectively. G.E. McKeever, who had served as General Salesman of The Star Stoneware Company, additionally pulled up stakes and accepted a sales position with Hull.

Location Site: China Street, Crooksville, Ohio

The A.E. Hull Pottery Company, located at the north end of China Street in Crooksville, Ohio, was modern in every respect. Hull's newly constructed pottery plant had four updraft kilns called "Bee Hives," and two small kilns used for decorative firing. The four largest kilns, twenty-two feet in diameter, were heated with natural gas produced nearby. The updraft kilns allowed the flames to pass through holes in the floor up, through, and around the stacks of ware and pass through apertures in the arched crown. The smoke was collected by the hovel, or cone-shaped chimney, which formed the roof. Records of an early engineer designated positioning of trialed wares in muffle kilns. This was no doubt shortly after Hull expanded to take in another facility. In this type of kiln, the chamber in which the ware was placed was closed to the flames by walls of fire clay, called a muffle. The flames passed under, around and over the chamber, being fired by heat which radiated through the walls. Edgar K. McClellan, an early ceramic engineer, included notations in his personal notebooks related to the company's additionally firing by use of the tunnel kiln, installed in 1923. The tunnel kiln, operated 24 hours per day, firing continuously while cars moved very slowly through the tunnel.

Edward Watts was 29 when the Hull plant was erected. His varied pottery experience began by assisting bricklayers and kiln makers at the Hull. After the completion of the pottery, Watts gained employment with Hull and processed the first clay used by the pottery from a pug mill. Watts, claimed to have had a hand in everything there was to do as a potter, and in 1966, concluded his work record at age 90, retiring from the Hull Pottery.

As the current market dictated, the company's production centered on stoneware and stoneware specialties. There was no question as to the impending success of the new organization headed by Hull, a young man respected in the community for his known abilities and expertise in the field of sales. He soon established the same excellent reputation as a manufacturer. Through successful management and honest dealings, Hull merited and maintained the confidence of his entire community, and in years to come, merited this enviable stature from an entire nation.

Need For Expansion: Purchase of The Acme Pottery Company

Demand for kitchenware items was so great that only two years into production, Hull found it necessary to expand operations. Keeping with current trends, Hull desired to continue all phases of stoneware manufacture, but also noted the acute interest in porcelain kitchenware items. Hull was anxious to make his move on a new market at the earliest possible date. In lieu of delaying production while current facilities were enlarged, and rather than building an entirely new plant, Hull secured control of The Acme Pottery's building, equipment and real estate. Hull suffered no delays in production, as Acme was readily equipped with the necessary machinery required for the manufacture of semi-porcelain items. In 1907, while Hull's Plant No. 1 continued production of stoneware and stoneware specialities, the conversion was quickly made to manufacture Hull's own porcelain kitchenware lines in Plant No. 2. Hull immediately discontinued manufacture of all Acme products.

The tiny Village of Crooksville offered no opposition to Hull's plan, considering this allowed the near 400 Acme craftsmen to retain employment. Hull's keen business sense had not only secured a readily equipped plant, needing only minor modifications, but also provided him with a predisposed, talented and qualified work force to man the operations. Hull was very fortunate indeed to enlist Acme's skilled dinnerware mechanics, imported from the West Liverpool pottery district, along with a select crew of hundreds of other highly experienced tradesmen for his new venture in porcelain production.

Construction of a new plant, installation of the required machinery and equipment, along with recruiting a skilled work force would have taken months, perhaps years to acquire. However, with the purchase of The Acme Pottery, the entire operations and crew were immediately at Hull's disposal. Hull had previously completed carefully detailed studies of the lines needed in the kitchen, and the Acme

Building, Hull's Plant No. 2 immediately converted production from Acme's semi-porcelain dinnerware to Hull's own style of porcelain products, such as bowls, nappies, casseroles, butters, baking dishes, cereal sets, etc. Hull's Plant No. 1 on China Street continued production of common stoneware and a line of stoneware specialties, heralding they were, "surpassed in quality and variety by no others."

A token accessory to the Acme building was Crooksville's first electric light plant. The Acme Electric Light Company was included as part of the package. One 75 K.W. two-phase generator had been installed in the pottery in 1905, and until 1908, the engine used for the pottery through the day was also the lighting generator at night.

In the earliest years that Hull occupied the old Acme building, there appeared to be a need for drinking water, and an enterprising eleven-year-old lad by the name of LeRoy (Sleepy) Moore, found he could collect 50 cents per week, per employee to whom he served water daily. Sleepy made several trips per day, carrying heavy bottles, jugs, and chamber pots brimmed with water, from Main Street, Crooksville, over the crest to Hull's Plant No. 2.

This postcard, illustrating Hull's No. 2 Plant, was printed by Edmiston Book & Stationary Company. It is marked, "Made in Germany, 1908."

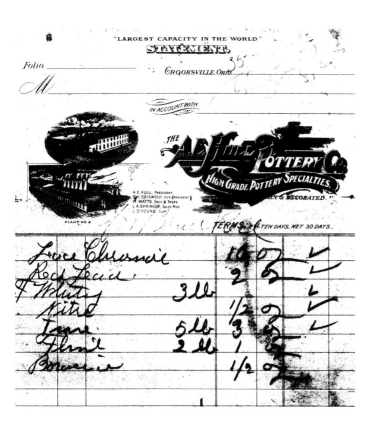

This early Hull Pottery statement listed company officers: A. E. Hull, President; F. H. Griswold, Vice President; W. Watts, Secretary and Treasurer; L. A. Springer, Sales Manager; and J. D. Young, Superintendent. William K. McClellan, Hull's head Ceramic Engineer of the day, apparently jotted necessary ingredients and formulas on whatever was handy, in this case, the firm's statement.

A.E. Hull's statement and envelope of about 1908, illustrates both Plants No. 1 and No. 2, and boasts the, "Largest Capacity in the World," further advertising production of "High Grade Pottery Specialties, Plain and Decorated." Plant No. 1 had four updraft kilns, while Plant No. 2 had six kilns, and two decorating kilns.

Traffic Expert Assigned to Manage Hull's Shipments

With the additional plant, Hull was afforded unexcelled shipping facilities by now being located on both The Pennsylvania and New York Central Railroads. Carloads were shipped daily and customers had the option of shipments being made by either railway. The two plants were responsible for shipping 900 carloads per year. Business was so great that Hull found it necessary to hire an expert traffic manager to take charge of all shipping arrangements.

Hull accepted all orders subject to, and contingent upon; strikes, legislation, fire, accidents, or other causes beyond the company's control. A.E. Hull Pottery, as well as other potteries, were forced to advertise that due to variation in materials used in manufacture it was impossible to produce earthenware (either porous, or semi-vitreous,) that would not craze eventually, therefore, their products could not be guaranteed against crazing after a long period of time. The guarantee to withstand crazing was for a reasonable period of time only, and the pottery reserved the right to refuse to adjust claims, when in their judgment, the merchandise had remained in stock too long.

Hull advertised their products to be fired with "stilts" and with the distinct understanding that stilt marks may be visible on any piece. For buyers who required pieces without these marks, special prices applied.

Although error was small, Hull could not guarantee sizes, capacities, and weights to be exactly as advertised. Shrinkage in the manufacture of pottery could not be precisely controlled due to varying materials and conditions, including the human element.

All goods were carefully packed, inspected and delivered to transportation companies in good condition. Prices for bulk packing in trucks or railroad cars were based on packing with straw between the items ordered and did not include containers of any kind. Excelsior packing was used if specified by the customer with an additional charge of 5% to regular prices. Containers supplied included crates, barrels, boxes and kegs.

More costly were the L.C.L. (Less than Car Load) shipments that were provided by Hull's expert packers using hand-made hardwood crates strapped with iron bands for strengthening. An additional 25% to the L.C.L. weight was the formula used to determine delivery cost and while 24 cents delivered 100 pounds of stoneware in a L.C.L. shipment to Columbus, Ohio, the costs to western and southern customers was $2.96 per 100 pounds for the same delivery. Prices for packing in containers was based on the use of the cheapest container that would suitably contain the items ordered and meet railroad company specifications for safe transportation to destination. Higher priced containers carried extra charges.

Accidents, delays in delivery, and loss by transportation companies were beyond the pottery's control, and all claims were made against the transportation company. However, Hull offered assistance to the purchaser in claim adjustments against the transportation companies.

Diversified Lines Offered

The company was afforded the opportunity of two different railway companies which ran beside their two plant facilities where the company's initial manufacture was separated: stoneware production in Plant No. 1, and semi-porcelain production in Plant No. 2.

Early Hull products centered on both stoneware and stoneware specialties and semi-porcelain products. Many types of wares were introduced to the market which included, a full line of quality blue and white stoneware, green tinted stoneware and brown stoneware with or without lined interiors, embossed with such motifs as plums, cherries, birds and cattle. Other products included Zane Grey banded ware, yellowware, and absolute white bodied semi-porcelain restaurant ware, hotel ware, toilet ware and kitchenware, in plain and embossed shapes which were decorated with bands, decalmonia, and stamps underglaze and overglaze, while others were air-brushed, blended, and hand decorated.

As numerous early designs, such as the blue and white and green tinted stoneware, were manufactured by more than one pottery company, in some cases identity truly cannot be established without a trademark. As far as items that were made exclusively by Hull, or glazing techniques that were exclusively Hull's, identification can be verified

Early Hull stoneware lines included the popular embossed designs illustrated above. These illustrations are reprinted from original company catalogues. These stoneware staples were offered in blue and green tints, mottled blue and white and brown ware lined with white.

THE A. E. HULL POTTERY CO.

MANUFACTURERS

Yellow Ware, Blended Ware, Stoneware, White Sanitary Cooking Ware

NEW YORK OFFICE: 200 5TH AVE.
WAREHOUSE: 57 HUDSON ST., JERSEY CITY

GENERAL OFFICES AND FACTORY
CROOKSVILLE, OHIO

An A.E. Hull Pottery Company letterhead of about 1910, advertised several of their distinctive lines: Yellow Ware, Blended Ware, Stoneware, and White Sanitary Cooking Ware. Add to this, Blue Band, Zane Grey, porcelain Toilet Ware, Cereal Ware and decorated kitchen ware, and you can readily see why Hull was considered to have offered the most complete kitchen lines in the United States.

through early brochure pages. First glimpses of many of Hull's earliest unmarked designs have been made available in a companion guide to this volume, which illustrates nearly 300 reprinted original company brochure pages. Additional early stoneware included black and white stoneware, used for food storage and preservation included 15 to 30 gallon meat tubs, churns, shoulder jugs, preserve jars, bean pots, milk pans, French pots and one-half to six gallon butters. Hull supplied many utilitarian wares to outside markets, as well as farms and households within the Ohio area which included milk crocks, preserving jars and refrigerator jars. Green glazed stew and bake pans with metal bails were used by nearly every area farm wife. Douglas Young, grandson of Jeptha Darby Young, began his work with the company around 1925, being paid 25 cents per hundred for attaching bails to those stew pans.

Hull was responsible for flooding the market with many banded semi-porcelain and stoneware utility items. These were decorated both underglaze and overglaze in nearly every color imaginable: blue, green, yellow, red, mauve, black, pink, ivory, brown, white and peach, as well as others. Some of these color bandings were additionally teamed with gold lines which varied in composition. Decorated items included, but were not limited to, range and refrigerator jars, bake dishes, jugs, nested bowls, casseroles with plates, handled individual casseroles, pie plates and bean pots. Hull's sales campaigns advertised many of the bowls, jugs and casseroles in sets for "bride's kitchen sets, pantry assortments and baking assortments." Bowl and nappy sets were advertised for baking as well as

serving, for "salads, fruits or as mixing bowls."

The company was prolific in its manufacture of semi-porcelain cereal ware sets which included cereal jars, spice jars, cruets and salt boxes. Semi-porcelain jars were of Hull's high-fired absolute white body, decorated in a variety of pleasing decalomania designs. Stoneware cereal sets, plain and embossed, were offered in banded, decaled or solid high gloss colors.

Early art lines included such items as vases, jardinieres, flower pots, hanging baskets and bulb bowls, which varied from stoneware to semi-porcelain bodies. Art lines were decorated in solid matte and high gloss glazes, blended matte and high gloss finishes, tinted glazes, and stark white mattes, as well as a full palette of colors. Embossed art designs included tulips, hearts and arrows, basketweave, ropes and tassels, birds, trees, stylized fans, harps, ferns and leaves. Plain and decorated florists' pots and saucers, and garden ware were also produced during Hull's earliest years.

Cookie jar collectors will be delighted with the Hull jars that have been authenticated by original company information. The early jars included both stoneware and semi-porcelain bodies in tinted and solid gloss and matte finishes with hand painted underglaze and overglaze decorations.

Clay bodies varied from that of absolute white, to ivory white, to dark ivory buff, yellowware and tile bodies. Much of the material used in Hull's early stoneware manufacture consisted of what was then known as yellow home clay, mined at Crooksville. Clay for tiling operations was obtained from Crooksville's Mineral Addition.

Hull Proclaims to be Largest Manufacturers
of Stoneware Specialties

A early billing, which dates about 1908, illustrates both Hull plants, proclaiming unprecedented products, as well as years of experience of officers, all natives, with exception of one, of Perry County, Ohio. Hull announced in 1910, to be the largest manufacturer in the United States of blue banded kitchenware and Zane Grey stoneware, which was also referred to as "Bristol glazed." In this billing, Hull said of it's two manufacturing plants:

"We are now without question the largest manufacturers of Stoneware Specialties in the United States. We have grown from four kilns, to a capacity of ten kilns, and two decorating kilns. All the officers are natives of Perry County except Mr. Griswold, Vice President, whose home is in Boston, Mass., and all are men of practical worth in the business. Mr. Griswold, who employs from twenty to thirty traveling salesmen constantly, is one of the largest users of the company's products."

"Almost all the staple articles in the Stoneware Specialty line have been originated by us, and we are at this time the exclusive makers of an entirely *new* line. We were the first to manufacture Decalcomania and Gold Decorated Stoneware, and have already placed these goods in all the principal markets of the United States."

"While the company was only organized in 1905, all of its officers have been engaged in the manufacture of Stoneware and Stoneware Specialities for twenty years or more, and are giving their undivided attention to the development of an industry the perfection of the product of which is contingent upon a superior quality of clay for its base. It is conceded that the very best clay for this purpose is found in the hills of Perry County, Ohio."

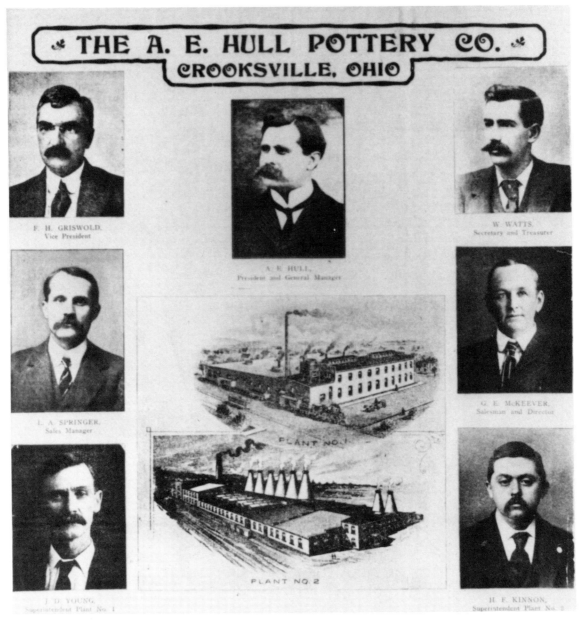

THE A. E. HULL POTTERY CO.
CROOKSVILLE, OHIO

F. H. GRISWOLD,
Vice President

A. E. HULL,
President and General Manager

W. WATTS,
Secretary and Treasurer

L. A. SPRINGER,
Sales Manager

G. E. McKEEVER,
Salesman and Director

PLANT NO. 1

PLANT NO. 2

J. D. YOUNG,
Superintendent Plant No. 1

H. F. KINNON,
Superintendent Plant No. 2

Production Of Zane Grey Ware

Kitchenware items such as salt boxes, jugs, nested bowls, nappies, custards, butters, and 1 to 6 gallon food containers were staple products in stoneware and were referred to as Hull's Zane Grey ware. Hull best described the evolution of Zane Grey in this early account.

"The Zane Grey line is being introduced to the trade to meet the growing demand for a lower priced kitchen ware. The A.E. Hull Pottery Co. ceramists, after a year of research and experiments, have devised a body made of refined clays and a glaze of extra soft, glossy texture free from excessive pinholes and crazing, to suit this body. The shapes of the bowls, nappies, jugs and butters are the same as the white and blue band ware with the above body practically vitreous and the blue band decoration under the glaze. Besides these kitchen specialties a line of food containers from one-half gallon capacity, including all sizes, to six gallons capacity are made, using the Zane Grey body, decoration and glazes. The quality of the whole line is on a par with the white ware and the price is substantially lower. With these qualifications we are recommending this line to the trade where cheapness, quality, design and texture, together with usual Hull service is desired."

Blue and White Stoneware and Yellowware Production

Collectors and dealers alike will be amazed to learn that Hull manufactured most every popular design of blue and white stoneware that affronts today's market. Add to this, green tinted wares and brown ware lined with white, in tankards, dairy jugs, butters, salt boxes, ewers and basins, and others, including a sanitary water keg embossed with deer decor, produced in three, four, five and six gallon sizes. Designs included, but were not limited to, embossed roses, birds, plums, daisies, cherries, and cattle.

Yellowware production comprised a large portion of the company's output. Early advertising tells the story of the gradual unfolding of Hull's yellowware production:

"Yellow bowls have come to be almost a household necessity. For the kitchen they find a multitude of uses such as bread mixing, as food containers, and for hand receptacles for anything the housewife uses in her kitchen. The yellow-bowl is first of all a more inexpensive bowl than most any other. The A.E. Hull Pottery Co. are manufacturing yellow bowls in large quantity at a remarkably low figure and combined with several other notable features. The Hull yellow bowl is made with a round spherical bottom which offers no hindrance to the housewife in stirring or cleaning the bowl. There are no sharp creases in the bottom. This yellow bowl is also made of a body that is fired until practically vitreous, thereby insuring a highly bonded and durable bowl with a bright glossy glaze and brown bands for decoration."

Production Of White Sanitary Ware

Tremendous volumes of plain white hotel and toilet ware, along with enormous numbers of cooking ware and kitchenware items were manufactured in Hull's early years in what was referred to as "American White Bodies."

Shapes were practical and items were advertised as "sanitary," made of absolute white-bodied semi-procelain fired at high temperatures to assure strength and durability. Hull's toilet and kitchenware was competitively priced and trade catered to both residences and hotels alike. The company listed toilet ware sets in both "Hull Shape" or "Rex Shape." Cuspidors were distinguished as either "hotel shaped," being flat-based, or "parlor shaped," which had a round base. Hotel ware offered sugars in two sizes, 30's and 36's; two sizes of oyster bowls, plain or decorated; and tapering and straight coffee mugs, either plain or decorated, along with what were referred to as Philadelphia coffee mugs.

William McClellan delineated his formula for the A.E. Hull White Body on this early Hull statement form, dating about 1915.

Hull boasted of being the first and original producers of the American White Body, underglazed, raised blue banded kitchenware. Hull reported their "careful and constant study of the lines needed in the kitchen, together with excellent modeler to transform ideas to actual plaster model, and ceramic engineers to supervise the manufacturing processes in one of the most modern potteries, insures the buyer of Hull Ware, the most practical shapes possible, made of absolutely white body, with the deep blue raised bands under the glaze. The ware is strong and durable on account of the selection of clays in the body, and the high temperature attained in the kilns."

In Hull's words, the quality of hotel and toilet ware was, "the same as the Blue Band Ware since the same body and glaze is used. Decorations are made over the glaze with decalcomania and color bands both selected for their pleasing colors and the fact that they fit nicely into the average color scheme of the ordinary room, be it hotel or residence." The glaze treatments were many, but some toilet wares included white, royal blue, or blue mottled combinets, ewers and basins, cuspidors, and chambers. Additional blue banding was offered to the plain or color glazed wares for an extra fifty-cents per dozen. Toilet sets were offered in five, six, seven, eight, nine, eleven and twelve piece assortments.

Jugs, bake pans, mixing bowls, bean pots, teapots and fluted nappies were also offered in white or blue mottled glazes. The term, "decorated goods," referred to the wares that were decorated in stamped or overglaze decalcomania, with or without color bands. The five-banded line was a refined semi-porcelain kitchenware line which included several combinations of nested bowls, three teapots and three coffee servers. This line was manufactured in a semi-porcelain, high-fired white body, and featured a series of five overglaze bands which encircled the wares' mid-line or top edge. The lowest band, being the thinnest, widened with each step of elevation.

Cereal Ware Production

Original company advertising introduced cereal sets to the retail market: "The square cereal set has been sold heretofore as a general rule in sets of fifteen pieces. We have decided to establish a new method in regard to the marketing of our standard square cereal set. Now, the buyer may make up his own set composition or buy open stock as he pleases. We offer seven decorations from which to choose, which are representative as to designs and colorings. The following names will be furnished in any of our decorations in any quantity. For cereal jars we have coffee, tea, rice, cereal, flour, sugar. For spice jars: cinnamon, ginger, pepper, allspice, mustard, nutmeg. For bottles either oil or vinegar. Salt boxes are furnished in every decoration. These sets are made by the casting process from the white body, used for our Blue Band Ware, which insures a close, durable body."

The May 31, 1917, issue of Pottery, Glass, and Brass Salesman, further praised Hull's cereal sets as follows: "The popularity of cereal sets still continues. The demand is growing every day and the manufacturers are hard pressed to keep abreast of it. In spite of this, the A.E. Hull Pottery, of which Guy Cooke, 200 Fifth Avenue, is the New York representative, has found time to work on four new decorations - a parrot in dark blue in a yellow panel, with dark blue bands on either side; a scroll effect in terra cotta color on both the top and bottom of the jars; a vine treatment in a combination of colors, including dark blue and green; and a classic design in green, blue and golden brown. In these new decorations the concern has gotten away from the old stereotyped forms usually seen on cereal sets. The ware is white, high fired and sanitary. Each set contains fifteen pieces, including large and small jars, vinegar and oil jugs, and salt box."

Cereal ware was not limited to square designs as Hull also produced round stoneware and round semi-porcelain cereal sets. These sets, banded in blue, gold or yellow with black lettering, consisted of large jars for rice, beans, prunes, tapioca, cereal, sugar, coffee and tea. Also available were jars in one-half gallon and one gallon sizes that were offered separately from the actual cereal set. The larger jars were complimented by spice jars for ginger, allspice, cloves, nutmeg, cinnamon, and pepper, and teamed with matching salt boxes. Additionally, banded round semi-porcelain utility jars were manufactured in two, four, eight and twelve-quart sizes which were lettered flour, bread, cakes, lard, sugar, etc. A complimenting round jar was available in two, three, or four-gallon sizes.

McClellan's Early Hull Bodies and Glazes

William K. McClellan was employed as Ceramic Engineer for Hull. His personal notebook of 1908, delineates glaze formulas for the pottery's output. Bright Glazes #4 through #14 are noted, along with formulas for, "stippled blended glazes, blue glaze #73, A.E. Hull Stoneware Glaze, Blue Green Glaze for Terra Cotta, Peacock Blue," as well as others known only to McClellan by their numerical coded designation. In McClellan's own hand, referring to firing processes, "wall pockets and decorated vases go in 11/10, will be out 11/14." Further notation included the kiln location of the ware McClellan waited to emerge from the fire, "3 rings, 4 saggers from bottom."

McClellan's personal papers include an A.E. Hull Pottery Co. letterhead from about 1910 with the following forty-seven colors listed:

1 — 567-Or.
2 — 1020-Or.
3 — 1055-Turq.
4 — 602-Brown
5 — 522-Brown
6 — 594-Mulberry
7 — 1078-Carmine
8 — 28-Carmine
9 — 792-Crimson
10 — 569-Blue Green
11 — 706-Ap. Green.

12 — 137-Moss Green
13 — 56-Dark Green
14 — 701-Dove Green
15 — 7231-Dark Green
16 — 100-Light Green
17 — 130-Green
18 — 104-Stamp Green
19 — 5-Russlin Green
20 — 504-O.K. Green
21 — 1033-Buff
22 — 1052-Old Gold
23 — 12-Mahogany
24 — 95-Brown
25 — 4002-Carmine
26 — 17-Pink
27 — 2-Pink
28 — 7-Pink
29 — 1023-Green
30 — 561-Green
31 — 770-Green
32 — 108-Blue
33 — 4-Blue
34 — 511-Blue
35 — 2-Blue
36 — 55-Ash Grey
37 — 1940-Yellow
38 — 1939-Yellow
39 — Hancock Black
40 — Pink Stain
41 — B. Stain
42 — Green Stain
43 — Pink Stain
44 — Kings Blue
45 — Hommel French Green
46 — 1-Blue St. 1 Pt.
47 — 100-Pink Plus 20 Gl.

The books which belonged to McClellan offer insight into an era for which there is no other present-day access. McClellan outlined formulas for a variety of bodies: "American White Body, Substitute for American Body, China White Body, English Body, Ferro Body, Garrett Body, Spinks Body, Regular Body, New Hull Body, Hall China Body, Acme Body, Electric Porselin, White Adas Hull Body, New Lexington Porselin, and a Sagger Body."

A.E. Hull's White Body was made up of, "Ten Ball Clay, Georgia Clay, Golden Clay and Flint Spar by mixing 3001 pounds of body with 39 buckets of water, 18 pints to bucket." This combination, plus soda ash and additional hot water made up Hull's casting slip. McClellan's listed formulas ranged in everything from a glaze for "Wedgwood Jasper," to a recipe of molasses, raisins, rain water and corn crack, for his "home made whiskey."

Preparing clay for the jiggermen and presses was a wearisome task. In Hull's earliest years it was necessary for many of the bodies and glazes to be ground and blended for hours by mixers which were turned by hand. Hull's Ceramic Engineers gave explicit instructions for compiling the components of the various mixtures, as well as instructions concerning the length of time necessary for

blending those mixtures. The workers charged with assisting the engineers in the preparation of clay bodies labored hours on end balancing buckets filled with heavy, wet clays and slips. A portion of Hull's Plant No. 2 had an upper story and it was necessary to lift the cumbersome clay buckets to overhead conveyor belts which moved the loads more easily upstairs and to other work sites within the plant. Safety was a major concern for those assigned the task of working in either plant near the conveyor systems. The machinery, when in operation, was reported to be treacherously dangerous enough to remove a limb if safety precautions were not painstakingly adhered to by all in immediate contact.

Little was left to the imagination, as McClellan offered an entire rainbow of colors: "Blended for Dec. Ware, A.E. Hull Yellow Glaze, Green for Pantry Sample, Tulip Yellow for Pantry, Osker Line Yellow, #100 Red Matt, Matt Blue Green, Shoulder Bowl Green, White Jep Young Stoneware Glaze, O.S.U. (Ohio State University) Glaze, Matt #2 for Art White Ware, Vellum Glaze #2, French Brown, Mission Green, Canary Crackele, Green Crackele #2 & #3, Cobalt Blue Ware #2, Yellow Glaze for Stoneware, Ivory Yellow Glaze, Yellow Matt Glaze Canary, Brown Pitcher Glaze, Soft Mahogany Glaze, Hard Glaze #12, Hard Green Glaze, Hard Yellow Glaze, Red Heat Glaze, Palace Glaze, White Enamel Glaze, Crystal Line Glaze, ABC Glazes, White Stoneware Glaze, New Royal Glaze, Robbin Eggs Blue, Cerulean Blue, Brown Stoneware Glaze, Greenware Bisk, Salmon, Coffee Pot Green, Matt Blue, Matt Rose, Matt Black, Black Enamel, White Porselin Glaze for Art, Zane Grey, Hawthorn Glaze, Art Green, #8 Matt Green, Egg Yellow Glaze, Blue Pan Glaze, French Matt Glaze, Rose Tint Tulip, New Buff Tint, Blue Matt Tint, Blue Green Tint," along with additional formulas for stains and banding colors. Stains included, "Lilack, Gold, Pink, Black, Dark Red, Lt. Red, Green, Light Blue," while lusters were noted as, "L.Y. Yellow, L.P. Purple, L.O. Orange, L. Lt. Green, L.M. Mulberry, and L.C. Chamois." Overglaze colors included: "Vellum #182, Flux #9, Black French #6, and Mazapine Blue #100."

Kiln and firing instructions of the teens, described by McClellan, included notations such as, "Bright Glaze - Red Stain, do not cover sagger tight; trile for stoneware glaze, OK for cusp.; blue cereal sets, clear white glaze OK on cereal sets; Blended Jars one fire; Stoneware glaze - Ads. Hull, O.S.U. OK; OK Royal Deep Blue Art Glaze; blue band bodies OK; kiln #1, White Enamel - Cone 9 OK; A.E. Hull in use - good; OK McC - fire white ware; White body #22 and White Glaze #5 - one out of tunnel kiln is in use for blue band bowls, mugs, Hall Boy; Lt. Green for Plain Luster; Mother Pearl - New Glaze on Bisk ware; New White Glaze for one fire - white ware; Redish Matt trile in the kiln #3 - OK color; Yellow glaze - trile in #4 kiln; green for cusp. - one fire; Yellow crystal - the trile of #6 kiln is good; blue band white stoneware glaze good, good; ivory glaze, OK glaze on square rim bowls, cone 9 in tunnel kiln; spool vase glaze OK, vase, wall pockets; Blend #4-1 for vase sample; #10 vase glaze; blue vase glaze - deep royal blue - OK blue vases; stipple vase - sample glaze; printing blue for Delft - June 7-17 trile blue."

McClellan's notebooks offer only shards of information which refer, most likely to contacts or potential buyers of early Hull wares. Names that are discernible are noted as, "Gimble Bros. J.T. Taylor, Edwin Knowles, Tom McNicke, Bill Clark, and Harry Roberts.

THE A. E. HULL POTTERY CO.

Date _____19_____   Plant No. 1

PLACERS—FETTLERS REPORT

ITEM	NO. SAGGARS FETTLED NO. SAGGARS PLACED	HOURS

THE A. E. HULL POTTERY CO.

Date _____19_____   Plant No. 1

GLAZING REPORT

ITEM	NO. GLAZED	HOURS	REASONS FOR DELAY

THE A. E. HULL POTTERY CO.

Date _____19_____   Plant No. 1

PRESS NO. _____

ITEM	PRODUCTION	HOURS OP.	REASONS FOR DELAY

Quality control measures included Placers - Fettlers Reports for the sagger makers and kiln workers; and Glazing Reports which totalled numbers glazed, hours, and reasons for delays. The Clay Presser Reports counted production numbers, hours, and again, reasons for delays. The Weekly Finishers Report tallied production as well as broken items, and shows us the plant worked at least six days per week. These forms, when completed and signed, were turned in at the office. They provided a very important service by allowing managers access to actual plant production and fall backs, and were also a necessary part of payroll processing. Orders of bisque stock were delivered to the glazing department, noting numbers and dates promised, and the glaze room was responsible for noting shortages and reasons for any delays. A separate Warehouse Shortage form was also necessary to keep abreast of delays and shortages of production. These forms date from the late teens and early 1920's.

THE A. E. HULL POTTERY CO.
Weekly Finishers Report   No. [   ]

Week Beginning _____, 192__ Ending _____, 192__																		
Product	Prod	Br	Prod	Br	Prod	Br	Prod	Br	Prod	Br	Prod	Br	Prod	Br	Prod	Br	Prod	Br
Thursday																		
Friday																			
Saturday																			
Monday																			
Tuesday																			
Wednesday																			
Total																			

Prod stands for Produce
Br stands for Broken   Signed _____
                                                              Finisher

BISQUE STOCK

Order No. _____

Date Promised _____

In Stock _____

Short _____

_____

_____

_____

Delivered to Glazing Dept. _____

_____

Return to Office At Once.

Signed _____

GLAZE ROOM

Order No. _____

Date Promised _____

Date Glazed _____

Shortages: _____

_____

_____

Reasons For Delay: _____

Return to Office At Once.

Signed _____

WAREHOUSE SHORTAGE

Order No. _____

Date Promised _____

Drawn From Kiln No. _____

Short Following Items:

Hull Recruited by The American Clay Products Company

In the early 1920's, there was unprecedented activity in all circles in this section of Ohio, and this boom in business was overshadowed only by the promised activity to come. A great campaign was drafted to accentuate the region's bountiful natural resources in an effort to entice businessmen to move into the area. Local reports boasted that never in this region's history had conditions been better than they were in the early 1920's. The potteries were all running and laborers were receiving a living wage much superior to that paid before the World War.

Karl Langenbeck, a chemist of note among potters and tile makers, and possessor of practical experience as a manufacturer, appealed to the business world by stating that "100 or more flourishing local clay-working industries could be added to those existing."

In existence as early as 1922, The American Clay Products Company, 416 Masonic Temple, Zanesville, Ohio, marketed Hull's Zane Grey stoneware items along with nested banded bowls, yellowware, hotel ware, toilet ware, and semi-porcelain cereal sets. The American Clay Products Company was such a large distributor of Hull products that invoices of accounts receivable were imprinted with ACP's name.

A. E. Hull Pottery Co. Factory No. 2
CROOKSVILLE, OHIO

Sold to THE AMERICAN CLAY PRODUCTS CO. DATE
ZANESVILLE, OHIO

Acct.

Shipped to   J.Lowenstein & Sons,
                     Valparaiso, Ind.

If cash in advance order place "X" here————

QUANTITY	DESCRIPTION
$1\frac{1}{2}$	Doz No.21 Cuspidors
$1\frac{1}{2}$	" No.30 "

Orders for The American Clay Products Company originated in both plants, (for combined stoneware and porcelain items). This particular order for three dozen cuspidors was generated in Hull's Factory No. 2, the porcelain plant. Another portion of the invoice provided a place for Hull to designate how the shipment was to be packed: crates, barrels, boxes or kegs.

The American Clay Products Company's stoneware plant, covered three acres and was said to have had a greater capacity than any of its kind in the world. The American Clay Products Company boasted of the world's finest potters and was comprised of The A.E. Hull Pottery Company, The Star Stoneware, Ransbottom Bros. Pottery, Logan Pottery, Muskingum Pottery, Crooksville Pottery, Nelson McCoy Sanitary Stoneware Company, Burley Pottery Company, Burley Winter Pottery, and perhaps others. All formed in an effort to share orders. Frank Ransbottom of Ransbottom Bros. Pottery served as President and Addis E. Hull, Sr., Served as Vice President of The American Clay Products Company. The company advertised "flower pots, all kinds of glazed specialties and high grade stoneware."

This formation served as a distribution campaign, and any one salesman could represent the ware of any firm involved. A common catalogue was shared and it was earlier believed, that all the firms involved manufactured at least a portion of the same products. It is becoming more apparent that the involved companies more than likely continued to maintain production of individual styles. The combined effort was in sales, wherein a fleet of salesmen existed that had access to all company catalogues which enabled them to sell for any one of the companies involved in this group. An early business card reads, "W. L. Brannon, Special Representative, The A.E. Hull Pottery Co. Lines, Crooksville, Ohio, for The American Clay Products Co., Zanesville, Ohio."

The American Clay Products Company was strictly a profit-making merchandising campaign that was formed much earlier than the Depression years. This was not a "beggar's plea'" for sales during slow economic times, as sales during the 1920's were reportedly extremely brisk and profitable. This was absolutely a money-making formation to monopolize orders and promote business for this group of businessmen, and perhaps more importantly, for advertising and promoting the area as a whole. There was an active campaign taking place to illustrate Zanesville and surrounding areas as a profitable mecca in order to bring new businesses to the area. Promotion included The Zanesville Chamber of Commerce's printed booklet entitled, *Zanesville - For the Manufacturer, Merchant, and Home Seeker.* The American Clay Product's effort to combine sales of the major firms of the "Clay Center of the World," was dissolved by the government which declared its formation a monopoly of merchandising efforts.

Hull's Rising Market Demands Met by Importation of European Wares

James Felz managed the New Jersey warehouse, which was eighty-six by two hundred and twenty-five feet in dimensions. Guy Cooke served as Hull's New York representative. Cooke later took over the position of Vice President of the company and Manager of Hull's eastern branch, a vacancy left by F.H. Griswold. L.A. Springer headed up Hull's team as Sales Manager. D.W. Worthington worked out of the Chicago office. G.E. McKeever, a director of the company, served as a salesman and Manager of the branch house in Detroit, Michigan. Western and northern sales areas were represented by G.W. Springer, and western and southern territories were represented by N.W. Leland. Also serving as a traveling salesman was V.D. Kinnon, a member of the board of directors.

The five-and-dimes, decorative shops and florists were buying massive volumes of artware throughout the teens and by the early 1920's, interest in artwares was so great that in order to supply the increasing market, Addis Hull traveled to Europe and arranged to purchase decorative earthenware, china, pottery and tile from England, Italy, France, Czechoslovakia and Germany.

The foreign items were delivered to New York at half the cost of local production. Hull continued the import of foreign products until 1929, by sending a company representative to Europe each year to procure pottery items and arrange for their shipment. This early account indicates just how successful Hull had become in this particular business aspect.

"The import division of the A.E. Hull Pottery Co., has made an auspicious start in the matter of its new importations for the fall trade, and as a result, a visit to its showrooms in the Fifth Avenue Building discloses an excellent display of items to tempt the buyer. They have the most interesting range of animal figures, consisting of dogs, elephants and cats. They are in both earthenware and china and present a varied range of sizes from small ones, which predominate to the larger animals.

They offer real values, which will be realized when it is stated they are priced to retail from 19 cents to $1.25. All of the animals are exceptionally true to life in every detail and they are all in natural colors. Scotties, wire-haired terriers, bull dogs, police dogs and sheep dogs are shown in the assortment. In addition to those mentioned above, the firm is also showing grotesque animals. These are in solid colors of red, dark gray and white. The little animals are comic and yet at the same time are quite artistic, having been designed by one of the leading European animal artists.

In addition to the new animals, the company has a number of other surprises. Naturally, when the name Hull is mentioned, one immediately thinks of kitchenware and the new samples in this respect are the very latest and most exclusive to be received from Europe. In fact, any line shown by Hull is classic in style and these newest importations are so exclusive that one cannot discourse upon them at very great length at this time. We can say, however, that they are most original and beautiful, and one can also comment upon their colors. Tints that are brand new and never shown before are included in their range, in addition to the other well known Hull colors.''

The eastern warehouse, located at 57 Hudson Street in Jersey City, New Jersey, provided storage for imports, numbering more than the entire output of domestic wares. The New York City office and showroom located at 200 Fifth Avenue, Room 207, became main headquarters and served as the distribution center for both domestic and imported wares. Hull also had a Branch House in Detroit and a Chicago office located at the Morrison Hotel which assisted in marketing both their domestic and foreign wares. Foreign wares were sold alongside Hull's domestic production for nearly eight years. Hull wisely closed the doors of the Jersey City Warehouse in 1929, due to the declining economy of the Depression Years.

Meanwhile, Back In Crooksville

Pottery was such a profitable business, that it was not uncommon for the area's leaders to have multiple interests in the pottery trade. By the 1920's, Addis E. Hull, Sr., in addition to managing the two Hull plants, served as President and Director of the Crooksville Pottery. Hull, and his director and Sales Manager, L.A. Springer, were both stockholders in The Muskingum Pottery Company. Springer additionally held the title of General Manager of The Muskingum Pottery.

The increase in demand for art lines of the 1920's, necessitated some major changes of equipment on the home-front and Hull installed the first continuous tunnel kiln during this period. The new kiln, 310 feet in length, at a cost near $75,000, proved to promote larger production numbers of artwares. In 1925, the pottery announced production totalling three million pieces per year. This

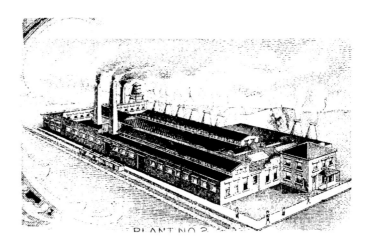

Hull's Plant No. 2, illustrated on this early letterhead of the mid-1920's, shows the extra kiln smoke stacks, those attributed to the first continuous kiln which was installed in 1923 at a cost of $75,000.00.

number excluded miscellaneous kitchenware items such as jugs, jars, custard cups and salt boxes. Hull remained constantly involved in market analysis and soon noticed that interest in stoneware items was decreasing slightly, due to improved canning and preserving methods for food staples. Keeping with movements dictated by the market, Hull, in 1926, converted Plant No. 1 to tiling operations. However, the pottery continued to manufacture stoneware items in very respectable numbers, making changes and improvements along the way.

Hull updated designs and decorations of their stone kitchenware items and produced large numbers of stoneware vases, jardinieres, flower pots and hanging baskets in plain or multi-colored blended glazes. Hanging pots and baskets were accompanied with chains. A miscellaneous assortment of art pottery consisting of jardinieres, flower pots and vases, were glazed regularly in matt colors Bermuda green and lotus blue. Special orders of matte oyster white and autumn brown were available when ordered in large quantities. Other typical color glazes of the day were maize yellow, egg shell white and turquoise.

In 1928, Hull offered newly designed kitchenware, based upon previously used designs, with updated features such as greater depth, projecting feet or bases, neater more precise decorations and round spherical bottoms. New shapes replaced old shapes in white blue banded bowls and the No. 701 shape yellowware bowls with brown bands replaced the No. 700 shape. White decorated luster band bowls were offered with the choice of a wide red band with small blue stripes, wide ivory brown band with small blue lines, or wide green band with small black lines. Hull stated they were, ''without doubt the finest appearing bowls we have produced in the past twenty-five years.''

Hull's nursery ware was offered in both new and old styles. This semi-porcelain nursery line included baby plates, cups, saucers, bread and milk sets in two sizes with a companion child's mug. Semi-porcelain cuspidors available in hotel, parlor or low parlor shapes were banded with gold, blue, green, maroon or luster colors. Also available were cuspidors which had been decorated with decals of rose or bird designs and those which were offered in glazed

The Hull Company, comprised of many adept leaders and salesmen, could not have survived the years without a loyal staff of front line pottery craftsmen, such as illustrated in this photo dated 1928. During this period, Hull employees numbered 285, and while Hull consistently had twenty-five to thirty salesmen stationed at various offices throughout the nation, seven salesmen traveled regularly from the home office in Crooksville.

mahogany with gold line trim.

Due to the failed economy and the depression years, Hull was prudent in closing the Jersey City warehouse in 1929. There was a lessened work force and sales staff in the eastern and northern areas. Hull had no recourse but to upgrade local production by concentrating his efforts on manufacturing only the highest quality domestic wares, which now centered on stoneware and semi-porcelain kitchenware and artware, and tile production. Markets indicated that new courses of production needed to be explored to remain solvent, and Hull continued to keenly watch manufacturing activities and retailing trends.

Hull knew that good business practice involved more than production of a quality item. He took took great pride in providing orders in a timely manner, and in his efforts to process orders more easily, provided customers the following classification systems for the bodies they produced. Earthenware classification was noted as that part of Hull production manufactured of white semi porcelain body, represented by a prefix number of three digits, such as, 300/13 Casserole, or 610/33 Vase.

Stoneware classification was designated as that part of Hull production manufactured of buff body, represented by a prefix number of two digits — 34/30 Jardiniere, or 34/35 Flower Pot.

Hull's marketing system included a second digit number which related to style. The number 30 represented jardinieres, 31 hanging pots and baskets, 32 flower and bulb bowls, 33 vases, 34 flower pots with unattached saucers, and 35 flower pots with attached saucers.

Hull's Tile Production

A Zanesville, Ohio, man by the name of F.H. Hall, had seen the opportunity in 1875 to utilize local clays for tile and soon patented his process. Several area tiling plants followed, The American Encaustic Tiling Company, The Mosaic, The Empire and The Standard Tile Companies. In 1926, Hull, who was always conscious of current market trends and demands, obtained fire clay in Crooksville's Mineral Addition and converted operations in Plant No. 1 to tile production. Operations in Plant No. 1 were mainly devoted to production of floor and wall tile.

J.D. Young, an able and experienced man, thoroughly schooled in his profession, and who had been associated with the company since 1905, served as Superintendent of Plant No. 1. Young, born in 1863, had married Minnie Watts, a native of Perry County, Ohio. They were the parents of six children, one being Earl Watts Young, who served as assistant to his father. Tony Donluvy was enlisted as a tile designer and William K. McClellan continued to head the company's glaze formulas for both Plants, inclusive of Hull's tile manufacture.

Hull's two plants, employed a total of 285 craftsmen from an annual payroll of $300,000. While Plant No. 1 employed 125 tile and stoneware workers with a total payroll of $150,000, Plant No. 2 employed 160 craftsmen with a payroll of $175,000 for its utility and artware output. When operating normally, Plant No. 1 produced 3,800 square feet of floor, wall and ornamental tile daily, or 10,400,000 square feet annually; Plant No. 2's capacity was 650,000 dozens, or 7,800,000 pieces of utility and artware annually.

Decorative tiling for floors, walls, fireplace mantles, etc., was made in a wide array of colors - both solid and stippled, including pastels and black, in both high gloss and matte finishes. Accessory items, such as towel bars and soap dishes were made in coordinating colors. Much of the company's tile business was on a "special order" basis, with two types of tiles manufactured; plain and faience, either being available with a "cushioned" or rounded surface.

Faience tile was characterized by a thicker body which usually contained grog, a mixture of dust made by pounding and sifting broken pieces of biscuit or unglazed pottery. Faience was usually distinguished by a coarse, porous body covered by a heavy opaque enamel instead of a translucent glaze. Tile was pounded or pressed into the mold and then trimmed with a wire drawn across the bottom. The surface of the tile could be made smooth with a dampened finger or given a sandy finish by sprinkling with fine grog. A too moist tile body cracked due to unequal shrinkage. Tile had to dry slowly and evenly to avoid warping and cracking. The edges were dampened if they were drying faster than the center of the tile. Shrinkage was lessened by mixing with the clay about a fourth part of fine grog dust.

The architects and decorators of the William H. Jackson Company, of New York, were Hull's largest tile customers, however, Hull also supplied buyers in the Chicago, Detroit and Cincinnati areas. McClellan's personal notebooks include tile formulas and their glazes and refers to supplying the William H. Jackson Company in Chicago, as well as New York. Other tile buyers referred to include Star Tile Company, Drake, Shaw, and Hawkinson, and specific notation of orders such as "356-W for Cran Brook School."

Specific notations regarding the W. H. Jackson Company include, "Jackson #1, blue trile good, outside on top - #1, 3 hrs. grinding; Jackson #2 blue green outside on top, 3 hrs. grinding; #4 turquoise trile Jackson, trile muffle kiln, OK; Blue Green Hi-fire Cone 10, W. H. Jackson Co., Chicago, Y.M.C.A. Job, OK; W.H. Jackson, Chicago, #171 good; #211-1 Detroit; 81-1 Detroit."

McClellan's notations in a notebook inscribed, "For Trile For Tile - 1926", encompassed tile glaze colors in, "gold, matt black, Blue Enamel, Enamel Green, matt blue, new black, yellow stain, pink stain, blue hi-fire, orange red, black enamel, MTC red glaze, lavendar, white matt, blue, slater blue, red brown, orange brown, copper, soft green, shamy yellow, Canary yellow, dark yellow, autumn leafe, crimson staine, olive green, rose, grey, bright red, blue green matt, yellow matt, ivory matt, brown bright, green bright, tan bright, Victoria green, blue green glaze- W.H. Jackson - YMCA, blood red, coral red, apple green, Hawthorne," and others. Tile bodies noted are, "Mosaic body, one fire body, Dust Pressed body, and Faience."

Interesting to note is the tile body composition noted in McClellan's own hand which consisted of, "63 buckets grog, 9 buckets ball clay, 13 wheel-barrow Ader H. Clay and 3 wheel-barrow Scott's ball clay," while the Casting Body (used for casting bath accessories and perhaps used for garden ware, statuary, and the like,) was listed as, "65 gal. water, 52 buckets clay, 3 lb. soda ash and 3 lb. sil. soda"

Further instructions for the "Pressing Body" were noted as, "24 shovel of body, 7 shovel of grog."

Instructions were penciled in the margins of McClellan's threadbare books: "#40 red bright, trile in muffle kiln; apple green, hand fire; Lt 107-1 samples OK, samples for Jackson in Chicago; P.O. Watts wall tile body, grinde to go thru 200 mesh screen; bright glaze for Shaw; new green Lt. 101, outside kiln; Lt Blue Colson Cone 8; sample 505-2 Drake; rec'd #1336A Special Bright Red, L. Reusche Co."

Special orders were taken in Hull's few years of tiling operations. Reproductions of art designs, along with free form and original art designs, in embossed clay tiles were executed. Douglas Young, now deceased, described a tiling mastery of "The Lord's Supper," many years ago during an interview. Another artistic tiling work, thought to have been executed and installed in a Catholic Church, illustrated STATIONS OF THE CROSS, the fourteen images or pictures which form in series the representation of the successive scenes of the Passion of Christ, and before which devotions are performed. This information has been researched through the Roman Catholic Property Administration, thus far, to no avail. While the locations of these works have not been verified, it is interesting to note that McClellan's notebooks contain the glaze formula, "Red for Christ's Robe."

In the 1930's, building construction declined and demand for tile decreased. Some tiling companies made attempts to lessen the costs of manufacturing faience tile in order to be competitive with others and to make their operations more profitable. The market price of dust-pressed 4¼" × 4¼" flat tile, which had previously dictated 65 to 70 cents per square foot, faltered to a mere 18 cents per foot. The Hull Company would not succumb to this type of operation, and rather than compromise quality, tile production was discontinued by 1931. Discontinuing tile production was Addis Jr.'s foresight, as Addis Sr. died in 1930, leaving the company to be run by his eldest son. Hull had most assuredly inherited his father's keen business sense, as the decision to end tiling operations was a very wise one. The nearby American Encaustic Tile, the largest tiling operation in the world, closed in 1935.

Plant No. 1, which had earlier converted almost exclusively to tiling operations, now housed outdated equipment in need of many modifications. This, combined with the current sluggish economy, prompted Hull, by 1933, to close the doors of Plant No. 1. Until that time, however, there was a unified effort of both plants to continue production of sizeable volumes of stoneware and semi-porcelain.

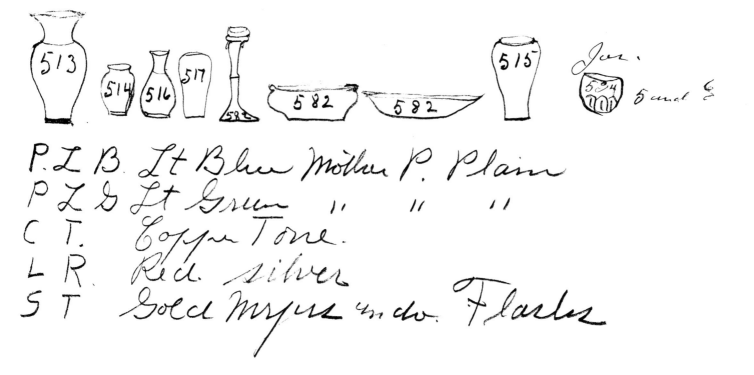

P.L.B. Lt Blue Mother P. Plain
P.L.G. Lt Green   "   "   "
C T. Copper Tone.
L R. Red. silver
S T. Gold Myers in do. Flashes

William McClellan has given us sample sketchings of Luster vases no. 513, 514, 515, 516, 517, jardiniere 534, and candle holder 582, and what is noted as bulb bowl 582, which may in fact be bulb bowl 562. These sketches of several of Hull's semi-porcelain luster items offer perhaps the only clues collectors will ever have to this unmarked line.

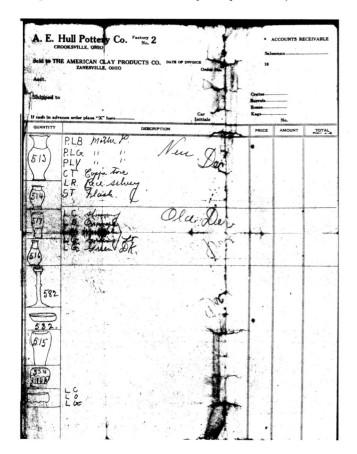

McClellan delineated some of the glaze treatments which were available in Luster shapes, noting these on an Accounts Receivable statement for Plant No. 2's sales to The American Clay Products Company of Zanesville, Ohio.

Hull's Luster Glazes

Hull had been experimenting with luster glazes since 1927. By the close of the 1920's, lusters were being used for banded bowls and Hull was working on a newly designed line of semi-porcelain art ware that was to sport luster finishes. Special expertise was needed when glazing in luster treatments and special care was necessary in the firing processes. Lusters, with two exceptions, were all the same color before fire, being a dark brown in the vial and a light yellow brown when applied. Lusters positively could not be successfully mixed in the liquid form, nor could one be painted over another without firing between the applications.

Alcohol was used as a thinner for luster glazes, as turpentine left a greasy film on the surface which caused streaks. Luster glazes could be fired on any type of clay, from domestic to finer clays, but lusters did pose problems that weren't typical to other glaze techniques. Each finger print showed after firing a luster and a too-thick coat cracked or peeled off. Humidity was also an enemy to luster glazes and some wares had to be fired while the lusters were still wet, while others needed to dry before lusters were applied.

The firing temperatures of luster colors had to be monitored at different levels for the various color techniques. Certain colors had to have light fire, while others required heavier firing. Some items had to be fired at once so the luster color didn't sink into the initial glaze color while others had to air dry before firing. A kiln that had not been heated very slowly at first, so that oils could be driven out gradually and allow fumes to escape before the kiln became too hot, dulled the lusters and also caused them to rub off easily after fire. Hull's semi-porcelain lusterware items were decorated in colors the company described as orange, shammy, lavender, slate, emerald, light blue, iridescent dark blue and golden glow. These lusters served as standard luster treatments. 10-inch luster artware vases wholesaled for $15.00 per dozen.

As you know, William K. McClellan was employed as Hull's Ceramic Engineer during the luster glazes. Pottery historians know too, that William McClellan also obtained employment with the American Encaustic Tile Company. Some of the luster colors Hull used match identically with those used by A.E. Tile. This coupled, with the fact that luster pieces were usually not marked, by either firm, causes much confusion in the market place. It was not uncommon for engineers, designers, modelers and tradesmen to take employment at several different potteries during their lifetimes. Nor, was it uncommon for a ceramic engineer that moved to another firm to take his livelihood with him, the formulas for bodies and glazes that he so carefully guarded.

McClellan noted on the reverse sides of company invoices, the luster colors as he knew them: "New Dec. P.LB Mother P., P.LG Mother P., PLY Mother P., CT Coffee Tone, L.R. Red Silvery, ST Flash; Old Dec. LC shammy, LO Orange, LM Mulberry, L Gr Green Lt., L Gr Green Dk.," which translates to: New Decorations: plain light blue Mother of Pearl, plain light green Mother of Pearl, plain light yellow Mother of Pearl, coffee tone, red silver or silvery, gold flashes; Old Decorations: light shammy, light orange, light mulberry, light green, dark green.

By theme designed outside the company, perhaps the Hommel Company, additional luster lines, Persian and Chinese Red Cracquell, were sold to the distributors in the Chicago area. One dozen of the same 10-inch vases, as used in the previous example, now cost $24.00 in the special luster glazes. It is believed that Persian refers to a turquoise blue luster and of course, the Chinese Red Cracquell refers to a red luster. McClellan's glaze books refer to several reds: bright reds, red stains and red mattes, and blues included hues that ranged from light blues to cobalts to Peacock blues and turquoises. If Persian actually referred to a blue green shade of luster it would have been necessary to have been applied in two or more applications in order to acquire something other than a gray tone. Gold luster glaze when used in two paintings provided a very rich purple, however, when the third painting used was a "covering" for gold luster, a pigeon-blood ruby was attained. This covering for gold luster was not used for any other purpose as it had little or no color when fired alone. In pure speculation, any of these colors, combinations thereof, the numerous applications of the gold lusters, or formulas contained in McClellan's glaze books could have been likely candidates for the special lusters. Cost alone tells us that Hull was using more expensive glazes indicative of gold content or the application and firing of wares in several stages.

A letter directed to McClellan, dated April 21, 1927, from The O. Hommel Co., "Importers and Manufacturers, Bronze Powders, China Colors, Oxides and Ceramic Chemicals,

Bronzing Liquids, Metal Leaf, Gold Paints, Enamels, Etc.," 209-213 Fourth Avenue, Pittsburgh, Pennsylvania, is no doubt in reference to Hull's luster glazes.

Dear Friend Bill:

You may think that I forgot my promise which I made you to send you the recipe for the Crystaline Glazes, but this is not the case. I have hunted a dozen times or more for the recipe but I have not been able to find it until just a short time ago. Ernest no doubt mentioned to you that I have not been well either and had been away on a trip so that for six weeks I did not attend to very much business. I am feeling considerably better again.

Hope you will let me hear from you what success you have with the crystalines. With many kind regards.

Another letter directed to McClellan from The Hommel Company is dated March 29, 1934, and may have referred to the color needed for the No. 300 Line semi-porcelain kitchenware decorated in overglaze Pimento Red stripes:

"We have matched the specimen of Overglaze Red, submitted, and are sending, under separate cover, sample of Overglaze Red #3154-A which you will find firing out very close to the desired shade.

We would like to receive your business for this color and would appreciate it if you could arrange to have this tried soon and favor us with your next order.

We assure you we would appreciate your kind consideration and would give your orders our very best attention."

The Hull Pottery was strongly comtemplating the art market when this photograph was taken, shortly after the tiling operations in Plant No. 1 were discontinued. All pottery production, both stoneware and semi-porcelain was now being conducted in Plant No. 2 (above,) as Addis E. Hull, Jr., further closed the doors to Plant No. 1 during this period. Changes were being made within Hull's one remaining plant to include more art lines, including lusters.

In this company photo, dated 1933, craftsmen are identified as follows:
Row 1, Bottom: Elmer Heskett, Billy Ansel, Don Lauterbach, William Woods, Ray Conaway, Jake Ansel, Ken Haymen, Harold Smith, Junior Williams, William Houk, Noah Watts. Row 2: Clifford Oliver, Burley Channel, Guy Eveland, Ralph Passon, Jay Young, Arthur Bayes, Lewis Woods, Pat Mooney, Orvil Bonifant, Guy Allen, Dick Cantor, Marshall Hall, Henry Tysinger. Row 3: Phyllis Rogers Stephenson, Grace Levering, Kathryn Mooney, "Click" Hinkle, Leona Orr, Grace Spung, Julia Dunn, Irene Williams, Loretta Presgrave, Elmer Conaway, Effie Ferguson, Cecila Adams, Zetta Wilson, Helen Bailey, Bertha McGuire, Ruth Russell, Cecil Hull. Row 4: Richard Rosser, Gerald Zinn, Tom Conaway, Gerald Conaway, Russell Lee, Dugan Kemmer, Cryil Burns, Raymond Underwood, Frank Stephenson, Bill Corbett, Clyde Allen, George Young, Arthur Levering, Cecil Wilson, Ralph Sherlock, Henry Russell.

The 1930's
A Time Of Turmoil

Addis Emmet Hull, Sr.'s accomplishments were many in his lifetime, he had been named postmaster of Rendville and was elected by his fellow townsmen to the town council. Hull served many years on the school board, taking an active interest in the education of his six children, Addis Emmet, Jr., James Brannon, Robert, Byron, Joy and Jane. Hull, who supported the Democratic party, was elected to the Ohio Legislature in 1898 in a Republican district, and in 1907-8 represented Perry County in the Ohio General Assembly. Hull, who had resided in Zanesville since 1911, at 1245 Maple Avenue, proved instrumental in all aspects of advancement of community, schools and legislation. Hull had married Etta Brannon, born in Morgan County, Ohio, in 1873. Mrs. Hull was very active in social, civic and church work, and served as director and trustee of the Bethesda Hospital in Zanesville.

Hull died in 1930, leaving the pottery trade in the experienced hands of his two eldest sons, Addis Emmet Hull, Jr. and James Brannon Hull. Robert was attending Ohio State University, taking courses related to factory management, and Byron had not been long out of high school at this time. Hull's two eldest sons were experienced in the pottery trade having previously worked for their father. At the time, Addis Jr., was serving as assistant manager of the Hull, and James Brannon, held the position of accountant and bookkeeper in charge of the order department. Neither son was a stranger to the

pottery business and each had inherited their father's keen market sense and prudence in decision-making abilities.

Both sons had graduated from Ohio State University. Addis, Jr. held the degree of Ceramic Engineer. Following their father's footsteps and the family tradition, both sons would prove to succeed in the presidency of the Hull Company. Addis Hull, Jr.'s position of top management came soon after the death of his father in 1930, however, James Brannon Hull would wait nearly twenty years for the same managerial advancement.

Addis E. Hull, Jr., resided in Zanesville at 1252 Euclid Avenue, and commuted to the Village of Crooksville, where he kept the pottery steadfast and strong during the Great Depression. Hull had married Lois Barnett in 1917, and had two children, A.E. III, and Richard D. Addis, Jr. was a veteran of the World War, and in 1918 served as chief inspector in the explosive section, army ordnance, being honorably discharged in 1919.

James Brannon Hull, a student at Ohio University during the late war, was attached to the federal reserve. Hull married Marie Hannum in 1924, and was now ready to devote his full attention to the family pottery business.

Imports had halted, and the doors of the Jersey City Warehouse had closed in 1929. After taking the helm of the family operation in 1930, Addis, Jr. ended tiling operations by 1931, and further closed Plant No. 1, in 1933. The major tiling manufacturers who remained in business faultered within the next few years. The A.E. Tile, the largest tile company in the world, closed it's doors completely by 1935. Interesting to note, is that Addis, Jr.

later acquired the A.E. Tile Company in 1937, and was instrumental in organizing another pottery on the premises, that being The Shawnee Pottery Company.

Although there was a definite trend to produce larger volumes of art pottery by the company's importation of nearly 20% of their clay for special items and glazes, the largest output continued to center on stoneware, kitchenware, garden ware and florist ware.

There was no guess work involved regarding market place demands. The Hulls that headed company production were very well versed in their trade. Economics and market trends ruled the ceramic industry and The Hull Company continued throughout its history to meet demands by maintaining quality and diversity at a pleasing price.

By 1935, Hull felt the lessening demand for stoneware, and decreased their numbers of stoneware utility and kitchenware production. Hull also closed the doors of the New York Showroom. While the company continued to manufacture some stoneware pieces in the form of vases, jardinieres and hanging pots, Hull's production emphasis was definitely taking a strong turn towards artware. Hull's preferred body for kitchenware items produced at this time was nearly always a porcelain-type body. It was increasingly clear that this medium was fast becoming the preferred body for the company's production of artware too.

Hull Accepts Contract With Shulton of New York

The 1930's proved to be a season of change. By the mid-1930's Hull employees had organized with the National Brotherhood of Operative Potters. The Hull Pottery and the Brush Pottery were the only two Union operated plants in the pottery region. This was also a time when Addis Hull, Jr., was interested in moving on. Hull had made the decision to accept a management position outside the family pottery.

Hull had previous insight into a declining stoneware market and had earlier decreased company production of these wares. Now, in 1937, in general, the stoneware business had died. Hull, not only offered stable guidance such as this, when in charge of the company, but at other times too. When confronted with outside business interests, Hull very carefully provided for the future employment of company personnel and for the future continuous flow of the production lines of his father's firm. Hull accomplished this by accepting a long-term contract with Shulton of New York for production of pottery cosmetic and soap product containers. Hull left the company knowing it was secure, jobs and production would continue under the direction of the company's new President, Gerald Watts, governed by provisions of this contractual agreement with Shulton.

While Plant No. 2's utility and artware production continued, the company made new space for the Shulton operations. Hull increased their 285 person work force to 450 personnel and worked around the clock in three shifts.

Addis E. Hull, Sr., died in 1930, leaving The Hull Pottery Company in the capable and experienced hands of his two eldest sons, Addis E. Hull, Jr., and James Brannon Hull.

The Hull Company manufactured in excess of eleven million Old Spice shaving mugs, after shave lotion, cologne, and after shave talc bottles over the next nine years.

The Hull Company began production of these containers in 1937, and Old Spice men's products were introduced to the market in 1938. Shulton was relatively small at the time, and it can be said with certainty that the Hull Company was the only producer of pottery containers for their firm during this period.

In planning for Old Spice men's products, William Lightfoot Schultz, president and founder of Shulton, Inc., and Mrs. Enid Edson, his art director, were confident that the time was ripe for a design excursion into Americana. It was perhaps natural that the country's increasing awareness and appreciation of its ancestry would influence Mr. Schultz to use an Early American motif.

Shulton journeyed into American history in search of an idea for containers that would duplicate hand made pottery and also demonstrate simplicity and strong masculine appeal. With colonial art of early America supplying a suitable atmosphere, Shulton created through their products and packaging, an aura of the days of sailing ships.

Shulton created a reproduction of an old shaving mug for Old Spice mug soap. A small colonial pottery medicine jar was the design inspiration for Old Spice men's cologne, after shave lotion and after shave talc bottles. These Hull pottery containers were decorated with fired-on illustrations of famous 18th Century sailing vessels; The Mount Vernon, The Grand Turk, The Recovery and The Friendship. The original illustration used was a sketch of a clipper ship.

The following article appeared in the September, 1953, issue of Modern Packaging Magazine, which described the evolution of Shulton's Hull Pottery.

"Introduced in 1938, at a time when the mere mention of "men's cologne" was a signal for loud guffaws, Old Spice demonstrated how simplicity, good taste, and strong masculine appeal in packaging could build a world market for quality men's products in the dollar-and-up price bracket.

The appeal of the packages as gift items was so great that by 1939, the men's line was outdistancing the women's items and accounting for 22% of the company's gross. Sales were reported at more than $3,000,000. It's success was perhaps even a little surprising to William Lightfoot Schultz."

Schultz, who had been in the soap business since 1910, was continually searching for THE idea that would create the promotional appeal that would sell millions. The famous ship replicas on Hull's bottles and shaving mugs created that level of success.

The advent of World War II and the resulting redirection of raw materials into the war effort, plus Shulton's necessity to advance to automatic filling and closing operations when the demand for talc and shave lotion rose to millions of bottles, forced a container material change. Shulton gave up the ceramic containers manufactured for them by Hull.

Hull manufactured millions of containers during this contract period, however, never fully met Shulton's specifications for the bottles and mugs. The requirements Shulton demanded for capacity control and neck tolerances were so stringent that quality control measures became an almost impossible feat. Soon this venture proved to be a profitless operation. It was vital that Shulton's requirements by fully met in order that the pottery wares could survive their machine production filling operations. Inaccurate fills due to irregularities of the containers, the percentage of leakers, and the porosity of the pottery, made handling and costs prohibitive on a large volume basis.

Both Hull and Shulton were relieved to see the "pottery-glass" bottles and mugs adopted, that first had been experimented with in late 1943, by T.C. Wheaton Co., Millville, New Jersey.

By 1944, all containers were being produced by Wheaton in an opaline glass which assimilated those made previously by Hull. Ceramic materials were added to the glass to give it a realistic clay-colored lustre which closely resembled the sheen of pottery. The glass containers duplicated the appearance of Hull's pottery containers and could be produced closer to desired specifications which better tolerated the need for mechanical filling and packaging operations.

Hull Pursues Career Outside the Family Business

When A.E. Hull, Jr., resigned in 1937, to accept management of The Shawnee Pottery Company of Zanesville, Ohio, there was no questioning his abilities. The May 6, 1937, Prospectus of The Shawnee Company assigned Hull to make an immediate appraisal of the works at Zanesville, purchased from American Encaustic Tiling Company, Inc. Hull, "was considered by the Company best qualified to make an appraisal of such machinery and equipment." The Shawnee Pottery Company anxiously awaited reorganizing the plant for use of new and improved techniques devised by Hull. Further account of the Shawnee Pottery Company's Prospectus clarifies how very highly regarded Hull was in the field of ceramics.

"Addis E. Hull, Jr. of Zanesville, Ohio, the President and General Manager, is a graduate of Ohio State University and holds the degree of Ceramic Engineer. He has been actively engaged in the pottery manufacturing business for more than twenty years, the last six as President and General Manager of A.E. Hull Pottery Company of Crooksville, Ohio, which was founded by his father and five associates in 1903. Mr. Hull has been devoting part of his time and attention to the affairs of the Company since its organization. His resignation from Hull Pottery Company will be effective not later than March 14, 1937, or at such prior time as may be convenient to Hull Pottery Company.

Mr. Hull has been employed by the Company as General Manager under an agreement terminating December 31, 1941, at a salary of $6,000 annually, plus 5% of the net profits for each fiscal year, resulting after deduction of all operating charges, including interest, depreciation and taxes, but excluding state and Federal income, excess profits and undistributed profits taxes. It is expected that life insurance in the amount of $100,000 payable to the Company will be placed on his life.

Mr. Hull will devote his entire time to the affairs of the Company. His principle activities will be market research by contact in the field with buyers and the design and development of new products. The success of pottery manufacture is greatly dependent upon the design and development of products having popular appeal, so that current sales trends may be anticipated and guided. Mr. Hull has outstanding ability as a designer and is thoroughly acquainted with the buyers of the large chain and department stores and wholesalers of pottery products."

The Forties Revisited

With Hull having moved on to accept the presidency at Shawnee, Gerald F. Watts, son of William Watts, was to succeed in the management of the Hull Pottery firm. This was the first time in the history of the company to be headed by someone outside the Hull family. The company had previously been clearly established as a giant in the field of ceramics by A.E. Hull, Sr., and A.E. Hull, Jr., and Watts continued to project the same strong and diversified image, by the major infiltration of the fluid and lovely pastel art lines for which this pottery is most famous.

In the late 1920's, Hull, as well as many other American companies, dealt in voluminous sales of foreign imports. Now, ten-plus years into this practice, the flood that overcame the market was nearly disastrous for local manufacturers. U.S. importers of foreign wares had created their own monster. Hull was seriously in need of great numbers of designs of artwares to compete not only with local competitors, but also with foreign competition. Times demanded American wares with a distinctively local look and feel. Necessity demanded that local manufacturers out-design, out-merchandise and out-distance all foreign competition.

Area competition remained constant, every pottery attempted to keep their corner of the market. Labor and materials were scarce during World War II, however, money was plentiful and the company was able to market all the artwares which could be produced. A minimum of fifty spray gun operators for tinting and twenty-five decorators were needed for coloring the artware lines. Numbers for trimmers and finishers were even greater. There was a separate "cold room" filled with additional decorators where masked and free hand designs were painted. Kiln operators, ceramic engineers for clay and glaze preparation, diemakers, moldmakers, casters, jiggermen, maintenance men, and the like, comprised an additional 100 workmen.

America reclaimed its retail market when the War abruptly halted any desire or demand for imported wares. The growing resentment toward both Japan and Germany, saw American-produced items outdistancing the sales of all foreign imports. "Buy American" campaigns were pushed by every available media - radio, newspapers, and magazines. The Hull Company, along with other local competitors could sell all the American-made artware and kitchenware that could be produced.

This was both good news and bad news, since the redirection of raw materials into the War effort created

A.E. Hull Company Pottery employees of the Casting Room, dated July 17, 1941.

The Potter-at-Wheel logo on company letterheads, as well as brochure pages and price lists remained a constant signet for the company, and echoed a pride in art pottery craftsmanship. Artlines of the 1940's were consistently marked with foil labels depicting the potter-at-wheel trademark.

problems, and modelers and other experienced craftsmen were scarce. The Hull Company remained open for production during the War years, while other companies were used for armed services headquarters, offices and warehouses. Hull produced casseroles for food provisions for the Navy while they kept as many of their regular lines in operation moving as well as they could with their decreased number of employees. Hull pottery officials proudly recognized those employees who left their pottery work tables to join the War effort. From 1942 to 1946, the Hull Company allotted servicemen $10.00 per month during the period each served their country.

Hull did its best to keep as many artware lines on the market as was possible. Perhaps situational to operations during War years, many shapes of the day were repeated three, and sometimes four times in a single pattern, gradually enlarging, i.e., Orchid, Tulip, Iris and Poppy. Although the pottery firm was determined that each design keep its individual identity, it was not uncommon for shapes, ideas and molds to be shared.

Watt's massive movement towards art pottery was definitely positive competition for other art pottery manufacturers, and soon, vases, baskets, ewers, wall pockets, rose bowls, console bowls, along with other styles were abundant. The pastel-tinted artwares of Hull, embossed with realistic floral sprays, virtually flooded the market, the lines for which The Hull Company is best remembered. Soothing to the senses, and simplistic in style, Hull's artware was air-brush blended in predominate matte colors of pink, blue, yellow and green. Hull was noticed in the market place to repeat these pastel colorations. This, combined with the pottery's distinctive look and feel, proved to be Hull's ''trademark'' of the Forties. It was an important time to keep everything ''American in appearance,'' and there definitely were no foreign-looking designs coming from this factory during War years. The realistic floral sprays that decorated Hull wares were taken straight from the American garden path or walkway.

Some art and novelty designs were supplied by Hull's potential buyers and chain store representatives. The company was guaranteed sales by allowing the buyer to supply the ideas and gather packages and assortments of their own liking for their sales campaigns. T.K. Kirkpatrick

of S.S. Kresge Co., W.W. Dixon of McCrory Stores Corp., H.H. Lindquist and Van Overschelde of F.W. Woolworth Co., and H.W. Smith of S.H. Kress Co. were instrumental in supplying basic production ideas to Hull and other pottery companies. Sears, Roebuck & Co. had a staff that assisted in designing kitchenware items which included Jane Miller, housewares stylist, James Butler, pottery buyer and F.R. Henniger, the division merchandise manager. Ideas were transformed by a Hull modeler and then dies and molds were made. Due to this merchandising assistance, there was very little need for a full-time designer at the plant. However, additional design work was contracted through Louise Bauer, who was free-lancing for many of the local potteries at the time.

Chain stores such as Mattingly, G.C.Murphy, F.W. Woolworth, McCrory, Federated Stores, Ben Franklin, and Kresge were leaders in Hull sales. Original price tags which remain on Hull wares show the matte Woodland hanging basket retailed for $2.69, Wild Flower vase 52-6" at $1.49, Calla Lily 11" ewer at $1.98, and Dogwood 521-7" low bowl at 98 cents. Merchants were guaranteed to double their investment since Hull set minimum retail prices for pottery leaving the plant. Higher rates were established for areas West of the Rocky Mountains. Hull's marketing of assortment packages included a system where the assortment number was in fact, the wholesale price, i.e., assortment #6502 cost $65.02, assortment #4690 cost $46.90.

Many prototype art lines came from the 1920's and 1930's, along with novelty items such as the Dancing Girl and Peasant Lady planters. Certainly the Sueno lines of Tulip, Calla Lily and Thistle were, and are today, considered prized art lines, however, Hull's most successful lines were yet to enter the market. The 1940's proved to be Hull's most important artware years. These were the years which actually marked Hull's success in time. Although the lines of Hull were many and varied, and all worthy of mention, those best remembered are the matte pastels of the Forties. Hull art lines represented the best of two worlds, combined in art and form. Hull's many intricate and flowing designs emerged thereafter. William McClellan's glaze books presented Sueno's art colorations as ''A - Blue and Pink, B - Blue TB (top and base), and C - Blue and Cream.'' Colors were designated numerically on company brochures in the same order: "Decorations 1 - blue base - pink top, 2 - blue base and top, and 3 - blue base - cream top."

The somewhat plain, yet refined Orchid art line was decorated in muted colors of blue and rose. Artistic lines with little use of handle designs made this line a classic, at home in almost any setting.Much to collector dismay, Orchid offered only one size ewer and one size basket. This is the only early art line known to offer a set of bookends. Company information listed Orchid's color combinations as "Dec. No. 1 - blue green bottom and pink top, Dec. No. 2 - blue green bottom and top, and Dec.No. 3 - pink bottom and ivory top."

Iris, the line everyone loves to call Narcissus, was offered in "Dec. No. 1 - blue bottom and rose top, Dec. No. 2 - peach bottom and top, and Dec.No. 3 - rose bottom and peach top." Original company information indicates this line was named Iris. This art design illustrated a classic combination of balance, from the plain lines used for rose bowls and jardinieres, to the more intricately scalloped vase tops and handles.

Shapes of the Poppy design were quite ordinary, and centered on bulbous designs. As with Orchid, here again, we saw a handful of shapes in graduated sizes. Intricacy in the embossed floral itself made the simple lines appear rich in detail, when in fact the floral design was responsible for this feeling. Two sizes of baskets and ewers were presented in this line, as well as a wall pocket.

The handles and lines of the Wild Flower numbered series design marked this ware the most delicately intricate of all art lines manufactured by Hull. In this line handles were more than functional, or for balance, being extra "lacy" in double and triple forms, high-standing on the tea set, vases and ewers. In addition to the lovely raised floral design, butterflies graced certain shapes. Two baskets, a handled bon-bon dish and double candle holders were featured. Company information listed color combination "A" as pink top, brown base, and "B" as mauve top, green base.

Camellia, often referred to as Open Rose, was Hull's most fanciful art design. There were no duplications in graduated sizes, each item in this line possessed an individual personality; vases with leafy handles, baskets with bows, jardinieres with ram's heads, hand-held fan vases, candle holders flanked by perched doves, the reclining mermaid with shell planter, and more. The stark white color treatments were somewhat "chalky" in comparison to the pink and blue combinations offered, however, no other line illustrated such a wide diversification of styles, which more than compensated for the white infiltration. Camellia was the actual company designated line name.

The Red Riding Hood cookie jar, patented June 29, 1943, immediately and most assuredly, made great impact on the novelty and kitchenware market. Design Patent Number 135,889 was issued to Louise E. Bauer of Zanesville, Ohio, assignor to the A.E. Hull Pottery Company, Inc., of Crooksville, Ohio, for "Cookie Jar." "Red" stole everyone's heart in which she came into contact. The story book character proved to be a tremendous seller and soon, various complementing accessories appeared which continued to be made well into the 1950's. And while, Hull began the livelihood of this best-seller with the assignment of the patent, the largest numbers of Red Riding Hood items were manufactured by the Regal China Corporation, of Chicago, Illinois.

Also, many of the Hull-produced Red Riding Hood items were decorated by The Royal China and Novelty Company, a division of Regal China Corporation. Louise Bauer modeled additional Red Riding Hood characters for Regal China during the two, 7-year terms of patent assignment. It was apparent that some type of contractual agreement existed between Hull and Regal since it appears the patent number remained assigned to Hull until June 29, 1957. It is possible, however, that the patent number was sold, or legally transferred entirely, by Hull to Regal.

Although matte finished lines dominated this period of art pottery production, there were exceptions. In 1946, the Rosella pattern offered a high gloss ivory or coral finish. Rosella's term of production was relatively short, due partly to the expense incurred in producing its special clay formula. The pink-based clay of coral Rosella was produced of imported clay ingredients mixed within the factory.

The excitement surrounding the new Rosella line was apparent in advertising campaigns which were launched immediately. The Company's pride of master craftsmenship was advertised, as well as promotion of an expected allure to buyers of this new, modern ware.:

"An eloquent tribute in pottery to modern American homes. The beauty of your home will be enhanced by the smoothness and warmth of texture in Rosella–exquisitely designed, with the charming floral motif sculptured on a body of flawless coral. Pottery in its finest sense must have qualities of velvet-like feel to produce an emotional stir and justify a place among your finest possessions. This is a dominant characteristic in our new Rosella pattern. In Rosella there is a balance of subdued color and style seldom obtained but always sought. See and feel the actual piece of ware to become as keenly enthused as were the inspired craftsmen producing them. Your best gift displays will show this ware as rapidly as it can be produced."

Rosella was produced at a time when the Company was torn between the comfort and stability of the old, and the need to move on with updated, innovative new styles and glazes. The Hull Company was somewhat ahead of it's time, as Rosella was produced in that small span of time before high glazed artware items were truly trendy. While Hull tested their markets with Rosella, they at the same time maintained constant production of matte wares. On the retailer's shelves, Rosella competed not only with Hull matte wares, but also with Hull's competitors' products. Rosella did not take the retail market by storm, matte designs prevailed.

The Hull Pottery cut their losses and commenced a full regiment of matte pastels in Wildflower "W" series and Magnolia lines with an additional matte line, Water Lily, waiting in the wings. The company did not attempt a similar major gloss line for nearly two years, that being New Gloss Magnolia.

Wildflower "W" series design was a second-generation line. The earlier line marked in numerical sequence, was changed in name by the division of the word, Wild Flower. The company was apparently in need of a completely new and/or inexpensive line, or perhaps it was the demanded volume of artware which dictated the immediate need for the new retail market line up. Whatever the reasons, Hull found it necessary to bring back a previously used line with added newness, and described it to be "fashionable foundations for your favorite flowers hand-painted in the gay colors of Spring to brighten the Fall and Winter months of indoor living ... styled to dwell in graceful harmony with any interior."

Wild Flower numbered series had 29 shapes, while Wildflower listed only 22. Six of the earlier used molds remained near the same, some with different cut-outs or laces to the handles. Some molds were used with only slight modifications of floral design. Some of the molds disappeared altogether, as did the "butterfly" used for Wild Flower numbered series line. Additional molds used for the Wildflower line were redesigned and updated. Simpler, more angular shapes appeared, many of the earlier used fanciful handles were lost.

Matte glazes dominated and another new line, Magnolia, emerged which was comprised of 27 newly designed molds. Although new colors seemed to have appeared in Wildflower and Magnolia, they were actually toned-down versions of the previously used pink and blue standards of earlier lines such as Orchid, Iris, Dogwood and Poppy. The russet and yellow glazes were newly formulated. Again, Hull took control of a market filled with new ideas, colors and concepts by way of using old tried-and-true ideas, colors and concepts, with a special "touch" of added newness which captured and amazed their wholesale and retail audiences, yet all the while, assured their past customers' comfort by allowing them to reacquaint with "an old friend."

In decorating Hull's embossed duo-tone pastels, leaves and flowers were first decorated by brushwork. Paint glaze was thinned by Epsom salt when it thickened and was difficult to work with. Wares were then transferred to spray gun operators who spray tinted, first the top, and then the base of the item being decorated. Wares were carried throughout the pottery on boards to a hand decorating room. From there the items moved to tinters, drying and kiln areas. Daine Neff recalled the day he disastrously dropped five 15-inch vases from the board he was carrying.

A small group of glaze books which belonged to Edgar McClellan, who followed his father's footsteps as Ceramic Engineer for Hull, remain and offer but a glimpse into the years of prosperity in which Hull relished during the Forties and Fifties. Glazes inscribed in McClellan's own hand record a history in itself. His artistry relating to Magnolia included, "Pink paint for Magnolia underglaze; yellow/green for Magnolia; Brown tint Magnolia; Pink flower engobe; Rose tint; Lt. blue tint; New Yellow underglaze for Magnolia; Oct. 28, 1946 - New Blue Tint;

New Green Tint - Nov. 15, 1946; Trial Pink Tint #20; Green Tint Magnolia; Peach Tint; Silver Grey Tint Trial; Blue Green Tint #2 - Trial Feb. 11, 1947, O.K.; Pink Tint #2 - Trial Feb. 11, 1947."

As directed by Hull, the Wildflower and Magnolia designs took the "front-row seat" of the nation's art pottery market and truly became major successes in the company's history. This, as in other times of Hull's prosperity, the conservative and traditional nature of the company came to light giving us insight into the men behind the scenes and how they used this to their advantage. Gerald Watts seemed to possess the same sixth sense as prior Hull managers regarding current market trends demanded by a nation of consumers. Crooksville, centered in the "hub" of pottery production, was surrounded by major potteries producing tremendous volumes of art lines. The Hull Company had wisely chosen to keep its personal identity of pink and blue tones, a trademark which most assuredly helped the company survive, while others failed.

By 1947, Hull ventured to present another high gloss artware line in the midst of the retail market's matte wares. However, instead of creating a newly designed mold system, as Hull had used when creating Rosella, the company opted for using shapes already familiar to the public. This proved to be a less expensive venture for the company, of course, with exceedingly less risk. The known shapes of Magnolia in updated glazes proved to be far more comforting to the buying audience and were advertised as, "Gracefully styled, handsomely decorated with hand-painted florals ... glazed overall for shimmering, enduring beauty." Any speculation of failure on the company's part regarding this high gloss artware and its timeliness would have been unfounded as, Hull's New Magnolia was a success.

Even with the major success of a high gloss artware, Hull's conventional nature emerged again in 1948. Hull used the basic molds of Wild Flower numbered series #58 cornucopia, #53 vase, #71 vase, and #55 pitcher, (although already redesigned for Wildflower) for the New Water Lily line. Flower pots with attached saucers were apparently back in vogue after being absent from the market for several years, and there was also a reemergence of the large jardiniere. Water Lily, consisting of 28 shapes, was decorated in matte colors of Walnut and Apricot or Turquoise and Sweet Pink. Company ads listed Water Lily as "practical, useful and handsome sculptural beauties, each with hand-painted floral, each in a choice of two duo-tone pastel combinations to assure complete harmony with your home's decorative motif."

McClellan's specific glaze formulas which related to Water Lily included recipes for, "Matt Green Paint for Water Lily; Water Lily Blue Green Tint now in use; Golden Brown Tint and Tangerine Trial (which were crossed out and replaced with) Brown Tint for Water Lily; Turquoise Matt - Trial good; White Matt For Lily; Paint for Flower; Pink Matt - Trial very good for tinting over brown; Silver Grey Matt trial good." Notations relating to other lines included, "Tint Turquoise for Painting Morning Glory; #70 Green; Velvet Green we used on Morning Glory."

Edgar McClellan's listed formulas for bodies included, "#5 Trial Body, White Body, Ohio China Body, Press Body, and C-5 Body." Interesting to note is the fact that Hull was instrumental in supplying other area potteries the clays they needed for producing competitive wares. Ungemach Pottery of Roseville, Ohio, purchased Whiting from Hull, while the Maurice A. Knight Pottery of Crooksville bought Peerless clay which was air-floated.

McClellan had a recipe listed for "Brown Tint," followed by numerous pages of graphs and alphanumeric identifications, along with a code for the ciphers, which no doubt can be decoded only by the engineer himself. Experimentation was noted, "Red Paint for Flowers for cherries and lambs and came out very good on the new line." Despite all the formulas produced by ceramic engineers, some glazes continued to be formulated by outside sources as McClellan noted, "received June 4th, 1946, pink glaze stain; green v.g. mixture; v.g. yellow mixture; pink; coral; blue."

As a quality control measure, decorators were assigned numbers to incise on the bases of items they were responsible for decorating. If the decoration was not acceptable, the decorator was easily located and instructed to do better work. Since Hull was commercially produced pottery, the craftsman's "squiggle" adds no real significant value to items being considered for purchase, however, they do add interest to those who are delving into Hull's history.

More than one mark incised in the base identifies both the decorator and tinter. It is also not unusual to find the decorator's or tinter's initials, rather than their assigned number, or the two combined. Hull items bearing the incised name of the modeler, caster, or decorator is more uncommon and does warrant a boost in price.

Hull's well-known "theory of diversification," which kept two or three new and different lines on the market at all times, was truly a diversification of carefully planned strategies to assure that they neither completely rid themselves of the old, nor totally and fully embraced the new. Although Hull's designers were capable of mastering completely new concepts in every aspect of artware, it's apparent the company chose not to. The conservative, well thought-out management plans dictated differently; plans which allowed the Hull Company to prosper years longer than local competitors of art potteries.

Production of the late 1940's was fully centered on artware, however, Hull continued to manufacture down-to-earth utilitarian kitchenware items, which too, emerged in redesigned shapes and updated glazes. Kitchenwares remained on the market alongside Hull's art designs. Hull remained in a position to please not only the retail buyer of artware, but also the customer needing utility and kitchenwares. New in 1948, The Cinderella Blossom and Bouquet lines of kitchenware, hand-painted under the glaze, entered the market. Blossom design was originally marketed with yellow florals, which was substituted ten months later, March 1, 1949, to pink decor. Bouquet pattern continued to be produced in the multi-colored spray throughout its tenure.

The years 1948 and 1949 saw an interesting combination of artware and kitchenware in the Sun-Glow line. The assortment was composed of nested bowls, casserole, grease jar, and shakers, which headed up the kitchenware, along with art and novelty pieces which featured four different wall pockets, a basket, assorted vases and two styles of tea bells. Decorations offered were allover yellow gloss with pink decor, or allover pink with yellow decor. The Sun-Glow line's mold numbers, a series of both 50's digits and 80's digits, divide the artwares and kitchenwares.

In 1949, the introduction of Bow-Knot proved to be a completely new concept of Hull artware. This apparent overnight change in form and content was due to the genius of designer, Louise Bauer, who was responsible for modeling the line. The company apparently saw the need for refining artware productions and made the major change in operations to offer Bauer, a free-lance modeler, who had earlier been responsible for designing individual Hull items, with full-time employment. Bow-Knot shapes included Sun-Glow's molds for wall pockets and the small basket. The company advertised Bow-Knot as, "the epitome of smartness ... beautiful new art pottery to match the natural beauty of your favorite flowers. Styled in twenty-nine pieces, including novel hanger pieces for unusual wall decorations."

During this same period, Louise Bauer created yet another full artware line, that being Woodland. This design's thirty shapes were billed, "an artware creation of the A.E. Hull Pottery Co. in gay, hand-painted florals, in a choice of Dawn Rose or Harvest Yellow body pastels." Hull continued their marketing campaign by describing the teaset as, "from the pages of the 'Arabian Nights' ... from the wonderful lamp of Aladdin come the graceful, flowing lines of this exquisite 3-piece Tea Set."

A news account, dated May 1, 1950, reports, "The A.E. Hull Pottery is now producing a new line called Modern Kitchenware in green plaid decoration. Among the items offered is a four-piece bowl set, ranging in width from five to 8 inches, the largest bowl having a lip for pouring. The retail price is about $2.65 a set. Also included in the line are the following: Cookie jar, $1.69; casserole, $1.29; range set, $1.89; cream and sugar set, 98 cents; and cereal or vegetable bowl, 39 cents. All items are ovenproof and are for delivery within 60 days." The company pricelist, dated April 20, 1950, listed the 12-piece "Modern Kitchenware," in decorations of green plaid or red plaid.

While the nation's major art pottery companies had shown deficits in their bookkeeping departments since the end of World War II, The Hull Pottery Company remained steadfast and strong. The company identified known trends and anticipated and guided future markets. This anticipation, an art form in itself, was necessary in order to survive a market place overflowing with foreign competition.

Hull remained cautious, in that potteries in business for decades, concluded their clay histories at this very time. The Weller Pottery had faltered for more than a decade, finally closing its doors in 1948. The Roseville Pottery, which had declined steadily after the World War, maintained only a fragment of the market they had earlier held. Roseville had switched to several high gloss lines of art and kitchenware, some were revived shapes from the past, none of which attracted the attention of retail buyers. Roseville closed in 1952.

Hull's decision to employ full-time designer, Louise Bauer, proved to be not only a wise, but a profitable market strategy. The new designs of Bow-Knot and Woodland attained acceptance in numbers which astounded even Hull company officials. More importantly, The Hull Pottery had most assuredly captured the attention of a nation-wide art pottery market with their new designer and their new creations. The future seemed promising in all respects ...

Hull Pottery Destroyed By Flood And Fire

Fire and flame, the potter's most impairing plague, became a reality to the Hull Pottery on June 16, 1950. *The Columbus Evening Dispatch* reported:

"Cloudburst and flash flood caused an avalanche of water which started from Black Fork Creek rushed northward in Jonathan Creek, south of Crooksville, and then poured into the three communities of Crooksville,

Roseville and Rose Farm. Cascading water rushed up a narrow valley, smashed five homes in Rose Farm (also called Tropic) and caused an explosion and fire which destroyed the Acme Pottery."

"Besides the Acme Pottery, a kiln of the Crooksville China Co. exploded and it was destroyed."

It had also been reported that five miles southeast of Crooksville, the Misco Mine Co. dam had succumbed to the water. State Highway Patrol officials later stated that the dam held but that water had rushed over and around the dam. Some families were able to flee their homes and search for higher ground, while others were trapped. A 55-year-old woman was a drowning victim when flood waters swept her house across the road. In the confusion, several families were reported missing. By daybreak when waters had receded to two feet in the downtown area of Crooksville, all had been accounted for.

A four-hour downpour that day changed Hull history. The Jonathan and Moxahala Creeks poured over their banks, flooding a 25-square-mile area in Muskingum, Perry,

This aerial view of the A. E. Hull Pottery was taken June 17, 1950, when all that remained were structural walls, billows of smoke and flood waters which had partially receded.

and Morgan Counties. In the Village of Crooksville, water ran seven feet deep on Main Street and stood four feet deep inside the Hull plant. When covered by water, the fiery pottery kiln of the Hull Company exploded, setting the plant ablaze. The tremendous pressure, by combination of rising waters and the great tunnel kiln, firing at 2000 degrees, caused the pottery's roof to ignite when expansion joints bolted apart.

The Zanesville Times Recorder, reported, the downpour began at about 10:00 p.m., and flames broke out at the pottery after the kiln blew up about midnight. Between 30 and 35 persons who had taken refuge in the Hull pottery to escape flood waters were safely rescued after the fire started. One man waded through water up to his neck to get out of the plant.

The deep waters kept most firemen from being able to get near enough to fight the fire, and the few firemen able to reach the scene stood by helplessly without equipment. The firemen, as well as local townspeople and employees of the pottery were forced to stand by and watch the pottery burn.

By dawn it was certain that the Hull Pottery was no more than a rubble of smoke and ashes. In a matter of a few hours, earth's elements had rendered the pottery totally useless. The kiln had exploded, the roof was gone and fire had razed the entire plant. All that remained were structural walls and charred waste within.

Brannon Hull, Vice President of the Company, declined to make an immediate estimate of the damage for reporters, however, Gerald F. Watts, manager of the pottery, told newsmen the loss would run at $500,000. News headlines proclaimed "The Acme at Crooksville" was completely destroyed. Harold Showers, Plant Superintendent, had earlier given an estimate at $1,000,000. Showers stated the pottery was a complete loss and all that was left standing was a portion of the walls. All areas of the plant, including the offices, which housed important documents, accounts receivable, and even payroll records, were affected by the flood and fire. The flood waters rose so rapidly that even the few workmen inside who operated the kiln had little, if any notice of the impending tragedy. Very, very few records survived the disaster.

A total of 1500 pottery workers in the region were affected by the flood, 350 of these were employed by Hull. Payroll was carried out immediately by having employees line up at a vacant room on Main Street in Crooksville to declare what was due them.

Hull's foundation of good will was sound. Hull creditors felt an obligation to the company and many satisfied customers rushed to pay their bills before they were due. $100,000 came in immediately after the fire.

The flood was devastating and there was only one pottery in the village unaffected by the high water which retained the use of its kiln.

By June 19, 1950, leaders of the community met in the offices of the Nelson-McCoy Pottery, and estimated the Roseville loss at $136,000 to business places, and $182,000 to residences. The loss in Crooksville, excluding the loss of the Hull plant, was not estimated in a dollar figure, but was believed to be even greater.

Industrial firms sent their employees to assist with the general cleanup whenever possible. In Roseville, The Robinson-Ransbottom Pottery sent its full force to assist. The few potteries that were not damaged severely, and other industries in the two towns were ready to resume operations on June 19th, but employers instructed their workers to return to the cleanup and salvage on company payrolls.

Still, with all added assistance, cleanup was slow. Many businesses and residences were destroyed, traffic was jammed as onlookers traveled through observing the storm damage, several miles of road bed were damaged, even the Ohio Power Company transformer station was thrown out of commission when it exploded. For several days, the only lighting in the area was from autos and emergency equipment.

The first shipment of pottery from Crooksville after the disastrous flood was sent on the Pennsylvania Railroad by the Worthington Pottery. Life in the Village of 3000 had resumed and area potteries recovered and were soon back in action.

A New, Modern Pottery Rises From The Ashes

Potteries were typically plagued by fires, they were a fact of life to workers in this industry. Few burned-out potteries survive, but fewer had the dynamic forces that the Hull was afforded. The people behind this pottery proved to all that they were survivors and this company would rise from the ashes. Hull's foundation was sound, support was strong, and their reputation unquestioned. Nearby towns quickly offered incentives to secure the business. Hull stockholders felt bound by moral obligation to remain in Crooksville where the firm had been founded. The skilled craftsmen Hull employed and their families lived in this tiny village. Ninety-five percent of the stockholders voted to rebuild a new and modern pottery plant. While Hull Company President, Gerald F. Watts, was not in favor of rebuilding, Vice President of the firm, James Brannon Hull, vigorously declared his conviction that it was indeed essential to reconstruct the factory.

"Bump" Showers, son of one of the original founders of The Acme Pottery, took on the job of rebuilding the pottery, a job in which he asked for shares of company stock rather than pay. The firm was able, through insurance provisions, to continue company officials, ceramic engineers and select key staff on the payroll during reconstruction of the new plant. This group staffed a pilot plant which remained operational during the months of reconstruction. Here new bodies and glazes were formulated expeditiously.

While architects and engineers were busy designing future processes of the modern plant, Hull salesmen were far from idle. The Hull Company maintained usual display space at all shows. Salesmen had little to display until mid-1951, but they met customers, and promised resumption of production. Salesmen were armed with a retail pricelist, dated July 1, 1951, entailing twenty-one pieces of the New Woodland design, again, as before the plant fire, available in matte glazes of Dawn Rose or Harvest Yellow. This same price listing of July, 1951, included #65 Lady Basket, #66 Lamb and the #68 Kitten planter.

Production was a reality by August 29, 1951. Hull's Just Right Kitchenware in Floral and Vegetable patterns, along with Blue Ribbon Bowls, headed up the utility lines. By September of 1951, the company's salesmen had secured an excess of $95,000 in orders on Woodland pattern alone. The first Woodland shipment was made in mid-October, 1951. Hull was assured that $150,000 of Woodland orders for the holiday season would follow.

On October 24, 1951, additional items were placed on pricelists, including the novelty pieces #90 City Girl, #91 Country Boy, #92 Baby, #93 Elephant, #60 Parrot, #61 Pheasant, #86 Pig, #87 Boy with Dog, #88 Pup with Yarn, #89 Kitty with Spool. A listing for December 10, 1951 added to the novelty line up by featuring #71 Ribbon Wall Pocket, #72 Fan Vase, #73 Peacock Vase, #78 Flamingo Vase and #79 Floral decorated Daisy Basket. Following closely were additional lines of Parchment and Pine and Crescent dinnerware.

A year and a half was necessary for architects and builders on construction of the plant and officially, January 1, 1952, the pottery was fully restored and the name changed, from The A.E. Hull Pottery Company to The Hull Pottery Company.

Although the name changed, the trademark did not, Hull continued throughout its production to use the potter-at-wheel logo on letterheads, seals, company brochures and advertising. J.B. Hull was elected President, Robert W. Hull, Vice President, E.D. Young, Secretary-Treasurer and Credit Manager, and Harold Showers, served as Plant Superintendent. All were Members of the Board of Hull Directors, along with a fifth member, John Hull. Byron Hull continued in his expertise as Hull's Sales Manager.

Hull Pottery: Behind The Scenes

Hull's new plant was built for in-line pottery production with only the latest and most modern equipment installed. Only air floated clay was used which prevented imperfections in the finished ware and two 50-ton ram presses were installed which formed ware many times faster than the old jigger and mold methods.

Hull's disasterous flood and fire enabled the plant to reconstruct with the assurance that its new pottery contained only the most organized methods for ease and speed of pottery production and handling. This organization was shown in mold making, casting, pressing, finishing, glazing, firing, sorting and packaging.

Electric conveyor belts carried ware through various stations within the plant where workers finished and glazed it. Additional conveyor belts lifted ware to overhead drying ovens. The circular Allied continuous kiln fired at 2000 degrees and operated 24 hours a day, seven days per week. Up to 52 cars entered the kiln per day, one car entered and another exited every 25 minutes, turning out nearly 100,000 pieces of ware per week. Booster portions of the kiln threw heat to the press units and drying ovens.

The installation of the modern time and energy saving equipment, and the search for a modern look in the new art lines to follow, prompted Hull to deter from local clays which had a yellow burn. Hull had actually used little local clay since the production of tile, stoneware and utilitarian wares, and had imported clays in the Forties from the Dakotas, Tennessee, New York and Kentucky for artware production.

By the 1950's, it was imperative that Hull achieve the desired "white burn," and also use a pottery plaster which allowed them the highest production and plant efficiency. Hull teamed its modern plant and equipment with high content kaolin clay mixtures whose consistency, basically free of impurities, fired with a white porcelain-type body, and allowed for the best and most efficient plant production. Less impurities in the clay meant less imperfections in the final product. Quality, consistency and speed were effected with use of kaolin clay mixtures.

Only clays which can be made plastic and will partially vitrify in the fire are desirable to pottery production. When dry, clay is very hard, but when moist it becomes plastic; that is, it yields under pressure and does not return to its original form when pressure is removed. Its plasticity can be increased by adding more water until it becomes too soft to retain its shape. Coarse clays and those containing much sand, as well as some of the primary clays, have little plasticity, and are known as being short, while some of the very fine clays are very plastic, or long.

Clay has never been found in a perfectly pure state, being more or less mixed with impurities such as small stones, silt, sand or rock dust and other nonplastic materials, which contain magnesia, soda, potash, iron oxides, lime and similar materials. Chemical analysis shows that a perfectly pure clay is composed of alumina, silica and water. The nearest to this found in nature is the relatively pure natural clay kaolin which is used in making porcelain. Other clays, such as ball clay, china clay, fire clay, pottery's clay, etc., contain kaolin's same elements, but in different proportions which are mixed with various quantities of impurities.

Vitrification of a clay depends upon its fusing or melting point. This vitrification point can be changed by altering the clay's ingredients. Some clays are refractory, or infusible, meaning they will not melt in a potter's kiln, while others are very fusible. A potter's clay needs not only to withstand the fire, but to have a binding quality to transmit durability to the ware. The Chinese spoke of the "bone and the flesh of their porcelain," giving reference to the clays from which it was made, the short refractory kaolin as the skeleton or framework to support the feldspar clay which bound it together.

It was also necesary for potteries to desire highly infusible clay materials for other aspects of their production, that being for the manufacture of saggers. Hull was surely not concerned with sagger production in this highly modern plant, and in actuality, had not produced saggers for years.

Setters and saggers were receptacles in which the ware was placed to protect it during firing. Because of the intense heat to which saggers were subjected, it was necessary for saggers to be made of a highly refractory or infusible material which would not warp or crack easily in the fire. Saggers were usually made from fire clay and a grog made from old broken saggers which had been ground and sifted.

Although McClellan's ceramic books referred to detailed formulas for sagger bodies, the company was not always responsible for producing their own saggers. It is speculated that saggers may have been made in Hull's earliest years, perhaps up to the 1920's, in Plant No. 1, where an abundance of grogged clay was available for stoneware and tile production.

Crooksville's Cesco Plant, The Refractories Division of The Ferro Corporation, was responsible for production of Hull's saggers in later years. This refractory plant was conveniently located nearby, almost at Hull's back door.

The Cesco Plant was originally founded as the Ceramic Supply Division of Ferro Corporation in 1936. At that early day, most pottery and ceramic manufacturing plants made their own setters and saggers, basically out of necessity, because commercially there was little available in the way of "kiln furniture." Ferro organized for the specialized fabrication of these products for a ceramic area that was bursting at the seams with manufacturers.

Their earliest production was devoted to dinnerware saggers almost exclusively. However, after World War II, the tiling boom made it necessary for Ferro to develop tile setters and saggers. Nearly all of the major ceramic manufacturers, those producing tile, dinnerware and pottery products, have been customers of the Cesco Plant.

This expansive aerial view of the pottery is quite impressive. Only the latest, most up-to-date equipment and operations were housed within.

Company President, J.B. Hull, at the controls of the circular Allied kiln. Photo taken 3-28-52, Zanesville Times Recorder.

This photo shows J. B. Hull surveying the physical plant and recent installation of kiln and electrical fittings.

Vice President, Robert W. Hull, was second in command at the opening of the reconstructed modern plant.

Byron Hull continued to serve as the Hull Company's Sales Manager after reopening of the plant.

Herbert Coulson, Ceramic Engineer who formulated bodies and glazes and operated the kiln. This Allied kiln was the most modern available in 1950, and required close attention of the engineer. The electrically driven fans, blowers, gauges, and pyrometers governed automatically under controlled conditions, so as to leave the result as little as possible to chance. The kiln made possible the recovery of expanded heat for other manufacturing processes. The process of drying ware was completed by equipment almost as large and complex as the tunnel kiln.

The die enabled the moldmaker to cast hundreds of working or production molds. Hull turned over its working molds three times during a single 8-hour shift. The life of a production mold was usually 150 "pours", before the
design and trademark were no longer detailed and crisp. In some cases the mold cracked or broke completely. The work of a diemaker and moldmaker was constant.

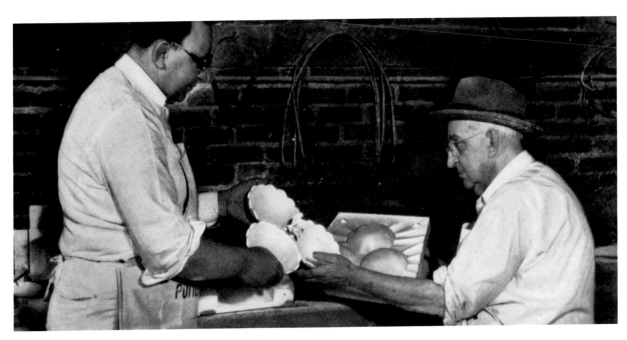

Casting is the technique used in making a series of identical pottery items. All Hull ware involved this process. A block or die was made by expert craftsmen such as the father-and-son team, Clarence H. Garrett and Warren E. Garrett, shown above. Other diemakers and moldmakers remembered are Sylvanus Burdette "Mose" Wilson, Paul Trussell, Tom Conaway, Homer "Jake" Ansel, Chester Cantor and Paul Heskett.

An advertisement which appeared in the June, 1956, *Ceramic Industry*, stated:

At Hull Pottery, in Crooksville, Ohio, 90% of the pottery plaster used is Certain-teed K-59. Robert W. Hull, production manager and purchasing agent, depends on the advice of his moldmakers and other pottery workers to guide him on purchases for the firm. Of his employees' attitude towards K-59, Mr. Hull says:

"Their reaction has always been that K-59 is the better quality plaster. The lasting qualities of K-59 are better. Its low expansion factor prevents the breakage of case molds. Our designs are more intricate than those of most potteries, and K-59 lends itself well to such detailed work."

Clarence H. Garrett, veteran Hull diemaker and moldmaker, with 57 years' experience behind him says: "Certain-teed is the best I've ever used!"

Ralph Passon, who has been with Hull since 1915, adds: "We use K-59 exclusively whenever possible. It has no "swell" to it. Another plaster has "flowers" or "detail" which make it swell and push pieces off the block. We get an average of 150 "pours" from the working molds. That's twice what it used to be."

In industry, when a large number of duplicate molds are to be made and it is desirable to preserve the original pattern, a plaster case is made around which the duplicate molds are cast.

A liquid clay slip, after being mixed, was allowed to stand in order for it to settle leaving the clear water which formed on top to be siphoned off before casting. The casting slip actually improved with age as the particles more finely dissolved. The feel of clay was only learned through experience and liquid slip had to be of the desired creamy thickness for casting purposes. Larger pieces required a thicker slip.

Slip casting in plaster molds was the most common method used in making commercial pottery, especially for light weight ware. Each plaster mold was used for up to 150 pours, and in between pours, it was necessary for workers to wipe the insides of the molds with a damp sponge and constantly be on guard for worn or damaged molds.

To increase production numbers, liquid slip was transported to slip casters by way of rubber hosing. This pressurized method, while faster, created a need for molds to be filled carefully to prevent air bubbles. As the slip settled it was necessary to pour in more liquid clay to keep the mold full. The small hose tips made it easier to fill tiny mold mouths.

New operations enabled the pottery to produce an upwards of 100,000 pieces of ware per week. The plant was responsible for manufacturing 5,000 Corky Pig Banks per day in 1957.

In the technique of casting, a liquid form of clay, called either slip or soup was poured into the plaster molds which had a large number of very small pores that absorbed the water from the clay slip wherever the mold came into contact with the slip. A wall of solid material gradually built up along the face of the mold. When this wall reached the desired thickness, the excess slip was poured out of the mold leaving the layer of slip solids that were in contact with the mold surface. This layer contained a considerable amount of water and through absorption, sufficient water had been removed, making the item essentially solid. As the water evaporated and was further absorbed, the layer started to shrink and break away from the mold. The cast piece was then removed, and after further drying, was ready for the finishing processes.

It was necessary for mold makers to construct additional molds if the design called for appendages or ornaments, such as basket and ewer handles, knobs, lids and attached ornamental pieces. Sometimes it was necessary that the foot or base of a particular item be molded and attached separately. Handles and knobs had to be designed to suit or match the body to which they were attached and needed to be affixed in clay of the same consistency and moisture as the primary piece so that shrinkage would be near the same. Usually, the area where the appendage was to be attached was covered with a spot of thick slip to aid in adhesion. Sometimes a scratch with a pointed tool, served not only as the point where the piece was to be joined, but also roughed the area so the handle or attachment adhered more readily.

Another view of mold makers and die makers at work.

Hull used additional methods for production of their wares. Many kitchenware items were formed by the jiggering method. This technique, although similar to hand turning, was faster and easier and produced wares more uniform in shape and thickness. The wheel used had a plaster mold on it. Items were formed by pressing the clay against the sides of the mold with a "bat," also referred to as a pull-down or paddle.

Jiggering lids for casseroles is Russell "Peanut" Lee.

The machines known as the jigger, for making flatware and hollow ware; and the jolley, for primarily making hollow ware; consisted essentially of a revolving mold mounted on a vertical spindle, used in conjunction with a descending profile held by a supporting arm. Flatware was made inverted on the revolving jigger mold which formed the inside of the ware while the descending profile cut the revolving clay and formed the bottom or outside surface of the ware. In earlier times it was difficult to make flatware of a desirable thinness except on a jigger. Hollow ware was made right side up in a revolving jolley mold which formed the outside surface of the ware while the descending profile formed the inside surface. As if jiggering and jolleying were not time consuming enough, it was also necessary that plaster molds as well as the wheel bats used in throwing be cast and cut directly on the wheel head to insure a perfect fit. The hinged arm and the flange or ring that kept the mold from slipping had to be in perfect alignment.

Jiggering hollow ware was a time consuming task that consisted of precision movements which required an experienced clay worker. The hollow ware mold was placed on the jigger head and a dab of soft clay was pressed down firmly under the low side of the mold if the mold did not run true. A profile, or designed cross section of the design to be made, was attached to the supporting arm of the jigger. The jiggerman next adjusted the profile so that it would stop at the desired thickness from the mold. After this adjustment, the profile was lifted out of the way and a sufficient amount of soft clay was wedged. The jigger was started and the worker wiped the inside of the revolving mold with a damp sponge. With his left hand controlling the profile, the craftsman's right hand slapped a handful of clay against the inside of the mold and roughly plastered the base and sides with it. The jiggerman's work also included eliminating air bubbles in the clay and wetting the clay when necessary. The jiggerman brought down the excess clay as it collected, and repeated this process until he had acquired the desired thickness. Holes or scratches were filled with soft clay and the jigger profile was lowered one last time to smooth the interior surface. Jiggering flatware was similar to this procedure but was done with the mold reversed or turned upside down on the wheel. With both procedures, the clay-filled molds were set aside for the ware to dry. A wet brush was run around the edge if the rim dried faster than the base. When the ware was leather-hard the piece was removed from the mold and any further air holes were filled with stiff clay and wiped carefully with a soft, damp sponge. In the reconstructed pottery, the jigger and jolley were soon replaced by ram presses which allowed for higher production numbers and greater quality control.

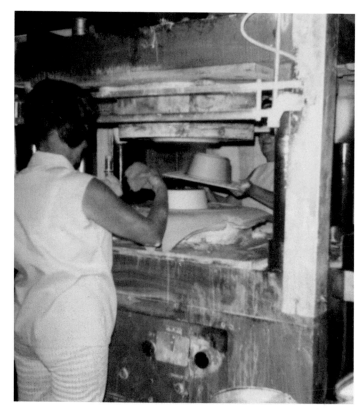

Another method used for producing hollow ware items, called ram pressing involved the compression of moist clay into molds under great pressure. Many shapes such as plates, bowls and casseroles were manufactured by this method.

Clay from a pug mill, pressed through a circular tube 12-14 inches in diameter and 36-40 in length, was wire cut into halves and fourths. The clay was then cut into smaller pieces for use with the ram presses, depending on the amount of clay needed for the piece being pressed.

Clay used in the ram presses needed to be plastic enough to wedge, similar to the consistency of fresh putty. It had to be soft and pliable, but not sticky, and free of air bubbles so that it pressed smoothly. It was necessary to keep the clay damp as it soon dried out and became unworkable. In addition to the presser, a second workman was closeby to remove excess clay as it collected and was being pressed away from the item produced.

The pottery plant was in constant motion. Conveyor belts, moving carts and rotating tables moved items with ease and speed through production processes.

The finishing processes were attended to as soon as the clay was tough enough to be handled without breakage or leaving fingerprints. Finishing processes included removing any waste materials at the top of the ware and then moistening and rounding rims carefully. Next the finisher fettled or scraped off the cast lines or mold marks with a knife and smoothed the area down with a wet finger or a soft, damp sponge. It was necessary to weld and smooth spouts on teapots and pitchers with the fingers, using clay slip or a modeling tool. Sponging usually took care of filling areas with tiny air holes, bubbles or depressions. Appendages and ornaments were attached during the finishing processes and inscriptions, dates, numbers and initials were scratched in the still moist clay at this time.

The delicate task of trimming was done by hand as the ware was still in a green, or unfired condition. This was too delicate an operation for a machine, and special tools were necessary, some in knife form, to enable the trimmer to smooth rough seams. Another tool, referred to as a "knobber," enabled trimmers to nudge the excess clay from handle and lid knobs or rims. Intricate, angular, or elongated portions of wares were given special attention to keep them from cracking during the firing process.

Tenured hand decorators Esta Marshall, left; and Bernice Walpole, right.

Every station had baskets or buckets beneath their work tables for the greenware which became damaged by these finishing processes. The clay was recycled by its being returned to the pug mill, and after additional water and mixing, was ready for reuse.

Finishers' work included pinching excess clay, rounding ends, smoothing joints carefully with the finger or modeling tool and attaching appendages.

With craftsmen desirous of only the best product, the ware was then moved on to another finishing process. Many times, the clay had minor imperfections such as, bumps, tiny holes or indentations that could not be perfected by trimming. However, rubbing the pottery with a damp sponge removed imperfections and any scratches left by the knives and knobbers in the trimming process.

Before the glaze was applied, a thin coating of wax was placed on the foot or base of the item so that portion remained unglazed in the process.

The business of trimming and sponging was most often left to female employees. These were very delicate operations and small hands were better able to handle the damp greenware which was so susceptible to breakage. Too little pressure did not give the desired finish, while too much pressure resulted in the ware crumbling in the hands.

This area of the plant was equipped with large mixers which ground and mixed glaze formulas. These glazes were stored in huge stoneware crocks, and sometimes in gallon jars as shown.

An additional finishing process involved the application of separate attachments, such as the mermaids of Ebb Tide's ashtrays. Many basket and ewer handles were molded or pressed separately and attached during the finishing processes while the ware was damp and in greenware form. The type of finishing processes needed depended on the ware being made. Elsie Robinson, shown above, punctured House 'n Garden greenware shakers before their fire.

The work area of the Ceramic Engineer was nearby, and shown is Paul Sharkey who worked the glazes, testing color formulas daily.

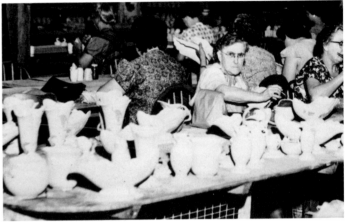

By the late 1950's, nearly all items of solid high gloss colors were hand-dipped in enormous crocks of glaze. This continued to be a necessary part of production until the plant's closing. The 50-gallon stoneware jars used for the glazing process were Star Stoneware products, made at the turn of the Century.

House 'n Garden and Imperial wares in solid high gloss colors with tinted sprays or foam edges were also hand-dipped in this method. The item was dipped in the glaze and, before the firing, the top edge was coated with a contrasting glaze. During the firing process the last application of glaze slowly melted down the sides of the ware over the first coat, making its own decoration, known as "run down". The contrasting glaze was of a thicker consistency and was usually contained in squeeze bottles which made application easier and more uniform.

While hand decorating gradually began being phased out with the installation of new equipment, most every art line between 1950 and 1959 required some type of special hand decorating skill. These lines included the sprayed effects of Parchment and Pine and Ebb Tide, to the necessary hand detailing of New Woodland, Blossom Flite, Butterfly and Serenade, and continued into lines of the late Fifties, such as Tropicana, Tokay and Tuscany.

Tinters, also referred to as spray gun operators, remained active in the company longer than the hand decorators. These operators continued to decorate art, novelty and florist lines through the late 1950's. Masks were also used for speed and continuity in decorating 1950's lines with fruit or berries, such as Fiesta, Tokay and Tuscany. A lead mask was designed to duplicate the embossed area to be decorated. The mask was held over the embossed design and a spray gun could be used for a quick spray of color.

Shown glazing House 'n Garden's French-Handled Casseroles is Mrs. Douglas Young, wife of Hull's Assistant Plant Superintendent. Some novelty and artware items were dipped in glaze and later splattered with a spray gun to effect a desired outcome, such as the Royal glaze.

Bernice Walpole is shown above decorating a Woodland ewer. On her right, decorating Floral shakers is Zetta Wilson.

It is necessary to mention gold decorators of the area who added special touches to Hull wares. Shown at his shop in 1978, is Granville, "Grany" Shafer.

Crooksville and the surrounding area boasted many talented decorators, many which presented hand decorating demonstrations at the area's annual Pottery Festivals. Mrs. Loren Baughman displayed her talents at the 1968 Festival. Usually, the festival souvenirs were hand decorated on-the-spot, in "cold color" or lacquers, to wares which had previously been fired. Those wares were items from The Hull and other area potteries. Note in the background the boxed Hull wares which included swans, Tokay caladium leaf, and on the table, Hull dinner plates which had already been decorated.

This photo, taken 5-2-65, by The Zanesville Times Recorder, leads us to believe that J.B. Hull was still at that time, very proud of the increased production made possible by the kiln installed after Hull's fire. Shown with Hull is Douglas Thomas. The circular continuous kiln operated 24 hours a day, seven days a week. The "cars" remained on a track and were continually in motion. One section of the circle was open and this space was used to load and unload the cars as they slowly passed by. With the modern equipment in place, Hull was able to manufacture nearly 100,000 pieces of ware per week. Considered the most modern and efficient kiln of the day, tunnel kilns such as this were almost in universal use by 1947.

Having had the pleasure to meet many of Hull's workers, who so carefully and lovingly made the pottery the success that it was, it is necessary to give special mention to two of my favorites, who have since passed on. Shown are, Douglas Young, grandson of Jeptha Darby Young, who worked as Assistant Plant Superintendent, and this author with Daine Neff, who had worked at the pottery since 1939.

James Brannon Hull, President of the reconstructed Hull Pottery, urged customer satisfaction through better service and products. The newly equipped plant made it possible to better meet the demands of manufacturing on a large volume basis. Items were able to be packaged for shipment directly from the kiln stacks.

Ladies packing ware from left to right: Carol Snyder, Rhea Alderman and Betty Maines.

J.B. Hull carried the company successfully through many years of diversive production. He remained President of the Company until his death in 1978. Hull is shown with the 3-piece swan set made throughout his tenure as President of the firm. These swans became as recognizable as the Hull logo itself, and continue to serve as "signets" of The Hull Pottery Company.

Many appreciated the tremendous designing talents of Louise E. Bauer, whose artistic abilities are now much sought after in her Pre-1950 designs of Bow-Knot and Woodland, and certainly, all artistic endeavors from the 1950's through the plant's closing in 1985. During her near forty years exclusively with Hull, along with earlier free-lance work for Hull before taking full time employment, makes Ms. Bauer responsible for the multitude of artware items we enjoy every day. She additionally designed the varied and voluminous Imperial florist ware line, along with most of Hull's House 'n Garden casual servingware items.

Louise E. Bauer: modeler, designer for The Hull Pottery Company.

Byron Hull: The Man Who Headed Up Sales

Much credit rightfully belongs to the salesmen who were stationed far away from life in Crooksville. J.B. Hull's brother, Byron, continued the family pottery tradition and worked consistently throughout his lifetime as a salesman in the New York office. "Bike," concerned not only with Hull sales, kept a watchful eye on current market trends as far as items competitors were selling and their prices. He periodically shipped wares, which were being produced by other companies, back to Crooksville to inform Hull of new products being sold in New York.

No doubt, Byron's extra duty "in the field," was greatly appreciated, and certainly the company was fortunate to have such expert assistance. Byron's salesmanship and marketing abilities were especially beneficial during the time the company was under reconstruction.

Byron Hull's skillful marketing strategy was demonstrated in a letter he wrote "Brannie," dated September 15, 1951, regarding a sample of a "nicely shaped salad bowl," made by Taylor Smith and Taylor, a "part of their Luray shape which has been a good selling line for a number of years." Byron further states, "this piece is just under 10 inches in diameter but I think that ours should be a full 10 inches." It seems foolish to me to make something 9 and 7/8 inches unless it is done because of a tremendous difference in cost when by adding an eighth you can list the item as a full 10 inches. Mr. Burgheimer suggests very strongly that we emboss, or as he put it, 'engrave' on the bottom the size of the bowl, and definitely put the name salad bowl in large letters. He says we should be sure that people know it is a salad bowl, not a nappy or low mixing bowl. I think he is correct about this and we should put in good sized letters 'salad bowl'." This salad bowl, referred by a salesman, rather than by designers or modelers, was added to the production lines of Just Right Kitchenwares, Floral and Vegetable, being sampled in Crooksville at the time.

If this wasn't design inspiration enough, Byron continued his letter, "I also sent you two planters, one a duck with a hat on and the other a pig, that sell for 39 cents in McCrory Stores. Orrie Yonkers showed me these about a month ago and said their price was $2.16 a dozen. They are made by Vogue China. The guy that owns this company is related to Lou Butler. He makes, as you can see, bigger pieces for the money than Lou. In fact, his are the largest in the field. Only his limited production and poor colors permit others to even be in the field. I only hope his prices are low enough that he will silently fold his tent, but I guess this won't happen as he has been in the business for a good number of years now."

"I think we should send samples to the various firms in the following order: Woolworth, Newberry, Grant, McCrory, Kress, Murphy, Fishman, Green, McLellan, Neisner, Fisher-Beer."

"Keep me posted on the progress. It sounded good to hear that our clay making machinery was going to work. Also will be anxious to hear what Stewart has to say. How about Sears or Montgomery Ward?"

J.B.'s answer to Byron dated September 28, 1951, reads, "You are no doubt anxious to learn about the progress being made in our operation not only for yourself, but for the trade you have already contacted and is now waiting for samples."

"We are now casting a limited amount of ware on all three machines together with quite a number of open benches, all being the Hand Decorated Woodland pattern together with the three planters namely: Lady Basket, Lamb and big Kitten. Today we were able to light the booster portion of our kiln which throws heat into the jigger units and by the middle of next week, at least a portion of the samples will be released to your trade covering Kitchenware in the order indicated."

"You inquired about Kresge's reaction to samples which were only submitted on Tuesday the twenty-fifth, on which day we received a telephone call from Everett in Detroit, indicating an unusual and happy reaction from Mr. Stewart the buyer. He insisted that Everett leave all of his samples after the girls in his office admired what they claimed were California colors with emphasis upon the Coral. He has definitely stated that both complete lines of Kitchenware, the Vegetable and Floral, together with the Green banded bowls, would be placed on a listing at an early date and he requested colored illustrations covering all of this merchandise. The single exception is the pitcher in the Kitchenware line which he claims is overpriced. This is a very unusual reaction from Mr. Stewart, who is an extremely tough buyer, and I am still keeping my fingers crossed because they have always worked very closely with the Nelson McCoy Co."

(Note: Company information indicates the Just Right Kitchenware pitcher, claimed by a prospective buyer to be overpriced, was reduced in price from $8.10, to $7.50 per dozen.)

J.B. continued, "the strange thing is that the Nelson McCoy bowl set 4-piece that retails around a dollar seemed to present no particular problem to him. This is his reaction in front of John the salesman, and what might develop later remains to be seen. I am definitely a pessimist regarding this account, although the reaction is pleasing and might possibly work out to our advantage."

"We liked very much the salad bowl you purchased and have already produced this shape in both the Vegetable and Floral pattern samples of which might possibly be ready by the middle of next week and forwarded to you. We will attempt to establish prices by that time also."

"You will be glad to learn that we have received in excess of ninety five thousand dollars worth of orders on the Woodland pattern with only a limited number of samples and it is entirely likely that there will be in our hands for the holiday season an approximate one hundred fifty thousand dollars worth by the time the first order is released from our plant which we hope will be the week of October 14. Orders that are coming to us at this time should not be anticipated before the middle of November. We are passing this word along to several of the largest jobbing sources who have not started making inquiry."

"This amount of business has come to us even before Butler's catalog reaches the trade, which will be within the next few days and we can at that time anticipate a considerable volume of business. In other words, our neck is out plenty far, so far as promising holiday shipments is concerned. One thing in our favor is that Butler Brothers has assured us that they will continue to sell this line all through the year 1952, and that they expect to sell a lot of merchandise for release following the holiday season. This kind of word could be passed along to other trade since they are all in the habit of selling this type of merchandise simply for a holiday period."

"Just as soon as we get suitable Kitchenware samples which certainly will be by the middle of next week, we are going ahead with the production of color plates for colored illustrations to be placed in the hands of your syndicate operators. Since all of the catalogue information was destroyed in the fire we will have to get that detailed word from you again as soon as listings can be prepared."

The letter continued with regard to Boris Elias of Elias Brothers, Montreal, Canada and a possible method of distribution in that country. Ware was already being distributed in Canada, but according to Byron, not at a large enough volume. Brannie answered, "hoping that we can develop more business across the border in the future than we had in the past."

Byron was always very modest about his accomplishments for the pottery, and in conversations, nearly always made comments about being away in New York stating he, "was not really aware of the happenings in Crooksville." He kept the company alive with ideas, a designer of sorts, with the added knowledge of what was trendy and what the customer was willing to pay. Byron also seemed to be quite good at directing, perhaps even prodding his brother, Brannie, not only to the right sources, but also to the right pieces. And, Byron in New York, so close to the Canadian border, couldn't resist. Hull trade was in Canada both before and after 1950, compliments of "Bike."

Production Lines Of The Fifties

Hull proclaimed the theory of "security in diversification," and it was certain they had the right designer and head salesman for the job. Hull produced a minimum of three new and different designs each year to cultivate profitable sales. New ideas referred from Byron in New York, were designed in Crooksville. Samples were fired and returned to New York in a matter of a few weeks, ready to be shown to prospective buyers. This course continued in a pattern of one artistic design followed by another, and another, in a seemingly unending line up. The new, modern plant called for new, modern designs and finishes, and during the Fifties, we saw everything from striking high gloss finishes, to subtle textured pastels.

Edgar McClellan was still responsible as Ceramic Engineer and supplied most of Hull's glazes for the 1950's. His personal notebooks delineated formulas for, "Turquoise Glaze, White Enamel, White Matt 2, Beige Glaze #91, Pink Glaze, Buff Glaze, 40-D Opaque Turquoise Enamel, Yellow Glaze, Green Opaque, Burnt Orange, Black Glaze, Tan Glaze, White Spatter, Red V.G. Tint, Dark Green, V.G. Yellow Tint, Chain Store White Enamel, Bittersweet, Matt Royal Blue, Broken Turquoise, Matt Chartreuse, Chain Store Duck Yellow, Bright Red, Ripe Olive, New Avocado Enamel, and Golden Wheat," as well as others.

Some of the easily recognized glazes of the day were listed, "Woodland Pink V.G. Tint 4799-C; Peach Woodland; Pink V.G. Tint Woodland; Blue V.G. Tint, Blossom Flite; Seaweed, Wine (Ebb Tide); and Green V.G. Tint for Tokay; Chartreuse for bowls; Strawberry rundown; Soft Pink, Swans; Turquoise Beaded Glaze; Pink Beaded Glaze; Black V.G. Pink Beaded Glaze; Willow Green; Dove Grey; Dark Copper Green Glaze (for Blossom Flite); and Persimmon and Mountain Blue (for Continental)."

Notations from experimentals and trials were noted as well. One such designation, "Dark Matte Turquoise Spatter - trial batch no good," was later scribed, "Turquoise V.G. (very good) for White spatter." Other trials were designated, "White Enamel, for spraying ashtrays; Turquoise Enamel, for spraying ashtrays — when using for dipping ... alternate ingredients." Other notations related to experimentation included, "Autumn or Rancho Gold O.G. (over glaze) Tint and Green O.G. (over glaze) Tint - to tint over White rundown Spatter, Trial Turquoise Tint, and XX Green Tint #2."

A listing of McClellan's in-stock stains included: "Brown, Grey, Green, Coral, Mahogany, 1805 Gray, Pink, Green, F-4738 Grey, Red Underglaze, Black Underglaze, and Tan Underglaze."

An any given time, there were as many as half a dozen different designs in various stages of completion in the plant. Recognizable in the previous photographs which illustrated processing operations, were Woodland,

Parchment and Pine, Floral, Blue Ribbon green banded bowls, Crescent, Swans and novelties, along with other items, all in production during the same period.

Woodland, introduced in thirty shapes in 1949, (listed as numbers one through thirty-one, with number 20 omitted), prior to destruction of the plant, again surfaced. The company, however, was no longer carrying mold numbers 1, 5, 12, 17, 19, 21, 23, 25, or 31. This reemergence of matte Woodland in 1951, proved the delicate soft-bodied pastel glazes of Dawn Rose and Harvest Yellow could not be successfully duplicated, and Hull with little time to spare in claiming their portion of the market place, and the urgency in the need to get their shipments out, decided it was time to move on and leave the glazes behind that were giving them problems.

August 29, 1951, also saw the kitchenware lines, Vegetable and Floral, along with Blue Ribbon bowls being manufactured, as well as novelty planters. The lady basket and lamb planters, which had been introduced in the early 1940's, were back. These novelties were underglazed in pink with red trim or ivory with blue trim. Other figural planters included, three-piece swan sets, kitten, parrot, pheasant, pig, elephant, country boy, city girl, pup with yarn, kitten with spool, wishing well planter, ribbon wall pocket, peacock, and flamingo vases, as well as others.

Parchment and Pine was manufactured beginning in 1951. Production lines began soon after the reopening of the plant. Hull advertised Parchment and Pine as, "Parchment ... repeatedly varnished to preserve priceless contents, rolled, and yellowed with age ... lends its gracefully curved beauty to this fine art pottery, with just the right touch of texture and color provided by clusters of pine and cones." Parchment and Pine remained in production until 1954.

From 1951 to 1954, Matte, Two-Tone and Hi-Gloss Woodland, Parchment and Pine and Ebb Tide headed the art market. The novelties which had been introduced in 1951, remained in production through 1952 and 1953, with a number of new items added in late 1951 and early 1952. These items included the bandana ducks, Bird of Paradise and hippo flower inserts, unicorn and flying goose vases, poodle and giraffe vases, as well as others.

In 1952, Woodland entered the market in classy high gloss glazes which were advertised as New Hi-Gloss Woodland. Brochure pages illustrated the Hi-Gloss Woodland as duo-tone tinted pieces, reminiscent of earlier wares, while Two-Tone Woodland was illustrated as a one-color glazed ware with contrasting interior color. The company later classified both decorations of Woodland in the same category, that being Hi-Gloss Woodland. Woodland headed the art market, in mattes and high glosses, from the reopening of the plant until 1954. Many of the novelty planters listed above prevailed. Just Right Floral dinnerware remained in production while Crescent was added in solid green or wine, and Debonair was presented in chartreuse and wine.

Next in line was Ebb Tide, available on January 1, 1954. Described by the company as, "The shapes that inhabit the seas ... shells, coral, fish, and plants ... set the motif. Hull has captured them, in glowing colors, and fashioned them into art pottery of great beauty." This exotic line included sixteen shapes which were decorated in high gloss Seaweed and Wine or Shrimp and Turquoise.

Although Ebb Tide was still available in 1955, the year heralded the new art design of Blossom Flite, which presented a "distinctive new rendering yet stays within the bounds of the vastly popular floral theme." Blossom Flite was available in fifteen pieces. Decorations of charcoal gray on overall high gloss pink, or blue on overall high gloss pink with metallic green interior were available. Many of the same chain store assortments remained available with a few new additions, the rooster planter, colt figurine, Siamese cat with kitten planter, and knight on horseback, to name a few. Kitchenware of the day remained Just Right Floral, Debonair in updated two-tones with banding, and nested bowls in pink with charcoal veiling and black with pink veiling. Florist ware, referred to as #F1 List, forerunner to the Imperial line, was also included in the 1955 line up in tinted, air-brush blended and veiled decorations.

While Blossom Flite was still being offered, the art design, Butterfly, was the company's major attraction for the year 1956, to make up "the newest entrancing collection by Hull. America's finest from the kilns of Hull." Butterfly was offered in twenty-five pieces and was decorated in a combined gloss and matte finish of white on white, or matte white with turquoise interiors.

In 1956, the novelty ware and chain store assortments were still in abundance, but the new rage was pottery with wrought iron and brass accessories. Assortments included jardinieres in metal stands, lavabo sets in hanging racks, and ash tray and planter combinations in Royal glazes of pink and turquoise, air-brushed blended glazes, white on white, and the veiled decorations which were still in vogue. Jardinieres with stands were advertised as, "High Fashioned, Red Hot Year Around Best Sellers," for use as porch or patio containers, cemetery urns, ice buckets, or gift ideas. A softer side of Hull was shown with Sun Valley Pastels and the Royal line, referred to as "Mist," which both entered the market in 1956. Each line included items with metal accessories. During this time, several varieties of satin finished Madonna planters were also available.

Serenade headed Hull's art market in 1957. "Chipper chickadees on colorful boughs are the motif; fine art pottery from the kilns of Hull is the medium. The result ... Serenade ... is beautiful, functional and colorful." Items with metal accessories were still in demand, and available were all the same varieties of jardinieres, ash trays, and planters offered earlier. Three new chain store assortments emerged: Fiesta, Jubilee and Fantasy. Sun Valley Pastels were still available in 1957, as were the various satin Madonnas, accompanied at this time by the St. Francis planter.

Sharing molds and the artware spotlight for the year 1958, were Tokay, "The zest of a gypsy dance, the warmth of fiery tokay wine," and Tuscany, "Ornamental in relief with grapes and leaves from the valley of the silver Arno, bringing the peasant art of Italy to the homes of America." Tokay, "each piece trimmed in bright pleasing tints of pink and green," was also available in Milk White and Forest

Green. Tuscany was available in two decorations, Sweet Pink and Gray Green, or Milk White and Forest Green. Tuscany was introduced only slightly after Tokay entered the market, the dual line necessitated most likely due to serving two different syndicated buyers. By January 1, 1959, three new and distinct pieces had been added to the Tokay/Tuscany line up. The company, "influenced by a definite trend towards larger sizes," soon added the caladium leaf, a 15" pedestal vase and a 15" pitcher to the two grape lines. By mid-1959, Tokay's pink and green combination, and Tuscany's pink and gray green combination had been discontinued, leaving both grape designs available exclusively in white and forest green. In 1958, Heritageware kitchen line, and the chain store assortment, Mayfair entered the market.

Carry over items included Fiesta and Fantasy, along with the jardiniere assortments and ash tray and planter combinations in metal stands.

By January 1, 1959, Tropicana, "hand decorated pieces ... carefree and colorful like the happy days of a Caribbean Holiday," and Continental's sophisticated, modern shapes in rich bold colors were introduced. The Continental line was first available in "two strikingly lucid colors from nature ... accented with rich, bold stripes." Initial colors were Persimmon, "the completely captivating accent for today's interiors in the higher key of contemporary color," and Evergreen, "a delightfully subtle color that lends itself as a perfect foil to nature's own brilliant floral and leaf displays." A third color for Continental, Mountain Blue, followed, which was characterized as, "twilight in the Blue Mountains - modernized with stripes of white haze." Mayfair was still offered, as were Tokay and Tuscany, however, only in milk white and forest green.

Gold-Medal Flowerware also made its debut in 1959, and the jardinieres and ash tray and planter combinations continued to be on the 1959 retail lists. While Hull had produced special items for florists throughout it's tenure, and lines since the mid-1950's had included "F lists," the first glimpse of a line specifically named "Imperial, made especially for florists," gained attention, with a listing of thirty-two shapes and a twelve-color glaze key.

Imperial was advertised as, "New and colorful American ceramic designs by Hull to accentuate your beautiful flowers, and priced at preinflation levels through the medium of modern methods of production. This is our response to requests from many important suppliers. Months of exhaustive study and preparation have culminated in these pieces and colors to meet all your requirements. From ordinary low cost vehicles for transporting plants, to beautiful containers for luxurious floral arrangements, you'll find everything you need and want in Imperial."

The predominate line of 1960 continued with sales of Continental and the Tokay and Tuscany artware was still available in milk white with forest green. Gold-Medal Flowerware and a variety of jardinieres and planters with metal stands remained available. Coronet, in a new line of smoker stands and planter combinations emerged. Pagoda, with its Oriental flair, and previously introduced novelty planters now marked Regal, in milk white with green trim were new lines in 1960.

In 1961, Capri, "inspired by the Isle of the Sun," was the last assortment truly singled out as an artware with individual identity. 1961 saw also the introduction of Athena, "reflecting the classic beauty and perfect proportions of Greek architecture," named for, "Pallas Athena, goddess of peacetime industry. The fluted shapes, the graceful pedestals, the scrolled details were inspired by the Ionic, Doric and Corinthian columns of ancient Greece." Athena was introduced in Lilac or Spring Green with White Lava. By 1962, Athena was also offered in Satin White. Other artware pieces emerged from this point to the plant's closing, all seemingly falling into the Imperial category.

There were steady parades of chain store lines throughout Hull's history, however, during the 1950's there were more shared molds, referred to by alternate names, than at any other time. Identical designs with different line names were used to serve a variety of chain stores. Many times, the glaze, being the only clue, dictated the line for which the piece was actually intended.

Chain store sales representatives chose from groups of novelty wares, then designed and printed brochure pages of the lines or items they intended to retail. Buyers from the chain stores either singled out certain items for their particular sales agendas, or in some cases, opted for the entire line that Hull presented. These brochure pages were issued to all their stores and also forwarded to Hull. The reverse sides of the brochure pages sometimes contained the actual order form and an agreement between buyer and seller.

In this agreement, Hull had already dictated the minimum retail price expected for its wares. In return, Hull guaranteed to ship merchandise which met requirements of existing state and federal laws and provide articles that could be introduced into interstate commerce, more or less, assigning temporary trademark rights. Hull agreed to, "hold harmless and defend at its expense, the seller against all damage and expense from all claims of infringement of patents, copyrights, trademarks, or of unfair competition or bodily injuries or property damage arising out of the use, possession, consumption, or sale of said merchandise."

Chain store sales brochures read like a "who's who" of buyers. W.T. Grant sold a line they dubbed as Mayfair, which included familiar items of Imperial, Gold-Medal Flowerware and Fiesta. McCrory Stores Corp. advertised both a 13-piece and a 17-piece Sun Valley Pastel line, Jubilee teamed up with jardinieres with metal accessories and a combined line which included both Fiesta and Fantasy.

McCrory-McLellan marketed Gold-Medal Flowerware and Coronet, along with several additional items with metal accessories. H.E. Stewart, buyer for S.S. Kresge Co., made it his business to specialize in Sun Valley Pastels, Jubilee, Pagoda, Fantasy, Fiesta, Gold-Medal Flowerware, and a group of jardinieres, planters, and ashtrays with brass and wrought iron accessories.

J.J. Newberry Co. retailed Sun Valley Pastels and Coronet, spurred with a few Gold-Medal Flowerware items. McLellan Stores chose to sell Jubilee. S.H. Kress & Co. did a volume of business with Jubilee and a Regal and Coronet combination. B.M. Swarzwalder was a buyer for Athena, Coronet, Gold-Medal Flowerware and a large assortment of Regal. Rose's 5-10-25 Cent Stores Inc., marketed Gold-Medal Flowerware and Coronet. F.W. Woolworth was a leader in the sales of Flower Club Ceramics, a mixture of florist and novelty ware. H.L. Green Co. chose a mixture of Coronet, Gold-Medal Flowerware, Fiesta and Fantasy for their line up.

By having interspersed plain, sophisticated Imperial-type lines with their art designs throughout the 1950's, The Hull Company procured a new and demanding market in florist ware. This proved to be a successful and profitable market, and by 1960, Hull, quick to follow market trends, made the move to change total plant production to a combination of House 'n Garden servingware and Imperial florist line.

Times Dictate Changes In Production

In 1960, Hull who remained at the helm, having tremendous insight into current market trends and demands, convinced Board Members Robert Hull, Byron Hull, Harold Showers, and J.E. Everett to make major changes in production in order to retain the company's firm economic stance. The California movement toward the casual in nearly every aspect of daily living, along with the good fortune Pfaltzgraff Pottery laid at Hull's disposal, prompted Hull to make an abrupt change from artware to dinnerware. Hull knew what the nation's market demanded from this tiny little corner of the World, known as Crooksville. He was acutely aware that past style developments had moved from West to East, across the country. Hull's leadership was sure and steady, but all the while adaptable to change, and so began the twenty-five year success story of House 'n Garden ovenproof casual servingware.

Pfaltzgraff Pottery, which was being distributed in the early 1960's to finer department stores, declined marketing its dinnerware to chain stores such as J.C. Penney, Sears, Kresge's and the "five and dimes." Representatives from J.C. Penney asked Hull to duplicate the ware they were unable to purchase from Pfaltzgraff. J.B. Hull quickly and easily made his move to control a major portion of the dinnerware market by providing what Pfaltzgraff would not, and Hull's House 'n Garden entered the retail market by mid-1960. Pfaltzgraff soon after changed their design, leaving Hull in the market's major position to continue with the production of Mirror Brown, and the other lines which followed. Through the years, J.C. Penney remained loyal to Hull and proved to be the company's largest account.

The company's first mention of color was described as, "Old Fashioned Mirror-Brown, decorated with White Flow." Designed with strong masculine lines and expected to withstand constant daily use in the home or on the patio, House 'n Garden was first manufactured in what the company later decided to call, Mirror Brown trimmed with Ivory Foam. Many of the original shapes remained in production throughout the pottery company's remaining

years. In Hull's own words, "A few months later tangerine was added and now many items are also available in green and butterscotch. Combination of the four colors produced a Rainbow table setting unsurpassed on today's market." Rainbow House 'n Garden was offered until 1967. The company further said of the evolution of Rainbow dinnerware:

> "Nationwide inquiries for the famous Mirror Brown House 'n Garden serving-ware continue to be sensational.
>
> Imitations by many manufacturers of ceramics have not suppressed consumer desires for the originals as evidenced by the ever growing demands on our facilities.
>
> House 'n Garden serving-ware (now more than fifty items) excels for casual living — breakfast, luncheon, the patio, barbeque, at the T.V. along with table service.
>
> This serviceable ware is made for the American way of life - you'll like it in the living room or under the sheltering sky.
>
> For those who want a more colorful effect, many items are also available in Tangerine, Butterscotch, and Green which together with Mirror Brown produce a four color Rainbow Table."

Beginning with colors that could be mixed and matched, glazes were formulated for House 'n Garden colors that could be used as companions to the standard Mirror Brown, such as the Rainbow table setting where Mirror Brown was teamed with Butterscotch, Tangerine, and Green Agate.

Two colors of Rainbow, Tangerine and Green Agate, graduated to become separate lines of dinnerware, available to the consumer as complete sets. Green Agate, in an entire set, became known as Country Squire. Tangerine, identified as the "900" series, was further billed as Burnt Orange in an assortment made specifically for J.C. Penney. For promotional sales, Tri City Grocers advertised its 50th Anniversary gala with Tangerine House 'n Garden, which was referred to as "Golden Anniversary."

Hull's casual, down-to-earth dinnerware line was an instant success, not only with J.C. Penney, but with other retailers as well, and new shapes were continually added to the more than forty companion kitchenware items. By the late 1960's, House 'n Garden included over 100 items.

Provincial, which advertised improved features for, "perfect mixing and refrigeration," was offered from January 1, 1961, through 1963. This was the name used for Hull's Mirror Brown House 'n Garden with Milk White interiors and lids. The faces of dinner plates and saucers were additionally glazed in white, while the reverse sides remained Mirror Brown. Provincial was a spin-off from another manufacturer's design called Brown-Stone, brown glazed ware with chartreuse glazed interiors. The caladium leaf was used in this line up in stark white as a Chip 'n Dip. J.C. Penney, J.J. Newberry Co. and other major chain stores were the main customers of Provincial. New sales were cultivated from retail firms and grocers that used Hull's dinnerware as give-aways and promotional items.

In 1961, a House 'n Garden display by S.H. Kress advertised, "Today's Best Buys - Outstanding Money Saving Values," from 29 cents to $2.49 each, and illustrated the versatility of Hull's wares in a patio barbecue or picnic setting.

Hull's House 'n Garden competed with other manufactured dinnerware lines at showrooms in most major cities, as well as, the Atlantic City Shows, National Housewares Show, Chicago Gift Show, and New York Gift Show year after year, for twenty-five years. Byron Hull was always in attendance at these shows as salesman for the company, accompanied by John Everett and Marvin Hoffman. Moderately priced House 'n Garden Ware by Hull was advertised to their buyers as "an invitation to bigger, more profitable sales." Special pricelists applied to Hull's syndicate buyers who received discounts beyond those which Hull advertised to the regular wholesale trade. While wholesale lists were available to the trade for bulk orders only, Hull offered separate Armed Forces Exchange pricelists in which items could be purchased individually.

This photograph, taken 5-2-65, by The Zanesville Times Recorder, shows President J.B. Hull in the conference room of the Hull plant where wares were displayed in showcase fashion. Hull examines Crestone's Chip 'n Dip, with Vice President Robert W. Hull, and E.D. Young, Secretary-Treasurer. The shelved showcase in the background housed Mirror Brown House 'n Garden.

Crestone, a newly designed casual line for 1965, entered the market in lovely high gloss turquoise with ivory foam. Crestone was considered "the new and fashionable way of life, thirty beautiful items designed specifically for present day living habits in the breakfast nook, on the patio, at the T.V. or barbeque, as well as normal table service." The Crestone dinnerware line was in production for only two years.

Hull also entered into a campaign effort headed by the National Association of Variety Stores, Inc., for promotion of their products which proved to be, in Hull's own words, "extraordinary volume." In 1966, Hull's sales were equal to that of Pfaltzgraff's. Each company reported a one million dollar sales picture.

Mirror Brown was the "standard" for House 'n Garden for twenty-five years, while other colors danced their way in and out of Hull's production. Hull believed in, and followed, a pattern of adapting to change in order to maintain the status House 'n Garden dinnerware held in the market, and continuously added new items. Hull asked of his already established trade, "Why new items?" This question was best answered in Hull's own words:

> "The new items illustrated are meant to make sure that the consuming public does not have to turn to any other source to complete its casual serving and kitchenware needs.
>
> The sole object is to maintain consumer enthusiasm and preference for the nation's number one line, instead of the normal reason for offering new items, to stimulate sales, which we all realize would not contribute to our present welfare.
>
> But we are taking nothing for granted so far as the future is concerned and we are fortunately in a position to be very selective in our choice of patterns. Time and the privilege to choose from innumerable ideas and sketches is on our side so long as consumer acceptance through willing buyers remains at, or near, its present level.
>
> We are proceeding with dies and molds in anticipation of favorable reaction to these offerings."

In 1968, Avocado with Ivory Trim was a part of Hull's dinnerware line up. Hull advertised their most popular shapes available in this "timely" color, formulated surely in an effort to follow the trend of avocado kitchen appliances. Could there possibly be a homemaker that wouldn't be smitten by a lovely set of avocado dinnerware to match her appliances? Hull didn't think so, and his vision was correct, as Avocado was not discontinued until May 15, 1971.

Hull provided House 'n Garden to chain store buyers both large and small; F.W. Woolworth Co., King's Dept. Stores, Victory Merchandise Mart, Meadow Sales Company, E.A. Hinrichs & Co., Neisner Brothers, Inc., Nobel, Inc., The 2800 Shop, S.E. Nichols, Inc., J.A. Tepper Co., S.S. Pennock Co., G.C. Murphy Co., Standard Drug Co., Ben Franklin Stores, and more.

Orders were being accepted by Canadian customers as well. Thomas A. Ivey & Sons, Ltd., of Port Dover, Ontario, and D.H. Lisser & Company, Ltd., Montreal, Quebec, were two of Hull's Northern buyers.

House 'n Garden glazes were tested and approved under the guidance of U.S.P.A. working with the Federal Food and Drug Administration which permitted a lead emission of seven parts (7 ppm) per million. Hull's dinnerware tested one hundredth of one part (.01 ppm) which was next to none, and far below the established safety level.

Hull was spearheading an effort to upgrade ware leaving the plant and had extensive conveying equipment installed in order to accomplish all sorting of ware during the normal daytime hours. J.B. Hull reported, "A silly union inspired labor board decision prevented us from obtaining acceptable supervisory judgment by the former round-the-clock method."

The hen on nest casseroles entered the market place in 1968, and in 1969, Hull added the two larger bakers with figural chicken bases. These bakers, one two inches deep, the other three inches deep had an incised rooster design in the bowl of the dish. An oval individual salad bowl complimented with the same incised rooster decor.

To renew interest in sales, Hull also presented at this time a corn serving dish, gravy boat with an extremely elongated handle, a double serving dish and a tray that teamed with a sauce bowl became a chip 'n dip. Several of these items had become obsolete by December 1, 1970; the tray and sauce bowl, the double serving dish, and individual salad with rooster decor.

In 1970, Hull had more than one thousand customers who disposed of nearly three million dollars worth of ware annually at retail prices. Under the direction of J.B. Hull, the company assumed and maintained an enviable sales position throughout his tenure as President of Hull, despite labor and management disagreements, and rising costs of raw materials. In September, 1970, House 'n Garden casual serving and kitchenware was available in over 60 shapes and constituted 70% of the company's total production.

Hull forwarded to distributors price quotations that became effective on December 1, 1971. Inflation was a fact of life, uncontrolled by any type of business or service, however, Hull felt a need to give customers an explanation for the rise in prices.

"The enclosed quotations represent in large measure the increase granted labor the second year of our three-year union shop agreement.

Of course our sources of raw material are in the same bind and in many cases their increases now come to us on postal cards, seeming to take for granted that this is simply our new way of life.

All we can do is to ask that you please bear with us as we continue a policy of adjusting prices to meet conditions over which we have the most limited control."

January 1, 1972, saw J.B. Hull further reconciling any differences with customers by an additional notification.

"Prices quoted are in compliance with Executive Order No. 11627, and if any price is found to be illegal, resulting in a price roll back, refund will be made of any such overcharge(s).

Established through collective bargaining the second year of our three year labor contract exceeds the government guide line but has been granted to labor by law.

We now find ourselves in the position of having to attempt next year's production on the basis of a 3% price increase which is less than half what is needed to continue the normal advancement of our business.

It is no secret that government guide lines were established on the basis of big business where labor is generally less than 30% of their costs but this does not apply to our business in which labor exceeds 50%. Nevertheless, we are caught in the process and will have to absorb the losses a price increase of only 3% will bring about. The increase will not become effective until March 1, 1972.

The investment and added yearly expense to improve the quality of ware combined with the fact that government controls prevent us from seeking equitable price adjustment establishes an unprecedented challenge to management.

Thank you very much for all past business and for whatever consideration you choose to extend to us at this time. We will surely do our best to justify your confidence whenever offered the opportunity."

Hull discontinued the larger chicken servers with incised decoration effective March 1, 1972, in order to make way for the introduction of items 5280, 5770, 5840, and 5950, the newly designed Chicken and Duck Casseroles.

At the same time the success of Hull's dinnerware and floristware was unquestioned by a nation of consumers, Hull Company employees began to question their employment rights. The company was plagued by employee strikes throughout the 1970's and 1980's, eight to be exact. Inflation created rising costs of the product, and this, coupled with plant shutdowns and worker's demands which had to be met in some form, put the company in a precarious position. J.B. Hull begged indulgence of consumers in an Official Notification after a seven week strike:

"We are pleasantly surprised by the volume of business left in our hands during these many troubled weeks and our position is to see that orders are processed as rapidly as possible in a fair manner.

Cancellations have been almost negligible and orders have piled up which means that we must continue to seek your indulgence for the immediate future.

Our fight with the union was to keep labor costs (which exceed 50% of total costs) competitive in this area rather than to submit to discriminatory demands based primarily upon the degree of success we have attained.

It is true that our facilities have been fully utilized for several years and it is only through comparable prices that we can maintain that enviable position.

Some prices will have to be adjusted in the near future because of increased labor costs but all orders you have chosen to leave with us during this trouble (and this has been a tremendous boost to our morale) will be processed at the figures already existing. This seems to be about the least we can do in recognition of the favor extended to us.

You may be assured of our great desire to get merchandise into your hands at the earliest possible moment."

Wages still under government control in November 1, 1974, prompted Hull to again appeal to his consumer audience for their continued consideration:

"In spite of the good intentions of our national governing body and the degree of stability needed, the only thing that keeps a business going is the difference between costs and selling prices, now, not some time in the future.

This is true because we have consistently followed a conservative policy of pricing that prevented an accumulation of funds sufficient to carry us over a prolonged period of time.

Therefore, our well-intentioned plan to delay price adjustment to late next year must be interrupted to meet cost increases forced upon us by the raw material sources of supply necessary in our operation together with labor costs established under government guide lines (before they were removed) causing anticipated cost of production to be far out of line.

This explanation may seem as an apology, and indeed it is, since it causes you to, again, have to decide whether or not our line is worth the all-too-often revision of prices. Naturally, we hope it is worth both the inconvenience and new quotations.

We are definitely holding to a company policy of turning away from new potential trade, both national and international, and are putting great emphasis on the quality of ware being sent to your stores. Nobody can be perfect in the production and inspection of thousands of pieces daily, but we are resisting a trend, prevalent in the country today, to cheapen the line for any reason whatsoever. This puts a burden on supervisors and the ceramic department as we encounter both prices and shortages of raw materials."

Continued additional cost adjustments prompted the company to send Byron Hull to J.C. Penney representatives on September 15, 1975, with new price quotations. This was followed by a letter from J.B. Hull to John Fuchs, J.C. Penney Company, New York, dated October 1, 1975:

"The necessity for price advancement causes us to restate an important part of our company policy.

We have consistently rejected the opportunity to substitute lower cost materials that have a bearing on quality in the belief that a better made and better appearing line will continue to lead over-the-counter sales. And we will pursue this policy so long as the consuming public through willing buyers decides that our line is worth the needed price adjustments.

Many years ago when industry appeared to exercise too much control over the economy, Federal Laws governing monopolies came into existence. And similar treatment will have to be exercised over organized labor if we are to prevent the never ending upward movement of prices.

Our past fiscal year dollar sales figure was up but profits down with full factory operation which means that we absorbed a greater portion of increased costs of both raw materials and labor than quotations were expected to produce. Therefore, this present increase represents the third year wage increase in our labor contract, along with an effort towards partial recovery of lost profits.

And this is important because there is no way under existing circumstances for us (a union shop) to acquire contracts without granting higher wages which means higher prices. And we need not point out that only profitable companies can continue as your sources of supply.

For more than six years we have turned away from new potential trade and will continue this policy until normal 30 day deliveries can be accomplished. Our principal concern is that the consuming public can be reached for final judgment as to the worth of our line which is only possible under our present policy through sources similar to the one you represent. And beyond this is the expectation that we will remain able to furnish readily saleable ware."

In 1975, the company's dinnerware production now totalled nearly 75% of the company's total output. The company continued their vigorous advertising campaigns, "Open stock House 'n Garden offers startersets, dinnersets, party-packs and many more appealing serving pieces and they are all ovenproof. The American homemaker has chosen Hull's House 'n Garden for today's casual way of life, its popularity has earned it its rightful place as a nation's number one line." At this time, seventy-five all-purpose pieces of House 'n Garden were available in Hull's extensive open stock.

In that same year, The Village of Crooksville was accorded a certificate of official recognition by the American Revolution Bicentennial Administration as a Bicentennial Community. The Crooksville-Roseville area Pottery Festival Association agreed to sanction the 10th Annual Pottery Festival as a Bicentennial event. The Hull Company produced a Mirror Brown line to accent the Bicentennial, however, it was never in full production, nor entered the retail market. A company brochure page was designed which proposed to sell this ware in 16-piece sets, consisting of the plain Mirror Brown dinner and salad plates, with specially designed mugs and fruits with the embossed eagle and star decoration. 12-Piece sets were to include the plain Mirror Brown dinner plates teamed with the Bicentennial fruits and mugs. Additional accessory items included creamer and covered sugar, shaker set, jumbo stein, two quart pitcher, four pint casserole and a five pint bean pot.

Although new colors and styles of dinnerware were being market-tested all across the United States, the standard House 'n Garden in Mirror Brown, still a major seller in the States, was a beginning sensation in Australia, where it was being sold at in-home parties.

Popularity of the Mirror Brown glaze remained unquestioned, as Hull was contracted to glaze and fire porcelain drawer pulls by the thousands. Wisconsin

Porcelain initially contracted for Hull to glaze and fire 10,000 drawer pulls and second and third orders for 30,000, and 50,000 followed. The company received the drawer pulls already molded and in greenware form. After the glazing and firing processes, Hull shipped them to the Amerock Corporation of Rockford, Illinois. There they were given metal accessories and marketed.

During experiments in the Spring of 1978, the round canister set in Mirror Brown, was on the firing line. A few months later, production lines were ready, but not without much controversy over shape, size, and the fact they had no handles; practicality was questioned. The Hull Company went so far as to invite ladies in to make certain they could easily lift and use the largest canister when filled to the brim with flour. There were additional problems related to production after the company made the decision to move forward. The sides caved in quite easily during the finishing processes of trimming and sponging. Workers found it nearly impossible to keep the canister bowls round, which of course, led to still another problem — improper fitting lids. The company was also responsible for production of additional innovative accessory items such as a spoon rest, an egg plate, fish platter, ginger bread man server and a handled tray. Problems within the plant did not keep J. B. Hull from issuing new items. Although Hull wasn't soliciting new customers, he was certainly attempting to offer updated styles to create a continuing interest in Mirror Brown.

J.B. Hull's Death Leaves Company With Unpredictable Future

The production move to the innovative idea of casual servingware, combined with the massive Imperial florist line, served as J.B. Hull's final chapter in leading the company. J. Brannon Hull died June 23, 1978, leaving the Hull Company unprepared for what was to come. Although knowing all Hulls of the pottery region were decidedly aged, the company's stockholders had made no provisions which would provide strong leadership to move the family pottery tradition forward in time. At the time, the seventy-three year old company, in which the family's interest had prevailed, was naive, almost helpless to outside enterprises. Security within the family had cushioned the pottery from the rest of the world; stockholders failed to realize interests of a family-owned operation would most likely not remain the same when outsiders entered this protected circle. After Hull's death, consumers and local craftsmen alike pondered the outcome of a company, famous not only for its artware production, but also a leader in the manufacture of dinnerware and floristware.

J.B. Hull never forgot that the company's success was based on customer satisfaction and adamantly regarded the customer as "number one." He reminded his employees of this on a daily basis with an enlarged letter-on-poster-board which was positioned inside the plant worker's area, very near the time clock. It read:

To All Employees:

Our customers are our life line for job security and continued happiness for our families.

Keeping customers satisfied is everybody's business. As long as we continue to do the best we know how - our customers will remain loyal. Customers respond to better products - better service with more business. More business keeps each of us working.

There's real satisfaction for all of us when we keep customers satisfied.

Sincerely,

J.B. Hull

Hull never neglected obligation to his fellowmen and gave his earnest cooperation in the advancement of measures for the public good. Hull, who had dedicated his life to employing the people of Crooksville, believed in furthering one's education and in turn, left a generous endowment to the Village of Crooksville, in the form of "The J. Brannon Hull Scholarship Fund." The purpose of the scholarship was originally funded to "encourage and assist graduates of Crooksville High School and children of the Hull Pottery Company employees to obtain a degree in higher education." This scholarship fund is still in effect, eligibility requirements having been revised by the Board of Trustees after the Hull plant closed.

Sulens Heads Hull Pottery

Although Marie Hannum (Mrs. J. Brannon) Hull, had controlling stock in the company, the management in 1978 shifted to the hands of Henry Sulens as President. Robert W. Hull, served as Chairman of the Board, Byron Hull, as Vice President and Sales Manager, and Harold Showers, Vice President and Plant Manager.

This was only the second time in the company's history that a Hull had not personally headed the firm. Adapting to change was difficult for Hull employees as they found it difficult to relate to outsider Sulens who was not a pottery man, nor was he from the Ohio pottery region.

Management and personnel had may disputes and despite negotiations, the employee strikes increased. At times there was harmony within the pottery and the firm was profitable; at other times, the company lost as much as $100,000 per year. During this period the loss of work due to employee strikes caused the company to lose ground with solid, repeat customers. Many major contracts were lost, never to be regained. Hull, was at this time, centering primary interest on the production of dinnerware, nearly 90%, in fact.

Early 1981, began with a three-month employee strike which assisted management and stockholders in ousting Hull President, Henry Sulens.

Taylor Becomes Hull President

Larry Taylor replaced Henry Sulens on May 26, 1981, as Hull's President. According to Taylor, the company had lost $10,000 in May, 1981, alone, and never made a profit after that time. Taylor reports the reason for the company's becoming stagnate was due to its not having taken on any new accounts for nearly seven years. J.B. Hull had stated that no major accounts had been recruited since 1969. Due to Union disputes, labor strikes and increased inflationary costs, Hull wisely felt obligated to serving present customers before adding new customers, which in turn, created even more delays in services. The company had been unable to provide timely services for several years, and Hull believed more business would have only added to the number of problems the pottery faced.

The company needed leadership, but more than that, it needed to revive the pottery worker's spirit of craftsmanship and pride for a livelihood that had kept the Ohio Valley in business since the early blue-bird potteries. Workers and retailers alike waited for a miracle, wondering if this much-needed revival would take place.

Taylor, the first to admit he was not a potter, set forth to build on the solid reputation and respect Hull had earned from past years as a major supplier of quality dinnerware and floristware. What Taylor failed to realize was, at this time, the Hull Pottery was enmeshed in problems that were far beyond his ability to solve.

No doubt the greatest situation involved a letter from the Environmental Protection Agency instructing the company to clean up lead wastes in and around the plant. According to Taylor, this letter, delivered in April, 1981, remained unnoticed for nearly a year. With the EPA left unnoticed, Taylor focused his attention on employees and production.

Jack Frame came into the business as Taylor's Vice President on July 13, 1981, and a short time later, also served as Plant Superintendent, taking the place of Harold "Slim" Showers. Under new management, changes were to be made. In years past, company employees had been allowed to work far into their senior years, many worked well into their eighties. While new management allowed employees to remain gainfully employed for a number of years, mandatory retirement was set at age seventy, and tenured employees were released.

There were also major differences of opinion which kept the company from moving ahead. Although the company was responsible for 2000 ware presses per day, Taylor believed the company's production could have been more efficient with a semi-automatic jigger installed to leave the ram presses free for even greater output. Jack Frame, the Plant Superintendent, believed a smaller kiln was necessary for a more profitable year-end picture. With sales down, the great tunnel kiln was deemed worthless by Frame for a profitable operation. Once the kiln was lit, it burned continuously, 365 days per year. In the event of a kiln rack, where the kiln cars came off the track, a complete cool-down was necessary, leaving the cars to be rebuilt. The company lost several production days due to any kiln rack. Operational costs to fire the kiln were in excess of $10,000 per month, and it was estimated that in order to justify its operation, three million dollars in sales per year were necessary. Hull had not produced this sales volume since the early 1970's. Decisions for change were left unmade and Hull struggled with current equipment and operations.

An inventory was made and Taylor soon found several ideas for production that had been shelved with no follow-through, ideas which may have in an earlier day worked, but now were considered out-of-date. Although a few of

these designs were expanded upon and used, such as the souffle dish, fresh, innovative ideas were imperative. Larry Taylor retained Louise Bauer as designer, but when converting production to entirely new dinnerware lines, the company hired free-lance designer Maury Mountain, known for creating the popular Pfaltzgraff designs.

In complimenting yet another trend in colored kitchen appliances, Taylor initiated dinnerware with a glaze of Mirror Almond with Caramel Trim. First shipments were made in mid-1981, after having solved a few minor problems of glaze bubbling. Although appreciative of the almond glaze, Byron Hull didn't care for the contrasting caramel trim and asked for his dinnerware set to be void of the run-down decoration. Items such as a round one-piece sectional server, a rectangular bake dish and squat condiment shakers without the caramel trim were marketed in Ohio's area pottery retail stores. These items were special orders for a restaurant chain and did not carry the Hull trademark. The sectional server was marketed with a metal base provided by Chromex of Cleveland, Ohio. The almond glaze was produced and marketed for nearly two years.

In 1982, Don Foulds, a retired Ceramic Engineer from Cleveland, moved to the Crooksville area after his expertise was retained by the Hull Company. Foulds had brought with him, twenty-nine years' experience in glaze formulas and reportedly there was no glaze this man could not formulate. By this time, the Environmental Protection Agency had made clear their demands for lead clean up of the pottery, and since lead had been found in Hull's glazes, Foulds' first task was to formulate a glaze that was lead-free.

The EPA spotlight posed problems that were immense. If EPA's letter regarding the new legislation for the clean up had been adhered to in a timely manner, all could have been saved, Hull would have been afforded the same time period for waste clean up as other potteries. Regardless of management transition, and Taylor's good intentions to make up for lost time, the government considered the pottery's dealings in clean up action a blatant refusal to adhere to law. When EPA tested, they found lead in Hull's glazes, the same glazes that were being poured down the drains within the plant. The same lead glazes that eventually settled in the waste lagoon adjacent to the plant property.

During this time, management centered major emphasis on the talented pottery craftsmen of the Ohio Valley. Credit given to fine craftsmen was enlisted in all phases of Hull's new advertising campaigns. With a renewed meaning for pride and craftsmanship of the potter, the potter-at-wheel logo was relied on even more in these modern times. The use of "Crooksville, Ohio," or "Crooksville, O." being added to all newly designed molds and any molds that were updated or retooled further promoted the local pottery region.

The Ridge Collection was in production nearly three years. Shipments of Ridge began in Spring, 1982. Ridge was advertised as being, "a unique blend of contemporary style and country flavor. This highly functional casual servingware is produced with much the same care and artful expertise as our other pottery items." Ridge's name was derived from its distinctive "ridged" edges and also from the various local geographical ridges found in the Crooksville, Ohio, area. For this line, the new glazes of tawny ridge (tan) and flint ridge (gray), joined Hull's standard brown, referred to in this line as walnut ridge. Many molds were restyled, the flat pieces such as plates were a little deeper, and were "ridged" on outer edges. New shapes emerged for bowls and shaker sets. Taylor reported accounts had been enlisted with J.C. Penney and Woolworth Stores, at that time, the only national chains involved with the company.

Due in part to lost business accounts, Hull's advertising campaigns found it necessary to prove a point, and once again appealed heavily to the consumer, as it once had with the initial introduction of House 'n Garden. "The Hull Pottery Company was founded in 1903, (taking credit for Acme Pottery's beginning, rather than Hull's which was 1905), producing kitchenware, floristware, and many patterns of artware. Hull Pottery has grown considerably since then, but continues many of the same traditions of craftsmanship and artful expertise. This new, highly functional, casual serving-ware is the culmination of many years of skill and knowledge."

"Your Ridge Collection casual serving-ware is a natural for the freezer, the oven, the micro wave, conventional ovens, the dishwasher, and, of course, the table. All Ridge Collection pieces are dishwasher safe and resist marring from everyday use. If items do become moderately scratched or dull, the original gloss can be restored by using a mild, powdered cleanser. You will notice some minor differences in color, size, and shape. This is very normal and characteristic of handcrafted pottery such as your Ridge Collection serving-ware. Due to the nature of ceramics, care should also be taken to protect fine wood furniture from being scratched by the "foot" or bottom edges of your serving-ware. Care is taken at the factory to make the bottoms as smooth as possible."

Taylor took the 11 inch Serving Tray that was first introduced in 1978, and saw to it that it was glazed in colors other than Mirror Brown, those being tawny ridge (tan), and flint ridge (gray). When first introduced, it was made to use both in microwave and conventional ovens. But alas, almost as instructions, this item came to bear the incised mark "Serving Tray," on its base due to consumer use on the range top, which of course, ended in breakage. The earlier manufactured trays were not marked with the "serving" logo.

The Gingerbread Man server had been placed in production before Taylor's term of presidency. And now, it too, was being glazed in the Ridge colors. Taylor saw a need to expand this idea and Louise Bauer designed the cookie jar in 1982, as a companion piece. The cookie jar proved successful and soon afterward, a bowl, mug and coaster/spoon rest appeared on the market. This animated design soon gave way to production of a train canister set with Taylor setting the mode. His idea included bulging, animated characters, looking as though they had stepped straight from a comic strip. Taylor, although still not quite satisfied as to their appearance, set out a limited production run which was discontinued by employee strike. Taylor's next step, already planned, was to include, "Gingerbread Junction," a train station house for the train canister set. Although the die and mold was made for this

and a candy dish, they were never finalized or trialed for production.

Taylor further commissioned Maury Mountain to design an entirely new dinnerware, also referred to as part of "The Hull Collection," which was glazed in Mirror Brown. This dinnerware was designed in fluid lines with a band of "rings" added to plates, cups, bowls, as well as other pieces. Hull lines Heartland and Blue-Belle also benefited from the "banded" molds, although each kept a separate and distinct glaze and color treatment.

Heartland, a hand-stamped brown heart design on a satin background of cream with gold shadings, exhibited a distinctive country look. In this line, the bulbous-shaped canisters with "banded" tops were used, rather than the plain, cylinder-shaped Ridge canisters. Canister jars were stamped flour, sugar, coffee and tea, and companion jars for baked beans, chowder, chili and cookies were available. Embossed or raised lettering had been used in many previous kitchenware designs, however, this was the first time in many years that stamped lettering appeared on shakers and jars. Heartland was in production from late 1983, to early 1985, with large volumes being sold to major chain stores such as Wal Mart and Penneys, neither of which at this time were listed as syndicate buyers.

The final line produced by Hull, Blue-Belle, was glazed in a classic winter-white, alleged by Taylor to match Lenox China's glaze. This dinnerware line exhibited the epitome of class and style combined in one package. Blue-Belle's classic flair, combined with a serene country air, was decorated with a blue underglaze floral stamp of trailing blue bell florals. The Lenox China "look" of this glaze is most apparent in the number 71 swan which complimented this line. Hull's Blue-Belle brochure pages had been photographed and a limited number were produced. The complimenting swan was also a part of the promotional advertising for this line, although it had first been introduced as part of the Medley chain store assortment in 1962. Blue-Belle was made in limited quantities and was in production no more than six months. There had been little or no chance to promote this dinnerware before the company closed.

The Pfaltzgraff influence was quite apparent in Heartland and Blue-Belle, as both were designed by Maury Mountain, Pfaltzgraff's designer. Some of Hull's old standards, the casseroles with chicken and duck covers, were additionally decorated in the Heartland and Blue-Belle glaze treatments. The 32-ounce covered casserole came from a shelf of discontinued molds. This casserole had first been introduced in the 1965 Crestone line, the lid's handle is the give-away. The newly molded souffle and quiche dishes offered in these lines were other evidences of Pfaltzgraff's influence.

The stressed management and labor relationship continued to make all of Crooksville uneasy. This, in combination with decreased production, loss in contracts, and the fact that foreign-made wares were less costly to manufacture, made any attempt of stability by providing new lines and new marketing strategies futile. The new lines introduced had promise of becoming successful under normal conditions. However, issues surrounding the company were anything but normal. Problems within the plant greatly affected production output, which could have been close to 50,000 pieces per day.

The Hull faced continuing problems with the EPA, which ultimately resulted in Federal Court litigation, beginning in 1981. The outcome resulted in a two-year clean up effort at the cost of $150,000. Additional to this expense were court costs and fees for attorneys, engineers and expert witnesses. The final figures were staggering, and according to Taylor, an upwards of a quarter of a million dollars was necessary for this purpose. The funding needed for the EPA clean up was met through operations money of the pottery plant. The drastic reduction of operations money put yet another hardship on the already strained economics of the firm.

The Hull Pottery Succumbs

After having pioneered the early uncertain years with numerous area competitors of the pottery trade, the uncertainty of the depression years, reduced output and decreased materials necessary for the War effort, disastrous ends by flood and fire, conflicts over reconstruction of the plant, shaken stability due to loss of family leaders within the company's structural foundation, numerous employee lay-offs and strikes, and monumental problems with the Environmental Protection Agency, the Hull Company could withstand no more.

Hopes that ran high were soon doused, and the fate of the pottery operations that once gave the Village and surrounding area potters their much-needed employment was now certain. The Hull Pottery would not regain its status in the market of manufacturing pottery. There would be no more glaze fired after August 6th, 1985, when twenty-five employees began an eighth strike. This strike centered on negotiations for increased holiday and insurance benefits, it did not concern employee pay.

Whether it was a case of a company and its officials too weary to fight any longer or just plain economics, a tired old company closed its doors. The walls within, as well as the townspeople in the small Village of Crooksville, Ohio, continued to hope for a miracle, believing this was not a fitting end to the pottery tradition, or the area craftsmen which had made the Hull a showplace in the ''Pottery Center of the World,'' since 1905.

It was considered traditional for any pottery to fire the ware left inside a kiln, even during a strike. With discontinuance of pottery operations almost overnight, Hull's kiln was filled with ware that was reportedly fired by a handful of kiln workers in this pottery tradition.

Immediate actions to disperse the pottery and equipment soon showed the Crooksville community that workers would never return to the pottery. The largest portion of equipment and most of the florist dies and molds were sold within a few weeks to the Friendship II Pottery of Roseville, Ohio, in late September of 1985. This firm later purchased the Hull building and real estate. Additional molds from House 'n Garden dinnerware and accessories were sold to a firm in northern Pennsylvania.

The pottery was virtually gone, equipment, dies and molds were being discarded and sold every day, but the official letter, which allowed the company to close down picket lines and give employees the opportunity to receive unemployment benefits, was not drafted until March 24, 1986, nearly six months later.

A handful of the company's newest blocks and dies were stored by Taylor. These molds included the Imperial swan, duck and frog, along with a few of the most recent dinnerware molds, including the Gingerbread molds, some of which Taylor later sold.

The Hull Pottery was in full production when its doors closed, and the plant held an upwards of 10,000 pieces of ware in various stages of production. Overhead conveyor belts hung heavy with ware, carts and tables were full and the kiln was loaded. The Company's dispersal methods severely damaged any future collectability of these wares by allowing such a haphazard plan to take place.

Truckloads and truckloads of molds and greenware were driven to be dumped. Many molds, along with leftover greenware and glazes were transported to the Ohio Ceramic Center, located on State Route 93, between Roseville and Crooksville. Al Dennis, responsible for the Museum's operations, has glazed and fired many of Hull's greenware pieces, and has molded many items from original Hull molds. After Hull's remaining glazes were depleted, the Ceramic Center began firing in their own glaze formulas, including solid and spattered or sponged ware glazes. All the greenware items bore the Hull logo, and while the trademarks were to have been eliminated, most were not.

Jerry Beaumont, of Beaumont Bros. Pottery of Crooksville, became interested in some of Hull's molds when he aided in storing some of the blocks and dies for Dennis and the Ceramic Center. Beaumont purchased designs with plans to place them into production. One in particular, the Cinderella teapot, (which after 1950, was referred to as the Cook 'N' Serve teapot), has been produced by Beaumont in volumes. Beaumont, located at 410 Keystone Street, Crooksville, Ohio, specializes in Early American traditional stoneware and hand painted salt glaze pottery. They utilize local Crooksville clay for their products which are decorated in rich grays and vibrant blues. The teapot shape is definitely recognizable, the clay and glaze treatment are not. Beaumont has removed the Hull trademark.

Salvage efforts also included inviting in members of the community to buy and clean out complete rooms or sections of the plant. This included the tools, tables, boards from the conveyor belts, ware, molds, and anything else they cared to carry out. Many greenware items were taken home for glaze and decoration and many molds were put in use in the home due to this all-out effort to dispose of anything and everything inside the factory walls. The in-home decorated and molded items will carry the Hull trademark in most instances unless the new owner has made a concerted effort to scratch off the existing mark. Greenware items which have been exposed to the elements for an extended length of time normally will not take glaze treatments effectively. This perhaps, will assist in identification of the in-home decorated greenware items.

A salesman at heart, Taylor would not sit idle. He wanted something to sell. Taylor searched for other firms to produce Hull items shortly after Hull's doors closed. Taylor believed the market demanded additional Gingerbread cookie jars and his first endeavor was to contract with Western Stoneware of Monmouth, Illinois, for this production.

Blocks and cases for the Gingerbread Man cookie jar and Gingerbread Man server were sent to Illinois, along with glaze formulas. In a short time, Western Stoneware developed the glazes and produced nearly 5,000 cookie jars, and close to the same number of servers, which were packaged with Hull information and logo, and shipped as Hull manufacture.

Although Western Stoneware produces a fine grade of ware, the cookie jars and servers the firm produced for Hull were, in fact, not Hull production. Western-produced items did not entirely match Hull's previous glazes. Further, the clay content was noticeably different. The clay was darker, and even bordered on gray in appearance. While the darker clay may or may not have been responsible for the glaze differences, the glaze was noticeably darker and heavier, and carried more imperfections. The finishing processes for the cookie jar sometimes left the base "short" of glaze and a bare clay "foot" can be seen when the item is in a seated position. The items were marked with the Hull trademark, and although "Crooksville, Ohio" was removed from some of the molds, they were packaged with Hull leaflets pertaining to Ohio artisans.

A television commercial was developed by Taylor to promote the Gingerbread cookie jar and server combinations for $19.95. The commercial further promoted the Ohio Pottery area artisans, who had absolutely nothing to do with production of the Illinois-based products. The commercial aired and Taylor waited patiently for orders that were slow in coming. The company was left with a volume of non-Hull items and the Ohio Valley, as well as other regions, have now been fully infiltrated with them. Confusion met is understandable in these Western Stoneware Gingerbread cookie jars, since they were both trademarked and marketed as Hull.

Perhaps a less expensive way to produce pottery items was the answer, and with Taylor's strong salesmanship qualities unable to rest, he explored the possibilities. Taylor was interested in any market, including a foreign market, and quickly sent blocks and cases and glaze formulas for the Gingerbread mug and House 'n Garden French-handled casserole to Taiwan. He soon learned the foreign market could produce these items so closely to specification, that no noticeable difference was apparent.

While the French-handled casserole had cost 40-50 cents each to produce in the Hull plant, the foreign market offered production at 17 cents per item. Keep in mind, this was without the aid of any type of modern press. These items were to be produced by Taiwan with a hand-turned press. Workers in Taiwan were unable to get handle portions to release easily from the molds, whereas, the Hull plant's modern press had an air pressure release for this purpose.

Already in the works, are plans for limited production with certain Hull molds, such as the Gingerbread items. Only time will tell if these items will lend any interest to Hull collectors. There should be a great response from cookie jar collectors, however, Hull collectors may have a problem with these items, if, in fact, they are produced outside the Ohio Pottery region. Hull trademark or not, items produced by outside sources, with or without Taylor's endorsement, all border on reproductions. Some semblance of a plan for the dispersal of Hull molds could have created a place for safe reentry of wares in a limited edition for Hull collectors, but it appears too much has happened to counteract that strategy. All molds contemplated for production have definitely been at risk of being in other hands for the same purpose. Gingerbread molds were not only available to the public during the clean up of the plant, but some were actually sold to private industry. One such mold included the Gingerbread train canister set.

All of the above-described situations, plus the fact that Friendship II, and others purchased nearly all florist and House 'n Garden dinnerware blocks and dies after the company closed, could total tens of thousands of pieces immediately infiltrating the market, which are not Hull.

The haphazard dispersal of the pottery, allowing almost effortless access to hundreds of molds, has become a Hull collector's nightmare. There is no questioning, that blocks which remained in the plant encompassed several, perhaps many, that had been stored for near forty years. One has already surfaced, that being the Cinderella teapot produced by Beaumont Pottery. Many additional Hull designs have been, and are yet to be produced by outside firms and the in-home decorator.

It is only recently that Hull's wares have risen to prices which have caused others to purchase items only for remolding purposes. This includes not only older items such as the Red Riding Hood Cookie Jar and the Bow-Knot B-29 basket, but also newer items, such as the Gingerbread train canister set and additional accessories. It is assured that reproductions of Hull will become more and more apparent as long as prices rise. The easy accessibility to Hull molds, glazes and greenware during the pottery's closing has cast a displeasing shadow on Hull's illustrious history of manufacturing. Hull collectors are now part of a market in which they will be forced to question identity and origin.

The Hull Pottery had been for sale since it's closing, and although there was some immediate interest, there were no takers due to the EPA cloud which hovered overhead. Initially after the doors of the Hull Company closed, Larry Taylor, leased a portion of the building to Ludowici Celadon, Inc., sculptors of terra cotta tile. This firm never fired the kiln or manufactured products in the plant, but apparently produced designs while using a small portion of the building for storage. Approximately seven to ten workmen occupied the building, in hopes that if they met with success, they would take over the entire building within one year. This did not become a reality, however, the tile workers remained in the building for approximately two years. A portion of the Hull building also served as a retail for seconds produced by Hall China and Sterling China.

Terrance Zahn, owner of the Friendship Potteries of Roseville, voiced an interest in purchasing the failed pottery. However, this interest was overshadowed by Hull's EPA predicament. Zahn leased the building in September, 1990, and later purchased the property when Hull was released by the EPA. Hull Stockholders who were set to meet in November or December of 1990, waited until March of 1991, to meet. It was at that time, Hull settled with the EPA. By Spring of 1991, the property transaction was completed and Zahn took title of all Hull property and real estate, with the exception of the waste lagoon area.

My last glimpse of the pottery in 1986, was foreign. Walking through the vacant plant, making sure to avoid the clay slip on the concrete floors, brought to mind those days of a busy and bustling pottery. While memories of sights and sounds were deafening, now all was silent and still. Gone was the factory's usual busy state of workmen pouring liquid slip into the molds, the ram presses at work, the ladies trimming and sponging ware, overhead conveyor belts loaded with pottery items, workmen busy with packaging for shipment, and of course the pottery craftsmen who took time to shut down their machines or just stop what they were doing, look up, smile and explain their particular expertise.

Many have given their reasons as to why they believe the company failed. Some have speculated the company's demise was attributed to the EPA's clean up costs and the fact this took away large portions of the company's operating monies, the continued Union problems and employee strikes, or outdated equipment and a kiln too large for profitable output. Perhaps a combination of these, or other unmentioned reasons, were the final culprits. The pottery, a livelihood of countless area craftsmen, and a tradition coveted by a founding family, slowly succumbed to the stresses. Hull's tenure in an international market had ended.

With little or no dignity, the Pottery died a slow death. A pottery plant with no production in sight, seemingly worthless to Stockholders and Board Members, set plans in motion by President, Larry Taylor, to have the pottery dismantled piece by historical piece. The building's interior was sold for salvage, including the bricks of the great tunnel kiln.

All that remains of the Hull Pottery is the corporation name, a trademark which has had its price, a three-man Board of Directors consisting of Larry Taylor, Marlin King, and Jack Frame, a handful of shareholders and a small portion of real estate divided from the plant by the railroad. The parcel that in no way enticed the buyers of the remaining Hull real estate, or the Village of Crooksville when offered as a baseball diamond, the site formerly used to dispose of Hull's contaminated lead wastes.

Recognition To Hull Pottery's Craftsmen

It is fitting, that the final note be, not a sad one, but a glorious tribute to the history and tradition of the Hull Pottery, and to the unbounding talent and spirit its craftsmen so willingly shared with collectors of Hull. Compiled is a listing of those known to have worked at the Hull Pottery. Any omissions are regretable, for each and every worker of the pottery deserves recognition for their part in making the pottery a success, a success which will be shared by many in years to come.

The following compilation includes hundreds workers known to have worked at The Hull Pottery Company: company founders, directors, salesmen, moldmakers, diemakers, casters, jiggermen, trimmers, finishers, and the like, and of course, those persons responsible for Hull's beautiful art wares, the tinters and the decorators. A handful of numbers of the decorators and tinters have been traced to their owners, and they are provided for your information.

Adams, Cecila, Finisher
Adams, Cyril
Adams, Glen
Adams, Robert, Office Manager
Adkins, Bernice
Adkins, Clifford
Adkins, Lenora
Adkins, Virginia
Aichele, David, employed 2/1/78
Aichele, Donna
Aichele, George, kiln worker
Aichele, Helen, Decorator, number 31, incised initials also used, employed 12/20/29
Aichele, Louella, Tinter, employed 4/20/43
Aichele, Marilyn
Aichele, Rose
Aichele, William
Alderman, John, Poured liquid clay or "slip" into molds
Alderman, Rhea, sorted and packed ware for shipment, employed 8/8/72
Alexander, Nellie, Finisher
Alfman, Jeanette, employed 9/24/73
Allen, Clyde, Jiggerman
Allen, Guy, Poured liquid clay or "slip" into molds, dipped ware in glaze
Allen, Kate, Tinter and decorator
Allen, Pauline, employed 7/21/70
Allton, Edward, Jiggerman
Allton, Mae, Finisher, worked on Old Spice bottles
Altier, Isabelle
Anders, Patsy, employed 9/28/66
Anderson, Dorothy
Anderson, Olla, Packed ware for shipment
Ansel, Homer (Jake), Mold maker and foreman, also worked in casting and finishing
Ansel, William (Billy), Mold carrier
Ashley, Elizabeth

Auker, Margie Robinson, Decorator
Bailey, Helen, Finisher and decorator
Baker, Tim, employed 6/4/73
Ball, Velma, Finisher and decorator
Barnett, Jeannette, Office worker
Barringer, Louise, Finisher, dipped ware in glaze, employed 7/27/49
Bateson, Delmar
Bateson, Eva, Tinter
Bateson, Helen, Finisher, employed 3/12/52
Bateson, Joanna, employed 9/18/75
Bauer, Louise, Free lance modeler, designer in early 1940's who gained full time employment in 1949. Employed until Hull's closing.
Baughman, Betty Donaldson, Hand decorator
Baughman, Ernestine (Teeny), Finisher
Baughman, Jessie, Finisher
Bayes, Arthur
Bess, Charles
Bess, Henry
Bishop, Danny, employed 2/17/72
Bishop, Helen, employed 10/20/71
Bishop, Josephine
Bishop, Milton
Bishop, Wavelyn, employed 3/1/76
Blackford, Edna, Decorator, employed 10/22/39
Blackford, Perry
Blackson, Lucille
Blair, Hazel Miller
Bobo, Nellie
Bolyard, Anna, Tinter
Bolyard, Mildred, employed 2/14/70
Bolyard, Ray
Bonifant, Lucille, Finisher and decorator
Bonifant, Orvil, Jiggerman and caster
Boyce, E.
Boyce, Sarah
Bradshaw, Marie, Decorator, number 0, incised initials also used, employed March, 1934
Bradshaw, Nellie, Decorator and tinter, employed September, 1939
Braglin, Mildred
Brannon, W.L., Sales representative of Hull lines for American Clay Products Co.
Briggs, Bertha
Briggs, James
Brown, Albert, Controlled Hull seconds in mid-1930's
Brown, Louise Sturgill, employed 3/5/62
Brown, Mace
Brown, Mary Jane, employed 2/18/74
Brown, Wesley, Made liquid clay slip, employed 9/12/66
Buckley, Carrie
Buckley, Virginia, Finisher, employed 1946
Burns, Cyril, Hand decorator
Burns, Eileen, Finisher
Burns, Harlan
Burns, Howard (Pie), Kiln worker.
Burns, Jerry, employed 10/15/74
Burns, Marjorie
Burton, Clara

Butler, Ed, Caster
Caldwell, Albert
Campbell, Bouser
Campbell, Elizabeth
Cannon, Bernard
Cannon, Elsie
Cannon, James, Caster, employed 1939
Cannon, Trolis, Decorator, incised initials used
Cantor, Chester, Moldmaker
Cantor, Dick
Carletti, Frank
Carr, Joe, employed 8/24/76
Cavinee, Helen
Cavinee, Pearl
Channel, Burley, Jiggerman, many times including lamps
Channel, Ronald, Jiggerman
Cherry, Orland, Packed ware for shipment
Chevelier, Margaret
Clark, Hattie, employed 10/19/70
Colburn, John
Colburn, Lenora, Decorator, employed 2/15/50
Combs, Gertrude
Conaway, Elmer, Supervisor
Conaway, Gerald, Dipped ware in glaze
Conaway, Melvin, Salesman. also worked in inspection and warehousing
Conaway, Ray, Caster, jiggerman, worked in clay room
Conaway, Tom, Jiggerman, moldmaker
Cook, Della
Cook, Elizabeth
Cook, Lawrence
Cook, Viola, Decorator, incised initials used
Cooke, Guy, New York representative in Hull's early years
Corbett, Bill, Mechanic
Corbett, Bertha
Coulson, Herbert, Ceramic engineer, worked with bodies, glazes and kiln firing
Cox, Estle, employed 8/27/73
Crain, Earl
Crider, Della, Decorator, employed 8/27/46
Crooks, Adryenne, Tinter, employed 4/23/49
Cross, Blanche, Finisher and decorator
Cross, Charles, Poured liquid clay or "slip" into molds, dipped ware in glaze
Dalrymple, Dorothy Harper, Finisher, tinter, and decorator, employed 9/24/39
Danielson, John
Davis, Dorothy Donaldson, Designer, decorator
Davis, Earl, Worked on Old Spice bottles, mugs
DeCoursey, Charles, employed 8/28/69
Dennis, Fred, employed 10/16/74
Dennis, Virginia, employed 10/26/76
Denny, Burnette, employed 10/11/76
Denny, Junior
Dickens, Gusta, Decorator, incised initials used, employed 1936
Dillehay, Frank, Kiln worker
Dillehay, June, Packed ware for shipment
Dillie, Minnie, Finisher
Donaldson, Dorothy Davis, Designer, decorator

Donluvy, Tony, Tile designer
Dorsey, Pearl
Downey, Pauline, Finisher and decorator
Drinkwater, Harry, Caster
Dunn, "Boob", Caster
Dunn, Julia Ferguson, Finisher
Dusenberry, Clarence
Dusenberry, Gene, Poured liquid clay or "slip" into molds
Dusenberry, Isabella, Finisher on jigger wheel, sorted seconds, employed 8/15/49
Dusenberry, Mae, employed 2/19/62
Dusenberry, Michael, employed 11/28/73
Dusenberry, Pauline, employed 9/16/74
Dusenberry, Richard, employed 9/14/66
Dusenberry, Tim, employed 1/13/79
Ebert, Gladys, Designer, hand decorator, employed February, 1931
Ebert, Myrtle
Ebert, Oneida, employed 2/19/62
Elliott, Lucille
Eppley, Floyd
Eppley, Glenn
Ervin, Ethel
Eveland, Catherine, hand decorator, employed 1/4/72
Eveland, Charles
Eveland, Chester (Chet), Worked in the clay room
Eveland, Dennis
Eveland, Guy, Jiggerman
Eveland, Joe, Caster, jiggerman
Eveland, Opal, employed 11/4/52
Eveland, Richard
Eveland, Steve, employed 9/2/76
Eveland, Sue, Decorator, worked on Old Spice bottles and mugs
Everett, John, Hull salesman
Fair, Stanley, Caster
Fauley, Verna Delle Young, Hand decorator
Fealty, Sophia Mooney, Finisher
Felz, James, Managed the New Jersey warehouse
Ferguson, Effie, Finisher and decorator, employed 1939
Ferguson, Frances, Tinter and decorator, incised initials used, employed 10/15/39
Fisher, Linda, employed 9/23/74
Fisher, Mary, Decorator, employed 8/17/45
Fitzer, Ruth Sandborn Russell, Decorator, employed 1932-1945.
Forgrave, Allen, employed 4/28/76
Forgrave, Patricia, employed 1/19/76
Foster, Mildred, Finisher, employed 3/17/52
Foulds, Don, Ceramic engineer employed in early 1980's, to formulate lead-free glazes
Frame, Jack, Superintendent for Hull Company from 1982 to 1984
Frankson, Ceramic engineer
Frash, Ed, Packed ware for shipment
Garey, Lillian, Finisher, employed 3/17/52
Garrett, Clarence H., block and diemaker, moldmaker
Garrett, Warren E., block and diemaker, moldmaker, also operated kiln
Garvin, John

German, Mayme, Tinter and decorator, incised initials used, employed 10/3/39
Gibbs, Clyde
Gibbs, Edna, Finisher and decorator, employed 11/8/39
Gibbs, Harry
Gibson, James, employed 9/13/77
Gossman, Gloria, employed 6/16/65
Gossman, Grace, Tinter, employed 12/15/45
Gossman, Mabel
Gossman, Mary Allton, Office worker
Gottke, Lenora, Tinter, employed 6/27/49
Gottke, Tod
Grannon, William, employed 9/18/61
Griswold, F.H., Company Vice President during early years
Grubb, Juanita
Guinsler, Grace
Hall, Marshall, Jiggerman
Hambel, Alma, Finisher
Hambel, Lawrence
Hammer, Connie, employed 2/29/78
Hammer, Steve
Hampton, Alice, Finisher, employed 9/20/49
Harbaugh, Lewis (Jerry), Salesman
Harbaugh, Pat
Harper, Dorothy, Decorator
Harper, Florence
Harrah, Elizabeth (Jimmy), Tinter and decorator, incised initial used, employed 3/23/41
Harris, Norma, employed 7/15/74
Harvey, Alice, employed 8/14/73
Havelock, Jean, Finisher
Hayhurst, Leonard, Jiggerman
Haymen, John
Haymen, Ken
Hazlette, Karolyn, employed 9/15/69
Heath, Laura, employed 2/29/72
Heskett, Clarence, Worked in machine shop
Heskett, Elmer, Engineer, boiler room foreman
Heskett, Jean, Finisher and decorator, used incised numbers 5 and 17, employed 1938
Heskett, Paul, Jiggerman, diemaker, moldmaker, employed 1932
Hicks, Charles, Jiggerman, foreman
Hinkle, Marjorie
Hinkle, Maxine, employed 1/10/52
Hinkle, Robert "Click"
Hoffman, Marvin, Hull salesman
Holland, Oleen Cook, Finisher
Holmes, Bonnie
Holmes, Carlos, employed 11/3/52
Holmes, David, employed 10/7/74
Holmes, Wenzel, worked at Hull as early as 1930, one company seniority list shows a reemployment date of 9/15/65.
Hood, Fred
Hoops, Ethel, Tinter, employed 1/8/49
Hoops, Phoebe, Decorator
Houk, Forest, Caster
Houk, Ralph
Houk, William, Dipped ware in glaze

Hughes, Blanche, Finisher
Hughes, David
Hughes, Mary, employed 9/10/73
Hughes, Relda, Decorator, employed 4/20/29
Hull, Addis Emmet, Jr., Succeeded his father as President of Hull in 1930
Hull, Addis Emmet, Sr., Company founder, first President and General Manager of Hull
Hull, Byron "Bike", Son of founder, Sales Manager, New York office
Hull, Cecil, Truck driver
Hull, James Brannon "Brannie", Son of founder, reconstructed and was elected president of Hull in 1952
Hull, Robert W. (Bob), Son of founder, Vice President and Secretary-Treasurer.
Hurrah, Elizabeth, Decorator, incised initials used, employed 1939
Hurst, Damon
Hurst, Lucille Gheen
Hysel, Clara
Inman, Francine, employed 1/5/72
Inman, Leona, Finisher, employed 3/19/52
Inman, Mabel, employed 4/25/63
James, Barbara
Jirles, Jennie, employed 4/25/63
Jones, Vinnie
Joseph, Florence, Tinter
Justice, James (Nick), Carried glaze, employed 2/19/43
Keates, Veronica, Finisher and decorator
Kemmer, Dugan, Jiggerman
Kemmer, Gladys, Decorator
Kemmer, Paul, Jiggerman
Kennedy, Janet, employed 3/29/76
Kenny, Eileen Trout, Office worker
Ketchum, Ernest
King, Herman
King, Lawrence
King, Marlin, 20-year Hull Director
Kinnan, Kevin, employed 5/20/77
Kinnan, Rebecca, employed 8/19/77
Kinney, Albert, employed 5/9/79
Kinney, Robert, employed 3/12/79
Kinnon, H.F., Superintendent of Plant No. 2 in Hull's early years
Kinnon, V.D., Member of the Board of Directors, served as traveling salesman in early years
Kirkwood, Etta, Tinter
Klinger, Kenny, Caster
Knight, Nadine
Lanier, Madeline, employed 5/29/73
Lauterback, Don, Kiln worker
Lauterback, Iona, Finisher and decorator, employed 1918
Lear, Anna Mae, Tinter
Lear, Art, Mold runner
Lear, Nellie Appleman, Finisher and decorator
Lee, Lois, Finisher, tinter and decorator, trimmer, began work at Hull in 1937 at 26 cents per hour
Lee, Russell "Peanut", Jiggerman, caster, also finished lamps. Began his work at Hull in 1922 at 21 cents per hour

Leland, N.W., Company representative for Western and Southern districts during Hull's early years
Lemity, Arthur
Levering, Arthur, Poured liquid clay or "slip" into molds, glaze man
Levering, Augusta, Decorator
Levering, Grace, Finisher
Levering, Jeff, employed 7/20/77
Levering, Margaret, Decorator, employed 9/17/45
Levering, Norman, Poured liquid clay or "slip" into molds
Lewis, Harry
Lewis, Martha, Tinter, employed 8/16/49
Liff, Gerald
Lipps, Rita, employed 7/30/73
Lohman, Alma
Longstreth, Leo, Caster
Longstreth, William
Love, Elsie, Finisher and decorator
Luster, Charles Eugene "Bulldog", Prepared clay for the jiggermen and the pressers. Employed 1939-1942 at 37 1/2 cents per hour, returned 1/17/46, after the War and worked until plant's closing.
Luster, Clarence, Prepared clay for the jiggermen and the pressers and poured liquid clay or "slip" into molds. Employed 1919-1950.
Luster, Virgil, Poured liquid clay or "slip" into molds
Lyman, Jim, Caster, poured Old Spice bottles
Lyman, Wanda, Finisher
Lyons, Eileen, Worked on Old Spice bottles
Lyons, Eunice
Lyons, Martin
McCall, Gail
McClain, Anna Belle, Hand decorator
McClellan, Edgar, Ceramic engineer
McClellan, William K., Ceramic engineer
McGarge, Bill
McGuire, Bertha, Finisher, made knobs for lids
McHenry, Sam, Worked in clay room
McKeever, G.E., Salesman and director during Hull's early years
McKinney, Tom, employed 5/12/65
McMillan, Lenora, employed 10/15/52
McNeal, Georgianna, Finisher, decorator, dipped ware in glaze, employed 3/19/52-1985
McNeal, Kathy, employed 7/23/74
Maines, Betty, Tinter, decorator, sorted and packed ware for shipment, employed 1942
Maines, Kenneth, Decorator
Marolt, Mable Appleman, Tinter, employed 7/20/48
Marshall, Esta, Decorator, number 12, incised initials also used. Worked for Hull from 1920-1935. Returned in 1936 at 33 cents per hour and retired in 1979.
Martin, Everett
Mauller, Nellie
Mickey, Clara
Mickey, Zelma Cherry, Tinter
Miller, Hazel, Tinter
Miller, Linda, employed 7/15/74
Mills, Thomas, employed 8/9/66
Monroe, Florence, Flossie, Tinter, trimmed ware and

packed ware for shipment, employed 1945

Moody, Roy, Worked in clay room

Mooney, Kathryn, Finisher

Mooney, Pat, Jiggerman

Moore, LeRoy "Sleepy", Jiggerman, mold runner, dipped ware in glaze. Employed from 1926, at 33 1/2 cents per hour, until fire destroyed pottery in 1950.

Moore, Rolland

Moore, Virginia

Morrall, Stella

Morrison, Jean

Mullen, Orville

Mullins, Goldie, employed 9/15/76

Mumford, Dirk, employed 4/14/78

Mumford, Patricia, employed 5/25/63

Murray, Mabel, Finisher

Musgrove, Ollie, Decorator, employed 1/21/46

Napier, Jim, Engineer

Neff, Clinton, Kiln worker, began working at Hull with his father, Ira Neff, at age 11

Neff, Daine, Bottle machine operator for Old Spice containers, employed 1939. After returning from service Daine worked as caster, sorted ware for seconds, and was a bench boss

Neff, David, employed 3/14/61

Neff, Durwood, Pressman

Neff, Frances, Decorator, incised initials used

Neff, Ira, Kiln worker

Neff, Norma Jean Locke, Office worker

Neff, Willard

Nelson, Nettie

Newlon, Elizabeth

O'Hara, Elizabeth

Oliver, Clifford, Poured liquid clay or "slip" into molds

Orecchio, Curley Corbett, Designer and hand decorator

Orr, Fred, Kiln worker

Orr, Leona, Finisher

Pace, Anna

Pace, Gertrude, Tinter

Passon, Iva, Finisher and decorator, employed 8/14/32

Passon, Ralph "Shad" decorated lined ware, employed 1915

Penrod, Agnes

Penrod, Elizabeth

Perani, Norma, employed 8/29/72

Peterson, Gladys

Pettit, Harry, Jiggerman

Pettit, Samuel

Pettit, Walter

Pickrell, Florence, Finisher

Pierce, Dale

Pierce, Merle, employed 3/31/62

Plant, Patricia, employed 6/11/73

Poling, Earl

Poole, Jim, Engineer

Presgrave, Glenn, Dipped ware in glaze

Presgrave, Loretta, Finisher

Printz, Arthur

Printz, Esta, Tinter and decorator, employed 11/12/36

Printz, George

Printz, Harold

Printz, Nan, Finisher and tinter, employed 8/16/49

Printz, "Snort", Foreman

Rambo, George

Rarrick, Mary

Reed, Bert, Engineer

Reed, Gerald

Reed, Mary

Reeves, Harvey

Repeck, John

Rinehart, Goldie

Rhodes, Bertha, Decorator, employed 7/10/45

Rice, Alford, Poured liquid clay or "slip" into molds, dipped ware in glaze

Riffle, Eugene

Riffle, Harold

Riffle, Marjorie

Riggs, Gladys Dunn

Riggs, Wavalene Houk, Tinter, employed 9/21/43

Rinehart, Gladys, Finisher

Roberts, Merle

Robinson, Elsie, Decorator, number 24, incised initials also used, employed 6/15/43

Robinson, James, Carried boards of ware to decorators

Robinson, Irlena (Sis), Finisher

Rodgers, "Jiggs", Mold runner

Rose, Gladys, Finisher

Rose, Jessie, Decorator, incised initials used, employed 7/8/38

Ross, Betty, Finisher, employed 3/13/52

Ross, Beulah Lemity

Rosser, Richard, Mold runner

Rouanzoin, Irene, employed 8/29/72

Royan, Leonard

Russell, Henry, Poured liquid clay or "slip" into molds, employed from 1928-1945

Russell, Maggie, Finisher

Russell, Ruth, decorator, employed from 1932-1945

Russi, Mary

Ryan, Leonard

Sandborn, Fred, Sagger maker, caster, Union representative

Schofield, Joyce

Schuster, Francis

Scott, Janet, employed 8/5/75

Seaman, Mary Frances Sturgill, Tinter

Sharkey, Paul, Worked in ceramic engineer's room, employed 4/3/61

Sheeran, Cora

Sherlock, Mamie, Finisher and decorator

Sherlock, Pat, formulated glazes

Sherlock, Ralph, decorated lined ware

Shields, John, Jr.

Shoemaker, Minnie Walpole

Showers, Gladys, Plant nurse

Showers, Harold "Slim", Plant Superintendent, 1950's to early 1980's

Shrever, Laura, Decorator, employed March, 1945

Shuster, Charles, employed 3/26/79

Shuster, Michael, employed 6/10/74

Skeenes, Nadine, Finisher, employed 3/18/52
Slack, Richard, Press operator, employed 9/3/59
Sloan, Harold
Snyder, Carol, sorted and packed ware for shipment, employed 2/11/71
Snyder, Roger, employed 3/26/57
Smith, Harold
Sowers, Bea, Designer, tinter, hand decorator and finisher, employed 2/19/49
Sowers, Lillian Bash
Spears, Mary
Spears, Ruby, Decorator, employed September, 1932
Spencer, Ada, Finisher
Spencer, Harry, Electrician and truck driver
Spires, John
Spires, Karen, employed 5/16/73
Spring, Dorothy
Springer, G.W., Company representative for Western and Northern districts in Hull's early years
Springer, L.A., Sales manager in Hull's early years
Sprouse, Elizabeth
Sprouse, Loretta
Sprouse, Ruth
Spung, Grace
Stalling, Clarence
Stalling, John
Stansberry, Louella, Finisher
Stansberry, Raymond
Starner, Eleanor, employed 2/26/70
Starner, Leroy
Stephenson, Christine Snide, Finisher
Stephenson, Earl, Caster
Stephenson, Frank, Poured liquid clay or "slip" into molds
Stephenson, James
Stephenson, Louis
Stephenson, Louise, employed 7/28/75
Stephenson, "Tacky", night supervisor
Stephenson, Phyllis Rogers, Finisher
Stigler, George
Stine, Harry
Stoneburner, Dolores, Finisher, employed 3/4/52
Stover, Estel, Jr.
Stover, Ethel
Sturgill, Hattie, Decorator, Number 21, incised initials also used, employed 8/17/45
Summers, Francis, employed 8/27/65
Swingle, Georgia Watts, Designed themes for hand decorated wares
Tague, Fanny, Decorator, employed 2/15/50
Tague, Mary, Loaded conveyors with ware
Talbot, Beulah
Talbot, Frank
Tanner, Clara, Tinter, employed 1/20/49
Tatman, Dolores, employed 2/10/65
Tatman, Elsie, Loaded conveyors with ware
Tatman, Frank
Tatman, James
Tatman, Renea, employed 11/10/75
Tatman, Sharon, employed 9/15/76
Tatman, Theodore

Tatman, Vivian
Taylor, Larry, Hull Company President, employed May 26, 1981
Taylor, Max
Theisen, Rose, Finisher, employed 3/13/52
Thomas, Douglas
Thomas, Edna
Thomas, Helen
Thomas, Marvena, Finisher, employed 3/13/52
Thomas, Mary
Thomas, Roberta, employed 4/24/61
Thorne, Dorothy, Timmer and finisher, employed 1948
Thorne, Goldie, Finisher
Thorne, William "Fat", Caster
Tittle, Freda
Tolliver, Mildred, Finisher, employed 3/12/52
Trussell, Clark, employed 5/16/77
Trussell, Marlin, employed 5/20/65
Trussell, Paul, Mold foreman, also designed color schemes in Hull's early years
Tysinger, Della Carson, Tinter and decorator, employed 10/10/39
Tysinger, Henry, Worked in clay room
Underwood, Bertha
Underwood, John "Buckwheat", Jiggerman
Underwood, Raymond, Poured slip into molds, moldmaker
Vallee, Kathryn (Kate), Tinter and decorator, incised initials used, employed 11/21/42
Van Atta, Maxine Levering, Office Worker
Wahl, Lenora
Wainwright, Bertha, Decorator, employed June, 1946
Walpole, Archie, Caster
Walpole, Benny, Worked in boiler room
Walpole, Bernice Hicks, Decorator, number 19, incised initials also used, employed 9/3/38
Walters, Rosemay, employed 2/26/74
Warner, Helen, Decorator, employed 2/15/50
Warren, Harry
Watts, Curt, Worked in boiler room, maintenance bench
Watts, Donna
Watts, Edward, Processed clay, dipped ware in glaze, retired October, 1966, at age of 90
Watts, Faye, employed 10/19/71
Watts, Frank
Watts, Genevieve, "Jenny" Heath, decorator, finisher
Watts, George, Mold runner
Watts, Gerald F., Son of William Watts, succeeded A.E. Hull, Jr., in management of the Hull firm in 1937
Watts, James
Watts, Noah
Watts, Sue, Finisher
Watts, Sylvester, Worked in boiler room, maintenance supervisor
Watts, William, Secretary-Treasurer in Hull's early years
Wease, Florence Hicks, Mold runner
Weaver, Evelyn Gibbs, employed 1/13/71
Weaver, Virginia, Finisher, employed 2/10/65
Weisenstine, Vernie
West, Lawrence
White, Doris, employed 10/7/68

White, Izetta, Finisher, employed 3/19/52
White, June
Whitstone, Alva, Kiln worker
Whitstone, Katheryn, Packed ware for shipment, employed
    11/18/44
Williams, Boyd, Tinter and decorator, employed 11/15/43
Williams, Clint
Williams, Dale
Williams, Douglas
Williams, Irene, Tinter
Williams, Junior "June", Decorated lined ware, mold
    runner
Williams, Laura
Williams, Lloyd, employed 1944
Williams, Naomi, tinter, employed 2/12/49
Williams, Vernon
Williamson, Ethel
Willison, Berky
Willison, Vivian
Wilson, Betty, employed 5/17/76
Wilson, Cecil
Wilson, Emma Slack, Finisher
Wilson, Lewis "Lew"
Wilson, Sue Mooney, Decorator
Wilson, Sylvanus Burdette "Mose", Mold maker
Wilson, Zetta Hicks, Finisher and decorator, number 13,
    incised initials also used, single initial, "Z", quite
    commonly used
Wise, Doris, Tinter
Wise, Leo
Wolfe, Kathryn, employed 2/29/72
Wolfe, Paula, employed 7/12/66
Woods, Lewis, Decorated lined ware
Woods, William, Decorated lined ware
Worthington, D.W., Worked out of Hull's Chicago office in
    early years
Worthington, Sam, Sr.
Young, Douglas, Grandson of Jeptha Darby Young,
    employed 1925, worked all phases of pottery and
    became Assistant Plant Superintendent
Young, Douglas Mrs., dipped ware in glaze
Young, Elza
Young, Dunkle, Office worker
Young, E.D., Secretary-Treasurer in 1960's
Young, George, Caster, glaze man
Young, Helen, employed 9/9/69
Young, Jay, Caster
Young, Jeptha Darby, Superintendent of Plant No. 1 in
    Hull's early years
Young, Marjorie, Finisher
Young, Robert, Caster
Younkin, Hayward, employed 8/31/65
Zinn, Gerald, Worked in clay room
Zinn, Harley, Headed boards
Zinn, Nellie, Decorator and finisher, employed 1/1/46
Zinn, Robert
Zinn, Sam, Worked in clay room, caster

Lines And Dates Of Manufacture

Although the following listing cannot be considered complete, as new lines will continually be discovered through additional research of the Hull Pottery, it is provided for your easy access of line identification, dates of manufacture, color and glaze treatments, and number of pieces available. Dates entailing several years of production will be noted for categorized items such as cuspidors, combinets, early art, etc.

A separate listing of known factory lamps, cookie jars, canister sets, House 'n Garden serving ware, and a notation on clocks and reproductions immediately follows this section.

A

ALMOND: 1981-1983. Refers to the House 'n Garden casual servingware offered in Almond with Caramel Trim. Many accessory pieces glazed in Almond had no contrasting trim.

ADVERTISING SIGNS: At least four advertisers are available for collectors. 5" X 11" plaque, "The A.E. Hull Co. Pottery," The 2 1/2" X 5 1/2" plaque, "HULL," the 6 1/2" X 11 1/2" Regal plaque, "Featuring Little Red Riding Hood, Covered by Pat. Des. No. 135889," and the 4 1/4" X 4 1/4" tile advertiser, "TILE BY HULL, INSTALLED BY A. SCHIRMER, CINCINNATI."

ALPINE: 1915-1930. Refers to stoneware tankards, steins, and jars embossed with Alpine scene, high glazed in golden brown.

ART POTTERY: 1925-1935. Miscellaneous semi-porcelain and stoneware art items which included vases, jardinieres, pots and saucers, bulb bowls, hanging baskets, etc. Glazes included solid matte Eggshell White, Bermuda Green, Lotus Blue, Oyster White, Autumn Brown, Egyptian Green, Maize Yellow, and others, and a variety of blended glazes in blue, turquoise, maroon, green, maize yellow, as well as other combinations.

ATHENA: 1960. Chain store vase and planter assortment decorated in overall high gloss colors Lilac or Spring Green, trimmed with White Lava, or allover satin white. Eleven pieces were offered which included an oval picture frame/wall pocket planter.

AVOCADO: 1968-1971. Refers to the House 'n Garden casual servingware offered in Avocado with Ivory trim. Satin finished Avocado was also available during this same period. It most often was not trimmed in Ivory. Thirty items were available, including a cylinder-shaped cookie jar.

B

BAK-SERVE: 1915-1935. Also referred to as Banded "100" line. Semi-porcelain kitchenware line which included nested bowls, jugs, bakers, custards, range jars, refrigerator jars, cereal jars, spice jars, pie plates, etc., decorated with green or blue underglazed banding. Bak-Serve casseroles were glazed in overall high gloss brown, and two quart and four quart bean pots were glazed brown over white.

BANDED: 1915-1940. Any of the varieties of kitchenware items that were decorated by way of overglazed or underglazed color bands. Semi-porcelain, stoneware, yellowware, and Zane Gray bodies were banded. Color bands included, but were not limited to, blue, green, yellow, red, pink, black, brown, and white, as well as gold and luster banding.

BANDED ESSENTIALS: 1930-1940. Semi-porcelain kitchenware line which included nested bowls, jugs, custards, casseroles, etc., decorated with underglazed banding in combinations of pink and blue, blue and peach, maroon and peach, other colors also available.

BANDED NO. "18" LINE: 1915-1935. Semi-porcelain kitchenware nested bowls with prominent "foot", decorated in underglazed blue bands.

BANDED NO. "20" LINE: 1915-1935. Semi-porcelain kitchenware nested nappy set with yellow underglazed bands, available with or without gold lines.

BANDED NO. "23" LINE: 1915-1935. Semi-porcelain kitchenware nested nappy set with blue underglazed banding.

BANDED NO. "25" LINE: 1915-1935. Semi-porcelain kitchenware nested nappy set with blue underglazed bands, available with or without gold lines.

BANDED NO. "41" LINE: 1915-1935. Semi-porcelain kitchenware nested nappy set decorated with three underglazed blue lines.

BANDED NO. "100" LINE: 1915-1935. Also referred to as Bak-Serve line. Semi-porcelain kitchenware line which included nested bowls, jugs, bakers, custards, range jars, refrigerator jars, cereal jars, spice jars, pie plates, etc., decorated with Spring Green or Alice Blue underglazed banding.

BANDED NO. "100" LINE CEREAL WARE: 1915-1935. Refers to round semi-porcelain cereal ware jars, spice jars, cruets and salt boxes which were glazed in transparent high gloss with underglazed banding in Spring Green or Alice Blue. "Cereal" and "Spices" appear in embossed letters on front of utility jars.

BANDED NO. "300" LINE: 1915-1935. Semi-porcelain kitchenware line which included nested bowls, jugs, bakers, custards, ramekins, bean pots, pie plates, etc., decorated in overglazed banding of Pimento Red or Nubian Black, and underglazed banding of Spring Green, Alice Blue or Magenta, other bandings available.

BANDED NO. "400" LINE: 1915-1935. Yellowware line which included nested bowls, jugs, bakers, custards, range jars, refrigerator jars, cereal jars, spice jars, pie plates, etc., decorated with underglazed brown band with white lines, either side.

BANDED CEREAL WARE: 1915-1935. Any of the varieties of cereal ware in either semi-porcelain or stoneware bodies, both round and square shapes, with underglazed and overglazed band decoration in colors including, but not limited to, gold, blue, green, black and red.

BASQUE: 1915-1935. Refers to early semi-porcelain utility line which included nested bowls, covered utility jar, beater jug and refrigerator jar.

BEAUTY: 1905-1925. Refers to a large embossed open floral decoration used on early stoneware artware and

jardinieres.

BICENTENNIAL: 1975-1976. Experimental line of ovenproof House 'n Garden casual servingware. Items included mugs, steins, low casseroles, bean pots, creamer and sugar, large pitcher, glazed in Mirror Brown or Satin Avocado.

BLACK AND WHITE STONEWARE: 1905-1930. Utilitarian wares used for food storage and preservation which included meat tubs, churns, shoulder jugs, preserve jugs, milk pans, butters, and more, high fired stoneware bodies glazed black over white.

BLENDED: 1910-1940. Refers to semi-porcelain and stoneware jugs, jardinieres, cuspidors, vases, bulb bowls, hanging baskets and flower pots, in plain or embossed designs, which were finished in high glazed or matte blended colors.

BLOSSOM: 1948-1949. Ovenproof kitchenware glazed in allover white with hand painted six-petal floral, decorated in pink or yellow with green leaves and banding. Fifteen shapes were catalogued, which included a cookie jar in each color decoration.

BLOSSOM FLITE: 1955-1956. Background combinations of black lattice on overall high gloss pink or blue lattice on overall pink with metallic green interior, with additional multi-colored embossed floral decoration. It is not uncommon to find heavy gold detailing or overall gold veiling. There were fifteen catalogued shapes.

BLUE AND WHITE STONEWARE: 1905-1925. Refers to stoneware bodies whose decoration is characterized by various shadings of light to dark tinted blues. Items were utilitarian, shapes were both plain and embossed. Items included stoneware dairy jugs, butters, salt boxes, cuspidors, water jugs, water kegs, nested bowls and nappy sets, ewers and basins, and more. Embossed shapes included, but were not limited to, cherries, plums, birds, daisies, wild roses, stags, and cattle.

BLUE BANDED: 1915-1935. White bodied high glazed semi-porcelain kitchenware items which included bowls, custards, nappies, butters, and jugs, with overglazed or underglazed blue bands.

BLUE-BELLE: 1985. One of Hull's "Collection" dinnerwares offered in high glazed winter-white background with hand stamped underglazed decoration of trailing bluebell florals. A bulbous canister set and cookie jar were available.

BLUE BIRD CEREAL WARE: 1915-1935. Blue bird in flight or perched blue bird decal used for decorating early cereal ware jars, spice jars, cruets and salt boxes. Fifteen items were included for complete set.

BLUE FLEMISH: 1915-1935. Refers to variety of stoneware and ivory bodied utility wares, butter jars, jugs, etc., decorated with blue tint.

BLUE RIBBON: 1951-1954. White high glazed nested set of five bowls banded in green, with additional green lines either side.

BOUQUET: 1948-1949. Ovenproof kitchenware in overall white high glazed finish. Decoration included yellow tinted tops with hand decorated floral spray in pink, yellow and blue. Fifteen shapes available, which included a cookie jar. An unlisted square serving bowl was also offered. Additional items included square plates, cereal bowls and a compartment dish which are considered experimental.

BOW-KNOT: 1949-1950. Embossed floral in duo-tone matte finished pastel bodies of pink and blue or turquoise and blue combinations. Twenty-nine shapes are catalogued, with an additional square cup and saucer wall pocket available.

BOY AND GIRL: 1905-1925. Also known as Indian Boy and Girl, or Pilgrims. Refers to an embossed decoration used for blue and white stoneware jugs. This design was also available in blended glazes.

BROWN AND WHITE LINED WARE: 1905-1925. Stoneware utility items which were burned to a very high heat which vitrified and caused them to craze less. Items were glazed overall brown with white linings.

BUCKET JARDINIERES: 1959. Bucket or tub-shaped jardinieres with wire bailed handles. These items were included as part of Gold-Medal Flowerware. Hi-buckets were available in five, six, seven and nine inch sizes; Azalea, or Tub-buckets were available in eight and ten inch sizes.

BUFF GREEN: 1925-1935. Refers to a variety of stoneware and ivory bodied utility ware, dairy jugs, butter jars, etc., which were decorated in green tint.

BURNT ORANGE: 1963-1967. Refers to Tangerine House 'n Garden casual servingware offered specifically for J.C. Penney. At least forty items were available, including a cookie jar.

BUTTERFLY: 1956. Raised pastel butterfly and flower motif in a combined gloss and matte finish of white on white, or matte white with turquoise interiors. It is not uncommon to find gold detailing on either glaze treatment. Twenty-five shapes were catalogued.

BUTTER JARS: 1910-1925. Plain, cylinder-shaped open or covered jars in one-fourth gallon to six gallon sizes, glazed black over white.

BUTTERS: 1910-1930. Any of the varieties of open or covered butters, some with wire-bailed metal wood grips, some embossed "Butters." Included were Zane Grey, ivory or yellow bodied ware with blue bands, buff body green tinted, blue Flemish, and others. Also available were plain and embossed shapes in semi-porcelain, stoneware or yellowware bodies in blended or tinted glazes. Sizes available included 1 to 5 pounds.

C

CALLA: 1933. High glazed solid or blended stoneware jardinieres and flower pots with embossed "pod-shaped" floral.

CALLA LILY: 1938-1940. Also referred to as Jack-in-Pulpit due to embossed floral and arrow-shaped leaves. Various matte tints and duo-tone colors were available, i.e. solid matte pastels of blue, green, cream or turquoise, and matte duo-tone shades of blue to pink, cinnamon to dusky green, cinnamon to turquoise, rose to dusty green, rose to turquoise, other color combinations available. At least twenty-four items were available, several in graduated sizes..

CAMELLIA: 1943-1944. Also referred to as Open Rose. Hand decorated embossed florals on shaded pastel backgrounds of matte pink and blue or allover matte white. At least 44 highly diverse shapes were available.

CAPRI: 1961. Dish gardens and figural planter line decorated in Satin Coral with weathered limestone effect, or Seagreen to represent sea-washed rock formations. There were thirty catalogued shapes.

CASTLE: 1905-1925. Refers to an embossed decoration used for early stoneware which was glazed overall brown with white lining. The overall embossed fishscale background has an enclosed medallion which encases a castle design.

CATTLE: 1905-1925. Refers to an embossed cattle decoration used for early stoneware five-pint dairy jugs, brown overall glazed with white lining, blue tint and green tint.

CEREAL WARE, ROUND: 1915-1930. Round semi-porcelain and stoneware cereal ware sets decorated with gold, yellow or blue overglazed banding. The set consisted of six cereal jars lettered rice, beans, prunes, tapioca, coffee and tea, and six spice jars lettered ginger, allspice, cloves, nutmeg, cinnamon, and pepper, and a salt box.

CEREAL WARE, SQUARE: 1915-1935. Kitchenware sets consisting of canisters, spice jars, salt boxes, vinegar and oil cruets with underglazed decaled decoration. Plain sets in semi-porcelain and stoneware bodies were also manufactured in various solid colors. Fifteen items were included for complete set.

CHAMBERS: 1910-1935. Semi-porcelain and stoneware bodies, plain and embossed shapes, with or without lids. Decorations included banding or decals.

CHECKER: 1920-1935. Semi-porcelain nested bowls set glazed in yellow or green.

CHERRY: 1905-1925. Refers to an embossed decoration used for early stoneware which was glazed overall brown with white lining, blue tint and green tint.

CHINESE RED CRACQUELLE: 1928. Additional luster line in brilliant red, designed by theme outside the Hull plant. At least 15 shapes were offered.

CINDERELLA: 1948-1949. Overall line name for kitchenware designs of Blossom and Bouquet. Blossom is characterized by an overall white gloss with hand painted six-petal in pink or yellow with green leaves and banding. Fifteen shapes are catalogued, which included a cookie jar in each of the two designs. Bouquet is characterized an overall white high gloss finish. Decoration included yellow tinted tops with hand decorated floral spray in pink, yellow, and blue. An unlisted square serving bowl was also offered. Additional items included square plates, cereal bowls, and a compartment dish which are considered experimental.

CHURNS: 1920-1925. Two to six gallon stoneware open or covered churns glazed in black over white.

CLASSIC: 1942-1945. Items in overall high gloss colors of ivory or pink. Raised florals appear on only one side of this ware which was manufactured in mass for chain store sales. Factory lamps were made from several of the vase shapes offered in Classic.

CLASSIC, BLUE CEREAL WARE: 1915-1935. Decal in blue used for decorating early cereal ware jars, spice jars, cruets and salt boxes. Fifteen items were included for complete set.

CLASSIC, GOLDEN BROWN CEREAL WARE: 1915-1935. Decal in golden brown used for decorating early cereal ware jars, spice jars, cruets and salt boxes. Fifteen items were included for complete set.

CLASSIC, GREEN CEREAL WARE: 1915-1935. Decal in green used for decorating early cereal ware jars, spice jars, cruets and salt boxes. Fifteen items were included for complete set.

COLLECTION: 1982-1985. Refers to Hull's overall advertising designation for the late lines of dinnerware, i.e. Mirror Brown with Ivory Foam Ridge and molds with rings or bands, which included Heartland, and Blue-Belle.

COVERED OVENWARE: 1932-1935. Plain undecorated line of kitchenware bake dishes offered in ivory white semi-porcelain bodies glazed in transparent Maize Yellow or Lucerne Green.

COLORED CEREAL WARE: 1915-1930. Semi-porcelain and stoneware embossed cereal ware sets in solid high gloss colors of green, yellow, tan or blue. Sets included cereal ware jars, spice jars, cruets and salt box. Fifteen items were included for complete set.

COLORED TEAPOTS: 1932-1935. Teapots offered in dark ivory buff semi-vitreous bodies. Glazes included, but are not limited to Opaque, Lucerene Green and Burgundy Brown.

COMBINETS: 1910-1930. Any of the varieties of Toilet Ware and Hotel Ware items. Bodies included both semi-porcelain and stoneware, styles were plain or decorated embossed, banded, or decaled. Items were wire-bailed with wood hand grips, offered with or without lids.

CONTINENTAL: 1959-1960. Modern shapes in brilliant high gloss colors, first offered in Persimmon and Evergreen, with Mountain Blue following. There were a total of twenty-six items catalogued.

CONVENTIONAL ROSE CEREAL WARE: 1915-1935. Floral decalcomania design used to border early cereal ware jars, spice jars, cruets and salt boxes, (#132 Pink Double Border). Fifteen items were included for complete set.

CONVENTIONAL TILE CEREAL WARE: 1915-1935. Geometric decalcomania design used to border early cereal ware jars, spice jars, cruets and salt boxes, (#133 Yellow Double Border). Fifteen items were included for complete set.

CONVENTIONAL VINE CEREAL WARE: 1915-1935. Decalcomania design used to border early cereal ware jars, spice jars, cruets and salt boxes, (#131 Blue Double Border). Fifteen items were included for complete set.

COOK 'N' SERVE: 1952-1953. Kitchenware line which included a combination of Cinderella and Just Right Kitchenware shapes. Items were high glazed, air-brushed decorated in brown and yellow, pink and charcoal, overall mottled green, or overall high gloss white with black handles and lids. Nineteen items were catalogued, exclusively for A.H. Dorman, New York, which included the large and small skillet trays, and cookie jar.

CORKY PIGS: 1957-1985. Although a variety of pig banks were produced by Hull, this item refers to the style of bank which was marked "Corky Pig," and glazed in a variety of color treatments. Although first introduced in 1957, this bank was manufactured through 1985.

CORONET: 1959. Vases, jardinieres, dish gardens,

ashtray and planter combinations in metal stands, etc., produced in mass for chain store sales packages in solid or tinted high gloss colors, with or without contrasting foam decoration. While assortments varied per retailer, at least thirteen items were available along with high-styled ashtray and planter combinations with metal accessories.

COUNTRY SQUIRE: 1963-1967. Refers to Green Agate with Turquoise trimmed House 'n Garden casual servingware set. At least forty items were available, including the cookie jar.

CRAB APPLE: 1934-1935. Semi-porcelain and stoneware art pottery vases, hanging baskets and jardinieres glazed in matte Eggshell White; matte Peacock Blue on white semi-porcelain body; hand painted flowers in rose, leaves in green on stoneware buff bodies; or bright white on white semi-porcelain body. Eighteen shapes were catalogued.

CRESCENT: 1952-1954. Ovenproof line decorated in high gloss color combinations of chartreuse with dark green trim, or high gloss strawberry with maroon trim. Twelve shapes were available, including a cookie jar.

CRESTONE: 1965-1967. Ovenproof casual servingware in high gloss turquoise with white contrasting foam edge. At least thirty-five items were available.

CUSPIDORS: 1910-1935. Hotel, (flat based) and parlor, (tall, bulbous based) shapes offered in semi-porcelain and dark buff bodies, decorated both overglazed and underglazed with decals and/or color bands of blue, green, maroon, brown, yellow, gold and luster, sometimes combined with matching or contrasting lines. Some cuspidors were additionally banded and/or lined inside interior rim.

D

DAISY AND TRELLIS: 1905-1925. Refers to an embossed decoration used for early blue and white stoneware butters.

DEBONAIR: 1952-1955. Ovenproof kitchenware line in high gloss solid chartreuse, combination wine and chartreuse or high gloss duo-tone lavender and pink with black banding. There were fifteen items available, which included a cookie jar.

DELFT CEREAL WARE: 1915-1935. Blue ship and harbor scene and/or windmill decal in blue used for decorating early cereal ware jars, spice jars, cruets and salt boxes. Fifteen items were included for complete set.

DIAMOND QUILT: 1937-1940. Refers to "B" Series Nuline Bak-Serve ovenproof kitchenware in solid matte and high gloss colors blue, turquoise, peach, maroon, yellow and cream. At least eighteen shapes were available, which included a cookie jar.

DOGWOOD: 1942-1943. Also known as Wild Rose. Hand decorated embossed florals in shaded colors of turquoise and peach, blue and pink, or allover peach. Twenty-two shapes were available.

DORIC: 1928. Panelled nested bowl set in glazed white semi-porcelain, underglazed banded with three blue lines.

DRAPE: 1937-1940. Refers to "D" Series Nuline Bak-Serve ovenproof kitchenware in solid matte and high gloss colors blue, turquoise, peach, maroon, yellow and cream. At least eighteen shapes were available, which included a cookie jar.

DRAPE AND FESTOON CEREAL WARE: 1915-1935. Decalcomania border in rose, blue, green and black used for decorating early cereal ware jars, spice jars, cruets and salt boxes. Fifteen items were included for complete set.

E

EARLY ART: 1925-1938. Miscellaneous semi-porcelain and stoneware items which included vases, jardinieres, pots and saucers, bulb bowls, hanging baskets, etc. Glazes included solid matte Eggshell White, Bermuda Green, Lotus Blue, Oyster White, Autumn Brown, Egyptian Green, Maize Yellow, along with others and a variety of matte and high gloss blended and solid glazes in pink, blue, turquoise, maroon, green and maize yellow.

EARLY UTILITY: 1910-1938. Refers to the variety of kitchenware and utility items, bowls, nappies, jugs, butters, etc., in both semi-porcelain, stoneware, Zane Grey, buff and yellowware bodies. Items included plain and embossed shapes decorated in solid and blended high gloss colors with both underglazed and overglazed banding decorations, stamped decorations, and decals.

EBB TIDE: 1954-1955. Embossed fish and sea shell motifs, high glazed in Seaweed (chartreuse) and Wine, or Shrimp and Turquoise. Gold detailing is not uncommon, this line was available in sixteen shapes.

EMBOSSED: 1934. Semi-porcelain embossed nested bowl set high glazed in solid green.

EWERS AND BASINS: 1905-1935. Refers to ewers and basins from Toilet Ware sets, offered in Hull (smaller), or Rex (fancier, larger) shapes. Bodies included both semi-porcelain and stoneware bodies. Semi-porcelain sets, in plain or embossed shapes, were decorated in blended or tinted glazes, or allover high glazed white. Stoneware sets, in plain or embossed shapes, were decorated in tinted, banded, or allover glaze treatments.

F

FANTASY: 1957-1958. Chain store novelties and vases high glazed in various colors, such as pink, blue, or black, with or without contrasting foam decoration, other colors possible. Assortments varied with retailer. One assortment included at least sixteen shapes.

FIESTA: 1957-1958. Chain store novelty assortment which included plain decorations, embossed fruits and florals, jardinieres and flower pots with metal accessories. Glaze treatments included both solid and tinted high gloss treatments. Assortments varied with retailer. One such assortment included fourteen shapes.

FISH SCALE: 1937-1940. Refers to "C" Series Nuline Bak-Serve ovenproof kitchenware in solid matte and high gloss colors blue, turquoise, peach, maroon, yellow and cream. At least eighteen shapes were available, which included a cookie jar.

FISHSCALE AND WILD ROSES: 1905-1925. Refers to an embossed decoration used for early blue and white stoneware ewers and basins. The overall embossed fishscale pattern was further decorated by raised pleated bowl edges and an enclosed wild rose floral in medallion on front of ewer.

FIVE BANDED: 1915-1935. Semi-porcelain kitchenware line which included a variety of nested bowls and nappy sets, at least three coffee servers and teapots, graduated pitchers and jugs, bean pots, casseroles, cookie and utility jars, pie plates, etc., in overall high glazed transparent white with an overglaze banded decoration of five lines encircling the wares' mid-line or top edge. The lowest band being the thinnest, widened with each step of elevation in this over the glaze decor of Pimento Red or Nubian Black. This kitchenware, with highly refined lines, included desirable shapes, high standing handles on servers, dubbed handles on casseroles, bean pots and cookie and utility jars. This line was the ultimate in class and style for semi-porcelain kitchenware lines. Solid color kitchenware items in glazes including yellow, turquoise, blue, mauve, peach and others, were also available with or without cold color decorations of fruits and florals.

FLEMISH: 1928. Two to five pound embossed stoneware butter jars with tinted blue glaze treatments.

FLORAL: 1951-1964. White high gloss kitchenware with raised yellow air-brushed daisies, yellow air-brushed lids and brown banding. Florals appear on one side only. Fifteen items were available, which included a cookie jar.

FLOR-DES-LIS: 1905-1925. Refers to an embossed decoration used for early blended stoneware jugs. Embossed bandings on the jugs enclose a spiral or swirled pattern.

FLORIST WARE: 1928. Early listing offered specifically for floral arrangements; green jardinieres and vases ranging from 6 to 15 inches in height. At least thirteen items were available.

FLOWER CLUB: 1963-1965. Chain store florist line in both satin and high gloss finishes in wild honey, jade green, with or without contrasting foam decoration, or satin white. Fourteen shapes were catalogued, which included three swans and one Madonna.

FLOWERWARE: 1957-1958. Chain store assortment of vases, planters, and jardinieres and ashtrays in metal stands. High glazed solid black and pastel colors were used, as well as Satin White. Assortments varied per retailer, one such assortment included nine items.

FLYING BIRDS: 1905-1925. Refers to an embossed decoration used for early stoneware tankards and jugs, tinted in blue and white.

FRENCH POTS: 1910-1925. Refers to high glazed stoneware utility pots with wide shoulder. One-half and one gallon sizes.

FOOTED: 1920-1930. Refers to the varieties of early Hull kitchenware in both semi-porcelain and stoneware bodies with an extended "foot," or base.

G

GARDEN DISHES: 1963. A packaged Imperial line for the florist trade. Glaze treatments included high gloss Moss Green, Lilac, Spring Green, Carnation Pink or Satin White. Thirteen items were catalogued.

GINGERBREAD MAN: 1978-1985. Animated character shaped into useful kitchenware items. Server was first introduced in 1978, and in 1982 the idea was expanded to include a cookie jar, bowl and mug. A train canister set was being trialed when the factory closed. A train station and candy jar were created, however, never put into production. Most items are high gloss Mirror Brown, but

Ridge colors tawny (tan) and flint (gray) were also used for Gingerbread items.

GOLDEN ANNIVERSARY: 1963-1967. Refers to Tangerine House 'n Garden casual servingware made specifically as premium items for Tri-State Grocers, when celebrating their 50th gala anniversary. At least forty items were available, including the cookie jar.

GOLD-MEDAL FLOWERWARE: 1959. Chain store line which included vases, bucket planters, Chinese Sage Mask wall pocket, and jardinieres with metal accessories. Glaze treatments included both plain and stippled finishes, overglazed gold banding was included as part of the package. Assortments varied per retailer. One retailer listed as many as twenty-one items.

GRANADA: 1938-1946. Matte and high gloss art lines which spanned several years of novelty chain store assortments. Plain and embossed decorations in satin and gloss white or pastels, and matte shaded pastels of pink and cream or pink and blue.

GREEN AND WHITE STONEWARE: 1905-1925. Refers to stoneware bodies whose decoration is characterized by various shadings of tinted greens. Items were utilitarian, shapes were both plain and embossed. Items included stoneware dairy jugs, butters, salt boxes, cuspidors, water jugs, water kegs, nested bowl and nappy sets, ewers and basins, and more. Embossed shapes included, but were not limited to, cherries, plums, birds, daisies, wild roses, stags and cattle.

GRECIAN, BLUE CEREAL WARE: 1915-1935. Decalcomania design used to border cereal ware jars, spice jars, cruets and salt boxes, (#119 blue). Fifteen items were included for complete set.

GRECIAN, GOLD CEREAL WARE: 1915-1935. Decalcomania design used to border cereal ware jars, spice jars, cruets and salt boxes, (#121, gold). Fifteen items were included for complete set.

GREEN BUFF: 1933. Embossed stoneware cuspidors, butters and nested bowl sets decorated in glazed green tinted style.

GREEN TINT: 1933. Buff-bodied, fluted bowls and nested bowl sets, butters, 2-5 pint dairy jugs and cuspidors, glazed and tinted green.

H

HARP: 1905-1925. Refers to an embossed decoration used for early stoneware artware and jardinieres which were decorated in rich blended glazes.

HEARTLAND: 1982-1985. One of Hull's "Collection" dinnerwares which was offered in shaded satin cream with hand applied brown heart and flower stamp. A bulbous canister set and cookie jar were available.

HEARTS AND ARROWS: 1905-1925. Refers to an embossed decoration of hearts and arrows which decorated early stoneware blended jardinieres.

HERITAGEWARE: 1959. Ovenproof kitchenware in high gloss Mint Green or Azure Blue with foam edge, and a textured finish in the same body colors with contrasting white handles and lids. Thirteen items were available, which included a cookie jar.

HOTEL WARE: 1910-1935. Semi-porcelain plain and embossed chambers, cuspidors, combinets, jugs, some of which were decorated over-the-glaze by decals, color bands and stamps, or transparent white with no decor.

HOUSE 'N GARDEN WARE: Refers to any of the color glazes of casual servingware produced in volume from 1960-1985, i.e., Mirror Brown, Provincial, Tangerine, Country Squire, Avocado, Almond, and others.

I

IMPERIAL: 1955-1985. Began as "F1 lists," and refers to the massive florist line produced by Hull from late-1950 through 1985. Colors included both satin and gloss black, carnation pink, willow green, lilac, moss green, wild honey, bittersweet, coral, turquoise, mahogany, as well as others.

IRIS: 1940-1942. Hand decorated embossed floral on tinted backgrounds of blue and rose, rose and peach, or allover peach. There are fourteen catalogued shapes, some in graduated sizes.

IVORY: 1928. Ivory bodied butters, bowls, custards, casseroles, and jugs with red and blue banding.

J

JARDINIERES: 1920-1930. High glazed stoneware five to ten inch jardinieres offered with sixteen to eighteen inch pedestal bases.

JARS: 1910-1925. Stoneware utility and preserving jars offered as "tall" or "low", glazed in black over white. Low jars available in 10, 15, and 25 gallon sizes. Tall jars available in one-half to fifty gallon sizes.

JUBILEE: 1957. Chain store assortment of novelty planters and dish gardens, with a selection of jardinieres and ashtray and planter combinations with metal accessories. Glaze treatments varied from high gloss to satin finishes in a variety of colors. Combinations varied per distributor. As least one retailer offered seventeen shapes.

JUGS: 1905-1925. Refers to the varieties of stoneware dairy jugs with embossed decorations such as cattle, castle, cherries, birds, etc. Decorated in solid, blended, or tinted glazes.

JUST RIGHT KITCHENWARE: 1951-1954. Overall kitchenware designation for Floral and Vegetable embossed designs. Floral, manufactured from 1951-1954, was decorated in white high gloss with raised yellow air-brushed florals, yellow air-brushed lids and brown banding. Florals appeared on one side only. Fifteen items were available which included a cookie jar. Vegetable was ovenproof kitchenware manufactured in 1951, with relief vegetable decoration (one side only), in solid high gloss glazes of Coral, Yellow and Green. Fifteen shapes available, which included a cookie jar.

L

LEEDS: 1940-1944. Novelty elephant and pig bottles manufactured for liquor, in high gloss blue or pink, with underglazed hand detailing.

LOVE BIRDS: 1905-1925. Refers to an embossed decoration used for early stoneware tankards tinted in blue and white and glazed overall in brown with white lining. Embossed Love Birds also appeared on jardinieres and jugs with blended glazes.

LUSTER: 1925-1930. Kitchenware line of bowls and tankard jugs in white semi-porcelain bodies with luster banded decorations. Banding colors included wide red band with small blue stripes, wide ivory brown band with small blue stripes and wide green band with small black stripes.

LUSTERWARE: 1927-1930. Semi-porcelain art and florist line in overall very brilliant and iridescent luster glazes of lavender, slate, orange, shammy, golden glow, light blue, iridescent dark blue and emerald. At least thirty-five items available.

M

MAGNOLIA MATTE: 1946-1947. Hand decorated embossed florals on shaded matte pastels of pink and blue or dusty rose and yellow. There were twenty-seven catalogued items, with vase 21-12 1/2" available with either open or tab rope handles; and 10-10 1/2" basket which was available with either closed or laced handle.

MAGNOLIA, NEW GLOSS: 1947-1948. Hand painted, embossed floral decoration of blue or pink on allover transparent pink high glazed background. Many items were detailed in gold, quite common for this line. Twenty-four shapes were catalogued, with Basket H14-10 1/2" being available with either closed or laced handle.

MARCREST: 1958. Kitchenware line made specifically for Marshall Burns as promotional items. Decorations included high gloss solid pastel colors of azure blue, mint green, shrimp and yellow. Although all molds from Heritageware were not used, Marcrest shared molds from Heritageware. Marcrest ashtrays are found in both high gloss and satin finishes, in a variety of colors.

MARDI GRAS: 1940. Semi-porcelain line manufactured exclusively for F.W. Woolworth Company, which included Spanish pots, Italian pots, flower vases, jardinieres and mixing bowls. Spanish pots were plain, while other items had raised concentric rings. Decorated in solid matte or high gloss colors of mauve, cobalt, turquoise, yellow and others.

MARDI GRAS: 1938-1946. Matte art lines which spanned several years of novelty chain store assortments. Plain and embossed decorations in satin and gloss white or pastels, and matte shaded pastels of pink and cream or blue and pink.

MAYFAIR: 1958-1959. Chain novelty and florist assortment in solid high gloss pastels and black, all with white foam trim. Assortment numbers varied per retailer, however, at least one retailer offered sixteen shapes.

MEAT TUBS: 1910-1925. Stoneware utility jars in fifteen gallons to thirty gallons, decorated in black over white glaze. Heart-shaped stamp on front of jar indicated gallon size.

MEDLEY: 1962. Novel chain store assortment of swirled urn vases, swan, dolphin, teddy bear planter, cat vase and items with metal accessories. Decorated in satin white, green agate with turquoise trim or persimmon with yellow trim. There were twenty-five items available.

MEXICAN: 1930-1940. Early semi-porcelain kitchenware items which were cold color decorated with Mexican motif, i.e., "300" gallon-sized cookie jar, "850" two-quart jug. Smoking Mexican in sombrero, seated under a black cactus, is painted in colors of red, ivory, and yellow.

MILK PANS: 1910-1925. Stoneware, flat or round bottomed, wide shouldered pans decorated in black or white, in one-half to two gallon sizes.

MIRROR ALMOND: 1981-1983. House 'n Garden casual servingware line glazed in overall Almond with Caramel Trim. At least thirty items available which included a cookie jar.

MIRROR BLACK: 1955-1957. Refers to any of the various wares glazed in overall high gloss black. Fantasy, Fiesta, and a variety of kitchenware items and jardinieres with metal accessories were included.

MIRROR BROWN: 1960-1985. Refers to the wide variety of House 'n Garden dinnerware offered in high gloss Mirror Brown with Ivory foam trim. Over one hundred items were available during the 25-year manufacturing period.

MIST: 1955-1957. Also referred to as Royal. Various mold blanks such as Ebb Tide, Butterfly, Woodland, Imperial, lavabo sets, jardinieres, novelties and ashtray planters in metal stands, used for various chain store assortments decorated in overall high glazed backgrounds of pink or turquoise with charcoal gray trim, sometimes having contrasting interiors: outer turquoise with pink interior, outer pink with turquoise interior. Assortment numbers varied per retailer, however, one particular chain store assortment contained twenty-seven different shapes.

MODERN: 1950. Overall line name for Plaid kitchenware manufactured just prior to the company's being destroyed by flood and fire. The company most likely intended to use this overall name for lines that followed, lines which were interrupted by the company's tragedy. It does not appear that the company went back to this line after the fire, although the molds were used for other kitchen lines, i.e., Floral, Vegetable, Cook 'n' Serve.

MORNING GLORY: 1940. Embossed design featured trumpet-shaped florals in allover matte white, or tinted matte blue to pink. This appears to be a part of the Mardi Gras/Granada line, rather than an experimental line.

MOTTLED: 1905-1925. Refers to glazing and color decoration treatment used on early stoneware such as butters and cuspidors. This was a sponging, or mottling of the glaze, usually in blue, with or without additional banding.

N

NULINE BAK-SERVE: 1937-1940. Ovenproof kitchenware in solid high gloss colors blue, turquoise, peach, maroon, yellow and cream At least three embossed patterns: "B", diamond quilt, "C", fish scale design, and "D" drape and panel design. At least eighteen shapes were available, which included a cookie jar in each of the three designs.

NURSERY: 1920-1932. Refers to semi-porcelain or ivory bodied deep baby plates, referred to as old style and new style, cups, saucers, mugs, bread and milk sets.

O

ORANGE TREE: 1918-1930. Refers to the embossed orange tree decoration on semi-porcelain and stoneware utility and artware items. Items were decorated in both solid and blended high gloss and matte finishes.

ORCHID: 1939-1941. Hand decorated embossed floral on tinted matte backgrounds of blue and rose, rose and cream, or allover blue. Fifteen catalogued shapes, many in graduated sizes.

OVERLAP NO. 75: 1915-1935. Refers to yellow or green semi-porcelain kitchenware line which included nested bowls, bake dishes, jugs, teapot, casseroles, range and refrigerator jars, bean pots and covered sugar.

P

PAGODA: 1960. Plain jardinieres, flower bowls and vases with a distinct Oriental flair, offered in three high gloss solid glazes: Persimmon or Green with black trim, or white with gray trim. Twelve items were catalogued.

PANDORA: 1915-1935. Also referred to as "150" Line. Semi-porcelain kitchenware assortment which included utility jars, steins, and salt boxes high glazed in yellow or green.

PANELLED BLUE BAND: 1915-1935. Octagon designed semi-porcelain kitchenware, nested bowl and nappy sets with panelled design and raised underglazed blue bands.

PARCHMENT AND PINE: 1951-1954. High gloss artware with embossed pine sprays, decorated in pine greens and browns, interiors being either brown or black. There are fifteen catalogued shapes with later entries of S14 center bowl and S15, instant coffee server. All shapes offered through 1954, with the exception of S14 center bowl, discontinued January 1, 1954.

PARROT CEREAL WARE: 1915-1935. Dark blue parrot in yellow panel decal used for decorating early cereal ware jars, spice jars, cruets and salt boxes. Fifteen items were included for complete set.

PERSIAN: 1928. Additional luster line, which originated by theme outside the company. At least 15 shapes of vases and jardinieres were available.

PIG BANKS: 1935-1985. Hull manufactured several different styles of piggy banks that ranged in sizes from dime banks to foot-long banks. Corky pig was a popular and long tenured bank design, beginning in 1957, and manufactured to the plant's closing. Corky pigs were decorated in a variety of solid and air-brush blended glazes. Dime banks had both plain and incised bodies, and foot-long banks were both plain and embossed with florals. Glazes and decorations were most often underglazed high gloss. However, some of the foot-long banks were decorated overglazed in cold color treatment.

PINECONE: 1938. Simplistic raised pinecone spray on solid matte pastel backgrounds of blue, pink or turquoise. One vase shape known.

PLAID: 1950. A part of Hull's, "Modern" kitchenware lines, this ovenproof kitchenware was decorated with green or red crisscross plaid design on high glazed yellow over white horizontally swirled backgrounds. Eleven items were available, which included a cookie jar in each decoration.

PLAIN CEREAL WARE: 1915-1935. Refers to semi-porcelain cereal ware jars, spice jars, cruets and salt boxes which were glazed in transparent high gloss, devoid of any further decoration. Fifteen items were included for complete set.

PLAIN WHITE: 1933. High gloss white semi-porcelain kitchenware which was devoid of decoration, inclusive of Hotel Ware, Restaurant Ware, Toilet Ware lines.

PLEATED WARE: 1920-1930. Refers to stoneware kitchen line of utilitarian items, i.e., nested bowls, covered casseroles, jugs, etc. Solid high gloss colors were used on this ware which is characterized by its pleating or overlap pattern of decoration.

PLUM: 1905-1925. Refers to an embossed decoration used for early blue and white stoneware dairy jugs.

POPPY: 1942-1943. Hand decorated embossed florals on tinted backgrounds of blue to pink, pink to cream, or allover cream, in at least twelve shapes, several in graduated sizes.

PRESERVE JARS: 1910-1925. One-half to three gallon covered stoneware cylinder-shaped jars, glazed black over white.

PROVINCIAL: 1961. Ovenproof House 'n Garden casual servingware glazed in Mirror Brown with white interiors and lids. At least twenty-three shapes were available, which included a cookie jar.

R

RAINBOW: 1928. Kitchenware line of white semi-porcelain with red and yellow, brown, or red and blue underglazed banding.

RAINBOW: 1961-1967. Ovenproof House 'n Garden casual servingware in solid high gloss colors of Mirror Brown, Butterscotch, Tangerine and Green Agate with contrasting foam edge which formed a rainbow table setting. At least forty items offered, including cookie jars in each of the four colors.

RED RIDING HOOD: 1943-1957. Includes the varieties of kitchen and novelty items produced in the Red Riding Hood character form. Most items are referred to as Hull Red Riding Hood, even though most were manufactured by Regal China Corp. Items included teapots, cookie jars, shakers, canister jars, spice jars, etc.

REGAL: 1952-1960. Novelty assortments for chain store sales which included florist ware, novelty planters and vases in a variety of high gloss colors. Items produced in 1952 were glazed in colors of chartreuse and dark green or wine and dark green. Figural vases such as the unicorn, twin deer, flying duck, flamingo, and parrot planter were decorated in green and white combinations, trimmed in brown.

RESTAURANT WARE: 1910-1935. High gloss white semi-porcelain kitchenware devoid of decoration, also referred to as Plain White consisting of chili, oyster and St. Dennis bowls, mugs, tumblers, water jug, and others.

RIDGE: 1982-1984. One of Hull's "Collection" dinnerwares glazed in Tawny Ridge, (tan.) Flint Ridge, (gray,) or Walnut Ridge, (brown.) Four-piece stacked canister set, cylinder-shaped cookie jar and Gingerbread Man cookie jar were available, in each of the three colors listed.

ROSELLA: 1946. Embossed wild rose decor, hand tinted under the glaze of either coral or ivory body. While sixteen shapes were catalogued, there's an additional pitcher, teapot, three lamps, dimpled vase and window box.

ROYAL: 1955-1957. Also referred to as Mist. Various mold blanks such as Ebb Tide, Butterfly, Woodland, Imperial, lavabo sets, jardinieres, novelties and ashtray planters in metal stands, used for various chain store assortments decorated in overall high glazed backgrounds of pink or turquoise with charcoal gray trim, sometimes having contrasting interiors: outer turquoise with pink interior, outer pink with turquoise interior. One particular chain store assortment contained twenty-seven different shapes.

S

SALT BOXES: 1915-1935. Refers to variety of salt boxes offered in Hull's early years. Bodies ranged from stoneware to semi-porcelain, Zane Gray and yellowware, encompassing both plain and embossed shapes. Glaze treatments included overglazed banding, decals, stamped decorations and mottled glazes. Salt boxes were available in round, square, rectangular, panelled or octagonal shapes. Lids, both pottery and wooden, were original to the boxes.

SANITARY WARE: 1910-1935. White, high fired semi-porcelain in plain, banded, stamped or decaled decorations, which included kitchenware and cooking ware items, along with Restaurant Ware, Toilet Ware and Hotel Ware.

SCROLL CEREAL WARE: 1915-1935. Terra Cotta double border decal used for decorating early cereal jars, spice jars, cruets and salt boxes. Fifteen items were included for complete set.

SERENADE: 1957. Textured exteriors of matte Regency Blue with Sunlight Yellow gloss interior, matte Shell Pink with Pearl Gray gloss interior, or matte Jonquil Yellow with Willow Green gloss interior were backgrounds for embossed bough and chickadee decor. Twenty-four items were available.

SHAMROCK: 1925-1935. Yellowware nested bowl and nappy sets, referred to as "fancy shaped," having underglazed brown bands.

SHOULDER JUGS: 1910-1925. Stoneware jugs, black over white glazed, in one-half to five gallon sizes.

SHULTON: 1937-1944. Cosmetic containers for shaving soap, after shaving lotion and talcum for men, manufactured by Hull under contractual agreement for Shulton's Old Spice men's products. Items produced include white high glazed bodies with fired on illustrations of sailing vessels in blue, "The Friendship, The Mount Vernon, The Recovery and The Grand Turk."

SPIRAL: 1960. Florist line jardiniere bowls and vases with a spiral or swirled panel. Glazes included Satin White and high gloss Mahogany or Moss with contrasting white foam edge.

SQUARE CEREAL WARE SETS: 1915-1935. Semi-porcelain canisters, salt boxes, spice jars and cruets, plain white glazed and decorated with decalcomania decorations. Fifteen items were included for complete set.

SQUARE FOOTED: 1935. Dark ivory buff semi-vitreous square footed kitchenware with transparent Popcorn Yellow glaze and wide Colonial Blue stripe with one Shell Bloom Pink pin stripe on each side. Also offered in solid high gloss colors of yellow or turquoise with or without hand painted florals. A square footed one-gallon sized cookie jar was available in the various color treatments.

SQUARE RIM: 1920-1930. Any of the varieties of utility lines characteristic of having a deep rim for ease in handling. Bodies ranged from dark ivory semi-vitreous buff, to yellowware, to ivory, with assorted banded colors, solid high gloss colors or blended colors.

STAG: 1905-1925. Refers to the embossed decoration used for early blue and white stoneware sanitary water kegs, with spigot, in three, four, five and six gallon sizes.

STAR AND LATTICE, BLUE CEREAL WARE: 1915-1935. Latticed open work top bordering blue decal used for decorating early cereal ware jars, spice jars, cruets and salt boxes. Fifteen items were included for complete set.

STAR AND LATTICE, GOLD CEREAL WARE: 1915-1935. Latticed open work top bordering gold decal used for decorating early cereal ware jars, spice jars, cruets and salt boxes. Fifteen items were included for complete set.

STONEWARE, BLUE AND WHITE: 1905-1935. Refers to stoneware bodies whose decoration is characterized by various shadings of light to dark tinted blues. Items were utilitarian, shapes were both plain and embossed. Items included stoneware dairy jugs, butters, salt boxes, cuspidors, water jugs, water kegs, nested bowl and nappy sets, ewers and basins, and more. Embossed shapes included, but were not limited to, cherries, plums, birds, daisies, wild roses, stags and cattle.

STREAMLINE ARTWARE: 1930-1940. Chain store assortment of semi-porcelain vases, jardinieres, flower pots with saucers, round jardinieres and hanging baskets. A draped effect "streamlined" embossed design, vertically on all pieces except round jardinieres, added dimension to these rather plain shapes. Items were glazed in high gloss pastel colors of yellow, turquoise, rose beige and matte white.

SUENO: 1938. Refers to overall chain store line name for Tulip, Calla Lily, Thistle and Pinecone designs.

SUN-GLOW: 1948-1949. Combination kitchenware and artware line which included nested bowls, pitchers, wall pockets, etc., decorated in backgrounds of solid high gloss pink or yellow with embossed floral and butterfly motif. Molds were later shared with Bow-Knot line, and these items may be found with Bow-Knot's glaze treatments of pink and blue or blue and turquoise. Twenty-nine shapes were available, including four wall pockets and two styles of tea bells.

SUN VALLEY PASTELS: 1956-1957. A seventeen piece chain store assortment in which eleven items were offered in satin finished pink with high gloss gray interior, or satin finished turquoise with high gloss yellow interiors. An additional seven items were offered in satin exterior finishes of pink, willow green and white. Retailers selected assortments which suited their own needs, up to the seventeen mentioned, sometimes mixing these with items from other chain store assortments.

SUPREME: 1960. Experimental ware never placed on the market in which some Imperial molds were used. A series of wire brushes scraped the surface after glazing and before firing. Company workmen referred to this as being "tooled" ware. Nine shapes offered in combinations of Agate and Chartreuse or Ripe Olive and Orange.

SWING BAND: 1938-1940. Five-piece band, averaging 6" in height, in ivory matte, finished with gold trim and hand painted features. Included band leader, accordionist, clarinet player, drummer and tuba player.

SWIRL: 1965. An experimental line of Ovenproof House 'n Garden casual servingware with swirled design incorporated into the design. Plates, cups, saucers, two sizes of bowls, stein and french-handled casserole were made.

T

TANGERINE, "900" SERIES: 1963-1967. Refers to the House 'n Garden casual serving ware line produced specifically in Tangerine. At least forty items were available. Also referred to as Burnt Orange and Golden Anniversary, originally this color was taken from the Rainbow line.

TEAPOTS: 1935. Semi-vitreous dark ivory buff body in opaque Lucerne Green or Burgundy Brown glaze, and high gloss yellow or green semi-porcelain bodies, devoid of further decoration.

THISTLE: 1938-1941. Embossed realistic thistle motif on solid matte backgrounds of pink, blue or turquoise. There are four known shapes.

TILE: 1926-1931. Hull manufactured plain and faience floor, wall and ornamental tiles with matching accessories such as towel bars, soap dishes, etc., with special orders accepted, in a variety of solid, blended and stippled colors, both high gloss and matte glazes being offered.

TOILET WARE: 1910-1935. Plain and embossed toilet ware items for the home or hotel in semi-porcelain and stoneware bodies. Some items were decorated by decalcomania, banding, stamping, and tinting, while others remained glazed transparent white with no decoration.

TOKAY: 1958-1960. Relief grape and leaf decor in color glazes of Light Green and Sweet Pink or Milk White and Forest Green. Both glazes available during 1958. After 1958, only the White and Green combination was available. There were eighteen originally catalogued items with a 14" caladium leaf, 15 1/2" pedestaled vase and 14" ewer which followed.

TROPICANA: 1959. Decorated Caribbean characters depict the tropics in this line which was glazed in allover white background, edged in Tropic Green. The line included seven shapes.

TULIP: 1925-1935. Tulip embossed stoneware jardinieres, pedestals and vases, some with overglazed cold color detail to florals. Items were overall glazed in backgrounds of deep brown, with or without white interiors. 7 1/2" Jardinieres and 7 1/2" matching pedestals each wholesaled for $21.60 per gross.

TULIP: 1928. Graduated semi-porcelain line of tankard jugs in backgrounds of overall transparent white, decorated with overglazed tulip decal.

TULIP: 1938-1941. Hand decorated embossed tulip motif on shaded combinations of blue and pink, blue and cream, or allover blue. There were fifteen catalogued shapes, many in graduated sizes.

TUSCANY: 1958-1960. Relief grape and leaf decor in color glazes of Sweet Pink and Gray Green, or Milk White and Forest Green. Both glazes available during 1958. After 1958, only the White and Green combination was available. There were eighteen originally catalogued items with a 14" caladium leaf, 15 1/2" pedestaled vase and 14" ewer which followed.

U

URN VASES: 1962. Imperial florist line of jardinieres, many in graduated sizes, which were first offered in Satin White or high gloss Moss Green, additional colors followed.

UTILITY JARS: 1910-1935. Refers to two to four gallon plain-shaped covered jars of both semi-porcelain and stoneware bodies, plain or embossed shapes, some decorated with various color banding treatments. Available with or without lettering, "Cakes, Bread, Flour, etc."

V

VEGETABLE: 1951. Ovenproof kitchenware with relief vegetable decoration in solid high gloss glazes of Coral, Yellow or Green. Fifteen shapes were available, which included a cookie jar.

VEILED WARES: 1955-1957. Refers to a free-form line decoration, or "spider-webbed" treatment on overall solid high gloss or matte colors for kitchenware, artware and floristware. Area decorators also used veiled treatments.

VICTORIAN: 1974. Imperial line of heavily embossed dish gardens and florist ware in overall solid gloss glazes of Olive with Willow Green and Green with Turquoise. Also offered in Satin White.

W

WATER JUGS: 1910-1935. Refers to two to six gallon covered water jars with metal spigots. Bodies included both semi-porcelain and stoneware, plain or embossed shapes, one being a stag. Decorations included decals, banding or color tints.

WATER LILY: 1948-1949. Hand decorated embossed Water Lily floral on matte shaded backgrounds of Walnut and Apricot or Turquoise and Sweet Pink. Gold decoration is not unusual on this line. There were twenty-eight shapes available.

WATER LILY, NEW GLOSS: 1949-1950. Hand decorated embossed Water Lily on high gloss backgrounds of white or cream. There were twenty-eight shapes available in gloss Water Lily.

WEBBED: 1955. Refers to decoration treatment used by enlisting a heavy glaze with added ingredients which built up in the glaze, giving a rough or "coconut" texture. Some items decorated with webbing were lined with a high gloss contrasting color. Webbing was used for both kitchenware items and artware items.

WHEAT: 1915-1935. Refers to canister jars, spice jars, cruets and salt box with embossed wheat design, produced in both semi-porcelain and stoneware, glazed green, yellow, blue or tan.

WILD FLOWER NO. SERIES: 1942-1943. Artware line with embossed hand decorated florals on matte duo-tone tinted backgrounds of blue and pink, russet and pink or allover cream. Several of the items have an embossed butterfly motif included in the lid, handle or within the body of the embossed decoration. There were twenty-nine catalogued items available.

WILDFLOWER "W" SERIES: 1946-1947. Hand decorated embossed motif of "Trillium, Mission and Bluebell," on shaded backgrounds of pink and blue or yellow and dusty rose. There were twenty-two catalogued shapes.

WOODLAND: 1949-1950. Matte finished backgrounds of Dawn Rose or Harvest Yellow with hand decorated embossed florals. There were thirty catalogued shapes of pre-1950 Woodland.

WOODLAND, HI-GLOSS: 1952-1954. High gloss tinted backgrounds of blue-gray and forest green, chartreuse and pink, pink and shrimp, chartreuse with or without dark green interiors and trim, or allover high gloss glazes of white, cream or pink. The hand decorated embossed floral appears on only one side of this ware. Allover glazes with contrasting interiors were first called Two-Tone and later placed in the category as Hi-Gloss. Heavy gold detailing is not uncommon on the lighter shades. Twenty-one shapes were available in Hi-Gloss Woodland.

WOODLAND, NEW GLOSS: 1949-1950. High gloss backgrounds of white, cream and pink with hand decorated embossed floral. Heavy gold detailing on the lighter glazes is not uncommon. There were thirty catalogued shapes of pre-1950 New Gloss Woodland.

WOODLAND, NEW MATTE: 1950. Matte finished artware on backgrounds of Dawn Rose or Harvest Yellow with hand decorated embossed floral on one side only. Twenty-one shapes were available in post-1950 matte Woodland.

WOODLAND, TWO-TONE: 1952-1954. High gloss solid chartreuse backgrounds with contrasting dark green interiors and trim. Twenty-one shapes were available in Two-Tone Woodland.

Y

YELLOWWARE: 1910-1925. Any of the varieties of utility ware which included jugs, bowls, butters, casseroles, custards, etc., with yellowware body which was manufactured in durable bright glazes, either plain, embossed or banded.

Z

ZANE GREY: 1928. Stoneware body with durable high quality "Bristol" glaze with under glaze blue banding. The same basic shapes as blue banded semi-porcelain wares were used to provide a more economical product for the trade. Items offered included jugs, jars, bowls, nappies, custards, butters and food containers from one to six gallons.

Lamps

While it is far from complete, the following is a listing of Hull factory lamps that I have either had the opportunity to see or own. See page 148 for information regarding identifying factory lamps.

Water Lily, vase shape L-5, 7 1/2"
Classic, T-1, 7 3/4"
Classic, T-2, 7 3/4"
Rosella, vase shape R-2, 6 3/4"
Rosella, L3, 11"
Rosella, dimpled body, 10 3/4"
Matte Unnamed line, (similar to Poppy decor,) 9"
High gloss Unnamed line, with or without framed decal, L2, 13"
Matte Unnamed line, embossed framed floral, L-1, 13"
Tulip, vase shape 100-33-8"
Orchid, vase shape 303, 10 1/4"
Camellia, vase shape 139, 10 1/2"
*Red Riding Hood figural, 8"
Kitten figural, shape 61, 7 1/2"
Pig figural, bank shape 196, 6"
Rooster figural, shape 53, 5 3/4"
Leeds Elephant figural, 8"
Leeds Pig figural, 8"
Magnolia Gloss, shape H24, 4"
Bow-Knot, shape B4, 6 1/2"
Bow-Knot, shape B10, 10 1/2"

Woodland Gloss teapot, shape W26, 8"
Woodland Gloss ewer, shape W24, 14 3/4"
Woodland Gloss, free form shape, 14"
Woodland Gloss, handled ovoid vase-shape, 15"

*The Red Riding Hood Figural lamp is of Regal manufacture, while most additional lamps with decals matching Red Riding Hood decaled florals are neither Hull nor Regal China manufacture.

Cookie Jars

B-8: CRESCENT: 1953-1954. Round jar in high gloss Chartreuse and Dark Green or Strawberry and Wine, each with contrasting "crescent" tipped contrasting lid, 9 1/2"

B-20: NULINE BAK-SERVE: 1938-1942. Cylinder-shaped semi-porcelain jar with embossed Diamond Quilt design, assorted solid color glazes. Capacity - 2 quarts, 8".

C-20: NULINE BAK-SERVE: 1938-1942. Cylinder-shaped semi-porcelain jar with embossed Fish Scale design, assorted solid color glazes. Capacity - 2 quarts, 8".

D-20: NULINE BAK-SERVE: 1938-1942. Cylinder-shaped semi-porcelain jar with embossed Drape and Panel design, assorted solid color glazes. Capacity - 2 quarts, 8".

O-8: DEBONAIR: 1954, Cylinder-shaped jar. Decoration No. 1, in solid Chartreuse with Dark Green glaze. Decoration No. 2 in white high gloss background tinted in pink and lavender, with black contrasting band around the center of jar, 9".

0-18: HERITAGEWARE: 1958. "Milk can" shaped jar decorated in high gloss Mint Green or Azure Blue with white foam edge. A second decoration was a solid color semi-matte stippled finish in the same colors of Mint Green or Azure Blue, with contrasting lid in white, 9 1/2".

No. 18: COOK 'N SERVE WARE: 1952-1953. Plain cylinder-shaped jar decorated in green and mottled brown flow glaze, white high gloss jar with contrasting black lid, tinted brown to yellow top, or tinted pink to charcoal top, 9 1/2".

No 28: JUST RIGHT KITCHENWARE: VEGETABLE, 1950-1951. Embossed vegetable pattern, carrots, radishes and pea pods spell "Cookies" on front. Decorated in high gloss solid colors of Yellow, Coral or Green, 9 1/2".

No. 30: BLOSSOM: 1948-1949, from the Cinderella kitchenware line. Straight cylinder-shaped jar with underglazed mask-decorated designs. Yellow or Pink six-petal hand painted floral with green leaves and banding on overall white high glaze, 10 1/2".

No. 30: BOUQUET: 1948-1949, from the Cinderella kitchenware line. Straight cylinder-shaped jar with underglazed mask-decorated design. Multi-colored hand painted floral spray with air-brushed base in yellow on overall white high glaze, 10 1/2".

No. 48: JUST RIGHT KITCHENWARE: FLORAL design, 1952-1953. Cylinder-shaped jar in white high gloss with embossed yellow daisy with air-brushed base in yellow on overall white high gloss, 9 1/2".

No. 67: MODERN KITCHENWARE: PLAID. 1950. Plain cylinder-shaped jar decorated in overall white high gloss background which has been "striped horizontally," in yellow and teamed with red or green crisscross design, 9 1/2".

22/20: SQUARE FOOTED:1925-1935. Cylinder-shaped stoneware jar with square-edged, draped-effect base with dubbed handles. Dark ivory buff stoneware body glazed in a variety of transparent and opaque colors. Underglaze decorated with wide colonial blue stripe with one shell bloom pink pin stripe on each side. Overglaze cold color decorations include fruits and florals and hand-decorated designs such as Poppy, Rose, Tulip, Poinsettia, and others. Capacity - one callon, 9 1/2".

70/20: PLAIN: 1930, squat cylinder-shaped stoneware cookie jar, no handles. Glazed in transparent Leghorn Yellow with overglaze hand-decoration of Poppy, Rose, Tulip, Poinsettia, and others, 11".

92/20: ALPINE: 1915-1930. Embossed Alpine decor in ivory and brown, three quarts, 9 1/2".

123 COUNTRY SQUIRE: 1963-1967. Same shape as 523 House 'n Garden cookie jar glazed in high gloss blend of turquoise and green agate, 8".

300/20: SEMI-PORCELAIN: 1925-1940. Plain cylinder-shaped with four incised groves at base. The various solid high gloss colors, may additionally be teamed with overglazed or underglazed hand-painted decoration or decals. Decorations included florals, fruits and a Mexican theme. This jar was restyled for the 1948 line known as Cinderella. Capacity - one gallon, 11".

"400" LINE: 1930-1940. Straight sided, semi-porcelain cylinder-shaped cookie jar with embossed florals and leaves. Decorated in solid high gloss colors in turquoise, mauve, yellow, pink, cobalt, and others, 10 1/2".

401: PAINTED: 1934. No additional information available.

423: HEARTLAND: 1983-1985. Squat cylinder-shaped jar with domed lid, dubbed handles. Embossed "ring" pattern decorated top of jar and around lid. Gold-shaded, satin speckled cream glaze, with hand applied brown stamp decoration, 9".

523: HOUSE 'N GARDEN: 1961-1985. Plain cylinder-shaped glazed in Mirror Brown with Ivory Foam, 8".

723: PROVINCIAL: 1961. Same shape as 523 House 'n Garden cookie jar, glazed in Mirror Brown, with contrasting white lining and white lid, 8".

850/20: 1930-1940. Semi-porcelain squat cookie jar with dubbed handles. Overglazed or underglazed decorations of fruits and florals. You can expect to find jars in solid color glazes such as turquoise, yellow, blue, etc. One such overglazed decoration illustrates an apple, 3 strawberries and a pear on either side. Lid has an embossed star shape. Capacity - one gallon, 9".

923: TANGERINE: 1963-1967. Same shape as 523 House 'n Garden cookie jar, glazed in solid high gloss Tangerine. The tangerine glaze was also referred to as Burnt Orange for an exclusive House 'n Garden line for J. C. Penney, 8".

966: DUCK: 1940-1943. Figural jar, glazed in white with overglaze cold color details, 11 1/2".

968: HEN WITH CHICK: 1940. White overall glazed background. Hen has chick underneath edge of wing, hen's tail feathers flair up in a crescent curve. Overglaze cold color detailed in black, yellow and red, 11 1/2".

971: BOY BLUE: 1940. Little Boy Blue character sitting on hay stack holding horn. Overglazed cold color decoration, hay stack in brown, boy's pants in blue, shirt in red, blue hat with red feather, 12 1/2".

AVOCADO: 1968-1971. Same shape as 523 House 'n Garden cookie jar, glazed in solid high gloss Avocado with Ivory Trim, 8".

BLUE-BELLE: 1985. Squat cylinder-shaped jar with domed lid and dubbed handles. Embossed "ring" pattern decorated top of jar and around lid. Glazed in high gloss winter-white with underglazed decoration of bluebell florals, 9".

COLONIAL GIRL: 1930-1940. Straight-sided, cylinder-shaped ivory, yellow or turquoise high glazed backgrounds with cold color hand decorated colonial girl figure and floral sprays. 11".

FIVE BANDED: 1915-1935. This high fired white semi-porcelain kitchenware line included cookie and/or utility jars with dubbed handles. These are rather bulbous, yet curving, extremely attractive jars. Jars are decorated in allover transparent white with five overglazed bands near top edges of jars. The lowest band being the thinnest, widens with each step of elevation in this decor of Pimento Red or Nubian Black. Solid color jars in colors including yellow, turquoise, blue, mauve, peach and others have either hand painted cold color decor, or no decor at all, 9".

GINGERBREAD MAN: 1982-1985. Animated embossed story book character, glazed in gray, tan or brown with contrasting foam. Brown cookie jars were also manufactured in this mold by Western Stoneware Company of Monmouth, Illinois. These jars can be detected by a darker brown glaze with more imperfections, darker clay content, bordering on gray, and the fact that the glaze does not cover the base completely, 12".

LITTLE RED RIDING HOOD: 1943-1957. Designs were floral decaled and underglazed decorated, trimmed with gold. There is an open-end basket cookie jar and a closed or rounded-end basket cookie jar, with or without apron, 13".

RAINBOW: 1963-1967. Same shape as 523 House 'n Garden cookie jar, glazed in solid high gloss Tangerine, Butterscotch, Green Agate, along with Mirror Brown, all with contrasting foam, 8".

Canisters

BLUE-BELLE 6410, four-piece canister set. Squat cylinder-shaped jars with domed lids, dubbed handles. Embossed "ring" pattern decorated top of jar and around lids. The two smaller jars are identical in size, additional jars are graduated. Glazed in high gloss winter-white with underglaze decoration of blue bell florals.

GINGERBREAD TRAIN four-piece canister set, Engine, Express Car, Kiddie Car and Caboose, embossed with animated characters, glazed in Mirror Brown.

HEARTLAND 490, four-piece canister set. Squat cylinder-shaped jars with domed lids, dubbed handles. Embossed "ring" pattern decorated top of jar and around lids. The two smaller jars are identical in size, additional jars are graduated. Gold-shaded, satin speckled cream glaze, with hand applied brown stamp decoration indicating flour, sugar, coffee and tea.

HOUSE 'N GARDEN MIRROR BROWN NOS. 556, 557, 568, 569, four-piece spherical canister set. Embossed with tea, coffee, sugar and flour, decorated in solid high gloss Mirror Brown with ivory foam.

HOUSE 'N GARDEN 5490 four-piece canister set. Squat cylinder-shaped jars with domed lids, dubbed handles. Embossed concentric "bands or rings" decorated top of jar and around lids. The two smaller jars are identical in size, additional jars are graduated. Glazed in Mirror Brown with ivory foam.

HOUSE 'N GARDEN CYLINDER STACK four-piece canister set. Straight sided, rimmed "grip" top for ease in handling, domed lids with bar handles. Glazed in flint (gray,) tawny (tan) and Mirror Brown with contrasting foam.

LITTLE RED RIDING HOOD: decaled jars with figural lids of Red Riding Hood character.

Decalcomania designs used on square cereal ware sets included, but were not limited to:

BLUE BIRD: at least two styles, blue bird in flight and perched bird.

CLASSIC: Double border designs offered in three separate colors: green, blue or golden brown.

CONVENTIONAL ROSE: Pink double border floral.

CONVENTIONAL TILE: Yellow double border geometric design.

CONVENTIONAL VINE: Blue double border trailing vine.

DELFT: Harbor, ship and/or windmill decor in blue.

DRAPE AND FESTOON: Top bordering decal in colors of rose, blue, green and black.

GRECIAN BORDER, BLUE: Greek key double border design in blue.

GRECIAN BORDER, GOLD: Greek key double border design in gold.

PLAIN: Items were marked as to contents, however, no decoration was used.

PARROT: Dark blue parrot in yellow panel, dark blue bands either side.

SCROLL: Terra Cotta double border scroll effect.

STAR AND LATTICE, BLUE: Top bordering decal in blue star and lattice design.

STAR AND LATTICE, GOLD: Top bordering decal in gold star and lattice design.

House 'n Garden Casual Servingware

The following listing of House 'n Garden Servingware is provided for collectors. Items listed are those which were available in Mirror Brown with Ivory Foam. Although some of these items were also offered in additional colors, this listing centers on those manufactured in Mirror Brown.

House 'n Garden typically used the same sequence of numbers for items that crossed over to different lines or colors, such as Provincial, Crestone, and Almond. While 501 was a Mirror Brown salad plate, 701 was a Provincial salad plate, 301 was a Crestone salad plate and 801 was an Almond salad plate. While the hundredth digit changed, the remaining digits remained the same for like items used in different House 'n Garden lines.

100 Series was Country Square, 200 Series was Rainbow, 300 Series was Crestone, 400 Series eventually became Heartland, 500 Series belonged to Mirror Brown, 600 Series was Avocado, 700 Series was Provincial, 800 Series became Almond and 900 Series was Tangerine. Items from the Mirror Brown Hull Collection also followed this numbering system with newly molded items designated as a 5,000 Series.

500 10 1/4" Dinner Plate
501 6 1/2" Salad Plate
502 9 oz. Mug
503 5 1/4" Fruit Bowl
504 4-Piece Place Setting (#'s 500, 501, 502 & 503)
505 2 Cup Covered Carafe
506 32 oz. Open Baker
507 32 oz. Covered Casserole
508 6 1/2" X 5 1/4" Oval Salad
509 5 Pint Jug
510 2 Quart Covered Bean Pot
511 16 oz. Gravy Boat
512 10 1/4" X 6" Gravy Boat Saucer
513 5 1/4" Open French Handled Casserole
514 2 Quart Ice Jug
515 3 3/4" Salt Shaker
516 3 3/4" Pepper Shaker
517 Shaker Set (#'s 515 & 516)
518 8 oz. Jug/Creamer
519 12 oz. Covered Sugar
520 Sugar/Creamer Set (#'s 518 & 519)
521 15" X 10 1/2" Leaf Shaped Chip 'n Dip
522 8 Cup Coffee Pot
523 94 oz. Cookie Jar
524 12 oz. Individual Covered Bean Pot
525 2 Pint Jug
526 16 oz. Beer Stein
527 5 1/4" Covered French Handled Casserole
528 4-Piece Coffee Carafe Set (1 covered carafe, 1 7 oz. cup, 1 deep well saucer)
529 6 oz. Cup
530 5 1/2" Saucer
531 8 1/2" Luncheon Plate
532 12-Piece Luncheon Set (8 1/2" luncheon plates, 6 oz. cups & 5 1/2" saucers)
533 6" Fruit
534 7 Pint Open Roaster
535 7 Pint Covered Roaster
535 9" Bud Vase
536 6" Mixing Bowl
537 7" Mixing Bowl
538 8" Mixing Bowl with Pouring Spout
539 3-Piece Mixing Bowl Set (#'s 536, 537 & 538)
540 12 1/2" X 7 1/2" Leaf Tray
540 Gravy Boat Set (#'s 511 & 512)
541 11 3/4" X 9" Individual Oval Steak Plate
542 10 3/4" X 7 1/4" Divided Vegetable
543 10" X 7 1/4" Open Oval Baker
544 10" X 7 1/4" Covered Oval Casserole
545 10 1/4" Bowl
546 3-Piece Salad Set (#'s 545 & 547)
547 Fork and Spoon Set (wooden accessories)
548 2 Quart Oval Covered Casserole
549 5 Cup Teapot

551 12 oz. Covered Jam/Mustard Jar (with plastic spoon)
553 11 oz. Soup Mug
554 9 3/4" Oval Tray (for Soup/Coffee Mugs or Cereals)
555 Soup 'n Sandwich (#'s 553, 11 oz. Soup Mug, & 554, Tray)
556 Snack Set (#'s 502, 9 oz. Coffee Mug, and 554, Tray)
556 Tea Canister
557 Toast 'n Cereal (#'s 503, 12 oz. Cereal, and 554, Tray)
557 13 3/8" X 10 1/2" Chicken Server
557 3 lb. Coffee Canister
558 13 3/8" X 10 1/2" Open Chicken Baker
558 5 lb. Sugar Canister
559 13 3/8" X 10 1/2", #557 Server with Chicken Cover
559 5 lb. Flour Canister
560 13 3/8" X 10 1/2", #558 Baker with Chicken Cover
560 8-Piece Canister Set
561 1/4 lb. Covered Butter Dish
562 3 Pint Covered French Handled Casserole
563 8" Ash Tray
565 3 Pint Dutch Oven
566 9 1/4" Pie Plate
567 3 Pint Open French Handled Casserole
568 3 Pint Open Square Baker
569 6 1/2" Soup/Salad Bowl
570 16-Piece Starter set (4 each: 6" Fruits, 7 oz. Cups, 5 7/8" Saucers & 9 3/8" Luncheon Plates)
571 10 oz. Continental Mug
573 9 1/4" X 3 3/8" Corn Serving Dish
574 10" X 5" Oval Service Dish
575 Chicken Top, Server & Baker Set (#'s 556, 557 & 558)
576 6 oz. Custard Cup
577 14 1/2" X 8 1/2" Double Serving Dish
578 3-Piece Place Setting (#'s 500, 502 & 503)
579 3 Pint Covered French Handled Casserole with Warmer
580 3-Piece Place Setting (#'s 500, 502 & 503)
581 10 3/4" Individual Oval Spaghetti Plate
582 12 oz. Cheese Shaker
583 11 1/2" X 8 3/4" Chip 'n Dip
583 11" Rectangular Salad Server
584 5 1/2" Sauce Bowl
584 12 oz. Oil Cruet
585 12" X 11" Tray
585 12 oz Vinegar Cruet
586 2-Piece Chip 'n Dip (#'s 584 & 585)
587 3 3/4" Mushroom Shaker
588 3 3/4" Mushroom Shaker
589 6 1/2" Bake & Serve
590 7 1/4" X 4 3/4" Individual Leaf Dish
591 12 1/4" X 9" Leaf Shaped Chip 'n Dip
591 9 1/4" Egg Plate
592 Two Tier Tid Bit Tray
592 Hen on Nest Casserole
593 14" X 10" Oval Well 'n Tree Steak Plate
594 Salt Shaker
594 6 3/4" Spoon Rest
595 Pepper Shaker
595 11 1/2" Handled Server
596 Shaker Set (#'s 594 & 595)
596 11 1/4" Individual Fish Platter

597 7 oz. Cup
598 5 7/8" Saucer
599 9 3/8" Luncheon Plate

Clocks

To date, there has been no documented information regarding Hull's manufacture of clocks of any type. The ceramic clock cases, with Sessions movements, selling in the range of $250-$400, were not produced at the Hull Pottery or for The Hull Pottery. Some of these clock cases were manufactured by The Shawnee Pottery Company, with no direct or indirect relationship to The Hull Pottery.

Reproductions

Reproduced items, which began infiltrating the market in 1992, initially in Ohio, have now interspersed throughout the United States.

Red Riding Hood items, very much in demand, were targeted as the initial reproduction. However, Bow-Knot, as well as other art lines are being purchased for remolding purposes only. These items contain the Hull trademark.

It was earlier felt that Hull collectors' primary enemy would be wares of the 1980's, due to the company's haphazard dispersal methods and buyers are cautioned to beware of all items looking suspect. Things to watch for in the remolded items include lighter weight, brighter colors, glazes which were not produced within the company and slightly smaller sizes due to shrinkage when remolded from the original item.

Items sanctioned as limited editions, such as Gingerbread wares, fall into a category very close to that of reproductions since these items have been produced no where near Hull Pottery's origin, that being Crooksville, Ohio, or by the pottery areas' local craftsmen.

While Gingerbread items manufactured outside the Hull firm have been glazed in Mirror Brown, very closely simulating the original glazes used within the Crooksville factory, the clay body originally used for the limited editions was of a darker, more gray composition. The clay body has since been changed to a whiter clay which is more uniform to Hull dinnerware clay bodies.

Hull Pottery Trademarks

1. This black ink stamp marked porcelain wares of the Acme Pottery Company (1903-1907,) of Crooksville, Ohio, purchased by The A. E. Hull Pottery in 1907.

2. This black heart ink stamp marked early black over white utilitarian stoneware, indicating gallon size within the heart's boundaries. This mark was used around 1912.

3. Most Hull wares remained unmarked until well into the Teens. The first trademark incised into the ware, appears to be the H in diamond form. This trademark is found most often on kitchenware and utilitarian wares.

4. By the 1920's, the incised bold capital (H) in circle trademark soon followed.

5. The (H) in circle trademark soon evolved into this far less bold designation.

6. This mark many times included incised numbers which indicated mold and size numbers for jugs, diameters for bowls, height for vases, etc.

7. The (H) in circle designation, used well into the 1930's, is found as illustrated in trademarks 4 through 7, as well as other similar variations. This trademark was used on a variety of both kitchenware and artware items.

8. Hull tile was manufactured in both plain and faience styles, with either a flat, or cushioned (rounded) surface. Faience tile was marked just that, "HULL FAIENCE." A cushioned tile was further marked, "Cushion." The faience cushion trademark is bold and deeply incised, and dates from 1926-1931.

9. The HULL TILE trademark is found in both raised and embossed form.

10. Hull Tile was sometimes embossed in one line, sometimes in two, size or shape of the tile did not usually affect the positioning of the trademark. "Cushion," was added to tiles with cushioned, or rounded surfaces. Hull tile was made from 1926-1931.

11. Another incised tile trademark, used during tile production 1926-1931, included this Hull Faience Cushion logo in crisscross fashion.

12. Some early utilitarian items indicated a registered patent assignment in incised form. This particular mark is found on yellowware batter bowls. This trademark was used as early as mid-1920.

13. This incised trademark incorporated the entire A. E. Hull firm name, and was used on kitchenware and novelties of the 1930's. It was most often followed by mold and size identification numbers. By the 1930's, nearly all Hull trademarks carried USA in some form. In fact, USA was indicated even when the Hull name was not. Many early stoneware, yellowware and kitchenware items were marked only with an incised USA.

14. The incised Hull Oven-Proof trademark was also used on kitchenware items from the 1930's, and into the 1940's. The trademark was usually followed by mold number and size identification.

15, 16, 17. Throughout the 1930's and 1940's, Kitchenware lines were additionally marked by ovenproof foil labels which indicated, "heat resisting, cold resisting." These foil labels, which marked many nested bowl and nappy sets, appeared in various colors including, but not limited to red, black, and silver, and were oval, round, rectangular and bowl-shaped.

18. Plain artwares from the Sueno line, being either shaded or overall white, carried no "Hull" mark, however, were incised with style or mold numbers, which usually included size identification.

19. Illustrated is a variation of the above-described trademark. These artware items most often carried the triangular Hull foil label to compensate for being unmarked.

20. Although many novelties from the 1930's and early 1940's carried no "Hull" designation, the incised "HULL MADE" trademark appeared on some of the novelty wares from this era. This trademark was usually followed by the mold number.

21. By 1938, this incised "HULL" mark, followed by "USA," or "U.S.A.," was widely used for matte pastel artwares.

22. Another version of the previously illustrated trademark shows little difference other than the "USA" designation. Hull soon learned that trademarks were good business, and Hull trademarks soon acted as representatives of a quality product. The advertising aspect was carried a step further with the offer of a complimentary A. E. Hull Pottery display plaque with orders totalling over $20.

23. During this same time, it was not uncommon for the Hull trademark to be absent on some very fine artware lines.

24. As with the above-described trademark, incised mold numbers and size identification were still apparent, sometimes being followed by USA. The Hull triangular foil label again, compensated for the ware's being unmarked.

1.	2.	3.	4.
5. 113 Ⓗ 7½	6. 30 Ⓗ	7. Ⓗ 60	8. HULL FAIENCE CUSHION
9. HULL-CUSHION TILE	10. HULL TILE	11. CUSHION HULL FAIENCE	12. PAT-APL-FOR USA 25-3-9
13. A.E. HULL U.S.A.	14. HULL USA OVEN-PROOF	15. HULL POTTERY HEAT RESISTING OVEN PROOF COLD RESISTING CROOKSVILLE OHIO	16. HEAT RESISTING OVEN PROOF COLD RESISTING MADE IN U.S.A.
17. HEAT RESISTING OVEN PROOF COLD RESISTING MADE IN USA	18. 930/33 3	19. 920/33 1 5"	20. HULL MADE USA
21. HULL USA	22. HULL U.S.A.	23. 500/33-8"	24. # 55-6½" USA

25. Part of the reasoning behind the trademarks which did not include the "Hull" name, was due to the additional placement of foil labels on the ware. These labels, elongated diamond or triangular in shape, are either black or maroon with lettering in silver or gold. The foil labels were used consistently to mark a variety of Hull's artware, novelty and kitchenware lines from the late 1930's to the mid-1940's.

26. Representative, or sample Hull items were marked with labels such as this paper seal which is green and white. Style No., Decoration, and Size number were noted directly on the label. The upper half of this seal is green with white lettering, while the lower half of this seal is white with green lettering. Sample seals are also found in black and red. The round sample seal was used prior to 1950, while a rectangular black and white seal was primarily used for post-1950 Hull wares.

27. By early 1940, the Hull trademark, identical to the previously used incised form, was now seen with raised or embossed letters.

28. Only a slightly different version than above-described, the raised versions proved to better meet the needs for manufacturing since embossed marking was less often obliterated by the remaining glazing processes when thick glazes filled the indentations of the incised letters.

29. From 1937-1944, product containers manufactured by Hull for Shulton's Old Spice, in the form of shaving lotion and talcum bottles, were marked with this incised trademark.

30. From 1937-1944, mugs for shaving soap, manufactured by Hull for Shulton's Old Spice were marked with this incised trademark.

31. This incised trademark is found on the figural elephant and pig liquor bottles of the mid-1940's. Patent designation is not always included, it is quite common to find items marked, "Leeds, USA," only.

32. Incised "Hull Ware" logos were typical trademarks for 1940's kitchenware nested bowl and nappy sets, as well as cookie jars

33. Mold numbers, sometimes with size identification, were also included in the above-described trademark as well as this variation of "Hull Ware".

34. There is no question as to the origin of items incised "Hull Ware Little Red Riding Hood." This mark is found on Hull-made "Red" wares, although some items were unmarked. This mark was also used without the "Hull Ware" designation. In this instance it included the patent design number, and was used most often for marking Regal-made cookie jars. (See Trademark No. 35.) Most all Red Riding Hood items, both Hull Pottery and Regal China, were accented with gold detailing. It is not uncommon to find items with foil labels stating, "Hand Painted Fired Ceramic Colors," indicating gold content, usually 23K.

35. This incised Little Red Riding Hood trademark was most often used on cookie jars which were large enough to accommodate the logo.

36. Many Red Riding Hood items were incised with the patent design number, 135889. Red Riding Hood items were produced from 1943-1957.

37. This incised script form served as trademark for the Boy Blue cookie jar in 1940.

38. An additional incised script trademark, "Hull, USA," was used for cookie jars and kitchenware of the 1940's

39, 40. Hull's art designs had gained wide acclaim during the 1940's, with artware sales making up a large portion of the company's retail sales. Provided with this stability, Hull chose to advertise their artwares as such, and designed the incised "Hull Art" trademark for this use.

41. Illustrated is another incised form of the company's "Hull Art" trademark used in the 1940's. This logo is found on the very plain, yet stylized art forms which did not have the typical floral embossing of the day.

42. In 1946, Rosella artware not only had its own special clay mixture, it was also accompanied by a specially designed foil label. This rose and banner "Rosella" label is brown with gold accents.

43. Interesting to note, the Hull Company had used the potter-at-wheel logo from its earliest inception throughout their history of production. This design, first used on advertising materials and brochure pages, later appeared in foil label form and was used on company letterheads after 1950. Many, many of the artware items from the Forties were consistently marked with this label. It has a black background with silver, gold or gray lettering.

44. The "Granada" potter-at-wheel foil label graced many chain store art and novelty items. While a specific matte artware line was manufactured from 1938-1946, the Granada line spanned years of the mid-1930's through the early 1950's. The Granada and Mardi Gras molds were used interchangeably. This label has a black background with gold or silver lettering.

45. The vase-form "Mardi Gras" potter-at-wheel foil label is found on assorted art and novelty items. While a specific matte artware line was manufactured from 1938-1946, the Mardi Gras line spanned years of the mid-1930's through the early 1950's. The Granada and Mardi Gras molds were used interchangeably. This label has a black background with gold or silver lettering. The company reports another foil label in white or silver, featuring a black silhouette of a female flamenco dancer with mask.

46. This crown and banner "Classic" foil label used in the early 1940's, marked many chain store pottery items. This label has a background of silver or gold and a contrasting green banner with gold and black lettering.

47, 48. Art lines carried the company through the Forties, and the "Hull Art" logo prevailed, however, by 1946, it was found in raised form.

25. HULL POTTERY USA / HULL POTTERY	26. SAMPLE THE A.E. HULL POTTERY CO. CROOKSVILLE, OHIO Style No._____ Decoration_____ Size_____	27. HULL USA	28. HULL U.S.A.
29. EARLY AMERICAN Old Spice MADE IN U.S.A.	30. EARLY–AMERICAN Old Spice SHAVING SOAP USA SHULTON	31. PaT. Appl'd For LEEDS U.S.A.	32. Hull Ware U.S.A.
33. Hull Ware U.S.A.	34. 967 Hull Ware Little Red Riding Hood Patent Applied For U.S.A.	35. Little Red Riding Hood Pat-Des-No- 135889 U.S.A.	36. Pat-Des-No-135889 U.S.A.
37. Hull Ware Boy Blue U.S.A.	38. Hull USA	39. Hull Art U.S.A	40. U.S.A Hull Art
41. U.S.A Hull-Art 750-13½	42. Rosella	43. HULL POTTERY CROOKSVILLE, OHIO Potter at Wheel	44. GRANADA POTTERY
45. MARDIGRAS POTTERY	46. CLASSIC HAND DECORATED UNDERGLAZE VASE	47. Hull Art U.S.A	48. U.S.A Hull Art

85

49. In 1948, a deeply incised bold block Hull, reminiscent of an earlier day, was the trademark used for Cinderella's Blossom and Bouquet kitchenware designs. Mold number and sizes, including ounces, were also incorporated into the trademark.

50. This blue and gold foil label indicating, "Hand Painted, Oven Proof," was additionally used for promoting Hull's Cinderella kitchenware items, produced in 1948 and 1949.

51. This incised Ovenproof trademark was used for Hull's Modern Plaid kitchenware of 1950.

52. This blue and silver "Hull-Ware" foil label, additionally advertising the A. E. Hull Pottery Co., Crooksville, Ohio, was used on Cinderella's kitchenware, as well as Hull's Modern Plaid kitchenware line.

53. This embossed, or raised beautiful flowing script Hull trademark was presented in 1949, prior to the company's flood and fire for the Woodland pattern. It was used to mark both matte and gloss Woodland shapes, both prior to, and after the company's flood and fire.

54. A very small brown ink stamp was the trademark used for Cinderella kitchenware items made immediately prior to the plant's destruction in 1950, or at the latest, during the time the company operated from a pilot plant in 1951.

55. The incised flowing script Hull Oven-Proof trademark was used on Hull's Just Right Floral and Vegetable kitchenwares in 1951.

56, 57, 58. These lovely incised flourishing trademarks carried both Hull artwares and kitchenwares successfully through the 1950's. While these trademarks appeared both in raised and incised forms, they varied very little, mainly in the style, size and intensity of the capital "H."

59. For identification purposes, the company used this label which indicated Style, Package and Price. It was used most often for representative or sample items of the 1950's.

60. This is the signature of Granville, "Grany" Shafer, who gold trimmed and decorated many Hull items from the 1940's through the 1970's. Many of his gold decorated wares included a hand-stamped gold block mark reading, "23K Gold Guaranteed, Shafer, USA, Zanesville, Ohio." Sometimes, only "Shafer, USA," was noted.

61. Some of Hull's novelty items of 1950, including the dime piggy banks, were marked with this impressed logo. It was also quite often used, (without the '58 designation,) on several House 'n Garden servingware pieces from the 1960's through the plant's closing in 1985.

62. The incised "Corky Pig" trademark was first implemented in 1958, as the mark indicates. This logo continued to be used, with the '58 designation, through the 1970's.

63. The "H. P. CO." trademark was used in embossed or raised form on ashtrays and novelties from the late 1950's into the 1960's.

64. The incised "Tokay" trademark was used on the grape embossed Tokay line. This logo did not appear on Tuscany, a line which shared the Tokay molds. Tuscany was marked with the incised script form of Hull.

65. The incised Marcrest logo was designated on premium items produced specifically for Marshall Burns, Chicago, in the late 1950's. There were other producers of pottery items for Marshall Burns, one being Western Stoneware, which produced brown Marcrest. Hull's Marcrest dinnerware was usually glazed only in solid pastel colors, and while Heritageware molds were used for this production, the line also included molds specifically for Marcrest production.

66. The raised block "Marcrest" logo appeared on a variety of ashtrays, again produced as premium items for Marshall Burns.

67. The raised block "Sinclair" mark was used for novelty banks made for premium items by Hull in the early 1960's.

68. "Regal's" majestic incised trademark was used for a variety of chain store vases and novelty assortments. Some earlier used molds of specific lines and assortments, sporting different glaze treatments were marked with the Regal logo. The Regal mark was enlisted for wares of both the 1950's and 1960's.

69, 70. The incised flowing Coronet trademark was used for a variety of chain store vase, novelty and planter assortments. Many of Coronet's designs were incorporated with brass and wrought iron stands, including a floor model planter and ashtray combination. The Coronet mark was used on wares produced in the 1950's and 1960's.

71. In 1960, the incised classical Pagoda trademark was used for a chain store line of vases and jardinieres of the same name. This chain store assortment had a marked Oriental theme.

72. In 1962, the incised "URN-VASE" trademark was used for a variety of floristware jardinieres.

49. HULL 29-16 OZ U.S.A.

50. HAND PAINTED Cinderella HULL POTTERY CROOKSVILLE OHIO OVEN PROOF

51. 60-5" OVENPROOF U.S.A.

52. A.E. HULL POTTERY CO. Hull·Ware CROOKSVILLE, OHIO

53. Hull W1-5½" U.S.A.

54. Hull USA

55. OVEN-PROOF Hull USA No 20-5

56. Hull USA

57. SALAD-BOWL Hull U.S.A No 44-10

58. Hull T10 USA ©'55

59. HULL POTTERY CO. CROOKSVILLE, O. STYLE $2 PACKAGE 4 cup PRICE

60. SHAFER 23 K. GOLD GUARANTEED Gravy

61. USA HP © 58

62. PAT PEND Corky Pigt © USA 1957 HP Co

63. H.P.©CO. PAT. PEND.

64. Tokay U.S.A

65. MARCREST OVEN PROOF QUALITY MADE IN USA

66. MARCREST

67. SINCLAIR USA

68. REGAL

69. Coronet 204 U.S.A.

70. Coronet 207 U.S.A.

71. Pagoda P3 USA

72. URN-VASE HULL-U.S.A.

73. Most all Hull House 'n Garden casual servingware was marked by this incised trademark. It was used from 1960 through the plant's closing in 1985. The exception being, when a new item was introduced, or when it was necessary for an item to be remodeled or retooled. In this instance, a later mold would have incorporated an incised, "Crooksville, Ohio," or "Crooksville, O." into the logo.

74. Another House 'n Garden casual servingware trademark incorporated the "H. P. Co." in an incised manner. This trademark was used primarily in the 1960's and 1970's.

75. In 1965, this flowing incised "Crestone" trademark was designed specifically for the House 'n Garden casual servingware of the same name. This mark appears additionally on Mirror Brown servingware as well as Crestone's turquoise dinnerware. The Mirror Brown ware not Crestone, went into production without a mold or trademark change.Brown ware with this Crestone mark is readily available and is not considered experimental.

76. This classical incised Imperial trademark was used from 1960 to 1980 for the massive assortment of floristware of the same name. In some cases, the lower cased, "hull" trademark additionally adorned the item.

77. This trademark, featuring the incised lower case, "hull," was used on both House 'n Garden casual servingware as well as Imperial floristware beginning in 1960.

78. This incised trademark was used for a chain store assortment of planters and floristware items in the 1960's.

79. The rectangular black foil label with gold lettering was used beginning in 1958 to mark novelty and floristware items.

80. The serving trays of 1978, soon enlisted this special incised trademark, almost as warning to keep it off the range top. It was a cooking utensil only in the microwave and oven. Earliest produced serving trays do not bear the "Serving Tray" logo.

81. This incised trademark was used on the Gingerbread Man server introduced in 1978.

82. By 1982, an increased interest in promoting area craftsmen provided the inspiration to include the incised, "Crooksville, Ohio," on all new molds or older dinnerware molds which were redesigned or retooled. This new trademark was specifically designed for Hull's 1982-1985 dinnerwares, most of which carried the revised trademark automatically. If limited mold space warranted, the origin was abbreviated to read, "Crooksville, O."

83, 84. Additional versions of the newly designed incised dinnerware trademark which included the product's origin, used from 1982 to 1985.

73. hull Oven Proof u.S.a.	74. Oven Proof H.P. © Co. u.S.a.	75. hull u.s.a Crestone © OVEN-PROOF	76. Imperial F 71 U.S.A.
77. hull u.S.a. F 14	78. planter, inc.	79. hull u.s.a. crooksville, ohio	80. Serving Tray Oven Proof hull © u.S.a.
81. hull © Gingerbread Man u.S.a.	82. hull © Crooksville, Ohio Oven Proof u.S.a.	83. hull © Crooksville, Ohio Oven Proof u.S.a.	84. Crooksville hull © Oven Proof u.S.a Ohio

Cereal Ware

PRODUCTION DATES: 1915-1935

COMPANY'S USUAL MODE OF MARKING:

These cereal ware items are unmarked, however, consistently bear the same type of glazed bases.

DESCRIPTION:

The cereal ware illustrated is of a white semi-porcelain body, decals were underglazed and appear only on the face side of the ware. Decals were used both in single and double border treatments. Company information indicated that double border decals were more costly than single borders, that difference being $1.00 more per 15-piece set. Decal lettering is black in color and appears in script form. The illustrated square cereal sets consisted of fifteen pieces: six canisters, (sugar, flour, rice, cereal, coffee and tea,) six spice jars, (ginger, nutmeg, cinnamon, allspice, mustard and pepper,) vinegar and oil cruets and salt box. The square cereal ware sets were initially sold in sets of 12, 14 and 15-piece sets. Later, cereal ware was available in open stock and the consumer was able to choose specific desired items.

Decalcomania designs used on square cereal ware sets included, but were not limited to: Blue Bird in Flight, Perched Blue Bird, Conventional Rose, Conventional Tile, Conventional Vine, Delft, Drape and Festoon, Blue Grecian Border, Gold Grecian Border, Blue Star and Lattice, Gold Star and Lattice, Plain, Parrot, Scroll and Classic.

KITCHEN

Ads taken from Blackwell Wielandy catalog reprinted by Antiques Research Publications

PLATE 1
Candle Holder, decorated underglazed blue and white stoneware, unmarked, 6½". Hull produced volumes of blue and white stoneware, and was additionally accountable for using this mold in a trademarked version in the Camellia line. This experimental piece was formerly owned by Hull Company employees.

PLATE 2
Row 1: 1. Blue Star and Lattice Spice Jar, "Ginger", 4¾"
2. Blue Star and Lattice Spice Jar, "Allspice", 4¾"
3. Blue Star and Lattice Spice Jar, "Nutmeg", 4¾"
4. Blue Star and Lattice Spice Jar, "Cinnamon", 4¾"
5. Blue Star and Lattice Spice Jar, "Pepper", 4¾"
6. Blue Star and Lattice Spice Jar, "Mustard", 4¾"

Row 2: 1. Plain Spice Jar, "Nutmeg", 4¾"
2. Blue Grecian Canister, "Cereal", 8½"
3. Drape and Festoon Spice Jar, "Cinnamon", 4¾"
4. Drape and Festoon Spice Jar, "Allspice", 4¾"
5. Drape and Festoon Spice Jar, "Ginger", 4¾"
6. Gold Grecian Canister, "Cereal", 8½"
7. Gold Grecian Spice Jar, "Mustard", 4¾"

Row 3: 1. Flying Blue Bird Spice Jar, "Nutmeg", 4¾"
2. Flying Blue Bird Canister, "Coffee", 8½"
3. Flying Blue Bird Canister, "Tea", 8½"
4. Flying Blue Bird Canister, "Rice", 8½"
5. Flying Blue Bird Spice Jar, "Ginger", 4¾"

Row 4: 1. Conventional Rose Spice Jar, "Allspice", 4¾"
2. Conventional Rose Spice Jar, "Ginger", 4¾"
3. Conventional Rose Spice Jar, "Cinnamon", 4¾"
4. Conventional Rose Cruet, "Oil", 9¾"
5. Conventional Rose Salt Box, "Salt", 6¾"
6. Conventional Rose Cruet, "Vinegar", 9¾"
7. Conventional Rose Spice Jar, "Nutmeg", 4¾"
8. Conventional Rose Spice Jar, "Pepper", 4¾"
9. Conventional Rose Spice Jar, "Mustard", 4¾"

Row 5: 1. Conventional Rose Canister, "Flour", 8½"
2. Conventional Rose Canister, "Sugar", 8½"
3. Conventional Rose Canister, "Rice", 8½"
4. Conventional Rose Canister, "Cereal", 8½"
5. Conventional Rose Canister, "Coffee", 8½"
6. Conventional Rose Canister, "Tea", 8½"

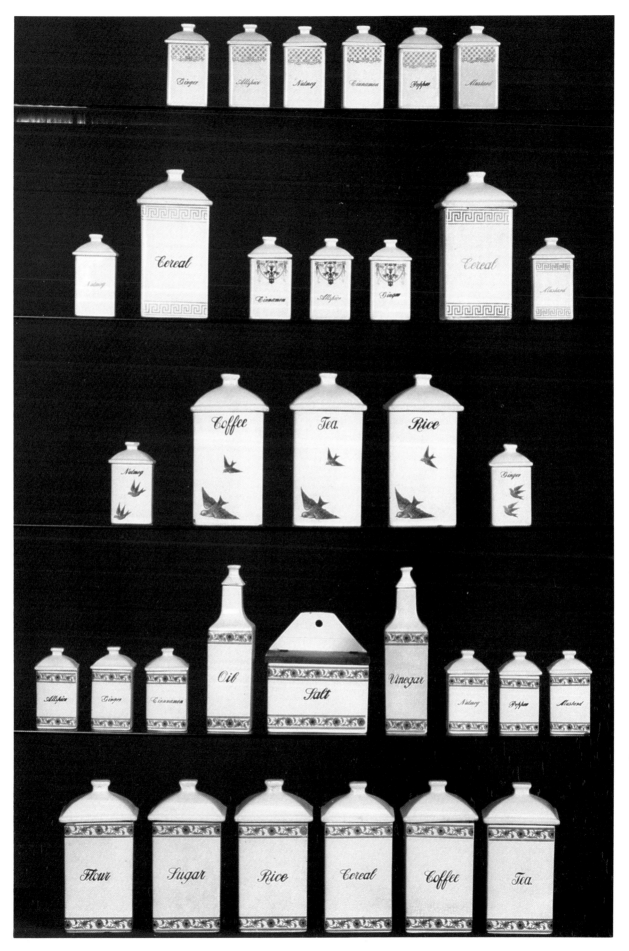

PLATE 2

Early Utility: Banded Semi-Porcelain

PRODUCTION DATES: 1915-1935

COMPANY'S USUAL MODE OF MARKING:

Banded items, rows one through three, are marked with an incised Ⓗ in circle and mold number. These items are also commonly found unmarked. Remaining items are incised with an ''E'' mold number, USA, and are also commonly found unmarked. A ''Heat Resisting, Cold Resisting, Ovenproof,'' foil label was also used for this utility ware.

DESCRIPTION:

Advertised as, ''Pantry and Cooking ESSENTIALS for the American home,'' utility wares comprised a large volume of Hull Company's production. The wares illustrated are both overglazed and underglazed banded. Slight inconsistencies are common in the banding decorations, which were blown on these wares. The salt boxes are pictured with semi-porcelain and wooden lids, both are original to the ware. The semi-porcelain salt box paired with semi-porcelain lid, is the more difficult to locate.

Illustrated by company brochure information, is an early kitchenware line, ''Five Banded,'' which included nested bowls, casseroles, cookie jar, pitcher, coffee servers and tea pots. This line, in white high gloss, was encircled by five bands at the wares' mid-line or top edge. The lowest band being the thinnest, widened with each step of elevation in this overglaze decor of Pimento Red or Nubian Black.

PLATE 3
Row 1: 1. Covered Casserole, 113Ⓗ, 7½"
       2. Pie Plate, unmarked, 9"
Row 2: 1. Salt Box, 111Ⓗ, 5", wooden lid
       2. Covered CasseroleⓇ, 7½"
       3. Pitcher, 107Ⓗ36, 4¾"
       4. Salt Box,Ⓗ, 5¾", porcelain lid
Row 3: 1. Bowl,Ⓗ, 8"
       2. Bowl, 100Ⓗ, 8"
       3. Covered Casserole, unmarked, 10"
       4. Spice Jar, 188Ⓗ, embossed, ''Spices'', 3¾"
       5. Spice Jar, 188Ⓗ, embossed, ''Spices'', 3¾"
Row 4: 1. Pitcher, E-7"
       2. Covered Casserole, E-13-7½"
       3. Bowl, E-1-7"
       4. Bowl, unmarked, 6½"
Row 5: 1. Bowl, unmarked, 7"
       2. Custard, E-14, 3½"
       3. Bowl, E-1, 9½"
       4. Custard, E-14, 3½"
       5. Bowl, E-1-10"

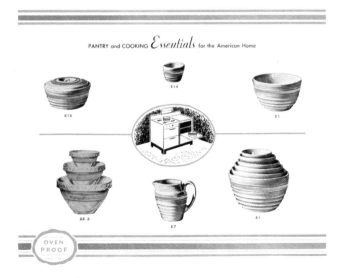

PLATE 3

Early Utility: Banded Semi-Porcelain

PRODUCTION DATES: 1930-1940

COMPANY'S USUAL MODE OF MARKING:

Utility items in Row 1 are incised script Hull Ware, USA, with an "A" series mold number and size identification. Additional early banded ware was marked with an incised Ⓗ in circle, or foil label which indicated the ware was "Heat and Cold Resisting."

DESCRIPTION:

Items shown illustrate Hull's underglazed and overglazed banding techniques. Few over-the-glaze banded, or "cold-color" items will be as showroom condition as those illustrated in Rows 3 and 4. This particular line which included casseroles, pie plates, bean pots, jugs, ramekins and custard cups was available with overglaze banding in Pimento Red or Nubian Black, and underglaze banding in Spring Green or Alice Blue.

The nested bowls wear a red and silver foil label which states, "Oven Proof, Heat and Cold Resisting." The yellow bands on the utility jar in Row 5 are further banded by gold.

PLATE 4

Row 1: 1. Bowl, Hull Ware A-1-9½"
      2. Bowl, Hull Ware A-1-7½"

Row 2: 1. Pitcher, unmarked, 3½"
      2. Bowl, unmarked, 7½"
      3. Bowl, unmarked, 7½"
      4. Pitcher, unmarked, 3½"

Row 3: 1. Bowl, 30 Ⓗ, 6½"
      2. Bowl, 30 Ⓗ, 5½"
      3. Custard, unmarked, 3½"
      4. Custard, unmarked, 3½"
      5. Pitcher, unmarked, 6¼"

Row 4: 1. Bowl, 30 Ⓗ, 7½"
      2. Bowl, 30 Ⓗ, 8½"
      3. Bowl, 30 Ⓗ, 9½"

Row 5: 1. Bowl, D-1-9½"
      2. Bowl, D-1-7½"
      3. Bowl, D-1-5½"
      4. Covered Jar, unmarked, "Lard", 8½"

5-Pc. MIXING BOWL SET

205/5361—Five Piece Set. Oven-proof pottery, resistant to heat or cold. Ivory body, decorated with wide band and narrow lines in two-tone maroon and peach; or blue and peach colors. Diameter of smallest bowl 5½ inches; largest bowl 9½ inches. ....Per set $2.00

COVERED CASSEROLE

205/5360 — Oven-proof pottery, resistant to heat or cold. Ivory body, decorated with wide band and narrow lines in two-tone maroon and peach; or blue and peach colors. Diameter 8 inches. 1 dozen assorted 2 colors in carton. (WE DO NOT BREAK CARTONS.) ....Per dozen $8.00

THE A. E. HULL POTTERY COMPANY, CROOKSVILLE, OHIO

KITCHEN WORK TABLE ENSEMBLE

No. 300/1—4½" BOWL   No. 300/7—½ PT. JUG   No. 300/7—1 QT. JUG
OVEN PROOF, COLD PROOF, IVORY WHITE WITH SPRING GREEN OR ALICE BLUE DECORATION

PLATE 4

Early Banded Utility:
Stoneware and Yellowware

PRODUCTION DATES: 1910-1935

COMPANY'S USUAL MODE OF MARKING:

Incised Ⓗ in circle, with or without mold number and size identification. It is not unusual for items to be unmarked, and some items bear an incised patent designation.

DESCRIPTION:

Hull's stoneware and yellowware banded items comprised many different shapes and designs. These items were both underglazed and overglazed decorated, in a rainbow of colors which included blue, pink, dark green, lime green, ivory, brown, white, gold, yellow, red, black, mauve, peach, and others. The yellowware items represented are banded underglaze. The nested bowls shown have four incised bands which have traces of their original green and orange overglaze, or cold color paint.

PLATE 5

Row 1: 1. Yellowware Batter Bowl,
　　　　　incised PAT APL FOR, USA, 25-3-9"

Row 2: 1. Stoneware Bowl, 428Ⓗ, 5"
　　　　2. Stoneware Bowl, 428Ⓗ, 6"
　　　　3. Yellowware Covered Casserole, 455Ⓗ, 9"

Row 3: 1. Yellowware Pitcher, 107Ⓗ36, 4¾"
　　　　2. Yellowware Covered Casserole, 113Ⓗ7"
　　　　3. Yellowware Bowl, 106Ⓗ6"
　　　　4. Yellowware Custard, 114Ⓗ2, 3¼"

Row 4: 1. Yellowware Bowl, 421Ⓗ, 12"
　　　　2. Yellowware Covered Casserole
　　　　　with Metal Bail, 455Ⓗ, 9"

Row 5: 1. Stoneware Bowl, 428Ⓗ, 7"
　　　　2. Stoneware Bowl, 428Ⓗ, 8"
　　　　3. Stoneware Bowl, 428Ⓗ, 9"

THE A.E. HULL POTTERY CO.

General Office and Factories:
CROOKSVILLE, OHIO
Offices:
NEW YORK — CHICAGO
Warehouse:
JERSEY CITY

PRICE LIST 1928

LEADER COOKING ASSORTMENT

COMPOSITION

1—No. 423, 7" Bowl.
1—No. 423, 9" Bowl.
1—No. 423, 5" Bowl.
1—No. 440, 30s Jug.
1—No. 440, 42s Jug.
1 No. 453, 7" Casserole.
6 No. 460/1 Custard Cups.

Price
95c
Per Set

96

PLATE 5

Early Utility Stoneware
Early Art Stoneware

PRODUCTION DATES: 1915-1930

COMPANY'S USUAL MODE OF MARKING:

Incised (H) in circle with or without mold number and size identification. Items are commonly unmarked.

DESCRIPTION:

The utility stoneware and artware items illustrated are decorated in both solid and blended high glazes. The tankard and mugs are glazed in tones which add dimension to the relief form Alpine scene.

PLATE 6

Row 1: 1. Mug, (H), 4½"
2. Mug, (H), 3¾", embossed, "Chocolate Soldier"
3. Mug, 497 (H), 5", embossed, "Happy Days Are Here Again"

Row 2: 1. Mug, 491 (H), 5"
2. Mug, 494 (H), 4¼", embossed, "Rhein Stein, Burg, Cochem, Stolzenfels"
3. Mug, 491 (H), 5"
4. Mug, 497 (H), 5", embossed, "Happy Days Are Here Again"
5. Mug, 265 (H), 4½", embossed, "Happy Days Are Here Again"

Row 3: 1. Alpine Tankard, 492 (H), 9½"
2. Alpine Stein, 492 (H), 6½"
3. Stein, 496 (H), 6½", embossed deer, "BPOE"
4. Stein, 498 (H), 6½", embossed, "American Legion"
5. Alpine Pretzel Jar, (H), 9"

Row 4: 1. Mug, 499 (H), 5"
2. Mug, 499 (H), 5"
3. Tankard, 499 (H), 8½"
4. Mug, 499 (H), 5"
5. Mug, 499 (H), 5"

Row 5: 1. Jardiniere, 536 (H), 9"
2. Flower Pot with Attached Saucer, 539 (H), 6"
3. Jardiniere, 551 (H), 7"
4. Flower Pot, unmarked, 4"

This early photo illustrates production of H in circle Alpine tankards and steins. Shown are finishers Iona Lauderbach and Zetta Wilson; Caster, Ray Conaway; and Workers, Richard Rosser, Ralph Sherlock and Ken Haymen.

PLATE 6

Early Utility: Stoneware And Semi-Porcelain

PRODUCTION DATES: 1915-1935

COMPANY'S USUAL MODE OF MARKING:

Incised Ⓗ in circle, with or without mold number and size identification or an incised Ⓗ in diamond. Items are commonly found unmarked.

DESCRIPTION:

Hull's early utility production included both stoneware and semi-porcelain items. Illustrated are solid high glazed finished wares. The incised banded items were glazed in white, green, yellow, blue and gray. The H in diamond marked cereal ware canisters, spice jars, cruets and salt box have an embossed wheat sheaf decor and have been found in yellow, green, blue and tan solid high gloss glazes.

Company information indicted the stoneware teapot was referred to as a "6-cup French-Process Coffee Maker." The teapot was marketed with an aluminum insert. The insert is not correct as illustrated on the following page, please refer to page 102 and the experimental section of this volume to see the correctly covered teapot, or to The Companion Guide to Roberts' Ultimate Encyclopedia of Hull Pottery, to see the complete set, inclusive of the aluminum insert.

PLATE 7

Row 1: 1. *Semi-Porcelain Individual Covered Bean Pot, Ⓗ, 3"
2. Semi-Porcelain Bowl, Ⓗ, 6"
3. Semi-Porcelain Pitcher, unmarked, gray interior, 6½"
4. Stoneware Bowl, 106 Ⓗ, 5"
5. Stoneware Pitcher, 107 Ⓗ 42, 3¾"

Row 2: 1. Wheat Semi-Porcelain cruet, unmarked, embossed, "Vinegar", 6½"
2. Wheat Semi-Porcelain Salt Box, unmarked, embossed, "Salt", 5¾"
3. *Semi-Porcelain Covered Bean Pot, Ⓗ, 4½"
4. Semi-Porcelain Pitcher, Ⓗ, 4¾"
5. Stoneware Custard, 60 Ⓗ, 2½"

Row 3: 1. Wheat Stoneware Spice Jar, H embossed in Diamond, "Spice", 3½"
2. Wheat Stoneware Spice Jar, H embossed in Diamond, "Pepper", 3½"
3. Stoneware Salt Box, 111 Ⓗ, 6"
4. Wheat Stoneware Canister, H embossed in Diamond, "Sugar", 6½"
5. Wheat Stoneware Canister, H embossed in Diamond, "Coffee", 6½"

Row 4: 1. Stoneware Teapot, incorrect insert, Ⓗ, 6¼"
2. Semi-Porcelain Bowl 25 Ⓗ, 7"
3. Semi-Porcelain Bowl, 25, Ⓗ, 6"

Row 5: 1. Stoneware Bowl, 421 Ⓗ, 7"
2. Stoneware Bowl, 421 Ⓗ, 10"
3. Semi-Porcelain Bowl, 30 Ⓗ, 7"
*lids sit inside deeply recessed rims.

PLATE 7

Early Art Stoneware

PRODUCTION DATES: 1925-1935

COMPANY'S USUAL MODE OF MARKING:

Incised (H) in circle and mold number. Items are commonly unmarked.

DESCRIPTION:

These stoneware items are decorated in both high gloss and matte glazes which are vertically striped, blended or mottled. Colors include pink, mauve, blue, turquoise, green, and mustard yellow, as well as others.

The numbering systems of this ware does not fully correspond to the Early Art illustrated on company brochure pages, however, does follow the company's early 1930's plan of identification used when they divided wares into Earthenware and Stoneware classifications.

Earthenware classification - that part of Hull production manufactured of white semi-porcelain body, in every instance represented by a prefix number of three digits - i.e., 300/13 casserole, or 610/33 vase; ·

Stoneware classification - that part of Hull production manufactured of buff body, in every instance, represented by a prefix number of two digits - i.e., 34/30 jardiniere, or 34/35 flower pot.

Not all items fit this classification system, and those that do not, are more than likely wares which were produced prior to the plan's formulation. This plan of identification was fully in place by 1935.

By 1935, the company's proposed system further gave classifications to second digit numbers by assigning:

30 as jardinieres,

31 hanging baskets and pots,

32 flower and bulb bowls,

33 vases,

34 flower pots with separate or unattached saucers and

35 as flower pots with attached saucers.

The number 22/20 Square Footed Stoneware Cookie Jars illustrated in the upper Brochure were cold-color decorated as shown, left to right, Poppy, Poinsettia and Rose. These designs, as well as others were painted over transparent yellow glazes. A 3 ¼ X 1 ¼ inch Red Bordered label placed on bases of the cookie jars read: "Important Notice: the decoration on this ware is of cold color paints and should not be washed in boiling water or strong soaps."

PLATE 8

Row 1: 1. Bulb Bowl, matte finished, unmarked, 8"

Row 2: 1. Vase, matte finished, 40(H), 7"

    2. Vase, high gloss, 39(H), 8"

    3. Vase, high gloss, 40(H), 7"

    4. Vase, high gloss, unmarked, 5½"

Row 3: 1. Vase, high gloss, 40(H), 7"

    2. Vase, high gloss, 32(H), 8"

    3. Vase, high gloss, 32(H), 8"

Row 4: 1. Vase, high gloss, 40(H), 7"

    2. Vase, high gloss, 32(H), 8"

    3. Vase, matte finished, 26(H), 8"

    4. Vase, matte finished, 32(H), 8"

A. E. HULL POTTERY CO.
CROOKSVILLE, OHIO

Listing with THE A. E. HULL POTTERY CO.

PLATE 8

Early Utility And Artware: Stoneware And Semi-Porcelain

PRODUCTION DATES: 1925-1935

COMPANY'S USUAL MODE OF MARKING:

Incised (H) in circle mark and mold number. Items are commonly unmarked.

DESCRIPTION:

Illustrated are solid high gloss turquoise semi-porcelain items embossed with the orange tree decoration and early art stoneware in predominately blue, mauve, green and turquoise solid and blended mattes as well as blended high gloss glazes.

PLATE 9
Row 1: 1. Stoneware Jardiniere, matte finished,(H), 6"
2. Stoneware Flower Pot with Saucer, matte finished,(H) 5"
3. Crab Apple Semi-porcelain Vase, matte finished, unmarked, 5"
4. Stoneware Flower Pot, matte finished, unmarked, 4¾"
5. Stoneware Jardiniere, matte finished, unmarked, 7"

PLATE 10
Row 1: 1. Orange Tree Semi-Porcelain Covered Batter Pitcher,(H), 7"
2. Orange Tree Stoneware Pitcher, 27(H)30, 7"
Row 2: 1. Orange Tree Semi-Porcelain Bowl, 26(H), 6½"
2. Orange Tree Semi-Porcelain Jardiniere, 546(H)7"
3. Orange Tree Semi-Porcelain Covered Bowl, 25(H)4"
Row 3: 1. Stoneware Hanging Basket, matte finished, 25(H)4"
2. Orange Tree Stoneware Jardiniere, matte finished, 546(H), 4"
3. Stoneware Hanging Basket, unmarked, 6"
4. Stoneware Hanging Basket, unmarked, 7"
5. Orange Tree Stoneware Jardiniere, 546(H), 3"
Row 4: 1. Stoneware Jardiniere, matte finished,(H), 5"
2. Stoneware Jardiniere, matte finished unmarked 8"
3. Stoneware Jardiniere,(H), 8"
4. Stoneware Jardiniere,(H), 5"
Row 5: 1. Stoneware Jardiniere, 550(H)7"
2. Stoneware Jardiniere, 530(H)10"
3. Stoneware Jardiniere, 551(H)7"

PLATE 9

104

PLATE 10

105

Early Art Stoneware
Early Art Semi-Porcelain

PRODUCTION DATES: 1925-1935
SHULTON PRODUCT CONTAINERS: 1937-1944
COMPANY USUAL MODE OF MARKING:

Early Art Stoneware and Semi-Porcelain items bear an incised Ⓗ in circle and mold number and are also commonly found unmarked.

Shulton Product Containers: Incised print, "Early American, Made in U.S.A.," with incised script, "Old Spice," in circle formation, or incised print, "Early American Shaving Soap, Shulton, USA," with incised script, "Old Spice," in circle formation.

DESCRIPTION:

The illustrated semi-porcelain wares include matte white, matte yellow and solid high gloss colors of yellow or turquoise. Other colors were available. Illustrated stoneware items are solid brown and blended high gloss glazes.

Hull produced Shulton Product Containers from 1937-1944. These high glazed stoneware bottles and mugs have underglazed blue ship transfers and block red lettering, "After Shaving Lotion," and "Talcum for Men," on bottles, and script red lettering, "Old Spice," on bottles and mugs.

Crab Apple, in an original company price list was described as, "Art pottery vases, jardinieres, hanging baskets, available in matte Eggshell White, matte Peacock Blue on white semi-porcelain body; hand painted flowers in rose, leaves in green on matte sun tan buff body; or bright white on white semi-porcelain body." This price list included eighteen shapes.

People of Crooksville have called this line "Acme" for years. (The locals have always had a habit of calling the Hull, "Acme" since Hull moved into the Acme Building when expanding operations.) The line is not particularly scarce, it has just been ignored, the cruder pieces taking back shelves to potteries which could be readily identified.

Although unmarked, this ware has been found with factory labels intact, and more importantly, some pieces bear permanent ink marks. The clay bodies and glaze colors correspond with company information, as do most of the labels and ink marks. Marking system and sizes correspond to Hull information as far as first digits of the series numbers are concerned, however, the last digit is dropped, i.e., 600/33 is 60/33, 670/30 is 67/30. This ware was produced in 1934-1935.

An early Hull company brochure, page 76 in *The Companion Guide,* illustrates a squat handled vase with an embossed branch, heavy with leaves and apples. This vase shows traits similar to Weller's Baldin, which entered the market about 1917. This is the first glimpse of an early Hull "apple" design, which may cause collectors to question the line they have dubbed Crab Apple.

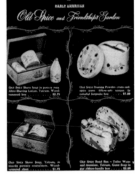

PLATE 12

Row 1:
1. Shulton "After Shaving Lotion" Bottle with original pontil closure, "Ship Grand Turk", 5"
2. Shulton Mug, "Ship Friendship", 3"
3. Shulton Mug, in original box, "Ship Grand Turk", 3"
4. Shulton "Talcum For Men" Bottle, "Ship Grand Turk", 5"
5. Shulton "Talcum For Men" Bottle, "Ship Grand Turk", 5"

Row 2:
1. Orange Tree Semi-Porcelain Jardiniere, 546Ⓗ, 4"
2. Orange Tree Semi-Porcelain Jardiniere, 546,Ⓗ, 5"
3. Orange Tree Semi-Porcelain Jardiniere, 546Ⓗ, 6"
4. Stoneware Jardiniere,Ⓗ, 4½"

Row 3:
1. Mardi Gras Semi-Porcelain Spanish Pot, unmarked, 4½"
2. Crab Apple Stoneware Vase, 65/33 ink mark, 9"
3. Crab Apple Stoneware Vase, unmarked, 9"
4. Stoneware Cuspidor, unmarked, embossed daisies, 7½"

Row 4:
1. Streamline Semi-Porcelain Flower Pot with Attached Saucer, unmarked, 6½"
2. Streamline Semi-Porcelain Flower Pot, unmarked, 8½"
3. Semi-Porcelain Vase, 660/33-8"
4. Semi-Porcelain Vase,Ⓗ, 5½"

Row 5:
1. Tulip Stoneware Jardiniere, unmarked, 10"
2. Tulip Stoneware Jardiniere, unmarked, 9"
3. Love Birds Stoneware Jardiniere, embossed birds, unmarked 7½"

PLATE 11:
Crab Apple Vase, semi-porcelain, unmarked, 6½"

PLATE 12

Early Utility And Artware: Stoneware And Semi-Porcelain

PRODUCTION DATES: 1925-1940

COMPANY'S USUAL MODE OF MARKING:

Incised Ⓗ in circle mark and mold number, commonly unmarked.

DESCRIPTION:

Utility wares shown include banded semi-porcelain and yellowware, semi-porcelain Nuline Bak-Serve, embossed orange tree items, decaled kitchenware and cookie jars in semi-porcelain and stoneware.

THE A. E. HULL POTTERY COMPANY, CROOKSVILLE, OHIO

No. 308/6 BAKE DISH
No. 308/15 FRENCH HANDLED CASSEROLE
HEAT PROOF, COLD PROOF, IVORY WHITE BODY AND GLAZE, DECORATED WITH PIMENTO, RED OR NUBIAN BLACK STRIPES.

PLATE 13
Row 1: 1. Crab Apple Stoneware Jardiniere, unmarked, 6 ½"
    2. Donkey Planter, advertised as 1940 campaign item, 6"
    3. Pleated Stoneware Utility PitcherⒽ, 6½"

PLATE 14
Row 1: 1. Crab Apple Vase, unmarked, 5"
    2. Cookie Jar, semi-porcelain with overglaze decoration, unmarked, 9"
    3. Five-Band Utility Pitcher with overglaze decoration, unmarked, 8"
    4. Tankard, 499, Ⓗ 8½"

PLATE 15
Row 1: 1. Semi-Porcelain French-handed casserole, underglaze banding, unmarked, 6½"
    2. Semi-Porcelain Covered Bean Pot, banding over glaze, unmarked, 4 ¼".
    3. Semi-Porcelain Nuline Bak-Serve Pie Plate, B-14-9½".
    4. Semi-Porcelain Pitcher, underglaze banding, 107Ⓗ, 42, 4".
Row 2: 1. Semi-Porcelain Reeded Spanish Pot,Ⓗ, 3".
    2. Semi-Porocelain Salt Box,Ⓗ, incised groves, 5¼" X 4½".
    3. Semi-Porcelain Casserole, unmarked, 8¼".
    4. Stoneware Teapot, gray-lined, unmarked, 6½".
    5. Stoneware Mug, honey-comb pattern, unmarked, 3¼".
Row 3: 1. Semi-Porcelain Bowl, decal decorated, 50Ⓗ6".
    2. Orange Tree Semi-Porcelain Compote, 26Ⓗ, 10¼".
    3. Orange Tree Semi-Porcelain Custard,Ⓗ 2¾".
    4. Semi-Porcelain Ice Lip Pitcher, 429, 8¾".
Row 4: 1. Yellowware Square Shoulder Bowl, underglaze banding, USA, 9½".
    2. Harp Stoneware Jardiniere, unmarked, 7½".
    3. Yellowware Bowl, underglaze banding, 421Ⓗ9.
Row 5: 1. *Stoneware Square Footed Cookie Jar, minus lid, blue matte with hand painted cold color fruit and blossom decor, USA, 9½".
    2. Semi-Porcelain Cookie Jar, high gloss turquoise, unmarked, 11". This jar has previously had an overglaze Mexican motif, Mexican in red pants, ivory shirt and sombrero leaning against black cactus.
    3. Semi-Porcelain Cookie Jar, white gloss with decoration apple, pear and strawberries over the glaze, unmarked, 11".
    4. *Stoneware Square Footed Cookie Jar, matte turquoise with hand painted floral over the glaze, unmarked, 9½".

*The Square Footed cookie jars characteristically have red glaze covering the open stoneware edge of the top of jar and tip of handle.

PLATE 15

109

Early Utility And Artware: Stoneware and Semi-Porcelain

PRODUCTION DATES: 1925-1940

COMPANY'S USUAL MODE OF MARKING:

Incised mold number, with or without (H) in circle mark and USA. These items are also commonly found unmarked.

DESCRIPTION:

The illustrated solid high glazed items in both stoneware and semi-porcelain bodies encompass rainbow colors of shrimp, pink, deep mauve, turquoise, blue, yellow, green, rust, and a matte gray, with shapes ranging from plain to ribbed, to floral embossed. For identification purposes, the cylinder vases contain thirteen raised ribs or bands.

PLATE 16

Bear Figural, marked Hull and dated Nov. 11, 1931. Additionally marked by caster, William "Fat" Thorne, 12½".

Ads taken from Blackwell Wielandy catalog reprinted by Antiques Research Publications

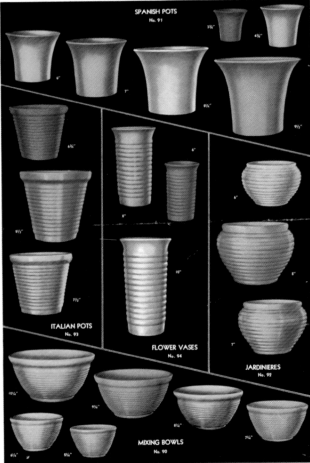

PLATE 17

Row 1: 1. Semi-Porcelain Jardiniere, 95-4¼"
      2. Stoneware Flower Pot,(H), 4"
      3. Stoneware Flower Pot with Separate Saucer, 538(H), 4"

Row 2: 1. Stoneware Custard, unmarked, 3¼"
      2. Mardi Gras Semi-Porcelain Spanish Pot, unmarked, 5"
      3. Streamline Semi-Porcelain Jardiniere, 690-6"
      4. Mardi Gras Semi-Porcelain Spanish Pot, unmarked, 5"
      5. Stoneware Custard, unmarked, 3¼"

Row 3: 1. Semi-Porcelain Pitcher, 407, 5"
      2. Semi-Porcelain Bean Pot, 219-6"
      3. Semi-Porcelain Bean Pot, 219-5"
      4. Semi-Porcelain Pitcher, 207, 5"
      5. Semi-Porcelain Custard, 214, 3½"

Row 4: 1. Stoneware Bowl, 300/1-8"
      2. Mardi Gras Semi-Porcelain Jardiniere, unmarked, 7½"
      3. Mardi Gras Stoneware Bowl, unmarked, 10½"

Row 5: 1. Stoneware Bowl, E-1-9"
      2. Mardi Gras Stoneware Vase, unmarked, 6"
      3. Mardi Gras Stoneware Vase, unmarked, 10"
      4. Mardi Gras Stoneware Vase, unmarked, 6"

PLATE 17

Nuline Bak-Serve

PRODUCTION DATES: 1937-1940

COMPANY'S USUAL MODE OF MARKING:

Impressed block A. E. HULL, USA, or HULL, USA followed by appropriate "B," "C," or "D," and mold number with size identification. Many times the identification of this kitchenware was concealed during the glazing method when the too-thick glaze filled the impressions of the trademark. Foil labels indicating "Heat and Cold Resisting," were also used for these kitchenware lines.

DESCRIPTION:

This ovenproof embossed semi-porcelain kitchenware line was available in three distinctive designs:

"B" series - an embossed diamond quilt design.
"C" series - an embossed fish scale design.
"D" series - an embossed drape and panel design.

Solid matte and high gloss colors of blue, turquoise, peach, maroon, yellow, and cream were featured. This line included at least twenty-nine shapes

PLATE 18

Row 1: 1. Diamond Quilt Teapot, B-5, 5½"
      2. Drape and Panel French-handled casserole, D-15, 4½"
      3. Fish Scale Mug, C-25, 3½"
      4. Diamond Quilt Teapot, B-5, 5½"

Row 2: 1. Diamond Quilt Custard, B-14, 2¾"
      2. Diamond Quilt Covered Casserole, B-13-7½"
      3. Drape and Panel Covered Casserole, D-13-7½"
      4. Drape and Panel Mixing Bowl, D-1-9½"

Row 3: 1. Fish Scale Mug, C-25, 3½"
      2. Fish Scale Batter Jug, C-7-1 Qt., 6"
      3. Diamond Quilt Batter Jug, B-7-1 Qt., 6"
      4. Diamond Quilt Batter Jug, B-7, 5"
      5. Fish Scale Mug, C-25, 3½"

205/5363 — Made of pottery, in all over diamond design, narrow style with ice lip. In solid pastel colors of green, rose or biege. Capacity 2 quarts. Height 8¼ inches; width 4½ inches. 1 dozen assorted, 3 colors in carton.
......Per dozen $14.40

205/5365 — Jardiniere or Rose Bowl, Hull pottery. Combination of pastel colors of pink, blue and ivory, or blue and ivory, decorated with raised tulip and leaf design in ivory, pink and green colors. Diameter 4¾ inches; height 4 inches. 1 dozen assorted in carton. WE DO NOT BREAK CARTONS.
..................Per dozen $7.50

205/4901 — Jardiniere. Diameter 6½ in. White lustre finish pottery with line decoration. 1½ dozen in carton.
.............Per dozen $4.00

205/4902—Larger, diameter 7½ in. 1 dozen in carton.
.............Per dozen $7.68

205/4903—Larger, diameter 8½ in. ½ dozen in carton.
.............Per dozen $9.60

205/4904—Hanging Flower Holder. Pottery flower pot in assorted colors of white, rose-beige, or yellow, with metal chain for hanging. Diameter of pot 4¾ inches. 1 dozen assorted colors to carton. ..... Per dozen $3.90

Ads taken from Blackwell Wielandy catalog reprinted by Antiques Research Publications

Row 4: 1. Fish Scale Ice Lip Pitcher, C-29, 8½"
      2. Fish Scale Ice Lip Pitcher, C-29, 7"
      3. Diamond Quilt Bean Pot, B-19-5½"
      4. Diamond Quilt Ice Lip Pitcher, B-29, 8½"

Row 5: 1. Diamond Quilt Nested Mixing Bowls, B-1, 5", 6", 7", 8", 9"
      2. Fish Scale Cookie Jar, C-20-2 Qt., 8"
      3. Drape and Panel Cookie Jar, D-20-2 Qt., 8"
      4. Diamond Quilt Cookie Jar, B-20-2 Qt., 8"

PLATE 18

Early Art, Novelty And Tile

COMPANY'S USUAL MODE OF MARKING:

Hull Company marked tiles in both raised and incised form, the designation of faience or cushion was usually noted. Most of the novelty items illustrated are unmarked, however, some do bear incised mold numbers and size identification.

PLATE 19
TILE: 1926-1931
Tiles illustrated in Plate 19 are 4¼" x 4¼".

Row 1: 1. *Satin black, incised Hull Faience, Cushion, ink stamped "8,".
2. *Mottled wash of green and aqua, satin finished, incised Hull Faience, Cushion, ink stamped "03,".
3. Stippled beige, matte finished, incised Hull Faience, Cushion.
4. Mottled golds, satin finished, incised Hull Faience, Cushion.
5. Mottled cream satin finished, incised Hull Faience.
6. Gloss black, raised Hull Tile.

Row 2: 1. Mottle greens, satin finished, incised Hull Faience, Cushion.
2. Stippled beige with brown, satin finished, unmarked.
3. Gloss green with indigo, incised Hull-Cushion, Tile.
4. Satin salmon, raised Hull Tile.
5. Mottled Green, aqua, satin finished, incised Hull Faience, Cushion.
6. Satin lavender, raised Hull Tile.

Row 3: 1. Gloss black, raised Hull Tile.
2. Gloss green, incised Hull-Cushion, Tile.
3. Satin ivory, raised Hull Tile.
4. Stippled brown matte, incised Hull Faience, Cushion.
5. Satin pink, incised Hull Faience, Cushion.
6. Stippled black with gold flecks, matte finished, incised Hull Faience, Cushion.

Row 4: 1. Mottled green, satin finished, incised Hull Faience, Cushion.
2. Stippled gray with ivory, satin finished, incised Hull Faience, Cushion.
3. *Olive green matte, incised Hull Faience, Cushion, ink stamped "4-2,".
4. Satin beige, incised Hull Faience, Cushion.
5. Gloss mint green, incised Hull Faience.
6. Stippled gray with green, satin finished, incised Hull Faience.

Row 5: 1. Satin lavender, incised Hull Faience, Cushion.
2. *Stippled bronze matte, incised Hull Faience, Cushion, ink stamped "7-3,".
3. Matte gray, incised Hull Faience, Cushion.
4. Matte blue, incised Hull Faience, Cushion.
5. Satin tan, incised Hull Faience, Cushion.
6. Mottled Green with tan, satin finished, incised Hull Faience, Cushion.

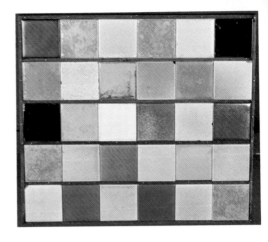

PLATE 19

PLATE 20
TILE: 1926-1931
Row 1: 1. *Tile, satin green, hand painted, incised Hull Faience, Cushion, ink stamped "360," 4¼" X 4¼".
2. Tile, Crest design, featuring six satin colors, incised Hull Faience, 6" X 6". This was the only Hull item, tile or pottery, housed in the famous Purviance Collection at White Pillars, Norwich, Ohio.
3. Advertising Tile, embossed Potter-at-Wheel, "TILE BY HULL, INSTALLED BY A SCHIRMER, CINCINNATI, 4¼" X 4¼", satin gray.
4. *Tile, satin lavender, hand painted, incised Hull Faience Tile, Cushion, ink stamped "349," 4¼" X 4¼".

Row 2: 1. Tile, satin turquoise and cream, raised Hull Tile, 2¾" X 6".
2. Tile, satin turquoise and cream, raised Hull Tile, 2¾" X 6".
3. Tile, matte blue and gold, incised Hull Faience, 2¾" X 2¾".
4. Tile, matte orange, incised Hull Faience, Cushion in crisscross form, 2" X 2".
5. Tile, dolphin decor, matte pink and blue, incised Hull Faience, 2¾" X 2¾".
6. Tile, boat decor, matte pink and blue, incised Hull Faience, 2¾" X 2¾".
7. Tile, boat decor, matte blues, raised Hull Tile, 2¾" X 6".

*The additional ink stamps referred to glaze color designations. These tiles were part of a sample set used by Hull retailing and order departments.

EARLY ART AND NOVELTY: 1930's
Row 3: 1. Puss 'n Boots, decorated bisque, unmarked experimental, 5½", 1936.
2. Pig, decorated bisque, unmarked experimental, 5½", 1936.
3. Crab Apple Semi-Porcelain Jardiniere, unmarked, 4", 1934-1935.
4. Vase, unmarked, 5½".
5. Monkey, unmarked experimental, 5¼", 1938.
6. Jardiniere, unmarked, 3", 1938.
7. Crab Apple Semi-Porcelain Vase, 3", 1934-1935.

Row 4: 1. Lusterware Pitcher, unmarked, 4¾", 1927-1930.
2. Sueno Vase, 930/33-1, 5", 1938.
3. Lusterware Wall Pocket, unmarked, 8½", 1927-1930.
4. Vase, 216-9", 1938.
5. Crazy Horse Planter, 959, 5", 1938.
6. Vase, unmarked, 5½", 1938.

PLATE 20

Early Art And Novelty

COMPANY'S USUAL MODE OF MARKING:

Swing Band items are unmarked and the bases are unglazed. Most items have a hole in the base, part of the manufacturing process. There are several look alikes on the market in several compositions. One such set is marked "Coventry."

Lusterware items are usually found unmarked, although some pieces have incised mold numbers and size identification. Bases of unmarked items are glazed, some with the same splotchy colorations as the body of the ware, others are glazed to match the interior of the item.

Acme wares are marked with a black shield and eagle ink stamp. The Acme pieces illustrated and described are for historical reference only and have very minimal, if any, monetary value in a Hull collection. The Hull Pottery operated, after Acme dispersed, in the old Acme plant building, and collectors of Hull ware should not entertain the idea that Acme is Hull.

DESCRIPTIONS:

SWING BAND, 1938-1940: Ivory matte finished with gold trim and hand painted features. Some band sets have been entirely decorated overglaze. In 1940, Blackwell Wielandy Company retailed the five-piece set for $3.50.

LUSTERWARE, 1927-1930: Hull lusters are exceedingly brilliant, and very iridescent where rainbow colorings play over the surface in changing lights. Intensity of luster colors vary since some colors did not accept the sheens as readily as others and settled primarily on the surface. It is believed Hull used a technique that caused the moisture to condense in drops to show white spots or splotching after fire. This method called water-smoking could have been achieved by not warming the kiln before stacking the ware or by covering the items during firing.

This modest artware line of vases, ashtrays and jardinieres was decorated in high glazed iridescent colors the Company referred to as shammy, orange, lavender, slate, emerald, light blue, iridescent dark blue and gold glow indicating at least thirty-five items were available. Chinese Red Cracquelle, a brilliant red, and Persian, an unidentified color, most likely blue or turquoise, were two additional Lusterware lines offered in fifteen shapes.

PLATE 23
Row 1: 1. Swing Band Accordionist, unmarked, 6"
2. Swing Band Clarinet Player, unmarked, 6"
3. Swing Band Drummer, base unmarked, "Swing Band" incised on side of drum, 5½"
4. Swing Band Band Leader, unmarked, 6½"
5. Swing Band Tuba Player, unmarked, 5¾"
Row 2: 1. Lusterware Candle Holder, unmarked, 3"
2. Lusterware Candle Holder, unmarked, 3"
3. Lusterware Candle Holder, unmarked, 3"
4. Lusterware Pitcher, unmarked, 4"
Row 3: 1. Lusterware Pitcher, unmarked, 4"
2. Lusterware Vase, unmarked, 9"
3. Lusterware Vase, unmarked, 10"
4. Lusterware Vase, unmarked, 9"
5. Lusterware Vase, unmarked, 8"
6. Lusterware Vase, unmarked, 3½"
Row 4: 1. Lusterware Pitcher, unmarked, 5¾"
2. Lusterware Vase, unmarked, 8"
3. Lusterware Vase, unmarked, 12"
4. Lusterware Jardiniere, incised 91-7½"
Row 5: 1. Lusterware Vase, unmarked, 12"
2. Acme Plate, eagle ink stamp, 11"
3. Acme Plate, eagle ink stamp, 11"

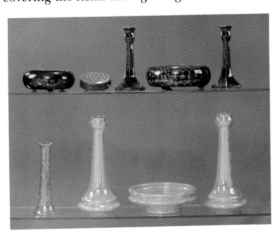

PLATE 21
Row 1: 1. Lusterware Bulb Bowl, unmarked, 7½"
2. Lusterware Flower Frog, unmarked, 4½"
3. Lusterware Candle Holder, unmarked, 9"
4. Lusterware Bulb Bowl, unmarked, 9½"
5. Lusterware Candle Holder, unmarked, 9"
Row 2: 1. Lusterware Vase, unmarked, 10"
2. Lusterware Vase, unmarked, 13"
3. Lusterware Console Bowl, unmarked, 10"
4. Lusterware Vase, unmarked, 13"

PLATE 22
Row 1: 1. Shell Planter, 202, 5"
2. Lusterware Candle Holder, unmarked, 9"
3. Lusterware Candle Holder, unmarked, 9"
4. Horse Doorstop, tile body, deep indigo and black, 8¾"
5. Vase, unmarked, 7½"
6. Stoneware Jardiniere, unmarked, 4¾"

PLATE 23

Early Art And Novelty

PRODUCTION DATES:
Early Novelty as Shown: 1938
Classic: 1942-1945
Sun-Glow: 1948-1949

COMPANY'S USUAL MODE OF MARKING:

Although these novelty wares do not bear the Hull trademark, many are incised with the mold number and USA. Classic wares are additionally marked with a gold or silver banner and shield foil label with the "Classic" name printed on the green banner.

PLATE 24

Illustrated is one of several time books belonging to William McClellan and Edgar McClellan, father and son, who both served as Ceramic Engineers for Hull. Also shown is one of several personal glaze formula books used by William McClellan. The particular page opened, dated September 12, 1917, is a formula for A. E. Hull White Body, in McClellan's own hand.

Obviously salvaged by an employee after some disastrous outcome at the plant, the base of a Woodland W25-12½" Vase was further decorated and glazed in this whimsical art form. Utensils in this piece are early tools used by Hull Company employees. The brushes were artistically used by Zetta Hicks Wilson and the metal trimmer, referred to by the pottery workers as a "knobber," was once used by Lois Lee.

PLATE 25

Row 1:
1. Rabbit, 952 USA, also marked with sample seal, 4½"
2. Monkey, unmarked, 5½"
3. Cactus Cat, 964, 2¾"
4. Experimental Monkey, unmarked, 3¾"

Row 2:
1. Elephant, unmarked, 5¼"
2. Rabbit, 968, 6"
3. Rabbit, 968, 6"
4. Rabbit, 968, 6"
5. Elephant, unmarked, 5¼"

Row 3:
1. Sun-Glow Rope-Handled Tea Bell, unmarked, 6¼"
2. Sun-Glow Rope-Handled Tea Bell, unmarked, 6¼"
3. Classic Vase, T-1-6½"
4. Classic Vase, T-2-6½"
5. Classic Vase, T-3-6½"
6. Sun-Glow Tea Bell, unmarked, 6½"

Row 4:
1. Cornucopia, 203-5½"
2. Classic Vase, 4-6"
3. Classic Vase, 5-6"
4. Classic Ewer, 6-6"
5. Cornucopia, 201, 5"

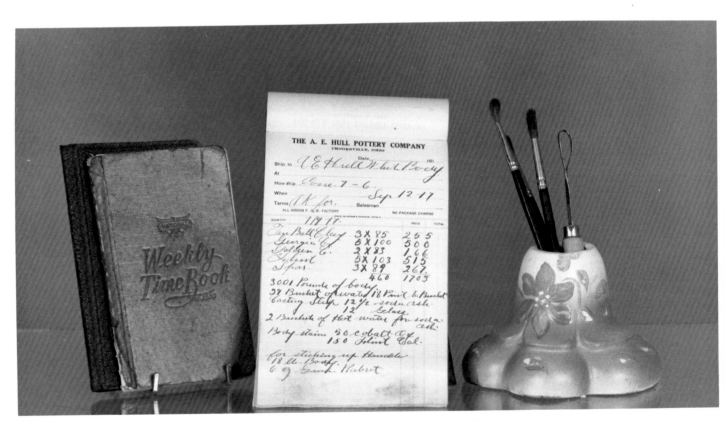

PLATE 24

PLATE 25

Calla Lily

PRODUCTION DATES: 1938-1940

COMPANY'S USUAL MODE OF MARKING:

This ware does not carry a Hull trademark in the mold. However, it carries an incised "500" series mold number and size identification. This line bears the triangular or elongated diamond foil labels which state, "HULL POTTERY," in two lines. These seals are found with black or maroon background and gold or silver lettering.

DESCRIPTION:

The company shows Calla Lily as part of its Sueno line, most likely an overall name for chain store package sales. The Calla Lily line is also referred to as Jack-in-Pulpit due to its embossed floral and arrow-shaped leaf decor. Colors included solid matte pastels of blue, green, cream or turquoise, and matte duo-tone shades of blue to pink, cinnamon to dusky green, cinnamon to turquoise, rose to dusky green, and rose to turquoise, as well as others.

An early Hull price list makes reference to "Calla", blended jardinieres with embossed "pod-shaped floral." Additional information is unavailable, however, we can assume these jardinieres were of a stoneware body.

PLATE 26

Row 1: 1. Candle Holder, unmarked, 2¼"
2. Console Bowl, 500/32-10"
3. Candle Holder, unmarked, 2¼"

Row 2: 1. Vase, 503-33-6"
2. Vase, 530/33-7"
3. Vase, 530/33-5"
4. Vase, 550/33-7½"

Row 3: 1. Vase, 501-33-6½"
2. Vase, 520/33-8"
3. Vase, 500/33-8"
4. Vase, 540/33-6"

Row 4: 1. Vase, unmarked, 9½"
2. Vase, 560/33-13"
3. Ewer, 506-10"

120

PLATE 26

Calla Lily
Thistle
Tulip

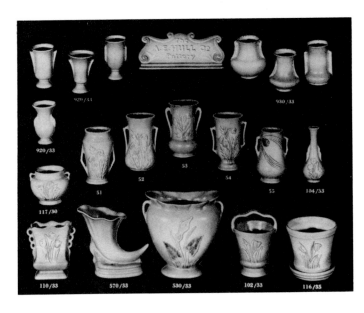

PRODUCTION DATES:
Calla Lily: 1938-1940
Thistle: 1938-1941
Tulip: 1938-1941

COMPANY'S USUAL MODE OF MARKING:
CALLA LILY: Incised "500 series mold number and size identification. This ware does not carry a Hull trademark in the mold.

THISTLE: incised "50" series mold number and size identification. There is no Hull trademark on the mold.

Calla Lily, Tulip, Thistle and the plain design Sueno vases all bear the triangular or diamond foil labels which state "HULL POTTERY" in two lines. These seals are found with black or maroon background with gold or silver lettering.

TULIP: Incised block HULL, U.S.A., "100" series mold number and size identification.

DESCRIPTION:
Calla Lily, Tulip and Thistle are all shown as Hull's Sueno line, most likely an overall name for a chain store sales package.

CALLA LILY: This line is also referred to as Jack-in-Pulpit. Colors include various solid and duo-tone matte pastels. At least twenty-four items were available, several in graduated sizes.

THISTLE: Embossed thistle floral on solid matte finishes of pink, blue or turquoise, four known vase shapes.

TULIP: Hand decorated embossed tulips on duo-tone matte pastels of blue and pink, blue and cream or allover blue. Fifteen catalogued shapes, many offered in graduated sizes.

PLATE 27
Several color combinations of the Calla Lily design were available, some of which are illustrated.
1. Calla Lily Vase, 560/33-13"
2. Calla Lily Ewer, 506-10"
3. Calla Lily Vase, 560/33-13"
4. Calla Lily Ewer, 506-10"
5. Calla Lily Vase, 560/33-13"
6. Calla Lily Ewer, 506-10"
7. Calla Lily Vase, 560/33-13"
8. Experimental Calla Lily Ewer, stoneware glaze 506-10"
9. Calla Lily Vase, 560/33-13"

PLATE 28
Row 1: 1. Sueno Vase, 920-33-1-5"
       2. Calla Lily Console Bowl, 590/32, 13"
       3. Sueno Vase, 930-33-3-5"
Row 2: 1. Tulip Jardiniere, 117-30-5"
       2. Tulip Bud Vase, 104-33-6"
       3. Tulip Jardiniere, 115-33-7"
       4. Tulip Vase, 100-33-6½"
       5. Tulip Vase, 100-33-4"
Row 3: 1. Thistle Vase, #51-6½"
       2. Thistle Vase, #52-6½"
       3. Thistle Vase, #53-6½"
       4. Thistle Vase, #54-6½"
Row 4: 1. Tulip Vase, 105-33-8"
       2. Tulip Ewer, 109-8"
       3. Tulip Vase, 101-33-9"
       4. Sueno Vase, 750-33-9½"

PLATE 27

PLATE 28

Calla Lily
Tulip

PRODUCTION DATES:
 Calla Lily: 1938-1940
 Tulip: 1938-1941

COMPANY'S USUAL MODE OF MARKING:
 CALLA LILY: Incised "500" series mold number and size identification. This ware does not carry a Hull trademark in the mold.
 TULIP: Incised block HULL, U.S.A., "100" series mold number and size identification.

DESCRIPTION:
 Calla Lily, Tulip and Thistle are all shown as Hull's Sueno line, most likely an overall name for a chain store sales package.
 CALLA LILY: This line is also referred to as Jack-in-Pulpit. Colors included various solid and duo-tone matte pastels. At least twenty-four items were available, several in graduated sizes.
 TULIP: Hand decorated embossed tulips on duo-tone matte pastels of blue and pink, blue and cream or all over blue. Fifteen catalogued shapes, many offered in graduated sizes.

PLATE 29
Row 1: 1. Calla Lily Cornucopia, 570/33-8"
        2. Tulip Flower Pot with Attached Saucer, 116-33-6"
Row 2: 1. Tulip Vase, 108-33-6"
        2. Tulip Basket, 102-33-6"
        3. Tulip Vase, 111-33-6"
Row 3: 1. Tulip Vase, 107-33-6"
        2. Tulip Vase, 110-33-6"
        3. Tulip Suspended Vase, 103-33-6"
        4. Tulip Vase, 106-33-6½"
Row 4: 1. Tulip Vase, 100-33-8"
        2. Tulip Ewer, 109-33-13"
        3. Tulip Vase, 100-33-10"

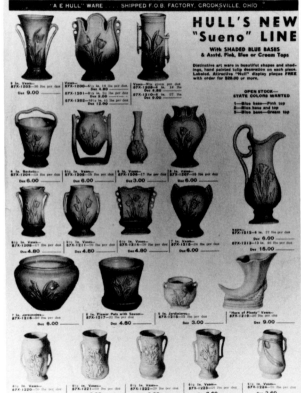

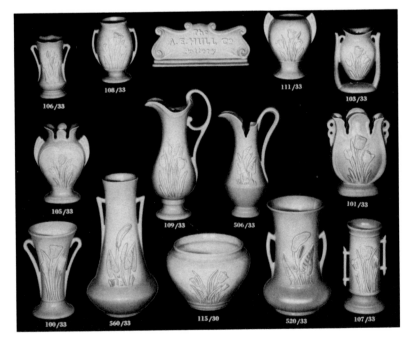

124

PLATE 29

125

Orchid

PRODUCTION DATES: 1939-1941

COMPANY'S USUAL MODE OF MARKING:

Incised block HULL, U.S.A., "300" series mold number and size identification. This line bears the triangular and diamond foil labels which state, "HULL POTTERY," in two lines. These seals are found with black or maroon background with gold or silver lettering.

DESCRIPTION:

Hand decorated embossed Orchid on duo-tone shaded matte backgrounds. The Hull Company described the color combinations as, "Dec. No. 1, blue green bottom and pink top; Dec. No. 2, blue green bottom and top; and Dec. No. 3, pink bottom and ivory top." At least fifteen shapes were catalogued, many offered in graduated sizes.

PLATE 30

Row 1: 1. Vase, 303-4¾"
      2. Vase, 308-4¼"
      3. Bulb Bowl, 312-7"
      4. Bud Vase, 306-6¾"

Row 2: 1. Vase, 307-6½"
      2. Vase, 307-4¾"
      3. Basket, 305-7"
      4. Vase, 303-6"
      5. Vase, 302-6"

Row 3: 1. Vase, 304-6"
      2. Candle Holder, 315, 4"
      3. Console Bowl, 314-13"
      4. Candle Holder, 315, 4"
      5. Vase, 308-6"

Row 4: 1. Vase, 302-8"
      2. Jardiniere, 310-9½"
      3. Jardiniere, 310-6"
      4. Jardiniere, 310-4¾"
      5. Vase, 301-8"

Row 5: 1. Vase, 301-10"
      2. Lamp Base, unmarked, 10"
      3. Vase, 304-10¼"
      4. Ewer, 311-13"

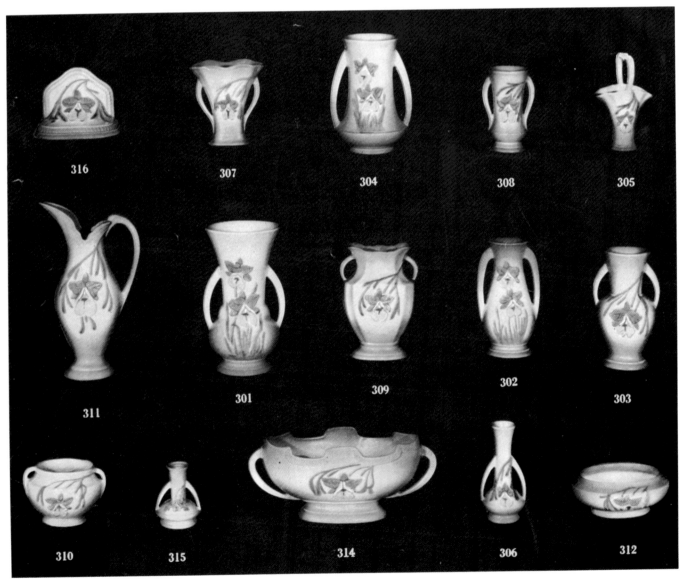

316   307   304   308   305

311   301   309   302   303

310   315   314   306   312

PLATE 30

Advertising Plaques

Iris

PLATE 31

These are all such hard to locate items, they deserve a closer look. The tile advertiser is a rarity.

Row 1: 1. Advertising Tile, embossed Potter-at-Wheel, "TILE BY HULL, INSTALLED BY A SCHIRMER, CINCINNATI," satin gray, 4¼" X 4¼", 1926.
2. Regal China Red Riding Hood Advertising Plaque, "Featuring Little Red Riding Hood, Covered By Pat. Des. No. 135889," 6½" X 11½", 1945.

Row 2: 1. Advertising Plaque, "The A. E. HULL POTTERY CO. POTTERY," 5" X 11", 1938.
2. Advertising Plaque, "HULL," 2¼" X 5½", 1938.

PRODUCTION DATES: 1940-1942

COMPANY'S USUAL MODE OF MARKING:

Incised block Hull, USA, "400" series mold number and size identification. This line bears the triangular and diamond foil labels which state, "HULL POTTERY," in two lines. These seals are found with black or maroon background with gold or silver lettering.

DESCRIPTION:

Hand decorated embossed florals on matte tinted backgrounds of blue and rose, rose and peach, or allover peach. There are fourteen shapes catalogued, several in graduated sizes.

PLATE 32

Row 1: 1. Candle Holder, 411-5"
2. Console Bowl, 409-12"
3. Candle Holder, 411-5"

Row 2: 1. Vase, 407-8½"
2. Vase, 402-4¼"
3. Vase, 404-8½"
4. Vase, 403-4¾"
5. Vase, 402-8½"

Row 3: 1. Vase, 404-10½"
2. Vase, 414-16"
3. Ewer, 401-13½"

PLATE 31

PLATE 32

Iris

PRODUCTION DATES: 1940-1942

COMPANY'S USUAL MODE OF MARKING:

Incised block Hull, USA, "400" series mold number and size identification. This line bears the triangular or diamond foil labels which state, "HULL POTTERY," in two lines. These seals are found with black or maroon background with gold or silver lettering.

DESCRIPTION:

Hand decorated embossed florals on matte tinted backgrounds of blue and rose, rose and peach or allover peach. There are fourteen shape catalogued, several in graduated sizes.

PLATE 33

Row 1: 1. Basket, 408-7"
2. Advertising Plaque, "The A. E. Hull Co. Pottery," 5" X 11" 1938.
3. Vase, 406-4¾"

Row 2: 1. Vase. 402-7"
2. Advertising Plaque, "HULL," unmarked, 2¼" X 5½" 1938.
3. Bud Vase, 410-7½"
4. Vase, 405-8½"
5. Ewer, 401-8"

Row 3: 1. Rose Bowl, 412-7"
2. Rose Bowl, 412-4"
3. Jardiniere, 413-9"
4. Vase, 404-4¾"
5. Jardiniere, 413-5½"

Row 4: 1. Vase, 407-8½"
2. Ewer, 401-5"
3. Vase, 414-10½"
4. Vase, 407-4¾"
5. Vase, 403-7"

130

PLATE 33

Dogwood
Wild Flower No. Series

PRODUCTION DATES: 1942-1943

COMPANY'S USUAL MODE OF MARKING:

Dogwood items are marked with an incised block HULL, USA, "500" series mold number and size identification. This line bears the triangular foil label which states, "HULL POTTERY," in two lines. This seal is found with black or maroon background with gold or silver lettering.

Wild Flower No. Series is marked with a raised print Hull Art, U.S.A., mold number and size identification. This line also bears the triangular foil "HULL POTTERY" label.

DESCRIPTION:

DOGWOOD: Known also as Wild Rose, this hand decorated embossed single or double rose motif is shaded in duo-tone matte finished pastels of blue and pink, turquoise and cream, or overall cream, with twenty-two shapes offered.

WILD FLOWER NO. SERIES: Embossed hand decorated florals on matte duo-tone tinted backgrounds of blue and pink, russet and pink or allover cream. There are twenty-nine catalogued shapes available.

PLATE 35
Row 1: 1. Dogwood Vase, 509-6½"
        2. Dogwood Ewer, 505-6½ (actual height is 8½")
        3. Dogwood Vase, 513-6½"
Row 2: 1. Dogwood Vase, 515-8½"
        2. Dogwood Ewer, 516-11½"
        3. Dogwood Vase, 502-6½"
Row 3: 1. Dogwood Vase, 510-10½"
        2. Dogwood Vase, unmarked, 14"
        3. Dogwood Ewer, 519-13½"

PLATE 34
Row 1: 1. Wild Flower No. Series Vase, special decoration 77-10½"
        2. Wild Flower No. Series Vase, 54-5¼"

PLATE 35

Dogwood
Sun-Glow Tea Bells
Wild Flower No. Series

PRODUCTION DATES:

Dogwood: 1942-1943

Sun-Glow: 1948-1949

Wild Flower No. Series: 1942-1943

COMPANY'S USUAL MODE OF MARKING:

DOGWOOD items are marked with an impressed block HULL, USA, "500" series mold number and size identification. This line bears the triangular foil label which states, "HULL POTTERY," in two lines. This seal is found with black or maroon background with gold or silver lettering.

WILD FLOWER NO. SERIES is marked with a raised print Hull Art, U.S.A., mold number and size identification. This line also bears the triangular foil "HULL POTTERY" label.

DESCRIPTIONS:

DOGWOOD: Known also as Wild Rose, this hand decorated embossed single and double rose motif is shaded in duo-tone matte finished pastels of blue and pink, turquoise and cream, or overall cream, with twenty-two shapes offered.

WILD FLOWER NO. SERIES: Embossed hand decorated florals on matte duo-tone tinted backgrounds of blue and pink, russet and pink or allover cream. There are twenty-nine catalogued items available.

SUN-GLOW: While Sun-Glow's usual glaze decoration of 1949 was high gloss pink or yellow, the tea bells were finished in the matte duo-tone treatment of the day, that being Bow-Knot. It is not known how many of the matte finished tea bells actually exist and it appears they are experimental. They are available in considerably lesser quantities than the glazed versions. Other Sun-Glow items as well have been found in matte glazes.

PLATE 36

Row 1: 1. Wild Flower No. Series Ewer, 57-4½"
2. Wild Flower No. Series Ewer, 63-7¼"

PLATE 37

Row 1: 1. Dogwood Vase, 517-4¾"
2. Dogwood Vase, 516-4¾"
3. Novelty Dancing Girl, 955, 7", 1938
4. Experimental Sun-Glow Tea Bell, unmarked, 6¾", 1949
5. Experimental Sun-Glow Rope-Handled Tea Bell, unmarked, 6", 1949

Row 2: 1. Dogwood Ewer, 520-4¾"
2. Dogwood Jardiniere, 514-4"
3. Dogwood Low Bowl, 521-7"
4. Dogwood Cornucopia, 522, 3¾"

Row 3: 1. Dogwood Basket, 501-7½"
2. Dogwood Window Box, 508-10½"
3. Dogwood Teapot, 507-6½"

Row 4: 1. Dogwood Candle Holder, 512, 3¾"
2. Dogwood Console Bowl, 511-11½"
3. Dogwood Candle Holder, 512, 3¾"

PLATE 36

PLATE 37

Wild Flower No. Series

PRODUCTION DATES: 1942-1943

COMPANY'S USUAL MODE OF MARKING:

Raised print Hull Art, U.S.A., mold number and size identification. This line bears the triangular foil label which states, "HULL POTTERY," in two lines. This seal is found with either black or maroon background with gold or silver lettering.

DESCRIPTION:

Embossed hand decorated florals on matte duo-tone tinted backgrounds of blue and pink, russet and pink or allover cream. Several of the items have an embossed butterfly motif included in the lid, handle or within the body of the embossed decoration. There are twenty-nine catalogued items available.

PLATE 38

Row 1: 1. Double Candle Holder, 69-4"
        2. Handled Bon-Bon Dish, 65-7"
        3. Double Candle Holder, 69-4"

Row 2: 1. Double Candle Holder, 69-4"
        2. Console Bowl, 70-12"
        3. Double Candle Holder, 69-4"

Row 3: 1. Jardiniere, 64-4"
        2. Creamer, 73-4¾"
        3. Teapot, 72-8"
        4. Open Sugar, 74-4¾"
        5. Vase, 56-4½"

Row 4: 1. Vase, 52-5¼"
        2. Vase, 67-8½"
        3. Vase, 52-5¼"
        4. Cornucopia, 58-6¼"

Row 5: 1. Vase, 51-8½"
        2. Vase, 59-10½"
        3. Ewer, 55-13½"
        4. Vase, 76-8½"

PLATE 38

Poppy

PRODUCTION DATES: 1943-1944

COMPANY'S USUAL MODE OF MARKING:

POPPY is marked in a raised block HULL, U.S.A. form, "600" series mold number and size identification. This line bears the triangular foil label which states, "HULL POTTERY," in two lines. This seal is found in black or maroon background with gold or silver lettering.

DESCRIPTION:

POPPY: Hand decorated embossed florals on duo-tone pastel backgrounds of blue to pink, pink to cream, or allover cream. There are at least twelve shapes available, many in graduated sizes.

Listed under "gifts for the house," Spiegel, Chicago, Illinois, advertised on page 431 of their 1943 Fall and Winter catalogue, Poppy Vase, 607-10½" for $1.10, as "Pottery vase, ornate shape with convenient side handles. Cream colored with gold flower on each side. 7 inches, wide, 11 inches high."

PLATE 39
Row 1: 1. Poppy Basket, 601-12"
       2. Experimental Dogwood Suspended Vase, white with gold decor, 502-6½"
       3. Wild Flower No. Series Basket, 66-10¼"

PLATE 40
Row 1: 1. Vase, 607-6½"
       2. Basket, 601-9"
       3. Ewer, 610-4¾"
Row 2: 1. Jardiniere, 603-4¾"
       2. Wall Pocket, 609-9"
       3. Low Bowl, 602-6½"
       4. Jardiniere, 608-4¾"
Row 3: 1. Vase, 607-8½"
       2. Vase, 605-8½"
       3. Vase, 606-8½"
Row 4: 1. Vase, 607-10½"
       2. Ewer, 610-13½"
       3. Vase, 606-10½"

PLATE 39

138

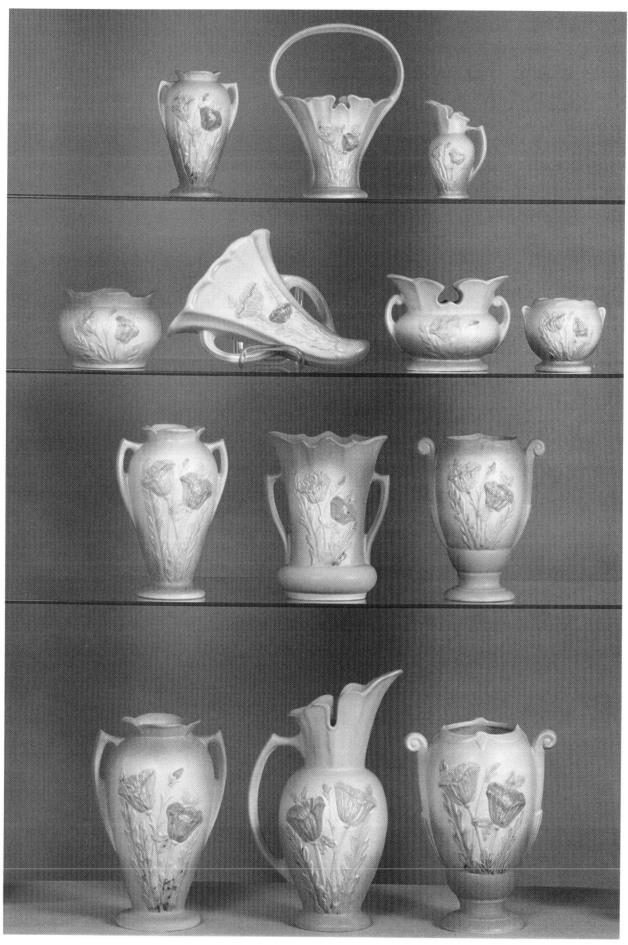

PLATE 40

Mardi Gras And Granada
Morning Glory

PRODUCTION DATES: 1938-1946

COMPANY'S USUAL MODE OF MARKING:

While Mardi Gras and Granada pieces are incised with mold number and size identification they do not carry the Hull trademark except in label form. Mardi Gras and Granada wares carry the triangular black or maroon foil label which states, "HULL POTTERY," with gold or silver lettering in two lines, and also carry separate line foil labels designed exclusively for these lines.

MARDI GRAS is marked with a vase-shaped black foil Potter-at-Wheel label which states, "Mardi Gras" in silver or gold lettering. The company reports another foil label in white or silver featuring a black silhouette of a female flamenco dancer with mask, which marked this ware.

GRANADA is marked with a vertically rectangular black foil Potter-at-Wheel label which states, "Granada" in silver or gold lettering.

DESCRIPTION:

MARDI GRAS AND GRANADA: This is a line with shared molds, being sold in assortments to different major chain stores. Molds included matte finished items with embossed florals and deco-styled wares finished in solid matte or gloss whites and pastels. Another variation is the duo-tone matte body of blue and pink.

PLATE 41
Row 1: 1. Experimental Vase, embossed star flower, unmarked, 8"
       2. Experimental Classic Vase, matte finished, T-1-6½"
       3. Experimental Wild Flower Candle Holder, unmarked, 3½"
       4. *Experimental Morning Glory Ewer, 63, 11"

PLATE 42
Row 1: 1. Mardi Gras/Granada Candle Holder, unmarked, 3¼"
       2. Novelty Planter, 204-5", 1938
       3. Mardi Gras/Granada Candle Holder, unmarked, 3¼"
Row 2: 1. *Morning Glory Ewer, 63, 11"
       2. *Morning Glory Basket, 62, 8"
       3. Mardi Gras/Granada Ewer, 31-10", signed "Grany" Shafer
Row 3: 1. Mardi Gras/Granada Basket, 32-8"
       2. Mardi Gras/Granada Teapot, 33-5½"
       3. Mardi Gras/Granada Basket, 65-8"
Row 4: 1. Mardi Gras/Granada Ewer-31-10"
       2. Novelty Cornucopia, 200, 9", 1938
       3. Mardi Gras/Granada Ewer, 66-10"

*Collectors have named this line Morning Glory, due to the embossed trumpet-shaped floral design. It has further been speculated by collectors that it is an experimental or trialed design. However, the number of pieces in circulation, their varied locations of purchase and the fact these pieces are usually mold marked, add discount to this theory. As easy to theorize is the concept that they belong to the Mardi Gras/Granada line.

PLATE 41

PLATE 42

141

Artware Mattes:
Mardi Gras And Granada
Pinecone

PRODUCTION DATES: 1938-1946

COMPANY'S USUAL MODE OF MARKING:

Mardi Gras, Granada and Pinecone pieces are incised with mold number and size identification but do not carry the Hull trademark. They usually carry Hull labels. While Mardi Gras, Granda and Pinecone all three carry the triangular black or maroon foil label stating, "HULL POTTERY," with gold or silver lettering in two lines, the Mardi Gras and Granada lines each have a foil label designed specifically for their separate identities.

MARDI GRAS is marked with a vase-shaped black foil Potter-at-Wheel label which states, "Mardi Gras;" in silver or gold lettering. The company reports another foil label in white or silver, featuring a black silhouette of a female flamenco dancer with mask, which marked this ware.

GRANADA is marked with a vertically rectangular black foil Potter-at-Wheel label which states, "GRANADA" in silver or gold lettering.

The "picture framed" lamps illustrated also are void of any Hull trademark.

DESCRIPTION:

MARDI GRAS AND GRANADA are lines with shared molds that were sold in assortments to a variety of chain stores. Mardi Gras/Granada items spanned many years of Hull production, from the 1930's throughout the Fifties. Items ranged from utility kitchenware items to artwares in both gloss and matte colors. The items illustrated are from Hull's most central years. These items are plentiful and are collected widely as the shaded items mix well with other Hull floral designs. The dual line items illustrated include matte finished items with embossed florals and deco styled wares finished in solid matte or gloss whites and pastels. Another variation is the duo-tone matte body of blue and pink.

PINECONE, shown on the company's Sueno brochure, appears to be an overall line name for a chain store sales package. This line features an embossed Pinecone spray on solid matte pastels of blue, pink or turquoise. Only one vase shape is known to have been retailed. Refer to experimental section of this volume for experimental Pinecone design.

PLATE 43

Row 1: 1. Pinecone Vase, 55-6½"
        2. Mardi Gras/Granada Vase, 207, 7½"
        3. Pinecone Vase, 55, 6½"

Row 2: 1. Mardi Gras/Granada Vase, 216, 9"
        2. Mardi Gras/Granada Vase, 47-9"
        3. Mardi Gras/Granada Vase, 215-9"

Row 3: 1. Mardi Gras/Granada Vase, 49-9"
        2. Mardi Gras/Granada Vase, 219-9"
        3. Mardi Gras/Granada Vase, 48-9"

Row 4: 1. Lamp, L-1, USA, Picture Framed embossed floral, 13"
        2. Lamp, L-1, USA, Picture Framed embossed floral, 13"
        3. Lamp, L-1, USA, Picture Framed embossed floral, 13"
        4. Mardi Gras/Granada Vase, 750-13½"

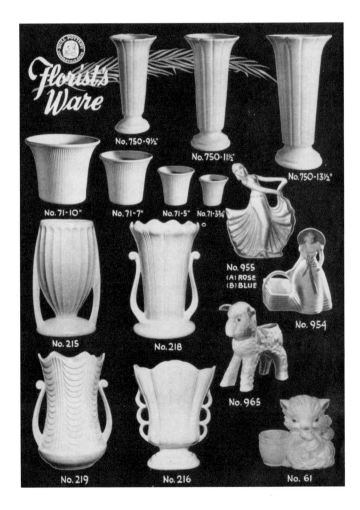

PLATE 43

Camellia

PRODUCTION DATES: 1943-1944

COMPANY'S USUAL MODE OF MARKING:

Raised block HULL, U.S.A., "100" series mold number and size identification. This line bears the triangular foil label which states, "HULL POTTERY," in two lines. This seal is found with black or maroon background with gold or silver lettering.

DESCRIPTION:

This line is also referred to as Open Rose by collectors, however, Camellia is the correct Company name. Featured are hand decorated embossed florals on shaded pastel backgrounds of matte pink and blue, or allover matte white. At least forty-four pieces are catalogued.

PLATE 44
Row 1: 1. Tulip Flower Pot with Attached Saucer, 116-33-4¼" 1938-1941
       2. Camellia Factory Lamp, Top is filled rather than open for use as a vase, base is open, side drilled for cord, unmarked, 10½".
       3. Camellia Vase, 123-6½"
Row 2: 1. Orchid Bookend, 316-7", 1939-1941
       2. Dogwood Vase, 504-8½", 1942-1943
       3. Morning Glory Vase, 61-8½", 1940
       4. Orchid Bookend, 316-7", 1939-1941

PLATE 45
Row 1: 1. Vase, 130-4¾"
       2. Vase, 136-6¼"
       3. Basket, 107-8"
       4. Vase, 121-6¼"
       5. Vase, 131-4¾"
Row 2: 1. Vase, 122-6¼"
       2. Vase, 138-6¼"
       3. Vase, 108-8½"
       4. Vase, 120-6¼"
       5. Vase, 134-6¼"
Rwo 3: 1. Vase, 141-8½"
       2. Vase, 135-6¼"
       3. Vase, 126-8½"
       4. Vase, 137-6¼"
       5. Cornucopia, 101-8½"
Row 4: 1. Vase, 102-8½"
       2. Lamp-shaped Vase, 139-10½", open top for vase use
       3. Ewer, 106-13¼"
       4. Vase, 143-8½"

PLATE 44

144

PLATE 45

145

Camellia

PRODUCTION DATES: 1943-1944

COMPANY'S USUAL MODE OF MARKING:

Raised block HULL, U.S.A., "100" series mold number and size identification. This line bears the triangular foil label which states, "HULL POTTERY," in two lines. This seal is found with black or maroon background with gold or silver lettering.

DESCRIPTION:

This line is also referred to as Open Rose by collectors, however, Camellia is the correct company name. Featured are hand decorated embossed florals on shaded pastel backgrounds of matte pink and blue, or allover matte white. At least forty-four pieces are catalogued.

PLATE 47
Row 1: 1. Basket, 142-6¼"
       2. Creamer, 111-5"
       3. Teapot, 110-8½"
       4. Open Sugar, 112-5"
Row 2: 1. Candle Holder, 117-6½"
       2. Console Bowl, 116-12"
       3. Candle Holder, 117-6½"
       4. Hanging Basket, 132-7"
Row 3: 1. Vase, 118-6½"
       2. Low Bowl, 113-7"
       3. Jardiniere, 114-8¼"
       4. Basket, 140-10½"
       5. Ewer, 128-4¾"
Row 4: 1. Wall Pocket, 125-8½"
       2. Vase, 103-8½"
       3. Vase, 124-12"
       4. Ewer, 115-8½"
       5. Ewer, 105-7"

PLATE 46
Row 1: 1. Mermaid with Shell Planter, 104-10½"

PLATE 47

147

Lamps

COMPANY'S USUAL MODE OF MARKING:

The lamps illustrated do not carry any Hull trademark in the mold, although some do have an "L" series system and some carry an incised USA. Please consult the index for lamps which appear in other sections of this volume.

PLATE 49
Row 1: 1. Water Lily, gloss, unmarked, 7½", 1949
Row 2: 1. Classic, T-1, 7¾", 1946
       2. Classic, T-2, 7¾", 1946
       3. Classic, T-1, 7¾", 1946
Row 3: 1. Rosella, dimpled body, unmarked, 10¾", 1946
       2. Unnamed matte line, unmarked, 9",
         Early 1940's
       3. Rosella, decorated over glaze, L3, 11", 1946
Row 4: 1. Rosella, unmarked, Rosella foil label, 6¾", 1946
       2. Rosella, L-3, 11", 1946
       3. Picture Framed rose decal, L2, 13", 1940
       4. Rosella, L3, 11", 1946
       5. Rosella, unmarked, 6¾", 1946

Buyer beware, lamps are at a premium and you must be sure you are purchasing a factory-made lamp. If the lamp has a metal base and/or top fitting, you would be wise to ask the owner's permission to disengage the lamp parts to assure it is factory made. The exception to metal fittings are the small Rosella and Classic lamps. These were either made at the factory or authorized by an agent, all fittings are consistently the same.

In considering other lamps, the absolute buyer's dream is locating a lamp base which has never been wired and is without metal fittings to be bothersome in your course of study. When the upper portion is factory filled-in, sometimes even built up in a rounded or stair-step fashion, you no doubt have a lamp base produced within the factory. The drilled area for cord placement is the second most important area to check, making sure it was drilled first then glazed, rather than drilled after the glazing process.

With prices for lamps at premium, expect to find home-fashioned items on the market. Also, there are some extremely close versions of the picture framed lamp in high glosses which are made of a heavier porcelain body.

There is no interest or value in the home-fashioned lamps which have been filled-in with cement or ceramic materials, and/or glass flowers. Additionally, vases which have been drilled with added attachments have only minimal value, that being much lower than the value of the vase itself. Any person can take an item and fashion a lamp and many have done so when retiring Hull vases or ewers in their redecorating efforts in the 1950's and 1960's. A specialty company, such as indicated in the kitten planter lamp ad would have better resources to make hand-fashioned lamps (those made outside the Company) presentable.

Kitten Planter Lamp for a nursery of hand-decorated underglaze pottery with plastic shade in pink or blue; 18″ high; $4.95, exp. coll. Gifford Specialty Co., 5849-B Northwest Hy., Chicago 31, Illinois.

BETTER HOMES & GARDENS, NOVEMBER, 1948

PLATE 48
Rooster Lamp, 53, 5¾"

PLATE 49

Rosella

PRODUCTION DATE: 1946

COMPANY'S USUAL MODE OF MARKING:

Raised print Hull Art, U.S.A., "R" series mold number and size identification. Cornucopia vases and ewers carry a "L" (left) and "R" (right) designation. Rosella was an expensive line to produce with its specially mixed clay, and further carried a foil label designed specifically for this ware. This banner and flower-form foil label is brown with gold accents.

DESCRIPTION:

Original advertising described Rosella as, "Distinctively designed by Hull master craftsmen: with the sculptured wild rose pattern hand-tinted under the glaze on a choice of ivory or coral body." The Rosella design included sixteen shapes with an additional pitcher, teapot, three lamps, dimpled vase, and a window box.

Rosella was produced at a time when the company was torn between the comfort and stability of the old, and the need to move on with updated, innovative styles and glazes. Hull tested their markets with gloss Rosella, and at the same time retained production of matte wares.

The Hull Company was a little ahead of its time, as Rosella was produced in that short span of time before high glazed artware items were truly trendy. Rosella did not take the market by storm, it was being teamed on retailer's shelves with matte wares belonging not only to Hull, but also the company's competitors, Roseville and Weller. Matte designs prevailed, and Rosella was neglected. The Rosella line was short-lived and the market numbers are deceptive. Rosella pieces that are taking a back seat to matte pastels are few in number, and only appear plentiful because they are being overlooked.

Better Homes & Gardens, January, 1946

PLATE 50
Row 1: 1. Basket, R-12-7"
     2. Vase, R-2-5"
     3. Basket, R-12-7"
Row 2: 1. Creamer, R-3-5½"
     2. *Covered Sugar, R-4-5½"
     3. Creamer, R-3-5½"
     4. *Covered Sugar, R-4-5½"
Row 3: 1. Ewer, R-11-7½"L
     2. Vase, R-6-6½"
     3. Wall Pocket, R-10-6½"
     4. Vase, R-5-6½"
     5. Ewer, R-11-7" R
Row 4: 1. Cornucopia, R-13-8½" R
     2. Ewer, R-9-6½"
     3. Vase, R-8-6½"
     4. Vase, R-1-5"
     5. Cornucopia, R-13-8½" L
Row 5: 1. Vase, R-15-8½"
     2. Vase, R-7-6½" (smooth)
     3. Vase, R-14-8½"
     4. Vase, R-7-6½" (dimpled)
     5. Ewer, R-7-9½"

*Many of the sugar lids were apparently discarded, please note prices for sugar with and without lid.

PLATE 50

Little Red Riding Hood

PRODUCTION DATES: 1943-1957

COMPANY'S USUAL MODE OF MARKING:

All Little Red Riding Hood pottery and china products have been referred to as "Hull" for the past twenty years or more, even though very few items were actually produced by Hull. Hull's trademarks included script "Hull Ware, Little Red Riding Hood, Patent Applied For U.S.A.," and script "Hull Ware, U.S.A." Regal China wares were marked with an incised Little Red Riding Hood script form, many carried only the patent design no. 135889, and some were unmarked.

DESCRIPTION:

The Hull company originated the Little Red Riding Hood design by issue of U. S. patent number 135,889 for "Cookie Jar." Interest was so great that this issue spurred demand for additional kitchenware characters. Regal China Company, not Hull, met this demand, although probably by way of some type of contractual agreement with the Hull Pottery Company.

Actual Hull-produced Little Red Riding Hood wares were few, and limited to the open basket cookie jar, covered "bow" jars and shakers. Although some of the same decals were used jointly by Hull Pottery and Regal China, identification of wares comes from the clay color and content.

I was uncertain as to whether or not to illustrate and list Little Red Riding Hood items which were not produced by Hull. The collector's need for accurate information of this ware helped solve this dilemma.

The collecting audience for Little Red Riding Hood is voluminous and most collectors began their collections in good faith that this ware was of Hull manufacture. Even with the 1989 publication of Mark E. Supnick's book, *HULL POTTERY'S LITTLE RED RIDING HOOD,* and further explanation of the ware's origins, Little Red Riding Hood is still referred to as Hull Pottery, being bought, sold and traded as such.

The original seven-year patent 135,889, was assigned to A. E. Hull Pottery Company by Louise E. Bauer, modeler of the design. The patent was filed April 12, 1943, and granted June 29, 1943. Interest was so great that the patent was extended once, expiring June 29, 1957. While Louise Bauer designed the cookie jar, small and large shakers for Royal China and Novelty Company, Chicago, Illinois, a division of the Regal China Corporation, most likely, Regal China hired modelers to design the additional items. Hull and Regal obviously had some type of contractual agreement, or the registered patent was sold and transferred totally to Regal. The Little Red Riding Hood advertising plaque, obviously produced by Regal China, incorporated the patent designation number into the design.

With the knowledge in hand that Hull Little Red Riding Hood is usually NOT HULL, Little Red Riding Hood collectors can continue to collect and call it whatever they wish, and people like Mark Supnick and I will continue to place it in volumes entitled, "Hull Pottery." Little Red Riding Hood items do have a rightful place interspersed with the rest of Hull's history and lines of manufacture since the design inspiration was in fact, Hull's.

To make the collecting dilemma even more confusing, you will see illustrated in the next few photographs, several additional items collectors value in their Little Red Riding Hood collections. It appears collectors gather various types of porcelain wares decorated with the same decal as was used on Hull and Regal Little Red Riding Hood items.

PLATE 51

Row 1: 1. Regal China Advertising Plaque, "Featuring Little Red Riding Hood, Covered By Pat. Des. No. 135889," 6½" X 11½"
       2. Regal China Butter Dish, 5½"

Row 2: 1 & 2. Regal China Shakers, 3¼"
       3. Regal China Creamer, 5"
       4. Pope Gosser Gravy with Attached Under Plate, 9"
       5. Regal China Sugar, 5"
       6. Regal China Mustard with Spoon, 5¼"

Row 3: 1. Hull Covered Jar, 9"
       2. Pope Gosser Platter, 13½"
       3. Regal China Teapot, 8"

Row 4: 1. Regal China Cookie Jar, 13"
       2. Lamp, maker unknown, 12"
       3. Hull Cookie Jar, 13"

PLATE 51

Little Red Riding Hood

PRODUCTION DATES: 1943-1957

PLATE 52
Row 1: 1. Regal China Handled Casserole, Pat. Des.
No. 135889, 11¾"

PLATE 53
Row 1: 1. Hull Covered Jar, decorated in matte pink and
blue, 9"

PLATE 54
Row 1: 1. Regal China Shaker, unmarked, 5¼"
2. Regal China Shaker, unmarked, 5¼"
3. Regal China Hanging Match Box, unmarked,
5½"
4. Regal China Wolf Jar, USA, 6"
5. Hull Shaker, unmarked, 5½"
6. Hull Shaker, unmarked, 5½"
Row 2: 1. Regal China Pitcher, unmarked, 7"
2. Hull Covered Jar, 9"
3. Regal China Covered Jar,
unmarked, 8½"
4. Regal China Standing Bank,
unmarked, 7"
Row 3: 1. Chic Pottery Wall Pocket, 4¾"
2. Pope Gosser Creamer, 3½"
3. Pope Gosser Dinner Plate, 10"
4. Pope Gosser Covered Sugar, 4½"
5. Chic Pottery Iron Wall Pocket, 5½"
Row 4: 1. Hull Cookie Jar, 13"
2. Lamp, maker unknown, 13"
3. Lamp, maker unknown, 12½"
4. Hull Cookie Jar, 13"

PLATE 54

155

PLATE 55

Little Red Riding Hood

PRODUCTION DATES: 1943-1957
PLATE 55
Row 1: 1. Regal China Crawling Sugar, unmarked, 3"
      2. Regal China Tab Handled Creamer, unmarked, 3½"
Row 2: 1. Hull Covered Jar, Hull Ware 932, 9"
      2. Regal China Canister, "Pretzels," Pat. Des. 135889, 10"
      3. Regal China Pitcher, Pat. Des. 135889, 8"
Row 3: 1. Regal China Canister, "Coffee," Pat. Des. 135889, 10"
      2. Regal China Covered Sugar, unmarked, 3½"
      3. Regal China Head Pour Creamer, unmarked, 3½"
      4. Regal China Canister, "Tea," Pat. Des 135889, 10"

PLATE 56

Little Red Riding Hood

PRODUCTION DATES: 1943-1957

PLATE 56

Row 1: 1. Regal China Shaker, unmarked, 5¼"
        2. Regal China Hanging Match Box, Pat. Des.
           No. 135889, 5½"
        3. Regal China Shaker, unmarked, 5¼"

Row 2: 1. Regal China Canister, "Cereal," Pat. Des.
           No. 135889, 10"
        2. Regal China Canister, "Flour," Pat. Des.
           No. 135889, 10"
        3. Regal China Canister, "Sugar," Pat. Des.
           No. 135889, 10"

Row 3: 1. Regal China Cookie Jar, Pat. Des. No. 135889, 13"
        2. Regal China Shaker, unmarked, 4½"
        3. Regal China Canister, "Salt," Pat. Des.
           No 135889, 10"
        4. Regal China Wall Hanging Planter, Pat. Des.
           No. 135889. 9"

157

Novelty

PRODUCTION DATES: Mid-1930's to Mid-1950's

COMPANY'S USUAL MODE OF MARKING:

Items illustrated range from unmarked to impressed print Hull Art, USA, to incised script Hull or Hull Ware, USA.

DESCRIPTION:

The experimental tumblers were used to test the day's glazes to assure quality control. These test pieces usually bear the inscribed alphanumeric markings in the base or side of the tumbler, which related to a certain glaze formula or color batch identification. These test tumblers were used from the reopening of the plant in 1950 to the plant's closing. Date of production is determined by the glaze treatment.

The novelty items shown were glazed in both matte or satin finishes and high glosses; the rooster planter was decorated in matte finish. The novelty pig and poodle planters were decorated in matte underglaze with air brush decoration and hand painted detail. In the early 1940's, basket girls were produced in satin white with both underglazed and overglazed detailing. They continued to be produced in both satin and high gloss throughout the 1940's, and into the 1950's. By 1953, basket girls and lamb and kitten planters were produced in high gloss pink or ivory with underglazed detailing. The lamb was also glazed in allover black. The pig planter was finished in high gloss while the cat door stop was finished in both high gloss and satin finishes.

The Hull Ware cookie jars illustrated are exceptional, each being decorated over the glaze. Both jars are difficult to locate and will most likely be on cookie jar collectors' want lists.

PLATE 57

Row 1: 1. Little Boy Blue Cookie Jar, incised Hull Ware, Boy Blue, U.S.A. 971-12½", 1940
2. Hen and Chick Cookie Jar, incised Hull Ware, 968-11½", U.S.A. 1940

PLATE 58

Row 1: 1. Experimental Tumbler, inscribed 36, 3½"
2. Experimental Tumbler, inscribed 68, 93, 94, 3½"
3. Experimental Tumbler, inscribed 54, 3½"
4. Experimental Tumbler, inscribed 12-7, 55, 3½"
5. Rooster, 951, 7", 1938-1942
6. Experimental Tumbler, inscribed 116, 3½"
7. Experimental Tumbler, inscribed 174, 3½"
8. Experimental Tumbler, inscribed 9-29, 175-V-31, 3½"
9. Experimental Tumbler, inscribed 5-24-1-10, 3½"

Row 2: 1. Vase, 38, 6½", 1955
2. Vase, 37 6½", 1955
3. Vase, 62, 6½", 1938-1940
4. Vase, 39, 6½", 1955

Row 3: 1. Basket Girl, 954, 8", high gloss pink
2. Basket Girl, 954, 8", matte white
3. Basket Girl, 954, 8", high gloss white

Row 4: 1. Kitten Planter, 61, 7½"
2. Pig Planter, 60, 8½", 1940-1943
3. Lamb Planter, 965, 7½"
4. Cat Door Stop, unmarked, 7¼", 1936

PLATE 57

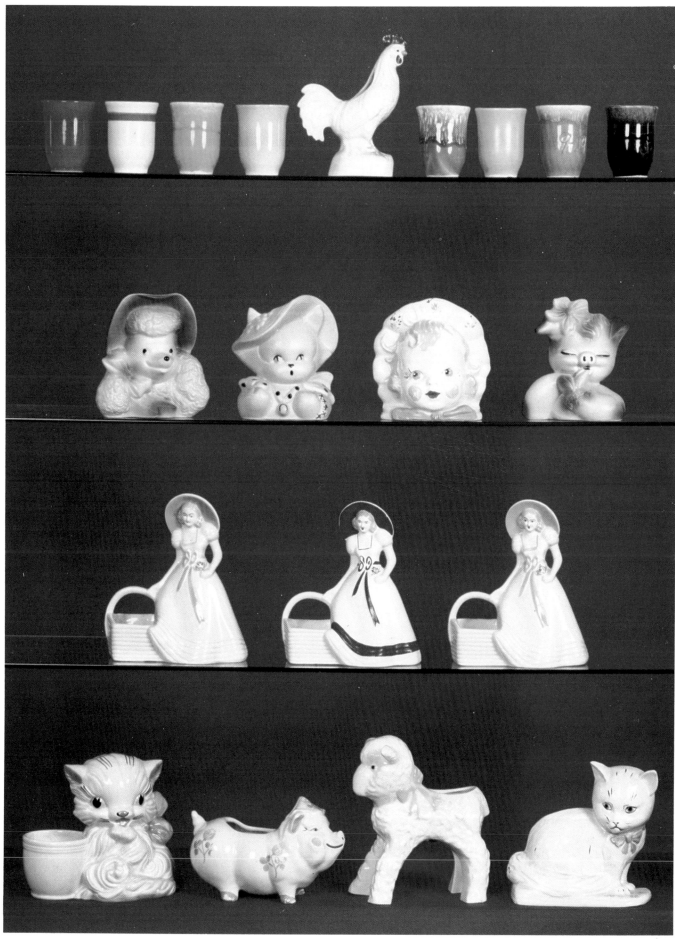

PLATE 58

159

Banks
Leeds Bottles

COMPANY'S USUAL MODE OF MARKING:

Corky Pigs are marked, just that, script "Corky Pig," ©57, USA. This mold was used from the time of its inception, to the plant's closing in 1985.

The largest pig banks from 1940 were marked USA only, and there is absolutely no way to identify the one without the embossed floral unless you buy it straight from a Hull family member or Hull employee. McCoy produced this pig bank too. The smallest pig, the dime bank, produced in the 1950's, was marked USA only. Hull employees boasted there was nothing small about these banks, since they proved they held $75.00 in dimes.

The sitting pig banks were manufactured from mid-1960 to the plant's closing in 1985. In production almost the same length of time, was the razor back hog bank.

Leeds Bottles are incised block "Leeds, USA."

DESCRIPTION:

These banks are as fun to display as they are to collect. Even though there was a limited number of mold shapes, the company was imaginative in its use of color combinations. You'll have your work cut out for you in trying to gather one in each color. Shown is a representative sampling, but colors shown are not inclusive of those which were available.

The Leeds bottles were air-brush decorated in high gloss pastels of pink and blue. The liquor bottles were made in the 1940's and many Crooksville citizens can relate stories of the many hundreds of bottles that floated through their Village during the flood of 1950.

PLATE 59
Row 1: 1. Dinosaur Bank, premium for Sinclair Oil Company, 7", early 1960.

PLATE 61
Row 1: 1. Pig Lamp, 196, 6"
2. Pig Bank, 196, 6", Tawny Ridge
3. Pig Bank, 196, 6
Row 2: 1. Corky Pig Bank, 5", Tawny Ridge
2. Leeds Elephant Liquor Bottle, 7¾", 1939-1944
3. Corky Pig Bank, 5"
4. Leeds Pig Liquor Bottle, 7¾", 1939-1944
5. Corky Pig Bank, 5", Flint Ridge
Row 3: 1. Corky Pig Bank, 5"
2. Corky Pig Bank, 5"
3. Corky Pig Bank, 5"
Row 4: 1. Pig Dime Bank, 3½"
2. Corky Pig Bank, 5"
3. Pig Bank, (underglaze decorated) 14"
4. Pig Dime Bank, 3½"
Row 5: 1. Pig Bank, embossed floral, (decorated over the glaze,) 14"
2. Pig Bank, 197, 8"

PLATE 60
Row 1: 1. Experimental Pig Bank, larger than the Corky Pig Bank, incised X's and O's pattern on back, unmarked, 6" X 9", 1957.

PLATE 61

Wildflower

PRODUCTION DATES: 1946-1947

COMPANY'S USUAL MODE OF MARKING:

Raised print Hull Art, U.S.A., "W" series mold number and size identification. This line carried the round black Potter-at-Wheel foil label which had silver, gold or gray lettering.

DESCRIPTION:

Hand decorated embossed floral spray of Trillium, Mission and Bluebell in two-tone matte pastel body shades of pink and blue or yellow and dusty rose. There were twenty-two catalogued shapes.

Wildflower

The sculptured beauty of the tasteful floral decoration . . . the exquisite delicacy of its hand-tinting and the artistry of its shapes, have made *Wildflower* the favorite of many in fine Art Pottery. 22 pieces, at better stores.

Wildflower is a creation of the master potters of The A. E. Hull Pottery Company, Crooksville, O.

This handsome console set admirably reflects the completeness of the *Wildflower* Art Pottery line by Hull. Two-tone spray tinting of the top and bottom distinguish each of the 22 pieces; each decorated front and back with exquisitely hand-painted floral group. Available at your favorite store.

Created and produced by the master potters of The A.E.Hull Pottery Co., Crooksville, Ohio

Fashionable foundations for your favorite flowers are these exquisite vases in the *Wildflower* Art Pottery line by Hull. There are 20 other equally delightful pieces, each with hand-tinted floral decoration embossed on a body of two-tone pastels. See *Wildflower* at your favorite store . . .

The A. E. HULL POTTERY CO.
Crooksville, Ohio

HULL
Modern Art Pottery

HULL'S GRACEFUL
Wildflower

Hand-painted in the gay colors of Spring to brighten the Fall and Winter months of indoor living . . . styled to dwell in graceful harmony with any interior. Twenty-two pieces from which to choose, each a masterpiece of ceramic art. See *Wildflower* at your favorite store.

Crafted by

THE A. E. HULL POTTERY CO.
CROOKSVILLE, OHIO

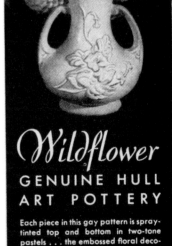

A favored setting for your favorite flowers is *Wildflower*, the new Art Pottery creation by Hull. You'll like the natural-colored floral motif of Trillium, Mission and Bluebell—embossed in tasteful trinity on a body hand-tinted in two-tone pastels. Twenty-two graceful pieces available at your favorite store.

Crafted by the master potters of The A. E. Hull Pottery Co., Crooksville, Ohio

HULL
Modern Art Pottery

Wildflower
GENUINE HULL
ART POTTERY

Each piece in this gay pattern is spray-tinted top and bottom in two-tone pastels . . . the embossed floral decoration front and back is hand-painted in natural colors. Twenty-two graceful pieces from which to make your choice, at leading stores everywhere. Created by the master craftsmen of **THE A. E. HULL POTTERY CO.** CROOKSVILLE, OHIO.

PLATE 62
Row 1: 1. Vase, W-1-5½"
       2. Vase, W-3-5½"
       3. Ewer, W-2-5½"
Row 2: 1. Vase, W-6-7½"
       2. Vase, W-9-8½"
       3. Vase, W-4-6½"
Row 3: 1. Cornucopia, W-10-8½"
       2. Vase, W-14-10½"
       3. Vase, W-12-9½"
       4. Ewer, W-11-8½"
Row 4: 1. Ewer, W-19-13½"
       2. Vase, W-15-10½"
       3. Lamp, not factory produced, 12½" pottery section

PLATE 62

Wildflower

PRODUCTION DATES: 1946-1947

COMPANY'S USUAL MODE OF MARKING:

Raised print Hull Art, U.S.A., "W" series mold number and size identification. This line carried the round black Potter-at-Wheel foil label which had silver, gold, or gray lettering.

DESCRIPTION:

Hand decorated embossed floral spray of Trillium, Mission and Bluebell in two-tone matte pastel body shades of pink and blue or yellow and dusty rose. There were twenty-two catalogued shapes

PLATE 63
Row 1: 1. Candle Holder, W-22, 2½"
      2. Console Bowl, 21-12"
      3. Candle Holder, W-22, 2½"
Row 2: 1. Cornucopia, W-7-7½"
      2. Vase, W-5-6½"
      3. Vase, W-8-7½"
Row 3: 1. Basket, W-16-10½"
      2. Vase, W-13-9½"
      3. Basket, W-16-10½"
Row 4: 1. Vase, W-18-12½"
      2. Vase, W-20-15½"
      3. Vase, W-17-12½"

THE
A. E. HULL POTTERY COMPANY
CROOKSVILLE, OHIO

THE **Wildflower** PATTERN

Nationally Known Hand Decorated Pottery

☆

Net Price List Effective January 1, 1947

PLATE 63

165

Magnolia

PRODUCTION DATES: 1946-1947

COMPANY'S USUAL MODE OF MARKING:

Raised print Hull Art, U.S.A., mold number and size identification. This line carried the round black Potter-at-Wheel foil label which had silver, gold or gray lettering.

DESCRIPTION:

Hand decorated embossed florals on shaded matte pastels of pink and blue or dusty rose and yellow. Twenty-seven items were included in this line, with vase 21-12½" being available with either open or tab handles.

PLATE 64

Row 1: 1. Cornucopia, 19-8½"
2. Basket, 10-10½"
3. Vase, 7-8½"

Row 2: 1. Candle Holder, 27-4"
2. Console Bowl, 26-12"
3. Candle Holder 27-4"

Row 3: 1. Vase, 4-6¼"
2. Ewer, 5-7"
3. Vase, 1-8½"
4. Vase, 2-8½"
5. Vase, 11-6¼"

Row 4: 1. Vase, 20-15"
2. Lamp, 15" pottery section, not factory produced
3. Vase, 16-15"

PLATE 64

167

Magnolia

PRODUCTION DATES: 1946-1947

COMPANY'S USUAL MODE OF MARKING:

Raised print Hull Art, U.S.A., mold number and size identification. This line carried the round black Potter-at-Wheel foil label which had silver, gold, or gray lettering.

DESCRIPTION:

Hand decorated embossed florals on shaded matte pastels of pink and blue or dusty rose and yellow. Twenty-seven items were included in this line, with vase 21-12½" being available with either open or tab handles.

PLATE 65
Row 1: 1. Creamer, 24-3¾"
         2. Teapot, 23-6½"
         3. Open Sugar, 25-3¾"
Row 2: 1. Vase, 12-6¼"
         2. Double Cornucopia, 6-12"
         3. Vase, 3-8½"
         4. Vase, 15-6¼"
Row 3: 1. Vase, 8-10½"
         2. Ewer, 14-4¾"
         3. Vase, 9-10½"
         4. Vase, 13-4¾"
         5. Vase, 21-12½" (open handles)
Row 4: 1. Ewer, 18-13½"
         2. Vase, 21-12½" (tab handles)
         3. Vase, 17-12¼"
         4. Vase, 22-12½"

THE A. E. HULL POTTERY COMPANY
CROOKSVILLE, OHIO

THE *New Magnolia* PATTERN

Net Price List Effective January 1, 1947

Nationally Known Hand Decorated Pottery

Art Pottery As Lovely As the Bride
The New Magnolia

Gracefully styled, handsomely decorated with hand-painted florals . . . glazed over all for shimmering, enduring beauty. Illustrated is but one of the twenty-four pieces available in *The New Magnolia* at fine stores everywhere. Created by the master potters of THE A. E. HULL POTTERY COMPANY, CROOKSVILLE, O.

Perfect Setting for Favored Flowers
HULL'S
New Magnolia

An art pottery masterpiece, with a beautifully hand-painted sculptured floral decoration . . . made enduringly lovely, forever lustrous under a rich glaze of transparent pink. Twenty-four smart pieces at your favorite store; crafted by THE A. E. HULL POTTERY CO., CROOKSVILLE, OHIO.

LOVELY
New Magnolia
TO BEAUTIFY YOUR HOME

For a new brightness, a new allure to home decoration choose this art pottery creation by Hull. The rich, hand-painted florals are made permanently durable under a soft over-all glaze. Your favorite store is now showing the complete line of 24 graceful pieces.

Crafted by
THE A. E. HULL POTTERY CO.
CROOKSVILLE, OHIO

IT'S THE LOVELY
New Magnolia
STYLED BY HULL

You'll say, too: "What lovely art pottery!" For *New Magnolia* is all of that with its twenty-four graceful pieces . . . its rich, hand-painted floral . . . its overall glaze of subdued pink. Women everywhere are choosing it to brighten their homes, to add extra beauty to their favorite flowers. See it now at your favorite store.

Crafted by the Master Potters of
THE A. E. HULL POTTERY CO.
Crooksville, Ohio

168

PLATE 65

169

New Magnolia

PRODUCTION DATES: 1947-1948

COMPANY'S USUAL MODE OF MARKING:

Raised print Hull Art, U.S.A., "H" series mold number and size identification. This line carried the round black Potter-at-Wheel foil label which had silver, gold or gray lettering.

DESCRIPTION:

Hand painted embossed floral decoration of blue or pink with allover transparent pink high glaze. Many items were detailed in gold outside the factory, not uncommon for this line. Twenty-four pieces were included in company catalogue.

Many of these shapes you will recognize as molds from the matte Magnolia line. Hull left behind use of the previous matte Magnolia molds; 13-4¾" vase and and 14-4¾" ewer and replaced them with new molds for gloss Magnolia: H-2-5½" vase and H-3-5½" ewer. The remainder Magnolia molds were used for firing both matte and high gloss wares.

Hull, in 1947, made the decision to place another high gloss artware line in the midst of the retail market's matte wares. Instead of creating a newly designed mold system as Hull had used when creating their high gloss Rosella, the company opted for using shapes already familiar to the public. Here was seen a less expensive venture, with exceedingly less risk to the company. The known shapes in updated glazes proved to be far more comforting to Hull's wholesale and retail audience, Hull's New Magnolia was a success.

PLATE 66

Row 1:
1. Vase, H-5-6½"
2. Candle Holder, H24,4"
3. Console Bowl, H-23-13"
4. Candle Holder, H24, 4"
5. Vase, H-1-5½"

Row 2:
1. Vase, H-2-5½"
2. Creamer, H-21-3¾"
3. Teapot, H-20-6½"
4. Covered Sugar, H-22-3¾"
5. Ewer, H-3-5½"

Row 3:
1. Cornucopia, H-10-8½"
2. Basket, H-14-10½"
3. Double Cornucopia, H-15-12"

Row 4:
1. Vase, H-8-8½"
2. Vase, H-6-6½"
3. Ewer, H-11-8½"
4. Vase, H-7-6½"
5. Vase, H-9-8½"

Row 5:
1. Vase, H-17-12½"
2. Vase, H-16-12½"
3. Vase, H-13-10½"
4. Ewer, H-19-13½"

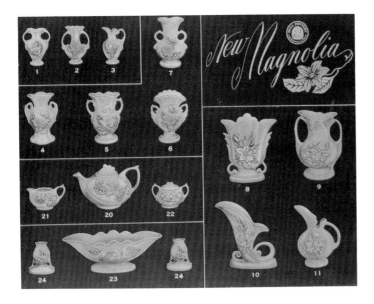

PLATE 66

171

Water Lily

PRODUCTION DATES: 1948-1949

COMPANY'S USUAL MODE OF MARKING:

Water Lily's trademark was usually raised, but occasionally incised print Hull Art, U.S.A., "L" series mold number and size identification. This line carried the round black Potter-at-Wheel foil label which had silver, gold or gray lettering.

DESCRIPTION:

Hand decorated embossed Water Lily floral on duo-tone matte backgrounds of Walnut and Apricot or Turquoise and Sweet Pink. Many items were detailed in gold outside the factory, not uncommon for this line. There were twenty-eight catalogued shapes.

PLATE 67

Row 1: 1. Creamer, L-19-5"
        2. Teapot, L-18-6"
        3. Covered Sugar, L-20-5"

Row 2: 1. Vase, L-1-5½"
        2. Cornucopia, L-7-6½"
        3. Vase, L-4-6½"

Row 3: 1. Vase, L-9-8½"
        2. Vase, L-A-8½"
        3. Vase, L-10-9½"

Row 4: 1. Vase, L-12-10½"
        2. Vase, L-15-12½"
        3. Vase. L-13-10½"

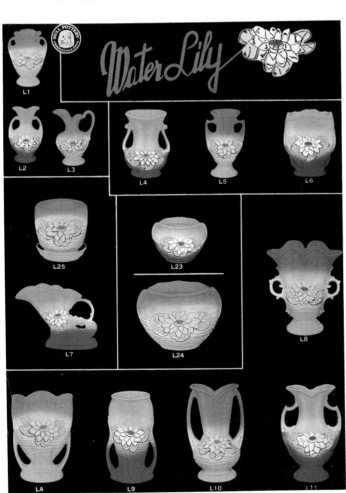

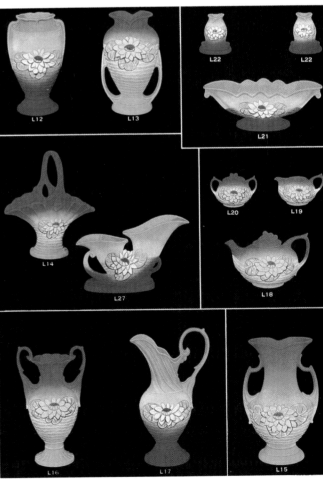

PLATE 67

173

Water Lily

PRODUCTION DATES: 1948-1949

COMPANY'S USUAL MODE OF MARKING:

Water Lily's trademark was usually raised, but occasionally incised print Hull Art, U.S.A., "L" series mold number and size identification. This line carried the round black Potter-at-Wheel foil label which had silver, gold or gray lettering.

DESCRIPTION:

Hand decorated embossed Water Lily floral on duo-tone matte backgrounds of Walnut and Apricot or Turquoise and Sweet Pink. Many items were detailed in gold outside the factory, not uncommon for this line. There were twenty-eight catalogued shapes.

PLATE 68

Row 1: 1. Candle Holder, L-22, 4½"
2. Console Bowl, L-21-13½"
3. Candle Holder, L-22, 4½"

Row 2: 1. Ewer, L-3-5½"
2. Vase, L-6-6½"
3. Vase, L-2-5½"
4. Vase, L-5-6½"

Row 3: 1. Jardiniere L-23-5½"
2. Jardiniere, L-24-8½"
3. Vase, L-11-9½"
4. Flower Pot with Attached Saucer, L-25-5¼"

Row 4: 1. Vase, L-16-12½"
2. Basket, L-14-10½"
3. Ewer, L-17-13½"

THE
A. E. HULL POTTERY
COMPANY
CROOKSVILLE, OHIO

The WATER LILY *Pattern*

Net Price List Effective January 1, 1948

Nationally Advertised Hand Decorated Pottery

PLATE 68

175

Cinderella Kitchenware:
Blossom And Bouquet

PRODUCTION DATES: 1948-1949
COMPANY'S USUAL MODE OF MARKING:

Incised bold block HULL, all upper case lettering, with a flourishing incised U.S.A. Sizes represented on molds identified volume in ounces. This kitchenware line carried a specially designed label, a blue and gold foil ''Cinderella'' label depicting horses and a carriage. Bouquet items beyond the fifteen catalogued pieces were usually marked with the small brown script ink stamp.

DESCRIPTION:

Cinderella was Hull's overall line name for kitchenware they designated as two distinct designs, known as Blossom and Bouquet. Each design had fifteen illustrated catalogued shapes while a company price list additionally specified the 9¾" salad bowl, which may refer to the square bowl with the brown ink stamp. Unlisted items that are so few they are categorized as experimental, include other dinnerware accessories, i.e., square cereal bowls, square dinner plates and a compartment plate.

BLOSSOM: Ovenproof kitchenware items, white gloss finish, with six-petal underglazed, hand painted flower in pink or yellow with green leaves and banding. The Blossom line was first introduced with yellow florals, which was substituted ten months later to pink florals.

BOUQUET: Ovenproof kitchenware in white gloss finish, yellow tinted tops with underglazed hand decorated floral spray of pink, yellow and blue.

PLATE 69
Row 1: 1. Blossom Creamer, No. 28-4¼"
        2. Blossom Teapot, No. 26-42 oz.
        3. Blossom Covered Sugar, No. 27-4½"
Row 2: 1. Blossom Shaker, No. 25-3½"
        2. Blossom Shaker, No. 25-3½"
        3. Bouquet Grease Jar, No. 24-32 oz.
        4. Bouquet Covered Casserole, No. 21-8½"
        5. Blossom Pitcher, No. 29-16 oz.
Row 3: 1. Bouquet Pitcher, No. 29-32 oz.
        2. Blossom Mixing Bowl, 20-5½"
        3. Blossom Mixing Bowl, 20-7½"
        4. Blossom Mixing Bowl, 20-9½"
Row 4: 1. Bouquet Bowl, brown ink stamp, 9¾"
        2. Bouquet Cookie Jar, unmarked, 10½"
        3. Bouqut Ice Lip Pitcher, No. 22-64 oz.

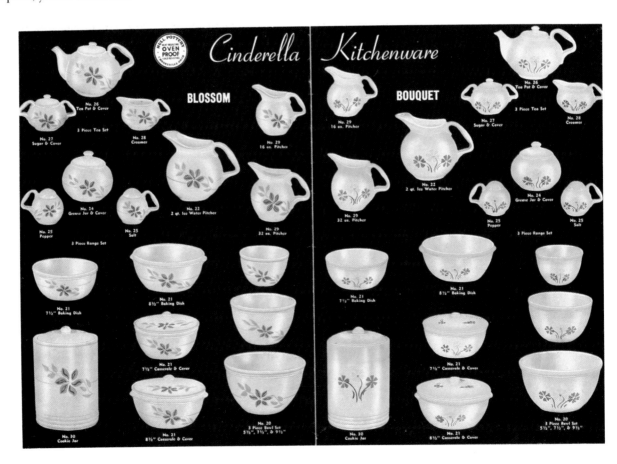

PLATE 69

177

Sun-Glow

PRODUCTION DATES: 1948-1949

COMPANY'S USUAL MODE OF MARKING:

Sun-Glow design does not carry the Hull trademark or a Hull label, most likely because it was used for chain store sales. Items are impressed with the mold number and size identification.

DESCRIPTION:

This line included hand decorated embossed florals in solid high gloss backgrounds of either pink or yellow. Two distinctly different florals appeared on this line; an embossed straw-like daisy and an embossed pansy, sometimes with an additional butterfly decoration. Gold detailing outside the factory was not unusual for these items. It is also not uncommon to see a piece decorated in the matte style of Bow-Knot, i.e., the tea bells, both rope and plain handled. Twenty-nine shapes were available.

PLATE 70

Row 1: 1. Shaker, 54, 2¾"
2. Grease Jar, 53, 5¼"
3. Shaker, 54, 2¾"

Row 2: 1. Vase, 100-6½"
2. Pitcher, 52-24 oz.
3. Vase, 93-6½"

Row 3: 1. Mixing Bowl, 50-9½"
2. Mixing Bowl, 50-7½"
3. Mixing Bowl, 50-5½"
4. Whisk Broom Wall Pocket, 82, 8½"

Row 4: 1. Cup and Saucer Wall Pocket, 80, 6¼"
2. Ice Lip Pitcher, 55, 7½"
3. Jardiniere, 98-7½"
4. Jardiniere, 97-5½"

SUN-GLOW.... By THE A. E. HULL POTTERY COMPANY, Inc., Crooksville, Ohio

All items available in Decoration No. 1, Pink, or Decoration No. 2, Yellow

No. 50 — 3 PIECE BOWL SET, 5½", 7½", 9½"
(Oven Proof)
Packed 6 sets, Weight 40 Pounds
Open Stock: 5½" Packed 4 Dozen, Weight 38 Pounds
7½" Packed 2 Dozen, Weight 48 Pounds
9½" Packed 1 Dozen, Weight 45 Pounds

No. 80 — CUP — SAUCER WALL POCKET
Packed 2 Dozen, Weight 24 Pounds

No. 81 — JUG WALL POCKET
Packed 2 Dozen, Weight 28 Pounds

No. 82 — WHISK BROOM WALL POCKET
Packed 2 Dozen, Weight 30 Pounds

No. 51 — 7¾" CASSEROLE WITH COVER
(Oven Proof)
Packed 1 Dozen, Weight 42 Pounds

No. 52 — 1½-PINT JUG
Packed 2 Dozen, Weight 38 Pounds

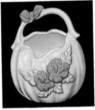

No. 83 IRON PLANTER — WALL POCKET
Packed 1 Dozen, Weight 16 Pounds

No. 84 — BASKET
Packed 1 Dozen, Weight 20 Pounds

No. 85 — 8½" VASE
Packed 1 Dozen, Weight 30 Pounds

No. 53-54 — 3 PIECE RANGE SET
(Oven Proof)
Packed 12 sets, Weight 30 Pounds
Open Stock: Range Jars Packed 2 Dozen, Weight 38 Pounds
Open Stock: Salt and Peppers Packed 2 Dozen Pairs, Weight 25 Pounds

No. 86 — TEA BELL
Packed 2 Dozen, Weight 15 Pounds

No. 87 — TEA BELL
Packed 2 Dozen, Weight 20 Pounds

PLATE 70

179

Sun-Glow

PRODUCTION DATES: 1948-1949

COMPANY'S USUAL MODE OF MARKING:

Sun-Glow does not carry the Hull trademark or a Hull label, most likely because it was used for chain store sales. Items are impressed with the mold number and size identification.

DESCRIPTION:

This line included hand decorated embossed florals in solid high gloss backgrounds of either pink or yellow. Two distinctly different florals appeared on this line; an embossed straw-like daisy and an embossed pansy, sometimes with an additional butterfly decoration. Gold detailing outside the factory was not unusual for these items. It is also not uncommon to see a piece decorated in the matte style of Bow-Knot, i.e., the tea bells, both rope and plain handled. Twenty-nine shapes were available.

PLATE 71
Row 1: 1. Sun-Glow Rope-Handled Tea Bell, unmarked, 6¼"
2. Sun Glow Tea Bell, unmarked, 6½"
3. Sun-Glow Rope-Handled Tea Bell, unmarked, 6¼"
4. Sun-Glow Tea Bell, unmarked, 6½"
5. Sun-Glow Rope-Handled Tea Bell, unmarked, 6¼"

PLATE 72
Row 1: 1. Cornucopia, 8½"-96
Row 2: 1. Iron Wall Pocket, unmarked, 6" (listed as No. 83)
2. Basket, 84, 6¼"
3. Ewer, 90-5½"
Row 3: 1. Jug Wall Pocket, 81, 5½"
2. Hanging Basket, 99-6"
3. Vase, 89-5½"
Row 4: 1. Vase, 94-8"
2. Covered Casserole, 51-7½"
3. Vase, 95-8½"

PLATE 71

PLATE 72

181

Bow-Knot

PRODUCTION DATES: 1949-1950

COMPANY'S USUAL MODE OF MARKING:

Bow-Knot carried an incised print Hull Art, U.S.A., "B" series mold number and size identification. The line was additionally marked with the round black Potter-at-Wheel foil label which had silver, gold or gray lettering.

DESCRIPTION:

Embossed floral in duo-tone matte finished pastel body colors of blue to pink or turquoise to blue combination. Twenty-nine shapes appeared in catalogue form. Add to this, another wall pocket, in square form, which was available.

A Hull Company price list dated January 1, 1949, established minimum retail prices West of the Rockies at $6.49 each for the B-29-12" Basket or console set, while the tea set retailed at $5.93 and the 10" plaque for $2.69. Wholesale prices were $3.00 each for the large basket, $2.90 for console sets, $1.50 per tea set, and $1.25 per plaque. A Bow-Knot assortment package of 14 pieces wholesaled for $102.40, while 186 pieces sold for $184.90.

PLATE 73

Row 1: 1. Vase, B-2-5"
        2. Creamer, B-21-4"
        3. Teapot, B-20-6"
        4. Covered Sugar, B-22-4"
        5. Ewer, B-1-5½"

Row 2: 1. Basket, B-25-6½"
        2. Cornucopia, B-5-7½"
        3. Vase, B-8-8½"
        4. Jardiniere, B-18-5¾"

Row 3: 1. Vase, B-4-6½"
        2. Double Cornucopia, B-13-13"
        3. Vase, B-3-6½"

Row 4: 1. Vase, B-11-10½"
        2. Basket, 8-12-10½"
        3. Vase, B-10-10½"

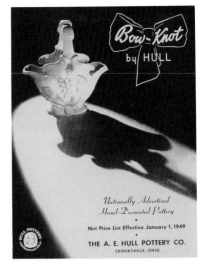

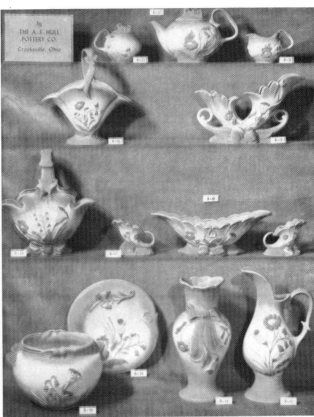

PLATE 73

Bow-Knot

PRODUCTION DATES: 1949-1950

COMPANY'S USUAL MODE OF MARKING:

Bow-Knot carried an incised print Hull Art, U.S.A., "B" series mold number and size identification. The line was additionally marked with the round black Potter-at-Wheel foil label which had silver, gold or gray lettering.

DESCRIPTION:

Embossed floral in duo-tone matte finished pastel body colors of blue to pink or turquoise to blue combination. Twenty-nine shapes appeared in catalogue form. Add to this, another wall pocket, in square form, which was available.

PLATE 74
Row 1: 1. Ewer, B-15-13½"

PLATE 75
Row 1: 1. Candle Holder, B-17, 4"
2. Console Bowl, B-16-13½"
3. Candle Holder, B-17, 4"
Row 2: 1. Pitcher Wall Pocket, B-26-6"
2. Whisk Broom Wall Pocket B-27-8"
3. Cup and Saucer Wall Pocket, B-24-6"
4. Iron Wall Pocket, unmarked, 6¼"
(listed as B-23)
Row 3: 1. Vase, B-7-8½"
2. Jardiniere, B-19-9⅜"
3. Vase, B-9-8½"
4. Flower Pot with Attached Saucer, B-6-6½"
Row 4: 1. Wall Plaque, B-28-10"
2. Basket, B-29-12"
3. Vase, B-14-12½"

184

PLATE 75

185

Woodland

PRODUCTION DATES: 1949-1950

COMPANY'S USUAL MODE OF MARKING:

Raised script Hull, USA, "W" series mold number and size identification. Woodland was also marked with the black Potter-at-Wheel foil label which had silver, gold or gray lettering.

DESCRIPTION:

Hand decorated embossed florals in matte finished duo-tones of pastel Dawn Rose or Harvest Yellow. An allover stark white high gloss ware with contrasting hand painted floral decoration was also part of the pre-1950 Woodland design. The white gloss items many times included gold detailing done outside the factory. There were thirty catalogued shapes of pre-1950 Woodland wares which were numbered one through thirty-one, with number twenty being skipped.

After the loss of glaze formulas in the fire of 1950, Hull soon had ceramic engineers experimenting with glazes, most being sub-standard to that which the market had been accustomed. Even though the molds were salvaged or reproduced, the company was unable to regain the quality of the pre-1950 Woodland glaze formulas.

PLATE 76

Row 1: 1. Ewer, W3-5½"
　　　2. Cornucopia, W10-11"
　　　3. Cornucopia, W5-6½"

Row 2: 1. Flower Pot with Attached Saucer, W11-5¾"
　　　2. Vase, W4-6½"
　　　3. Jardiniere, W7-5½"

Row 3: 1. Wall Pocket, W13-7½"
　　　2. Candle Holder, W30, 3½"
　　　3. Console Bowl, W29, 14"
　　　4. Candle Holder, W30, 3½"

Row 4: 1. Double Bud Vase, W15-8½"
　　　2. Hanging Basket, W12-7½"
　　　3. Vase, W17-7½"

Row 5: 1. Vase, W25-12½"
　　　2. Basket, W22-10½"
　　　3. Ewer, W24-13½"

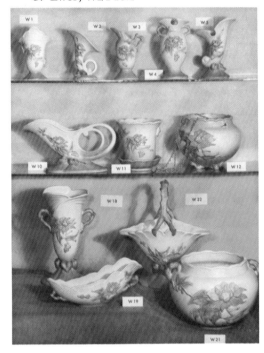

PLATE 76

Woodland

PRODUCTION DATES: 1949-1950

COMPANY'S USUAL MODE OF MARKING:

Raised script Hull, USA, "W" series mold number and size identification. Woodland was also marked with the black Potter-at-Wheel foil label which had silver, gold or gray lettering.

DESCRIPTION:

Hand decorated embossed florals in matte finished duo-tones of pastel Dawn Rose or Harvest Yellow. An allover stark white high gloss ware with contrasting hand painted floral decoration was also part of the pre-1950 Woodland design. The white gloss items many times included gold detailing done outside the factory. There were thirty catalogued shapes of pre-1950 Woodland wares which were numbered one through thirty-one, with number twenty being skipped.

PLATE 77
Row 1: 1. Ewer, W6-6½"
      2. Planter, W19-10½"
Row 2: 1. Creamer, W27, 3½"
      2. Teapot, W26, 6½"
      3. Covered Sugar, W28, 3½"
Row 3: 1. Vase, W1-5½"
      2. Vase, W8-7½"
      3. Basket, W9-8¾"
      4. Vase, W16-8½"
      5. Cornucopia, W2-5½"
Row 4: 1. Double Cornucopia, W23, 14"
      2. Vase, W18-10½"
      3. Jardiniere, W21-9½"

Created for You . . .
WOODLAND
ARTWARE BY HULL

This charming vase is one of the 30 graceful, smart pieces available in this new artware design . . . now at your favorite store in your choice of Dawn Rose and Harvest Yellow. Styled by THE A. E. HULL POTTERY CO., CROOKSVILLE, OHIO.

THE
A. E. HULL POTTERY COMPANY
CROOKSVILLE, OHIO

WOODLAND

In DAWN ROSE and HARVEST YELLOW

Net Price List Effective January 1, 1950

Nationally Advertised Hand Decorated Pottery

The Pages of the "Arabian Nights" Inspired This Gay Tea Set in
WOODLAND ARTWARE BY HULL

From the wonderful lamp of Aladdin come the graceful, flowing lines of this exquisite 3-piece Tea Set. These and 27 other exciting pieces in this new Woodland artware pattern are now available at your favorite store—each with hand-painted flowers, in your choice of two body colors. An artware creation of THE A. E. HULL POTTERY CO., CROOKSVILLE, OHIO.

PLATE 77

Pre-1950 Gloss Woodland
Pre-1950 Gloss Water Lily

PRODUCTION DATES: 1949-1950

COMPANY'S USUAL MODE OF MARKING:

PRE-1950 GLOSS WOODLAND: Raised script Hull, U.S.A., "W" series mold number and size identification.

PRE-1950 GLOSS WATER LILY: Raised print Hull Art, U.S.A., "L" series mold number and size identification.

DESCRIPTIONS:

PRE-1950 GLOSS WOODLAND

The only gloss Woodland from pre-1950 years is that which was glazed in high gloss colors of stark white, ivory or pale pink. These glazes appeared on the thirty mold shapes used before the flood and fire. Pay attention to the open floral and the side used for that floral, that's the basic key to identification of pre-1950 wares. Many of these glazed Woodland pieces have gold detailing from area artists, not unusual for these particular items.

PRE-1950 GLOSS WATER LILY

Water Lily items in high gloss colors of white, ivory or pink were made prior to the 1950 Company disaster. Glaze treatments overlapped and one glaze treatment at a glance is similar to the colorations of the Sun-Glow line. This vase has a white interior. Gloss Water Lily items typically have gold detailing which was done outside the factory.

PLATE 78

Row 1: 1. Woodland Vase, W1-5½"
      2. Woodland Jardiniere, W7-5½"
      3. Woodland Ewer, W3-5½"

Row 2: 1. Water Lily Vase, L-5-6½"
      2. Water Lily Vase, L-2-5½"
      3. Water Lily Ewer, L-3-5½"

Row 3: 1. Water Lily Creamer, L-19-5"
      2. Water Lily Teapot, L-18-6"
      3. Water Lily Covered Sugar, L-20-5"

Row 4: 1. Woodland Double Cornucopia, W23-14"
      2. Experimental Water Lily Vase, L-15-12½"
      3. Water Lily Vase, L-A-8½"

Water *Lily* TEA SET
A "HULL ART" CREATION

The three handsomely styled pieces makes this a delightful ensemble for informal entertaining moments. The embossed floral is hand-painted in natural colors . . . the body is tastefully tinted in duo-tone pastels. There are twenty-four other pieces available in this gay "Water Lily" pattern; see them at your favorite gift or department store today.

Styled by the Master Craftsmen of
THE A. E. HULL POTTERY CO.
CROOKSVILLE, OHIO

Smart—New—Styled for You . . .
WOODLAND ARTWARE BY *HULL*

This lovely double horn is just one of the 30 graceful, smart pieces of *Woodland*—now available at your favorite store. Gay hand-painted florals, in a choice of Dawn Rose or Harvest Yellow body pastels. Styled by THE A. E. HULL POTTERY CO., CROOKSVILLE, OHIO.

PLATE 78

191

Post-1950 Woodland:
Matte Woodland
Hi-Gloss Woodland
Two-Tone Woodland

PRODUCTION DATES:

Post-1950 Matte Woodland: 1951
Hi-Gloss Woodland: 1952-1954
Two-Tone Woodland: 1952-1954

COMPANY'S USUAL MODE OF MARKING:

Raised script Hull, USA, "W" series mold number and size identification.

DESCRIPTIONS:

Post-1950's items are identified first by mold use. Treatment and color glaze is secondary. One definite characteristic of the post-1950 ware is the reversal of the mold, in that the handles and decoration of the ware appeared on the opposite side from that used in earlier wares.

Matte production of Woodland in Dawn Rose and Harvest Yellow body pastels resumed after Hull's reconstruction. Most of these finishes were substandard, color was usually satisfactory, but the glaze and finish itself was coarser in most cases. After providing a short term of matte Woodland production, the company moved on to high gloss color treatments. Twenty-one shapes appeared in post-1950 Woodland wares.

Woodland's gloss finishes included several two-toned glazes such as rose and chartreuse, rose and peach, green and chartreuse, green and blue, allover green with either white or dark green interiors, and allover white or pastel pink. It is not unusual for the lighter colored items to have gold detailing done outside the factory. Glazes were first separated into the designations of Hi-Gloss Woodland and Two-Tone Woodland, but by January 1, 1954, all treatments were referred to as Hi-Gloss.

PLATE 79

Row 1: 1. Candle Holder, W30, 3½"
        2. Console Bowl, W29, 14"
        3. Candle Holder, W30, 3½"
Row 2: 1. Covered Sugar, W28, 3½"
        2. Window Box, W14, 10"
        3. Creamer, W27, 3½"
Row 3: 1. Jardiniere, W7-5½"
        2. Teapot, W26, 6½"
        3. Cornucopia, W10, 11"
Row 4: 1. Vase, W18-10½"
        2. Vase, W16-8½"
        3. Ewer, W24-13½"
        4. Basket, W9-8¾"

PLATE 79

Post-1950 Woodland:
Matte Woodland
Hi-Gloss Woodland
Two-Tone Woodland

PRODUCTION DATES:

    Matte Woodland: 1951

    HiI-Gloss Woodland: 1952-1954

    Two-Tone Woodland: 1952-1954

COMPANY'S USUAL MODE OF MARKING:

    Raised script Hull, USA, ''W'' mold number and size identification.

DESCRIPTIONS:

    Along with the matte finished wares in Dawn Rose and Harvest Yellow body pastels, there were several two-toned glazes such as rose and chartreuse, rose and peach, green and chartreuse, green and blue, allover green with either white or dark green interiors, and allover white, ivory or pastel pink. It is not unusual for the lighter colored items to have gold detailing done outside the factory.

    Remember, post 1950's wares are identified first by mold use, treatment and color glaze is secondary. One definite characteristic of the post-1950 ware is the reversal of the mold, in that the handles and decoration of the ware appeared on the opposite side from that used in earlier wares. Twenty-one shapes appeared in post-1950 Woodland wares.

PLATE 80

Row 1: 1. Ewer, W6-6½"

       2. Basket, W9-8¾"

       3. Vase, W8-7½"

       4. Ewer, W6-6½"

Row 2: 1. Teapot, W26, 6½"

       2. Vase, W8-7½"

       3. Console Bowl, W29, 14"

Row 3: 1. Ewer, W24-13½"

       2. Candle Holder, W30, 3½"

       3. Vase, W18-10½"

       4. Candle Holder, W30, 3½"

       5. Ewer, W24-13½"

The NEW HI-GLOSS *Woodland*

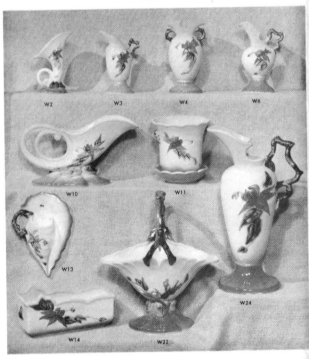

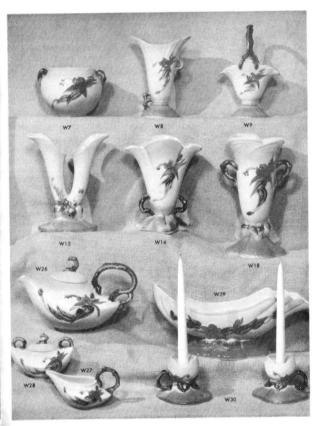

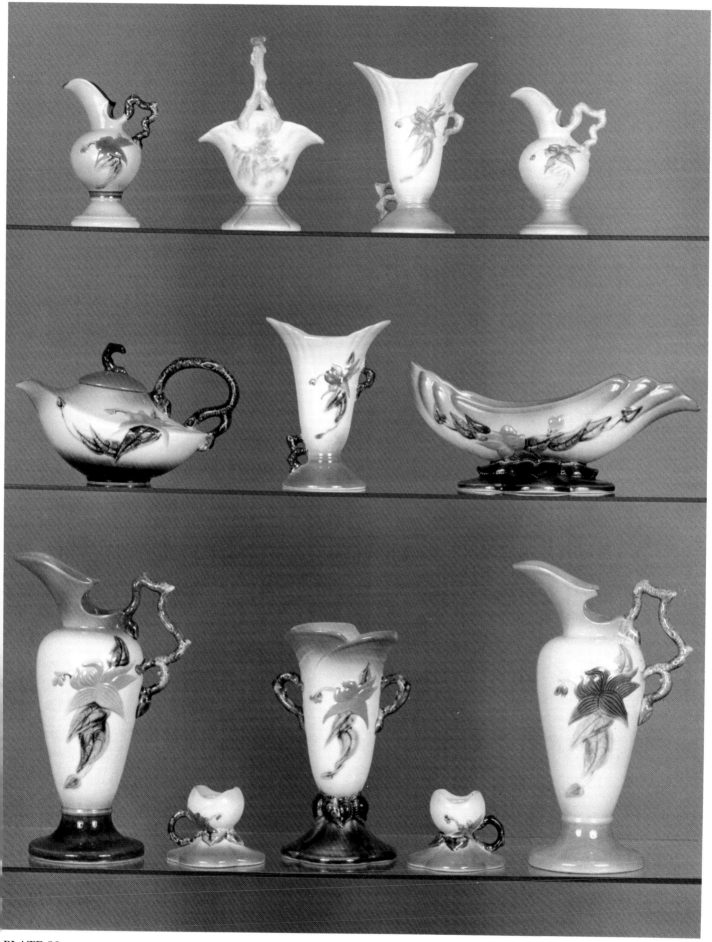

PLATE 80

Post-1950 Woodland: Matte Woodland Hi-Gloss Woodland Two-Tone Woodland

PRODUCTION DATES:
Post-1950 Matte Woodland: 1951
Hi-Gloss Woodland: 1952-1954
Two-Tone Woodland: 1952-1954

COMPANY'S USUAL MODE OF MARKING:
Raised script Hull, USA, "W" mold number and size identification.

DESCRIPTION:
Hand decorated embossed florals finished in Dawn Rose and Harvest Yellow body pastels, along with several two-toned glazes such as rose and chartreuse, rose and peach, green and chartreuse, green and blue, allover green with either white or dark green interiors, and allover white, ivory or pastel pink. It is not unusual for the lighter colored items to have gold detailing done outside the factory.

Introduced before the plant destruction, Woodland appeared in thirty catalogued shapes, numbered one through thirty-one, with number twenty being skipped. The original thirty Woodland shapes were used prior to the company's flood and fire in 1950, for both matte and high gloss finished wares. All Woodland production after the plant's destruction was limited to twenty-one shapes, again used for both matte and high gloss finished wares. The earlier Woodland molds numbered 1, 5, 12, 17, 19, 21, 23, 25, and 31 were not remolded, and were seldom used for wares after 1950. The molds which were used for post-1950 production were reversed, leaving the embossed floral on an opposite side from that used previously.

Although scarce, most Woodland lamps do not appear to be experimental, only in cases of glaze differentiation. The molds appear to have been well used.

PLATE 81
1. Experimental Woodland Lamp, unmarked, 15"

PLATE 82
Row 1: 1. Ewer, W3-5½"
2. Flower Pot with Attached Saucer, W11-5¾"
3. Vase, W8-7½"
4. Flower Pot, W31-5¾"
5. Cornucopia, W2-5½"

Row 2: 1. Vase, W4-6½"
2. Double Bud Vase, W15-8½"
3. Teapot Lamp, unmarked, 8"
4. Ewer, W6-6½"

Row 3: 1. Basket, W22-10½"
2. Free Form Lamp, unmarked, 14"
3. Experimental Ewer Lamp, incised into the clay, "M. Wilson," (Sylvanus Burdette "Mose" Wilson,) 14¾"

PLATE 81

PLATE 82

Parchment And Pine

PRODUCTION DATES: 1951-1954

COMPANY'S USUAL MODE OF MARKING:

Incised script Hull, USA, and "S" series mold number. Cornucopias carry a "L" (left) "R" (right) designation. Many pieces of this line do not carry any Hull trademark.

DESCRIPTION:

High gloss art ware with realistic embossed pine sprays, decorated in pine green and pearl gray with brown or black trim and contrasting interiors. The company illustrated fifteen catalogued shapes. Additionally offered were shapes noted as the 14" center bowl and the S15 instant coffee server. All shapes were offered through 1954, except the S14 center bowl, which was deleted from the company listing January 1, 1954.

PLATE 83

Row 1: 1. Teapot, S-11, 6"

Row 2: 1. Vase, S-1, 6"
2. Basket, S-3, 6"
3. Instant Coffee Server, S15, 8"

Row 3: 1. Basket, S-8, 16½"
2. Ewer, S-7, 14¼"

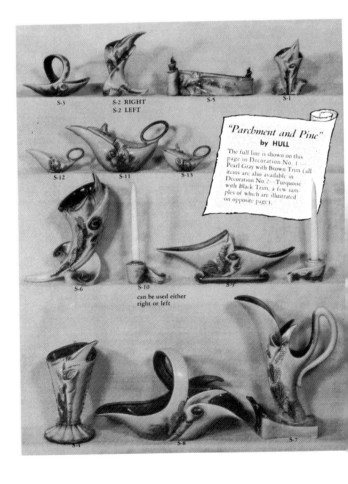

 Hull Pottery Co. • Crooksville, Ohio

198

PLATE 83

Parchment And Pine

PRODUCTION DATES: 1951-1954

COMPANY'S USUAL MODE OF MARKING:

Incised script Hull, USA, and "S" series mold number. Cornucopias carry a "L" (left) "R" (right) designation. Many pieces of this line do not carry a Hull trademark.

DESCRIPTION:

High gloss art ware with realistic embossed pine sprays, decorated in pine green and pearl gray with brown or black trim and contrasting interiors. The company illustrated fifteen catalogued shapes. Additionally offered were shapes noted as the 14" center bowl and the S15 instant coffee server. All shapes were offered through 1954, except the S14 center bowl, which was deleted from the company listing January 1, 1954.

PLATE 84

Row 1: 1. Candle Holder, S-10, 5"
2. Console Bowl, S-9, 16"
3. Candle Holder, S-10, 5"

Row 2: 1. Cornucopia, S-2-L, 7¾"
2. Window Box, S-5, 10½"
3. Cornucopia, S-2-R, 7¾"

Row 3: 1. Center Bowl, S-14, 14"
2. Vase, S-4 10"

This photograph, taken about 1952, shows the interior of the company's enclosed shelving unit in the plant's conference room. The company kept this area packed with wares of current production to entice customers who came to the factory site.

PLATE 84

Ebb Tide

PRODUCTION DATE: 1955

COMPANY'S USUAL MODE OF MARKING:

Incised script Hull, USA, "E" series mold number and size identification.

DESCRIPTION:

Embossed fish and sea shell designs in high gloss colors of Seaweed and Wine (chartreuse and wine), or Shrimp and Turquoise. Gold detailing was not uncommon but was done outside the factory. There were sixteen catalogued shapes in the Ebb Tide line.

PLATE 85
Row 1: 1. Teapot, E-14, 6½"
Row 2: 1. Basket, E-11, 16½"
Row 3: 1. Cornucopia, E-9, 11¾"
       2. Ewer, E-10, 14"

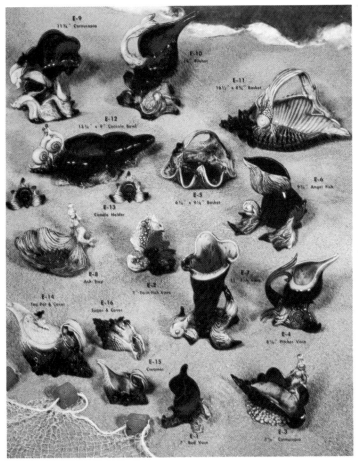

HULL POTTERY CO. Crooksville, Ohio

202

PLATE 85

Ebb Tide

PRODUCTION DATE: 1955

COMPANY'S USUAL MODE OF MARKING:

Incised script Hull, USA, "E" series mold number and size identification.

DESCRIPTION:

Embossed fish and sea shell designs in high gloss colors of Seaweed and Wine (chartreuse and wine), or Shrimp and Turquoise. Gold detailing was not uncommon but was done outside the factory. There were sixteen catalogued shapes in the Ebb Tide line.

Described in company literature, "Up from the sea comes the inspiration for Hull's newest, colorful, complete line of art pottery. In Ebb Tide, the shapes that inhabit the seas ... shells, coral, fish, and plants ... set the motif. Hull has captured them, in glowing colors, and fashioned them into art pottery of great beauty."

PLATE 86
Row 1: 1. Creamer, E-15, 4"
       2. Teapot, E-14, 6½"
       3. Covered Sugar, E-16, 4"
Row 2: 1. Basket, E-5, 6¼"
       2. Ashtray, E-8, 5"
Row 3: 1. Candle Holder, E-13, 2¾"
       2. Console Bowl, E-12, 15¾"
       3. Candle Holder, E-13, 2¾"
       4. Vase, E-6, 9¼"

Gene Whitlatch's display space at the 1958 Columbus, Ohio, State Fair is virtually packed with Hull wares. Items being sold included Serenade, Tokay, Fiesta, Fantasy, Corky pig banks and more. All items are of Hull production, with the exception of the small items in the foreground.

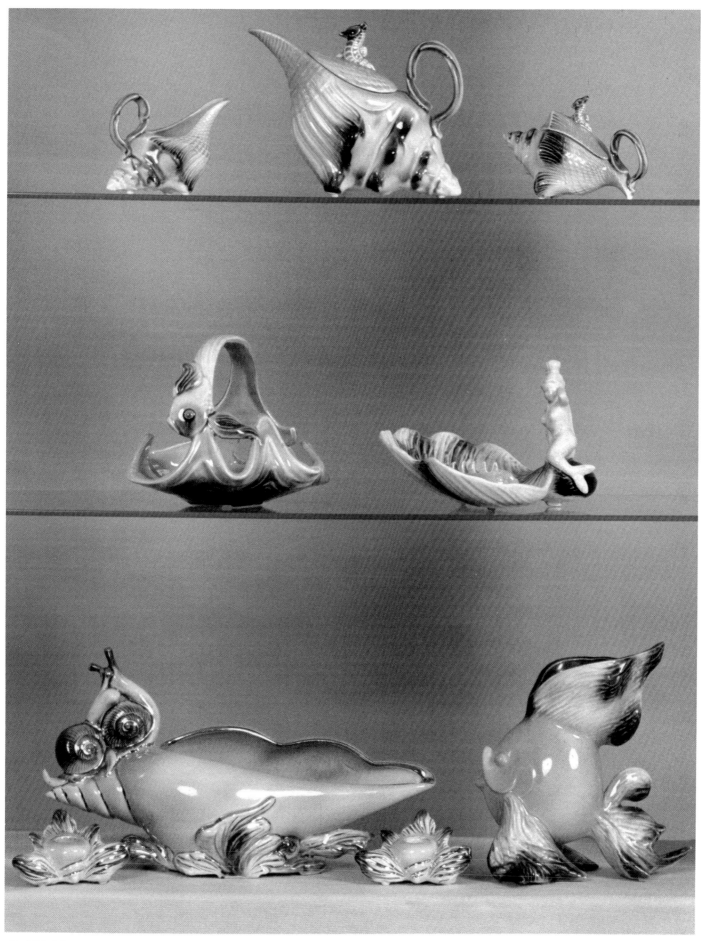

PLATE 86

Blossom Flite

PRODUCTION DATES: 1955-1956

COMPANY'S USUAL MODE OF MARKING:

Incised script Hull, USA, "T" series mold number and size identification.

DESCRIPTION:

Glaze treatments included charcoal gray on overall high gloss pink with pink interior, or blue on overall high gloss pink with metallic green interior. A multicolored relief spray of florals decorated this line of fifteen pieces.

Some of these molds can be found in transitional stages, i.e., with different placement or numbers of blossoms. These and additional pieces not catalogued represent experimental items. There were several experimental glazes considered for this line, and according to company literature, this new concept of "enchanting art pottery presents a distinctive new rendering, yet stays within the bounds of the vastly popular floral theme."

Company advertising described the embossed decor as, "a windblown pattern with blossoms of various colors." "As a summer storm subsides, the land is flooded with the rosy light of the reappearing sun, and a final gust of wind detaches flower petals from their stems to fill the air with form and color. This magic, fleeting moment in nature has been captured permanently by Hull to set the theme for Blossom Flite."

Company literature on this line additionally advertises the company's 50th anniversary, 1905-1955.

PLATE 87

Row 1: 1. Honey Pot, T1, 6"
2. Teapot, T14, 8"
3. Basket, T2, 6"

Row 2: 1. Candle Holder, T11, 3"
2. Console Bowl, T10, 16½"
3. Candle Holder, T11, 3"

Row 3: 1. Basket Vase, T4, 8½"
2. Cornucopia, T6, 10½"
3. Planter Flower Bowl, T12, 10½"

Row 4: 1. Ewer, T13, 13½"
2. Handled Low Bowl, T9, 10"
3. Ewer, T13, 13½"

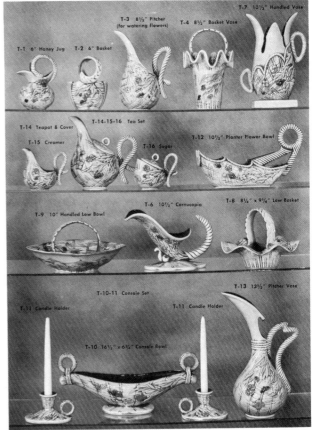

Hull Pottery Company - - Crooksville, Ohio

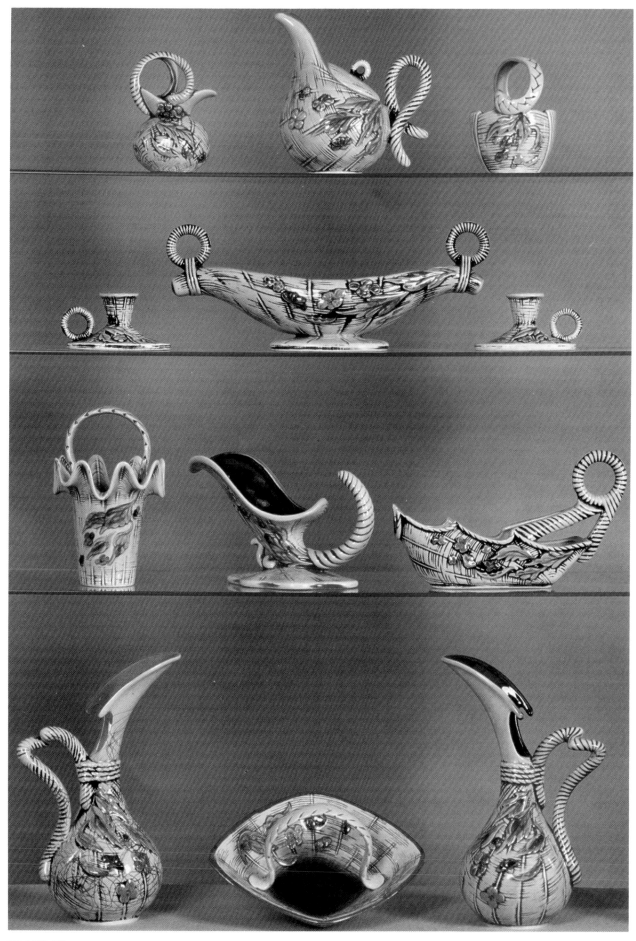

PLATE 87

Butterfly

PRODUCTION DATE: 1956

COMPANY'S USUAL MODE OF MARKING:

Incised script Hull, USA, impressed © 56, and "B" series mold number. Sizes do not appear on the molds. The round black foil "Potter-at-Wheel" label was used for this ware.

DESCRIPTION:

Original company description: "Raised pastel butterfly and flower motif in a combined gloss and matte finish of white on white, or matte transparent white with turquoise inner surfaces." Gold detailing was not uncommon but was done outside the factory. There were twenty-five catalogued items in the Butterfly line.

PLATE 88

Row 1: 1. Lavabo, B-24 & B25, in original hanger, 16"
Row 2: 1. Jardiniere, B5, 6"
      2. Vase, B10, 7"
Row 3: 1. Candle Holder, B22, 2½"
      2. Candle Holder, B22, 2½"
      3. Ashtray, B3, 7"
      4. Cornucopia, B2, 6½"
Row 4: 1. Cornucopia, B12, 10½"
      2. Serving Dish, B23, 11½"
      3. Ewer, B15, 13½"

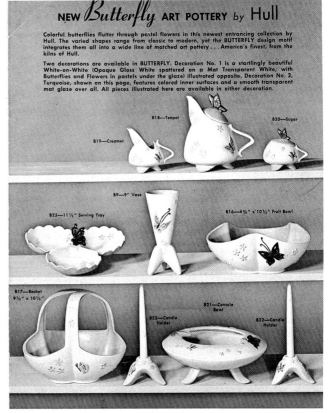

Hull Pottery Company - - Crooksville, Ohio

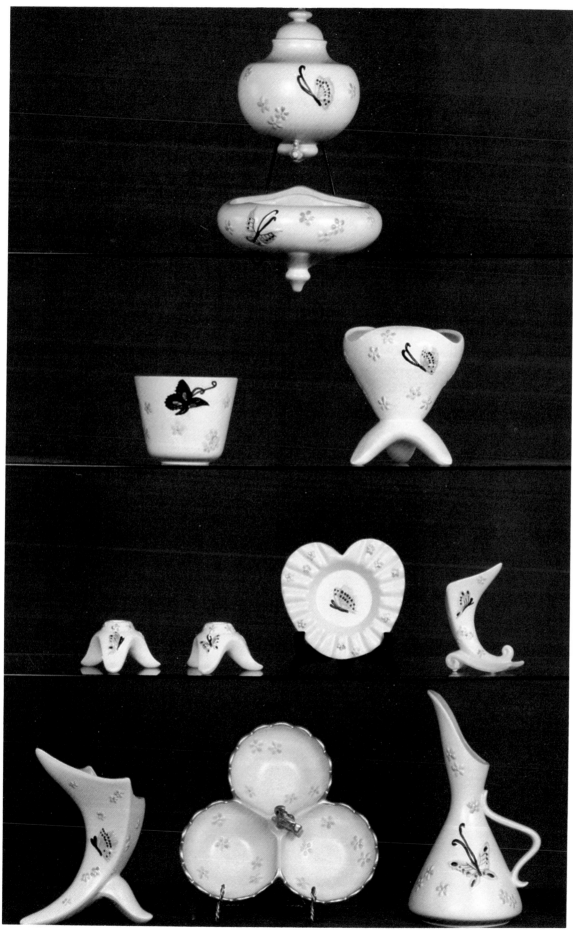

PLATE 88

Butterfly

PRODUCTION DATE: 1956
COMPANY'S USUAL MODE OF MARKING:

Incised script Hull, USA, impressed © 56, and "B" series mold number. Sizes do not appear on the molds. The round black foil "Potter-at-Wheel" label was used for this ware.

DESCRIPTION:

This design featured an embossed butterfly and flower motif in a combined gloss and matte finish of white on white, or matte transparent white with turquoise inner surfaces. Gold detailing was not uncommon but was not done in the factory. There were twenty-five catalogued items in the Butterfly line.

In the mid-1950's, Hull noticed there to be a tendency toward pottery items with brass and wrought iron stands. The introduction of such wares was a general trend, started on the West Coast, and believed by J. B. Hull to be a continuing craze, moving from West to East. Hull joined the bandwagon and produced a volume of wares with metal accessories from mid-1950 through early 1960. Items included jardinieres, ashtrays, planter with ashtray combinations, lavabos, and more. As shown in the following company information, Hull advertised them as "Red Hot, Year Around Sellers!"

PLATE 89
Row 1: 1. Creamer, B19, 5"
2. Teapot, B18, 8½"
3. Covered Sugar, B20, 5"
Row 2: 1. Basket, B-13, 8"
2. Basket, B17, 10½"
3. Ewer, B11, 8¾"
Row 3: 1. Vase, B14, 10½"
2. Console Bowl, B21, 10"

Red Hot . . .
Year Around Sellers!

G 8
Contemporary 10" Jardiniere
with Brass Stand
21" High

M 30 W
Classic 8" Jardiniere
with Brass Stand
15" High

K 30 W
Classic 6" Jardiniere
with Brass Stand
7½" High

O 75 W
Lantern 7" Jardiniere
with Brass Stand
19" High

(See your listing for prices and packages).

- Sell them for use on porch or patio!
- Sell them for use as cemetery urns!
- Sell them for use in living room!
- Sell them for use as ice bucket!
- Sell them for use wherever smart containers for plants or flowers are desired!

High Fashion

HULL POTTERY COMPANY   : :   Crooksville, Ohio

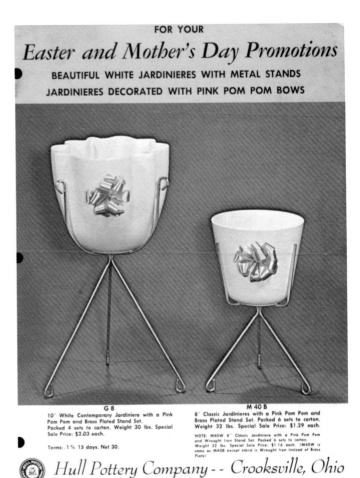

FOR YOUR
Easter and Mother's Day Promotions
BEAUTIFUL WHITE JARDINIERES WITH METAL STANDS
JARDINIERES DECORATED WITH PINK POM POM BOWS

G 8
10" White Contemporary Jardiniere with a Pink Pom Pom and Brass Plated Stand Set. Packed 4 sets to carton. Weight 30 lbs. Special Sale Price: $2.03 each.

Terms: 1 % 15 days. Net 30.

M 40 B
8" Classic Jardinieres with a Pink Pom Pom and Brass Plated Stand Set. Packed 6 sets to carton. Weight 32 lbs. Special Sale Price: $1.29 each.

NOTE: M40W 8" Classic Jardiniere with a Pink Pom Pom and Wrought Iron Stand Set. Packed 6 sets to carton. Weight 32 lbs. Special Sale Price: $1.16 each. (M40W is same as M40B except stand is Wrought Iron instead of Brass Plate!)

Hull Pottery Company -- Crooksville, Ohio

PLATE 89

Royal Ebb Tide
Royal Imperial
Royal Woodland

PRODUCTION DATES: 1955-1957

COMPANY'S USUAL MODE OF MARKING:

Raised or incised script Hull, USA, carrying mold numbers and size identifications of the molds shared with Woodland, Ebb Tide and Imperial lines. Since these pieces were designed for chain store sales, many carried no Hull trademark unless the trademark was already an existing part of the mold the ware shared with its previous owner.

DESCRIPTION:

Royal is characterized by its high gloss pink or turquoise glazes with an overall white spattered decoration. Air brushed charcoal gray appears on handles, lids and bands. The Hull Company noted this as their "W & E Line," (Woodland and Ebb Tide,) in pink or turquoise "Mist," edged with Dove Gray.

The chain store assortments included novelties as well as the Woodland and Ebb Tide mold shapes. The company brochure page illustrated shows one such assortment also included the St. Francis Planter.

PLATE 90

Row 1: 1. Royal Woodland Cornucopia, W10-11"

Row 2: 1. Royal Woodland Candle Holder, W30, 3½"
2. Royal Woodland Console Bowl, W29, 14"
3. Royal Woodland Candle Holder, W30, 3½"

Row 3: 1. Royal Woodland Wall Pocket, W13-7½"
2. Royal Imperial Jardiniere, 75-7"
3. Royal Woodland Vase, W4-6½"

Row 4: 1. Royal Lazy Susan, sections marked No. 81, center bowl marked No. 83, 18" overall
2. Royal Woodland Ewer, W24-13½"

Hull Pottery Company - - Crooksville, Ohio

146—Printed in U.S.A.

PLATE 90

Royal Butterfly
Royal Ebb Tide
Royal Imperial
Royal Woodland

PRODUCTION DATES: 1955-1957

COMPANY'S USUAL MODE OF MARKING:

Raised or incised script Hull, USA, carrying mold numbers and size identifications of the molds shared with Butterfly, Woodland, Ebb Tide and Imperial. Since these pieces were designed for chain store sales, many carried no Hull trademark unless the trademark was already an existing part of the mold the ware shared with its previous owner.

DESCRIPTION:

Royal is characterized by its high gloss pink and turquoise glazes with an overall white spattered decoration. Air brushed charcoal gray appears on handles, lids and bands. The Hull Company noted this as their "W & E Line," (Woodland and Ebb Tide,) in pink or turquoise "Mist," edged with Dove Gray.

Royal items were additionally offered with metal accessories as illustrated by this Hull Company brochure. Shown are lantern jardinieres, classic straight-lined jardinieres in single, double and triple stands, along with a lavabo set.

PLATE 91

Row 1: 1. Royal Butterfly Lavabo, 86, 87, original hanger, 16"

Row 2: 1. Royal Imperial Window Box, 82, 12½"
2. Royal Woodland Basket, W9-8¾"

Row 3: 1. Royal Ebb Tide Vase, unmarked, 7"
2. Royal Imperial Urn, unmarked, 5¾"
3. Royal Ebb Tide Bud Vase, E1, 7"

Row 4: 1. Royal Woodland Vase, W18, 10¾"
2. Royal Woodland Basket, W22, 10½"
3. Royal Ebb Tide Vase, unmarked, 10¾"

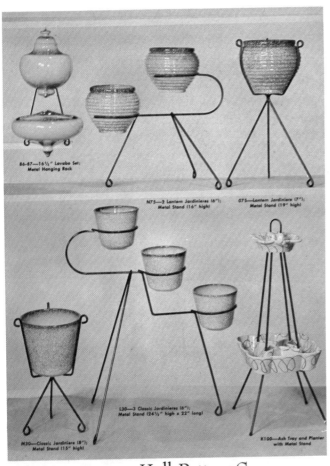

NEW Hull Pottery WITH METAL ACCESSORIES

86-87—16½" Lavabo Set; Metal Hanging Rack

N75—2 Lantern Jardinieres (6"); Metal Stand (16" high)

075—Lantern Jardiniere (7"); Metal Stand (19" high)

L30—3 Classic Jardinieres (6"); Metal Stand (24½" high x 22" long)

M30—Classic Jardiniere (8"); Metal Stand (15" high)

K100—Ash Tray and Planter with Metal Stand

26—Printed in U. S. A.

Hull Pottery Co. CROOKSVILLE, OI

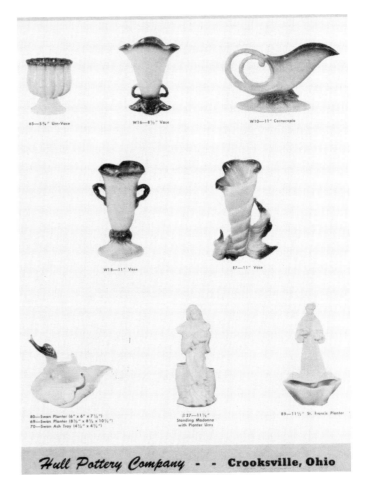

65—5¾" Urn-Vase

W16—8½" Vase

W10—11" Cornucopia

W18—11" Vase

E7—11" Vase

80—Swan Planter (6" x 6" x 7½")
69—Swan Planter (8½" x 8½ x 10½")
70—Swan Ash Tray (4½" x 4½")

#27—11½" Standing Madonna with Planter Urns

89—11½" St. Francis Planter

Hull Pottery Company - - Crooksville, Ohio

PLATE 91

Serenade

PRODUCTION DATE: 1957

COMPANY'S USUAL MODE OF MARKING:

Incised script Hull, USA, © 57, and "S" series mold number.

DESCRIPTION:

The Serenade line incorporated an embossed bough and chickadee decoration. Solid pastel colors included textured matte Regency Blue with Sunlight Yellow gloss interior, textured matte Shell Pink with Pearl Gray gloss interior and textured matte Jonquil Yellow with Willow Green gloss interior. Serenade included twenty-four catalogued shapes.

Items from the Serenade molds were additionally produced in solid textured pastel colors without further decoration of the embossed design. These items are not uncommon, and represent a separate line for chain store sales.

PLATE 92

Row 1: 1. Fruit Bowl, S15, 7"
      2. Ewer, S2, 6½"

Row 2: 1. Bud Vase, S1, 6½"
      2. Teapot, S17, 5"
      3. Vase, S-6, 8½"

Row 3: 1. Covered Casserole, S20, 9"
      2. Puritan Vase, S4, 5¼"

Row 4: 1. Vase, S11, 10½"
      2. Basket, S14, 12"
      3. Vase, S11, 10½"

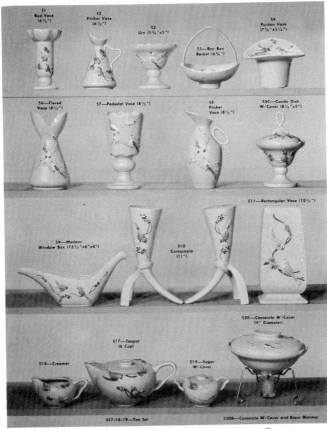

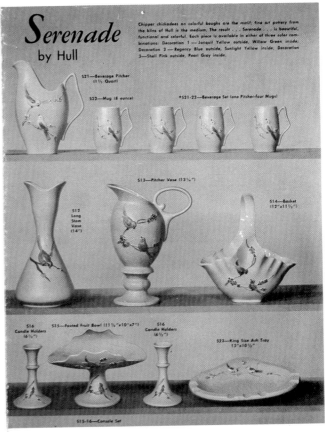

Hull Pottery Company - - Crooksville, Ohio

PLATE 92

217

Serenade

PRODUCTION DATE: 1957

COMPANY'S USUAL MODE OF MARKING:

Impressed script Hull, USA, © 57, and "S" series mold number.

DESCRIPTION:

The Serenade line incorporated an embossed bough and chickadee decoration. Solid pastel colors included textured matte Regency Blue with Sunlight Yellow gloss interior, textured matte Shell Pink with Pearl Gray gloss interior and textured matte Jonquil Yellow with Willow Green gloss interior. Serenade included twenty-four catalogued shapes.

Items from the Serenade molds were additionally produced in solid textured pastel colors without further decoration of the embossed design. These items are not uncommon and represent a separate line for chain store sales.

The Company brochure illustrated is from the line referred to as Sun Valley Pastels, produced in 1956 and 1957. The seventeen piece chain store assortment had eleven items which were offered in satin finished pink with high gloss gray interior, or satin finished turquoise with high gloss yellow interior. An additional seven items were offered in satin exterior finishes of pink, willow green and white. Retailers selected assortments which suited their own needs, and may or may not have included all items. McCrory Stores Corp. included all seventeen Sun Valley Pastel items in their assortment.

PLATE 93

Row 1: 1. Candle Holder, S16, 6½"
2. Candle Holder, S16, 6½"
3. Window Box, S9, 12½"

Row 2: 1. Beverage Pitcher, S21, 10½"
2. Candy Dish, S3, 8¼"
3. Cornucopia, S10, 11"

Row 3: 1. Basket, S5, 6¾"
2. Mug, S22, 5½"
3. Basket, S5, 6¾"

Row 4: 1. Vase, S12, 14"
2. Ashtray, S23, 13"
3. Ewer, S13, 13¼"

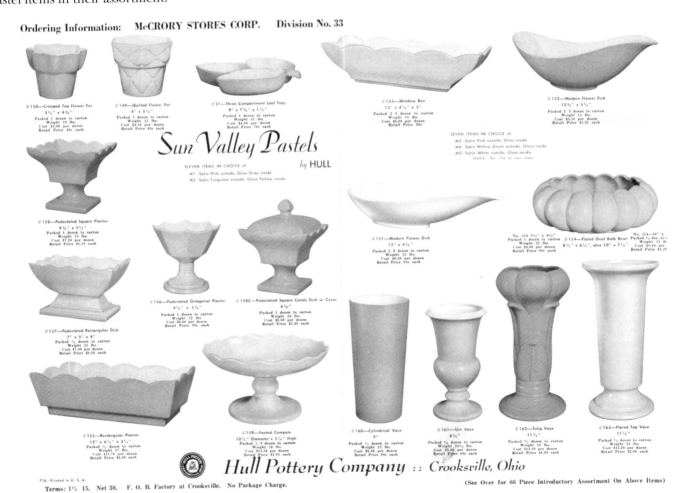

PLATE 93

Tokay And Tuscany

PRODUCTION DATES:

Tokay: Both Color Combinations: 1958

Tuscany: Both Color Combinations: 1958

Tokay and Tuscany: Milk White and Forest Green: 1958-1960

COMPANY'S USUAL MODE OF MARKING:

TOKAY: Molds bear an incised script "Tokay" signet, USA and mold number. The Hull name was not included on the Tokay mold.

TUSCANY: Incised script Hull, USA and mold number. Items were commonly unmarked.

DESCRIPTIONS:

TOKAY: Embossed leaf and grape decor in allover high gloss background of Milk White with Forest Green grapes and leaves, or high gloss duo-toned spray tinted Light Green and Sweet Pink with pink grapes and green leaves. Eighteen shapes were catalogued.

TUSCANY: Embossed leaf and grape decor in allover high gloss backgrounds of Milk White or Sweet Pink, each with green grapes and leaves. Eighteen shapes were initially catalogued.

Additional items to the Tokay/Tuscany line included the 14" leaf dish, a 10" pedestaled vase, a 15½" pedestaled vase, and a 14" ewer.

PLATE 94

Row 1: 1. Covered Sugar, No. 18, 3¼"
2. Consolette, No. 14, 15¾"
3. Creamer, No. 17, 3¼"

Row 2: 1. Basket, No. 6, 8"
2. Vase, No. 8, 10"
3. Cornucopia, No. 10, 11"

Row 3: 1. Covered Candy Dish, No. 9, 8½"
2. Leaf Dish, No. 19, 14"
3. Urn, No. 5, 5½"

Row 4: 1. Ewer, No. 13, 12"
2. Moon Basket, No. 11, 10½"
3. Vase, No. 12, 12"
4. Ewer, 21, 14"

PLATE 94

Tokay And Tuscany

PRODUCTION DATES:

Tokay: Both Color Combinations: 1958

Tuscany: Both Color Combinations: 1958

Tokay and Tuscany: Milk White and Forest Green: 1958-1960

COMPANY'S USUAL MODE OF MARKING:

TOKAY: Molds bear incised script "Tokay" signet, USA and mold number. The Hull name was not included on the Tokay mold.

TUSCANY: Incised script Hull, USA and mold number. Items were commonly unmarked.

DESCRIPTIONS:

TOKAY: Embossed leaf and grape decor in allover high gloss background of Milk White with Forest Green grapes and leaves, or high gloss duo-toned spray tinted Light Green and Sweet Pink with pink grapes and green leaves. Eighteen shapes were catalogued.

TUSCANY: Embossed leaf and grape decor in allover high gloss backgrounds of Milk White or Sweet Pink, each with green grapes and leaves. Eighteen shapes were initially catalogued.

Additional items to the Tokay/Tuscany line included the 14" leaf dish, a 10" pedestaled vase, a 15½" pedestaled vase, and a 14" ewer.

PLATE 95

Row 1: 1. Basket, No. 6, 8"
2. Basket, No. 15, 12"
3. Ewer, No. 3, 8"

Row 2: 1. Cornucopia, No. 10, 11"
2. Planter, No. 9, 8"
3. Fruit Bowl, No. 7, 9½"
4. Ewer, No. 3, 8"

Row 3: 1. Vase, No. 8, 10"
2. Moon Basket, No. 11, 10½"
3. Vase, No. 4, 8¼"

Row 4: 1. Ewer, unmarked, 15"
2. Leaf Dish, No. 19, 14"
3. Ewer, No. 13, 12"

NEW! additions to "TUSCANY" pattern by HULL

All three shapes available in Pink or Milk White with embossed motif in fashionable green.

Hull Pottery Company
CROOKSVILLE, OHIO

"TUSCANY" pattern by HULL

No. 1—Cornucopia 6½" (Reversible) — No. 2—2-Handled Vase 6" — No. 3—Pitcher Vase 8" — No. 4—2-Handled Vase 8¼" — No. 5—Urn 5½" x 5½"

No. 6—Basket 8" — No. 7—Fruit Bowl 9½" — No. 8—2-Handled Vase 10" — No. 9—Planter 5½" x 6½", No. 9C—Candy Dish W/Cover 7" x 8½"

No. 10—Cornucopia 11" (Reversible) — No. 11—Moon Basket 10½" — No. 12—2-Handled Spool Vase 12" — No. 13—Pitcher Vase 12"

No. 14—Consolette 13½" — No. 15—Basket 12" — No. 17—Creamer, No. 16—Teapot, No. 18—Sugar W/Cover, Nos. 16-17-18—3 pc. Tea Set

Hull Pottery Company -- Crooksville, Ohio

TUSCANY, known as the Garden of Italy, is the inspiration for this beautiful expression of the potters art. Ornamented in relief with grapes and leaves from the valley of the silver Arno, bringing the peasant art of Italy to the homes of America.

DECORATION 1—Sweet Pink with embossed grapes and leaves in fashionable Gray-Green.

DECORATION 2—Milk White with embossed grapes and leaves in cool Forest Green.

PLATE 95

Tropicana

PRODUCTION DATE: 1959

COMPANY'S USUAL MODE OF MARKING:

Incised script Hull, USA and "T" series mold number.

DESCRIPTION:

High gloss white background with colorful Caribbean figures, edged in Tropic Green. The company offered seven catalogued shapes.

PLATE 97

Row 1: 1. Flower Bowl, T51, 15½"

Row 2: 1. Slender Vase, T54, 12½"
      2. Flat-Sided Vase, T53, 8½"
      3. Ewer, T56, 12½"

Row 3: 1. Fancy Basket, T55, 12¾"
      2. Planter Vase, T57, 14½"
      3. Fancy Basket, T55, 12¾"

PLATE 96
Row : 1. Ashtray, T52, 10"

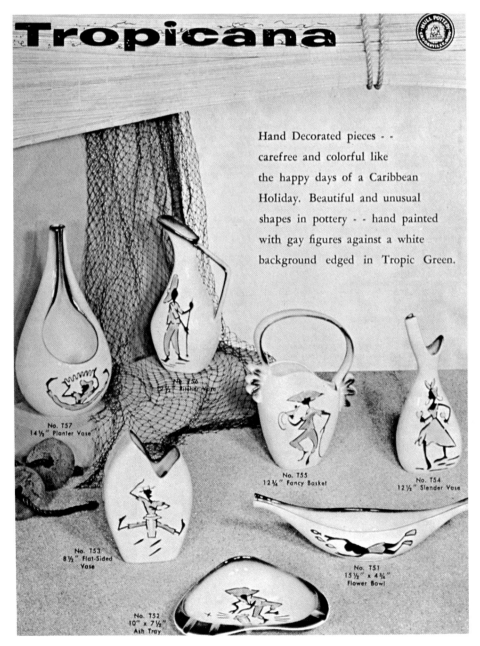

224

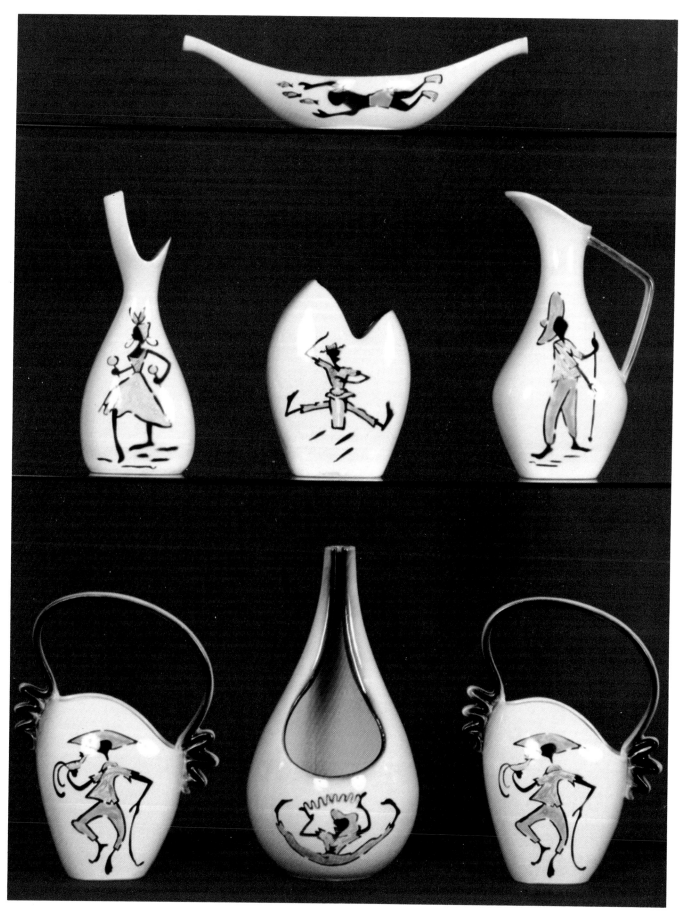

PLATE 97

225

Continental

PRODUCTION DATES: 1959-1960

COMPANY'S USUAL MODE OF MARKING:

Incised script Hull, USA, with a ''50'' series mold identification number and the © 59 designation. Many items did not carry the Hull trademark.

DESCRIPTION:

Modern shapes in brilliant high gloss colors of Evergreen, Persimmon and Mountain Blue with contrasting vertical stripes or ''run.'' Items with Evergreen and Mountain Blue glazes were decorated with contrasting white stripes, while Persimmon glazed items were striped in yellow. There were a total of twenty-six catalogued items. It is typical that some of these very bright shades vary in intensity.

The Continental line, first introduced in 1959, consisted of fourteen items in ''two strikingly lucid colors from nature ... accented with rich, bold stripes.'' Initial colors were Persimmon, ''the completely captivating accent for today's interiors in the higher key of contemporary color,'' and Evergreen, ''a delightfully subtle color that lends itself as a perfect foil to nature's own brilliant floral and leaf displays.''

The Continental line later included additional sophisticated, modern shapes which were offered in the earlier mentioned colors, along with a third color, Mountain Blue with white haze. Added items were ashtrays: A1, A3, A20, and A40; Vases C28, C29, C64, C66, and console pieces C67, C68, C69 and C70.

PLATE 98

Row 1: 1. Vase, 53, 8½"
Row 2: 1. Candle Holder/Planter, 67, 4"
       2. Flower Dish, 51, 15½"
       3. Candle Holder/Planter, 67, 4"
Row 3: 1. Ewer, 56, 12½"
       2. Basket, 55, 12¾"
       3. Bud Vase, 66, 9½"
Row 4: 1. Bud Vase, 66, 9½"
       2. Bud Vase, 66, 9½"
       3. Basket, 55, 12¾"
       4. Ewer, 56, 12½"

New **Continental**

Sophisticated, Modern Shapes In Three Delightful Decorator Colors.

MOUNTAIN BLUE   Imagine twilight in the Blue Mountains— modernized with stripes of white haze.

Hull Pottery Company -- Crooksville, Ohio

Continental

PERSIMMON -- the completely captivating accent for today's interiors in the higher key of contemporary color.

Hull Pottery Company -- Crooksville, Ohio

Lovely natural colors --- accented with rich, bold stripes

EVERGREEN -- a delightfully subtle color that lends itself as a perfect foil to nature's own brilliant floral and leaf displays.

Continental --- beauty that comes from expert craftsmanship, modern designs and finest glazes.

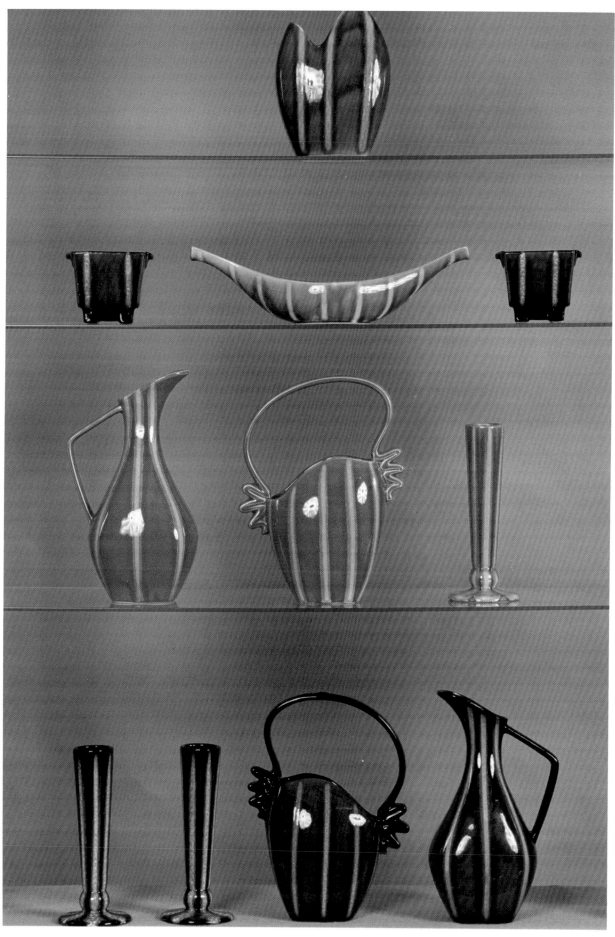

PLATE 98

Continental
Pagoda

PRODUCTION DATES:

Continental: 1959-1960

Pagoda: 1960

COMPANY'S USUAL MODE OF MARKING:

CONTINENTAL: Incised script Hull, USA, with a "50" series mold identification number and the © 59 designation. Many items did not carry the Hull trademark.

PAGODA: Incised script Pagoda, along with a "P" series mold number and USA.

DESCRIPTIONS:

CONTINENTAL: Modern shapes in brilliant high gloss colors of Evergreen, Persimmon and Mountain Blue with contrasting vertical stripes or "run." A total of twenty-six items were catalogued.

PAGODA: Plain jardinieres, flower bowls and vases with a distinct Oriental flair, offered in three high gloss solid glazes; persimmon or green with black trim and white with gray trim. The company catalogued twelve shapes.

PLATE 99

Row 1: 1. Continental Ashtray, 52, 10¼"
        2. Continental Ashtray, A-1, 7¾"
        3. Continental Ashtray, 52, 10¼"

Row 2: 1. Pagoda Vase, P3, 7¾"
        2. Pagoda Vase, P4, 10"
        3. Experimental Pagoda Vase, glazed in cobalt blue, unmarked, 7¾"

Row 3: 1. Pagoda Vase, P5, 12½"
        2. Continental Ashtray, A-4, 13"
        3. Pagoda Vase, P5, 12½"

No.	SIZE and DESCRIPTION
P1	6½" x 3¾" x 3¾" Footed Dish Garden
P2	10" x 6¾" x 2½" Low Flower Bowl
P3	7½" Hexagonal Vase
P4	10" Hexagonal Vase
P5	12" Hexagonal Vase
P6	15" Hexagonal Vase
P7	6" Hexagonal Jardiniere
P8	10" Hexagonal Jardiniere
P9	11½" Hexagonal Jardiniere
P10	6" Hexagonal Pot with Saucer Attached
P11	10" Hexagonal Pot with Saucer Attached
P12	11½" Hexagonal Pot with Saucer Attached

Choice of Colors   A—White with Gray Trim
                    B—Green with Black Trim
                    C—Persimmon with Black Trim

Oriental in Style

HULL *Pagoda* WARE

Hull Pottery Company -- Crooksville, Ohio

228

PLATE 99

Capri
Imperial Golden Mist

PRODUCTION DATES:

Capri: 1961

Imperial Golden Mist: 1967

COMPANY'S USUAL MODE OF MARKING:

Capri was marked with incised script Hull, USA, while Imperial items were usually marked with an incised lower case "hull", USA. It is not uncommon to find items of either line unmarked.

DESCRIPTION:

CAPRI: Original Company description: "Satin finished bowls and planters in Coral with weathered limestone effect, or Seagreen to represent sea-washed rock formations." The Capri line consisted of thirty shapes.

IMPERIAL: The Imperial items illustrated with Capri are decorated in what Hull referred to as "Golden Mist." While items from the Imperial brochure page are all inviting, the items glazed in "Golden Mist" have a special mystic.

PLATE 100

Row 1: 1. Capri Swan, 23, 8½"

Row 2: 1. Imperial Golden Mist Chickadee Planter, F473, 6"

2. Capri Leaf Basket, 48, 12¼"

3. Imperial Golden Mist Praying Hands Planter, F475, 6"

Row 3: 1. Capri Ewer, 87, 12"

2. Capri Covered Candy, unmarked, 8½"

3. Imperial Golden Mist Eagle Flower Bowl, 5¾"

4. Imperial Golden Mist Swirl Ewer, F480, 10¾"

Row 4: 1. Imperial Golden Mist Gurgling Fish Ewer, F482, 11"

2. Capri Vase, 58, 13¾"

3. Capri Lion Head Urn Vase, 50, 9"

PLATE 100

Novelty

PRODUCTION DATES: 1951-1954

COMPANY'S USUAL MODE OF MARKING:

Marks most commonly used for items illustrated included incised script Hull, USA, and incised script Regal, USA.

DESCRIPTION:

Hull's striking high gloss dark green and wine combinations included a wide variety of figural shapes and designs. Although some novelty items were in production for several years, most can be accurately dated by their color treatments. "Glazes of the day," are the key to dating many of Hull's 1950's wares. By referring to the major 1950 artware line of the day and its color glazes, you will be able to identify dates for the company's miscellaneous and novelty items that were glazed in that same treatment. The bulk of novelties with chartreuse glazes and trims were produced shortly after the Company's reopening, right along with Woodland's chartreuse. The deep green tones were also characteristically used after the reopening of the plant. Some of the novelty items illustrated also reflect 1954 tones of Ebb Tide's wine glaze.

PLATE 101

Row 1: 1. Window Box, unmarked, 11"
      2. Basket, unmarked, 6"
Row 2: 1. Flying Goose Wall Pocket, 67, 6"
      2. Clover Shaped Planter, 4½"
      3. Regal Rectangular Flower Dish, 124, 10"
      4. Rectangular Vase, 116, 6"
Row 3: 1. Giraffe Planter, 115, 8"
      2. Deep Oval Flower Bowl, unmarked, 10"
      3. French Poodle Planter, 114, 8"
Row 4: 1. Bandana Duck Planter, 75, 7"
      2. Bandana Duck Planter, 74, 9"
      3. Bandana Duck Planter, 76, 3½"
      4. Bandana Duck Candle Holder, 3½"
Row 5: 1. Flying Duck Planter, 104, 8½"
      2. Low Flower Bowl, 85, 13"
      3. Bird of Paradise Flower Frog, unmarked, 10½"
      4. Suspended Vase, 110, 9¼"

Hull Pottery Co. CROOKSVILLE, OHIO

Hull Pottery Co. CROOKSVILLE, OHIO

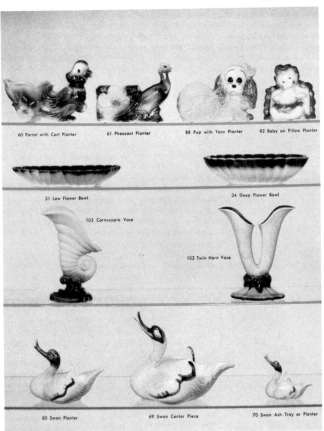

PLATE 101

233

Novelty

PRODUCTION DATES: 1951-1962

Keep in mind most of these novelty wares were in production two to three years, and dates listed refer to initial introductory dates of manufacture.

COMPANY'S USUAL MODE OF MARKING:

Although many of these novelty items were commonly distributed unmarked, those which are marked most often bear an incised script Hull, USA trademark.

The swan planters, produced from 1951 through the 1970's, were so plentiful that they became "signets" for the Hull Company, acting as Hull trademarks themselves. There were several variations of high gloss color treatments, but by 1961, the swan set was available only in Satin White. The Swan Centerpiece Planter was first introduced shortly after the reopening of the plant in 1951. The small Swan, 70, was introduced in price lists first as an ashtray. Later it was referred to as ashtray/planter.

PLATE 102

Row 1: 1. Console planter, F-3, 4", 1957
2. Mayfair Planter, 87, 10", 1958
3. Footed Planter, 410, 5", 1958

Row 2: 1. Daisy Basket, 70, 6½", 1951
2. Ribbon Wall Pocket, 71, 6", 1951
3. Kitten with Spool Planter, 89, 6", 1951
4. City Girl Planter, 90, 5½", 1951

Row 3: 1. Pig Planter, 86, 6¾", 1951
2. Medley Window Box with Metal Stand, 603, 13", 1962
3. Pup with Yarn Planter, 88, 5½", 1951

Row 4: 1. Baby with Pillow Planter, 92, 5½", 1951
2. Swan Ashtray/Planter, 70, 4", 1951
3. Swan Planter, 80, 6", 1951
4. Swan Centerpiece Planter, 69, 8½", 1951

Row 5: 1. Mayfair Leaf Dish, 86, 10", 1958
2. Jubilee, "The Duchess" Planter, 411, 12¼", 1957
3. Jubilee, "The Duchess" Ashtray/Planter, 5", 1957
4. Fantasy Vase, 71, 9", 1957

234

PLATE 102

Novelty

PRODUCTION DATES: 1951-1957

Most of the illustrated novelty wares were made for two to three years. The dates listed refer to introductory dates of manufacture.

COMPANY'S USUAL MODE OF MARKING:

While these items are commonly unmarked, wares which do have a trademark bear an incised script Hull, along with mold number and USA.

While novelty items were sometimes placed in use more than once, perhaps for different chain store lines, most can be identified by color glaze treatment. Some of these novelty items crossed over from pre-1950 lines to post-1950 lines. The Sun-Glow Flamingo No. 85 vase, first introduced in 1948, later referred to as No. 78 vase in 1951, was placed in production a third time in 1960, as No. 309 for the Regal line.

PLATE 103

Row 1: 1. Parrot with Cart Planter, 60, 6", 1951
       2. Fan Vase, 72, 8½", 1951
Row 2: 1. Jubilee Garden Dish, 402, 8½", 1957
       2. Peacock Vase, 73, 10½", 1951
       3. Jubilee Garden Dish, 401, 6¾", 1957
Row 3: 1. Jubilee Jardiniere, 425, 4", 1957
       2. Flower Dish, 81, 10", 1957
       3. Sun-Glow Flamingo Vase, 85, 8½", 1948-1949.
Row 4: 1. Unicorn Vase, 99, 11½", 1952
       2. Unicorn Vase, 98, 9½", 1952
       3. Jubilee Ashtray, 407, 11½", 1957

PLATE 103

Novelty

PRODUCTION DATES: 1951-1962

While most of the illustrated novelty wares were made for two to three years, dates listed refer to introductory dates of manufacture.

COMPANY'S USUAL MODE OF MARKING:

Items illustrated are most commonly marked with an incised script Hull trademark, mold number and USA. Urn-Vases from Imperial's "400 Series," bear the "Urn-Vase" name in incised print, along with USA.

Apparently another firm produced dachshund figurals in the 1950's. On the retail market is a molded dachshund which very closely resembles Hull's. The Hull dachshund is only slightly larger, and has the tail in a flipped-up or curved fashion. The look-alike dachshund's most conspicuous difference is a tail which curls under the back leg. Clay content on both is near same, as is weight, and colors of the look-alike dachshunds are very similar to Hull's colors of pinks, blacks and charcoals. The look-alikes even bear a slight indication of glazed over mold marks in the same position as Hull's.

PLATE 104
Row 1: 1. Caladium Leaf Dish, 14", 1957
Row 2: 1. Urn-Vase, 418, 5", 1962
　　　　2. Dachshund Planter, 14", 1952
　　　　3. Bubble Vase, 109, 9", 1952
Row 3: 1. Wishing Well Planter, 101, 7¾", 1951
　　　　2. Candle Holder, 455, 4½", 1963
　　　　3. Single Hippo Flower Frog, 83, 3½", 1951
　　　　4. Twin Geese Planter, 95, 6½", 1951
　　　　5. Flower Club Planter, 823, 5½", 1963
Row 4: 1. Gold-Medal Flowerware Egyptian Vase, 103, 12", 1959
　　　　2. Dachshund Figural, 14", 1952
　　　　3. Urn-Vase, 410, 7", 1962

Hull Pottery Co. CROOKSVILLE, OHIO

Hull Pottery Co. CROOKSVILLE, OHIO

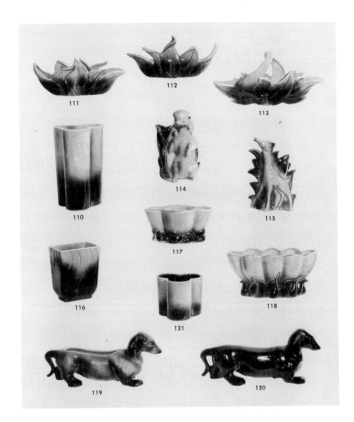

PLATE 104

239

Coronet: 1959-1960
Fantasy: 1957-1958
Fiesta: 1957-1958
Jubilee: 1957
Mirror Black: 1955-1957

COMPANY'S USUAL MODE OF MARKING:

Incised script Hull, mold number, USA. The Coronet smoker set base is marked incised script, "Coronet, USA," while the ashtray is incised with only the mold number and USA.

DESCRIPTIONS:

Ashtray/Planter Combinations were offered in a variety of glaze treatments beginning in 1956. While some stands were offered only in wrought iron, others were available in brass. The Coronet smoke stands were introduced in 1959. Glazed treatments of combination stands ranged from gloss to matte finishes which were additionally air-brushed, edged with foam and line veiled. Styles ranged from square and crimped cylinder to heart and star-shaped ashtrays. All metal stands are original to these Hull items.

The high gloss mirror black wares overlap from the Fiesta and Fantasy lines, some decorated with contrasting foam decoration. The florist list F#1, forerunner to the massive Imperial line, emerged in 1955, in tinted and veiled decorations. Kitchenware bowls in high gloss solid black backgrounds with pink veiling also entered the marked in 1955. The wall pocket is from the varied Gold-Medal Flowerware line.

PLATE 105

Row 1: 1. Ashtray/Planter, Ashtray 22, Planter 23, 26", 1955
2. Coronet Ashtray/Planter, Star-Shaped Ashtray A5, Planter 204, 24½", 1959
3. Ashtray/Planter, Ashtray 22, Planter 23, 26", 1956
4. Jubilee Ashtray/Planter, Ashtray T20, Planter T21, 26", matte finished embossed basketweave with charcoal edge, 1957

PLATE 106

Row 1: 1. Window Box, veiled decoration, 82 12½", 1955
Row 2: 1. Planter, veiled decoration, F1, 6¾", 1955
2. Fiesta Flower Pot, 40, 4", 1957
3. Fantasy Pedestaled Planter, 38, 4¾", 1958
Row 3: 1. Bowl, Ovenproof, veiled decoration, 16, 8½", 1955
2. Bowl, Ovenproof, veiled decoration, 16, 7", 1955
3. Bowl, Ovenproof, veiled decoration, 16, 5½", 1955
Row 4: 1. Fantasy Candy Dish, 8", 1958
2. Gold-Medal Flowerware Vase, 111, 15½", 1959
3. Gold-Medal Flowerware Chinese Sage Mask Wall Pocket, 120, 8", 1959
4. Fantasy Vase, 37, 8¼", 1958

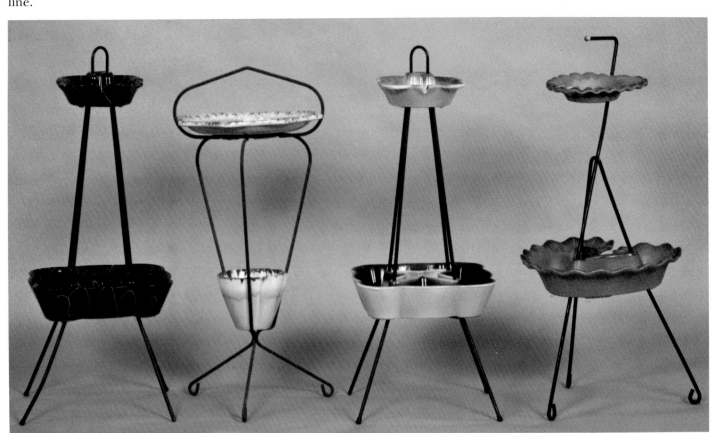

PLATE 105

240

PLATE 106

Novelty

PRODUCTION DATES: 1951-1960

COMPANY'S USUAL MODE OF MARKING:

Items illustrated are most commonly found with the incised script Hull trademark and mold number, along with USA.

PLATE 107

Row 1: 1. Ashtray/Planter veiled decoration, Ashtray 18, Planter, 19, 26", 1955
      2. Royal Lantern Jardiniere with Stand, 75-7", 19" overall, 1955

PLATE 108

Row 1: 1. Colt Figurine, unmarked, 5½", 1954
Row 2: 1. Regal Parrot with Cart Planter, 313 12½", 1960
      2. Colt on Flower Bowl, 7", 1953
Row 3: 1. Knight on Horseback Planter, 55, 8", 1953
      2. Double Bud Vase, 103, 9", 1951
      3. Rooster Planter, 54, 7½", 1953
Row 4: 1. Love Birds Planter, 93, 6", 1953
      2. Rooster Planter, 53, 5¾", 1953
      3. Flying Duck Planter, 79, 6", 1953
Row 5: 1. Flying Goose Vase, 97, 11¾", 1953
      2. Fiesta Fan Vase, 50, 9", 1956
      3. Twin Deer Vase, 62, 11½", 1953

PLATE 107

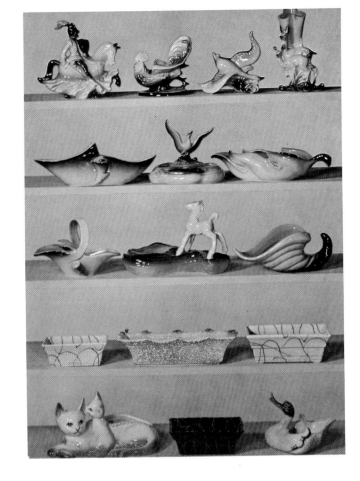

PLATE 108

Novelty

PRODUCTION DATES: 1955-1959

COMPANY'S USUAL MODE OF MARKING:

Items illustrated are most commonly marked with an incised script Hull trademark and mold number, along with USA. The Coronet ashtray/planter combination is marked with an incised script, "Coronet, USA."

DESCRIPTION:

Pink and charcoal glazes, very popular from 1955 to 1957 for novelty and dinnerware items, most often were used in high gloss finishes, but also included matte backgrounds. Decoration treatments of items illustrated included air brush blending and line veiling.

All items shown with metal accessories are high glazed. These shapes include cylinder and heart-shaped base planters, to heart and star-shaped ashtrays. Jardinieres are both plain and crimped cylinder form. All metal holders are original to these items.

PLATE 109
Row 1: 1. Jardiniere in Stand, 8" jardiniere, overall 14½", classic shape in Willow Green Mist
2. Jardiniere in Stand, 10" jardiniere, overall 21", crimped jardiniere in high gloss black with white foam
3. Coronet Ashtray/Planter, Ashtray A5, Planter 204, 24½"
4. Ashtray/Planter, Ashtray 18, Planter 19, 26"

PLATE 110
Row 1: 1. Ashtray, veiled decoration, 18, 7"
2. Planter, veiled decoration, F3, 8½"
Row 2: 1. Bowl, webbed decoration, 29-6"
2. Bowl, veiled decoration, 10, 5½"
3. Bowl, veiled decoration, 10, 7"
Row 3: 1. Cornucopia, 64, 10"
2. Scroll Window Bowl, 71, 12½"
Row 4: 1. Bowl, No. 10, 8½"
2. Covered Divided Casserole, 35, 8½"
3. Individual French Handled Casserole, 5"
Row 5: 1. Scroll Basket, 56, 6"
2. Telephone Vase, 50, 9"
3. Scroll Basket, 72, 8"

PLATE 109

PLATE 110

245

Fiesta: 1957-1958
Sun Valley Pastels:
1956-1957

COMPANY'S USUAL MODE OF MARKING:

Illustrated items are most commonly found with the incised script Hull trademark with mold number and USA.

DESCRIPTIONS:

FIESTA: Twenty-four items were included in the Fiesta line. Items included a varied assortment of high gloss and satin finished jardinieres with metal accessories, fancy vases, baskets and garden dishes with embossed fruit and floral decorations, classic flower bowls with candle holders, and more.

SUN VALLEY PASTELS: A seventeen piece vase assortment for chain store sales in which eleven items were offered in satin finish of pink exterior with high gloss gray interior, or satin finish of turquoise exterior with high gloss yellow interior. The additional seven items were offered in satin exterior finishes of pink, willow green and white with gloss interiors.

PLATE 111
Row 1: 1. Sun Valley Pastel Flower Dish, 152, 13"
Row 2: 1. Sun Valley Pastel Window Box, 153, 12½"
 2. Sun Valley Pastel Bulb Bowl, 154, 8½"
Row 3: 1. Fiesta Tulip Shape Jardiniere, 46, 6½"
 2. Sun Valley Pastel Footed Compote Bowl, 159, 5¼"
 3. Fiesta Jardiniere, 47, 6½"
Row 4: 1. Sun Valley Pastel Flower Pot with Stand, 150, 10"
 2. Fiesta Vase, 45, 8½"
 3. Fiesta Jardiniere, 43, 6"
 4. Sun Valley Pastel Square Candy Dish, 158, 6¾"
Row 5: 1. Sun Valley Pastel Vase, 163, 11½"
 2. Sun Valley Pastel Tulip Vase, 162, 11½"
 3. Fiesta Jardiniere, 92, 7"
 4. Fiesta Cornucopia, 49, 8½"

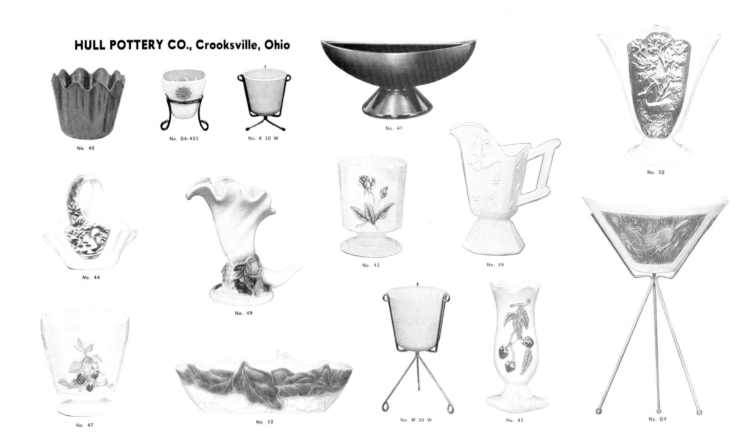

HULL POTTERY CO., Crooksville, Ohio

No. 40
No. G6-425
No. K 30 W
No. 41
No. 50
No. 44
No. 49
No. 43
No. 48
No. 47
No. 52
No. M 30 W
No. 45
No. G9

PLATE 111

Fantasy: 1957-1958
Gold-Metal Flowerware: 1959
Imperial: 1955-1985
Mayfair: 1958-1959

COMPANY'S USUAL MODE OF MARKING:

Marking variations included incised script Hull for the 1950's items, to incised lower cased "hull" on the later produced items. While the incised script Imperial name appeared on many of the line's earliest produced items, the incised lower case "hull" form became the trademark of choice. Items are commonly found without a Hull trademark.

The numbering system for Imperial is not fully consistent, most likely due to its many years of production and a number of items being retained each year, while a number of additional new items were introduced. A consistent trait was the inclusion of the incised "F" which appeared in front of many mold numbers, signifying floristware.

DESCRIPTION:

The massive Imperial floristware line, produced from 1955 to 1985, was first referred to by company salesmen as the "F1 List," and included planters, vases, flower bowls and baskets. Many colors in both satin and high gloss finishes appeared, some had contrasting foam or "run-down" trim. Earliest pieces of Imperial ware were veiled and webbed in free-form designs over contrasting color glazes.

Many of the 1950's designs, i.e., Fiesta, Fantasy, Jubilee, Mayfair, and others, are identified only by their color treatment, as shapes were used sometimes for more than one line. Color treatments assist in determining line names of many of the 1950 wares. As far as the Imperial line, identification of color treatments, usually other than Satin White, can be effectively used for determining dates of production.

Hull's Imperial line evolved from a variety of previously used designs of the 1950's. While Hull's earlier lines were separated one from another, the 1950's lines were characteristically combined for chain store sales, i.e., Fiesta teamed with Fantasy, Fantasy with Gold-Medal Flowerware, and others. Hull lines which had initially kept sole identities, later mixed with other designs to form the chain store sales packages dictated by the pottery's retail markets.

By the late 1950's, assortments which had been known earlier as Medley, Mayfair and others, were simply referred to as, "Flowerware." Interesting to note, is that first glimpses of Hull's Imperial line were interspersed in earlier variety packages. By the late 1950's, planters, jardinieres, flower bowls, flower vases, etc., were known as Imperial, and a short time later, the plant's entire output, other than the kitchenware that was being produced, was known as Imperial Florist Ware. While some of the Imperial items illustrated were manufactured for several years, only the initial dates of production will be listed.

PLATE 112

Row 1: 1. Imperial Candle Holder, 437, 2", 1970
      2. Imperial Swan, 23, 8½", 1961
      3. Imperial Candle Holder, 437, 2", 1970

Row 2: 1. Mayfair Mandolin Wall Pocket, 84, 7"
      2. Fantasy Cherub Planter, 90, 7¼"X 9"
      3. Mayfair Violin Wall Pocket, 85, 7"

Row 3: 1. Imperial Cherub Girl Planter, unmarked, 5¾", 1969
      2. Fantasy Candle Holder, 78, 6½"
      3. Imperial Basket, 457, 6½", 1964
      4. Fantasy Candle Holder, 78, 6½"
      5. Imperial Baby Planter, F51, 5½", 1969

Row 4: 1. Imperial Pitcher with Bowl, F91 & F92, 6", 1974
      2. Imperial Victorian Basket, B36, 9", 1974
      3. Gold-Medal Flowerware Bucket Jardiniere, 94B, 6"
      4. Gold-Medal Flowerware Bucket Jardiniere, 94B, 5"

Row 5: 1. Imperial Vase, 413, 8¾", 1955
      2. Fantasy Vase, 73, 9½"
      3. Fantasy Vase, 39, 12"
      4. Imperial Vase, F28, 9½", 1955
      5. Imperial Ewer, 461, USA, 12", 1964

FANTASY By HULL

HULL POTTERY COMPANY, Crooksville, Ohio

PLATE 112

249

Coronet: 1959
Fiesta: 1957-1958
Gold-Metal Flowerware: 1959
Imperial: 1955-1985
Jubilee: 1957
Mayfair: 1958-1959

COMPANY'S USUAL MODE OF MARKING:

Items shown are most commonly found marked with an incised script Hull, mold number and USA. Coronet line is marked with incised script "Coronet", mold number and USA. It is not unusual to find these novelty items unmarked. Imperial items were marked with either an incised script Hull, or an incised lower cased "hull", USA.

DESCRIPTION:

The green glazes of Hull ware were many, and varied in intensity, from chartreuse to olive. Some mid-1950's novelty wares were characterized by the chartreuse and yellow to green combinations. Coronet items were manufactured in high gloss solid glazes of turquoise, gray, green, orange and white, many having contrasting black, grey or white foam edge. Items from the Fiesta line featured embossed floral and berry decorations, somewhat reminiscent from earlier embossed themes. Jubilee consisted of a line of jardinieres with metal accessories, along with a number of novelty items.

PLATE 113

Row 1: 1. Wall Pocket, 112, 10½", 1952
       2. Coronet Swan, 213, 6½" X 10"
       3. Coronet Planter, 207, 8"

Row 2: 1. Flower Pot, unmarked, 3¾", 1958
       2. Mayfair Consolette, 91, 13½"
       3. Imperial Basket, F38, 7", 1958

Row 3: 1. Basket, unmarked, 12½", 1952
       2. Imperial Basket, B36, 9", 1971
       3. Bulb Bowl, unmarked, 10½", 1952

Row 4: 1. Fiesta Basket, 51, 12½"
       2. Madonna, 24, 7", 1956
       3. Fiesta Window Box, 52, 12½"

Row 5: 1. Imperial Pitcher with Bowl, A50 & A51, 7½", 1971
       2. Clover Vase, 110, 9½", 1952
       3. Jubilee Vase, 421, 12"
       4. Gold-Medal Flowerware Bucket Jardiniere, 94, 9"

HULL POTTERY COMPANY, Crooksville, Ohio

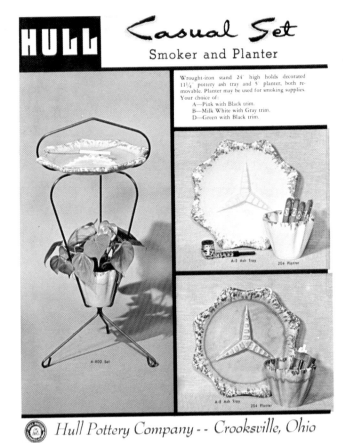

Hull Pottery Company -- Crooksville, Ohio

PLATE 113

251

Artware And Novelties

COMPANY'S USUAL MODE OF MARKING:

Items shown are most commonly found marked with an incised script Hull, mold number and USA. It is not unusual to find these novelty items unmarked. The latest Hull production illustrated is marked with an incised lower case hull and mold number.

PLATE 114

Row 1: 1. Imperial Vase/Candle Holder, 67 U.S.A. 4", 1957
2. Swan, unmarked, 8" (a previously used Medley mold from 1962, which was glazed to compliment the Blue-Belle dinnerware line in 1985.)
3. Imperial Planter, 405 U.S.A., 8¼", 1958

Row 2: 1. Athena Flower Bowl, 601, USA, 5¾", 1960
2. Pigeon Planter, 91, 6", 1955
3. Modern Flower Bowl, Hull USA, 11½", 1955
4. Capri Basket, F38, 6½", 1961

Row 3: 1. Mayfair Candle Lite Flower Bowl, 88, 11", 1958
2. Vase, 414 USA, 10½", 1958
3. Dove Ashtray/Planter, unmarked, 4¼", 1965
4. Imperial Leaf Planter, F24, 12½", 1955

Row 4: 1. Imperial Basket, embossed basketweave decor, unmarked, 8", 1985
2. Imperial Frog, unmarked, 6½", 1985
3. Ashtray, H.P. Co. Pat. Pend., 6¼", 1960
4. Imperial Planter, unmarked, 5", 1985
5. Imperial Basket, embossed strawberry decor, unmarked, 7½", 1985

Row 5: 1. Jubilee Top Hat Basket, 418, 8½", 1957
2. Gold-Medal Flowerware Gladiolus Vase, 112, 10", 1959
3. Tokay/Tuscany Vase, 20, 15", 1959
4. Pagoda Vase, P5, 12½", 1960
5. Gold-Medal Flowerware Vase, 101, 8", 1959

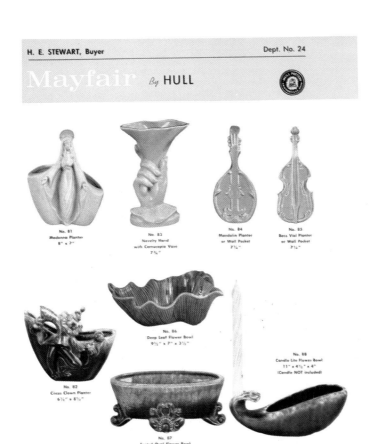

PLATE 114

Imperial

Imperial line, first referred to as the "F1 List," in 1955, was manufactured in volume through the plant's closing in 1985. Imperial's color treatments were many, and included both satin and high gloss finishes. Imperial glazes illustrated on the following page include Wild Honey, Olive Green trimmed in Willow Green, Green trimmed in Turquoise, Satin Avocado, Mirror Black and Satin White.

Many Imperial wares were in production for several years, sometimes the same shape in a variety of different glaze treatments. Certain glaze treatments for Imperial assist in determining production dates. While Olive Green, Green Agate, Moss Green and Satin White were used for many years, other glazes such as Satin Pink, Lilac, Coral, Mahogany and others, were used during specific years of production.

PLATE 115

Row 1: 1. Imperial Victorian Footed Dish Garden, B32, 7", 1974
2. Imperial Footed Bowl, unmarked, 3¾", 1982
3. Imperial Footed Pot, unmarked, 4½", 1982

Row 2: 1. Imperial Pedestaled Planter, B26, 6½", 1974
2. Imperial Jardiniere, 431, 6", 1968
3. Imperial Fancy Oval Vase, F33, 5¾", 1967
4. Dove Ashtray/Planter, unmarked, 4¼", 1965

Row 3: 1. Imperial Swirl Pedestaled Planter, F57, 8¼", 1969
2. Gold-Medal Flowerware Chinese Sage Mask Wall Pocket, 120, 8", 1959
3. Vase, Mirror Black, 9", 1980
4. Vase, Mirror Black, 6", 1980
5. Gold-Medal Flowerware Chinese Sage Mask Wall Pocket, 120, 8", 1959
6. Imperial Usubata Vase, 439, 9", 1968

Row 4: 1. Imperial Rose Vase, 9", 1974
2. Experimental Ashtray, unglazed base, 8", 1965
3. Imperial Jardiniere, F60, 5½", 1969
4. Imperial Jardiniere, Thunderbid decor, 4", 1978

Row 5: 1. Vase, 6", 1980
2. Vase, 9", 1980
3. Vase, 4", 1980
4. Jubilee Caladium Leaf, 405, 14", 1957

HULL POTTERY COMPANY -- Crooksville, Ohio

254

PLATE 115

Athena: 1960
Coronet: 1959
Mayfair: 1958
Regal: 1960

COMPANY'S USUAL MODE OF MARKING:

Trademarks on items shown range from unmarked, to incised script Hull, USA, to incised lower case hull, USA. Regal and Coronet are marked with an incised script form of their line name, USA, and mold number.

DESCRIPTIONS:

ATHENA: Eleven items were offered in this chain store vase and planter assortment which was decorated in overall high glaze Lilac or Spring Green, trimmed with White Lava. Items were additionally glazed in Satin White.

CORONET: A line of vases, jardinieres, dish gardens, ashtray and planter combinations, etc., manufactured specifically for chain store sales. Wares were decorated in solid and tinted high glazes, with or without contrasting foam edges. While assortments varied per retailer, at least thirteen items were available along with the high-styled ashtray and planter combinations in brass and wrought iron stands.

MAYFAIR: Comprised a chain store novelty and florist assortment in solid high gloss pastels and black, all with white foam trim. At least sixteen shapes were available.

REGAL: A line designed exclusively for chain store sales. Items offered included novelty planters, vases and florist ware items in a variety of high glazes, some with contrasting trim.

PLATE 116

Row 1: 1. Imperial Vase, F1, 4", 1961
      2. Siamese Cat Planter, 63, 12", 1953
      3. Imperial Vase, F1, 4", 1961

Row 2: 1. Regal Planter, 301, 3½"
      2. Regal Bowl, unmarked, 6½"
      3. Regal Planter, 6½"
      4. Regal Planter, 303, 5"

Row 3: 1. Athena Cornucopia Vase, 608, 8½"
      2. Athena Low Flower Bowl, 602, 9"
      3. Mayfair Hand with Cornucopia Vase, 83, 7¾"
      4. Athena Oval Picture Frame/Wall Pocket, 611, 8½"

Row 4: 1. Regal Flying Duck Vase, 310, 10½"
      2. Vase, B14, 10½", 1958
      3. Coronet Queen with Crown Vase, 209, 9"
      4. Regal Flamingo Vase, 309, 9"

B. M. SWARZWALDER, Buyer *Regal* Dept. 24

No. 301—5¾" Pedestaled Round Flower Bowl   No. 302—5¼" Square Top Urn Vase   No. 304—6½" Chalice Planter Vase   No. 305—6½" Butterfly Flower Bowl on Pedestal   No. 306—7" Scalloped Compote Bowl

No. 303—6¾" Pedestaled Free Form Flower Bowl Plant Not Included

No. 307—10" Cornucopia Planter   No. 308—10" x 4¼" Oval Flower Bowl   No. 309—9" Flamingo Vase

No. 310—11" Flying Duck Vase

No. 311—11" Unicorn Vase   No. 312—13" Twin Deer Vase   No. 313—12¼" x 7½" x 5¼" Parrot Planter   No. 314—10½" x 8" Flying Duck Planter

No. 315—7½" x 2½" Scalloped Low Flower Bowl   No. 316—9½" x 6" Free Form Low Flower Bowl   No. 317—8½" x 6¾" Contemporary Low Flower Bowl   No. 318—7½" x 6¼" Oriental Low Flower Bowl

HULL POTTERY COMPANY   Crooksville, Ohio

B. M. SWARZWALDER, Buyer *Athena* By HULL DEPT. 24

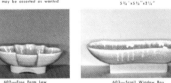 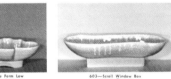

Reflecting the classic beauty and perfect proportions of Greek architecture, this gracious ware is aptly named for Pallas Athena, goddess of peacetime industry. The fluted shapes, the graceful pedestals, the scrolled details were inspired by the Ionic, Doric and Corinthian columns of ancient Greece. Made in two decorations: Lilac trimmed in underglaze White Lava or Spring Green trimmed in underglaze White Lava. These are pieces especially designed to enhance floral arrangements and are in the best of taste.

601—Fluted Square Low Flower Bowl 5¾" x5½" x2¼"

Colors may be assorted as wanted

602—Free Form Low Flower Bowl 8¾" x5½" x2¾"   603—Scroll Window Box 13" x4¼" x3½"   604—Fluted Window Box on Pedestal 9¾" x4" x5"

605—Flared Window Box on Pedestal 11" x4½" x6"   "606—Ruffled Round Planter on Pedestal 7" dia. x 6½"   "607—Paneled Square Planter on Pedestal 5½" x5½" x6½"

608—Cornucopia Vase 8½"   609—Ruffled Vase on Pedestal 9" x 7"   610—Fan Vase 9" Hi. x 9" Wide   611—Oval Picture Frame Wall Pocket Planter 8½" Hi. x 6½" Wide

*Note: No's 608 and 607 may be assorted as wanted in the one dozen carton.

 *Hull Pottery Company -- Crooksville, Ohio*

PLATE 116

Medley

PRODUCTION DATE: 1962

COMPANY'S USUAL MODE OF MARKING:

While many novelty items were unmarked, some were marked with the incised script Hull, USA, the incised lower case hull, USA, and with an incised lower case, "planter inc." The Medley urn vases are marked with an incised print, "URN-VASE," USA, in circle form.

DESCRIPTION:

MEDLEY: This chain store assortment of swirled urn vases, dolphin, swan and teddy bear planters, cat vase, Madonna planter, and items with metal accessories was decorated in Satin White, Green Agate with Turquoise Trim and Persimmon with Yellow Trim. Twenty-five items were catalogued for the Medley assortment, some being shared Coronet and Imperial shapes.

For those who appreciate the high gloss tangerine /persimmon glaze, illustrated are items in solids and spattered glazes, and those edged in contrasting foam. The Jack-O-Lanterns were produced in at least two face styles. McCoy Pottery also made these items, some reportedly being contracted through the Hull Company. Buyer beware ... there is little, if any difference. Glaze in this instance is not always the identifying clue since at least two varying shades were used by Hull for the pumpkins. Also, it is almost certain Hull provided McCoy the glaze formula in order to produce the like-items.

PLATE 117

Row 1: 1. Bulb Bowl, 107, 7", 1952
        2. Vase, 100, 9", 1952
        3. Medley Swan, 815, 4"

Row 2: 1. Imperial Window Box, unmarked, 14½", 1960
        2. Medley Jardiniere, 806, 5"

Row 3: 1. Jack-O-Lantern, unmarked, 5½", 1965
        2. Planter, Inc. Flower Pot, 25-3¼", 1962
        3. Medley Teddy Bear Planter, 811, 7"

Row 4: 1. Medley Urn-Vase Jardiniere, 801, 5½"
        2. Double Bud Vase, 103, 9", 1952
        3. Medley Round Flower Bowl, 44, 4½"

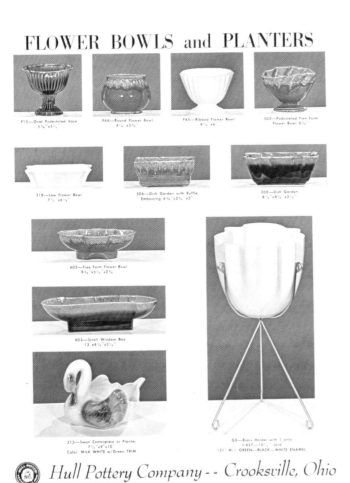

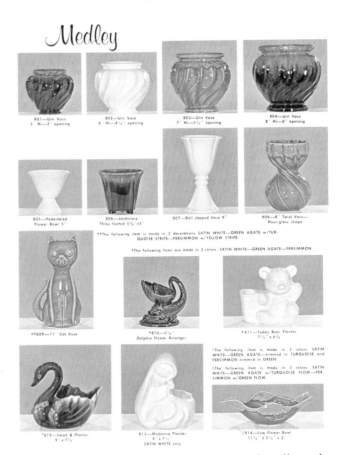

PLATE 117

259

Gold-Medal Flowerware: 1959
Imperial: 1955-1985

COMPANY'S USUAL MODE OF MARKING:

Trademark variations for items illustrated included incised script, "Hull," incised lower case, "hull," and script "Imperial." These items are also commonly found unmarked.

DESCRIPTION:

The Imperial floristware line included planters, vases, flower bowls and baskets produced from the mid-1950's, through 1985. Several Gold-Medal Flowerware items were later included in the Imperial line. Both satin and high gloss finishes were used, and illustrated are three vases decorated by Granville "Grany" Shafer, Shafer Pottery Company, Zanesville, Ohio. Two are decorated in lusters of blue and dark rose, while a third is a decoration Shafer referred to as his gold "daisy chain." Formulas for these decorations were Shafer's guarded secrets.

Hull's religious planters first entered the market in January, 1957, with numbers 24 Praying Madonna, 25 Kneeling Madonna, 26 Madonna with Child, 27 Standing Madonna with Urns, and 89 St. Francis Planter. Madonna planters were advertised in "new" satin finishes of yellow, ivory and carnation with hand painted underglazed features. While some Madonna planters were later glazed in high gloss white, yellow and pink, they eventually became available only in Satin White. Hull designer, Louise Bauer, a devout Catholic, was responsible for modeling these, and other religious planters for the firm.

The Imperial Spiral, "swirled panel" design of 1960, included a line of vases which doubled as pedestals for jardinieres. F86 included a F83 Vase and F84 Jardiniere, which together was an overall twenty-five inches in height. These items were distributed in glazes of Moss Green or Mahogany with White Flow and allover Satin White.

PLATE 118

Row 1: 1. Imperial Duck Planter, F69, 10", 1985
Row 2: 1. Imperial Jardiniere, F88, Shafer dark rose luster, 5¾", 1970
   2. Imperial Jardiniere, F34, Shafer gold "daisy chain," 5", 1970
   3. Imperial Jardiniere, F88, Shafer blue luster, 5¾", 1970
Row 3: 1. Imperial Madonna, F7, 7", 1974
   2. Imperial Madonna, 417, 9½", 1960
   3. Imperial Ewer, F480, 10½", 1965
   4. Imperial Madonna, 25, 7", 1957
Row 4: 1. Imperial Victorian Vase, B37, 9", Shafer gold, 1974
   2. Twin Swan Planter, 81, 10½", 1970
   3. Imperial Victorian Vase, B37, 9", 1974
Row 5: 1. Experimental Imperial Spiral Jardiniere, unmarked, 10" X 12", 1960.
   2. Gold-Medal Flowerware Jardiniere, 105, 11", 1959
   3. Gold-Medal Flowerware vase, 102, 11½", 1959

260

PLATE 118

Just Right Floral
Cook 'N' Serve Ware

PRODUCTION DATES:

Just Right Floral: 1951-1954
Cook 'N' Serve Ware: 1952-1953

COMPANY'S USUAL MODE OF MARKING:

JUST RIGHT FLORAL: Incised script Oven-Proof, Hull, USA, with "40" series mold number designation in circle formation. Sizes were not included in the mold.

COOK 'N' SERVE WARE: The trademark on this ware consisted of the incised script Hull, USA form, with mold number designation.

DESCRIPTIONS:

JUST RIGHT FLORAl: White high gloss kitchenware with raised yellow air-brushed florals, yellow air-brushed lids with brown banding. Florals appear on only one side of the ware. Fifteen items were available.

COOK 'N' SERVE WARE. Twenty-two piece ovenproof kitchenware line offered in high gloss yellow and brown, pink and charcoal, green with brown flow, and white with black contrasting trim, with other color combinations possible. Nineteen items were catalogued exclusively for A. H. Dorman, New York.

PLATE 119

Row 1: 1. Floral Salad Bowl, No. 49, 10"
2. Floral Mixing Bowl, No. 40, 9"

Row 2: 1. Floral Cookie Jar, No. 48, 8¾"
2. Floral Grease Jar, No. 43, 5¾"
3. Floral Salt Shaker, No. 44, 3½"
4. Floral Pepper Shaker, No. 44, 3½"

Row 3: 1. Floral Individual French Handled Casserole, No. 47, 5"
2. Floral Mixing Bowl, No. 40, 5"
3. Cook 'N' Serve Ware Mug, No. 33, 3¾"
4. Cook 'N' Serve French Handled Casserole, 5"

Row 4: 1. Cook 'N' Serve Ware Divided Covered Casserole, No. 35, 11½"
2. Cook 'N' Serve Ware Coffee Server, No. 32, 11"
3. Cook 'N' Serve Ware French Handled Casserole, No. 28-8"

"Just Right Kitchenware"

Floral Pattern

HULL POTTERY Co. - Crooksville, Ohio

PLATE 119

Cook 'N' Serve Ware

PRODUCTION DATES: 1952-1953

COMPANY'S USUAL MODE OF MARKING:

Incised Script Hull, USA, also commonly found marked only by mold number.

DESCRIPTION:

Skillet trays were available in two sizes and are found in a variety of high gloss color treatments. They are decorated both overglaze and underglaze. While some of these glaze treatments are considered experimental and may have been made for whimsey, others glazes were formulated for accessories to the Cook 'N' Serve dinnerware line. The Cook 'N' Serve Ware line is a combination of Cinderella and Just Right Kitchenware shapes. Glaze treatments included high gloss yellow and brown, pink and charcoal, green with brown flow, and white with contrasting black trim, with other color combinations possible. A total of nineteen items were catalogued, exclusively for A. H. Dorman, New York.

PLATE 120

Row 1: 1. Skillet Tray, cold color decor, No. 27, 9¼" X 15½"
2. Experimental Skillet Tray, unmarked, 9¼" X 15½"

Row 2: 1. Skillet Tray, No. 27, 9¼" X 15½"
2. Skillet Tray, 9¼" X 15½"

Row 3: 1. Skillet Tray, No. 30, cold color decor, 5" X 10"
2. Experimental Skillet Tray, unmarked, 9¼" X 15½"
3. Skillet Tray, No. 30, 5" X 10"

Row 4: 1. Skillet Tray, No. 27, 9¼" X 15½"
2. Experimental Skillet Tray, 9¼" X 15½"

264

PLATE 120

Kitchen Ware

COMPANY'S USUAL MODE OF MARKING:

These kitchenware lines most commonly bear the incised script form, Hull, USA, along with mold number and size identification. Plaidware does not carry the Hull trademark and was incised with mold numbers and size identification only. A foil label stating, "A. E. Hull Pottery Co., Hull Ware, Crooksville, Ohio, in three lines, accompanied Plaidware. The label had a light blue background with silver lettering.

The cylinder cookie jars remained in production throughout the 1930's and 1940's. The only jars in this plain cylinder shape which contained Hull trademarks appear to be the Cinderella cookie jars in Blossom and Bouquet designs. Other jars were marked with number and size designations only. There were two sizes of jars, one being slightly taller than the other, and the knob of the lid included two different styles. One knob was completely spherical, while the other knob was near half-round.

DESCRIPTIONS:

COOK 'N' SERVE WARE: 1952-1953. Nineteen-piece ovenproof kitchenware line offered in high gloss yellow and brown, pink and charcoal, green with brown flow, and white with black contrasting trim, with other combinations possible.

DEBONAIR: 1952-1955. Fifteen-piece ovenproof kitchenware line offered in high gloss wine and chartreuse or high gloss duo-tone lavender and pink with black center banding.

PLAIDWARE: 1950. An eleven-piece ovenproof kitchenware line offered in decorations of green or red plaid on overall high glazed white background with yellow horizontally striped decoration. Items included three nested bowls, batter bowl, cereal bowl, casserole, range jar, shakers, cookie jar, creamer and sugar.

VEGETABLE: 1951. Embossed vegetable patterned kitchenware in high gloss solid colors of yellow, coral and green. Carrots, pea pods, radishes and string beans were embossed in the design which spelled, "Cookies" on the cookie jar, and "S" for salt and "P" for pepper on the shakers. Fifteen Vegetable shapes were catalogued.

PLATE 121

Row 1: 1. Plaidware Creamer, 67, USA, 3"
2. Plaidware Covered Sugar, 68 USA, 4"
3. Plaidware Cookie Jar, 66, Ovenproof USA, 9½"
4. Plaidware Bowl, 60-5", Ovenproof, USA
5. Just Right Vegetable Batter Bowl, No. 21-9"

Row 2: 1. Debonair French Handled Casserole, 18-8"
2. Experimental Plaidware Cookie Jar, unmarked, 9½" (This jar is decorated just the opposite of what the company placed on the market. Instead of brush-striped yellow on overall white with red crisscross, this jar is brush-striped red on overall white with yellow crisscross.)
3. Cook 'N' Serve Ware French Handled Casserole, No. 28-8"

PLATE 122

Row 1: 1. Cook 'N' Serve Ware Creamer, No. 25, 3½"
2. Cook 'N' Serve Ware Covered Sugar, No. 24, 4"
3. Experimental Shaker, 3½", 1958
4. Experimental Cookie Jar, 18, 9½", 1958

Row 2: 1. Cruet, 984, 5", 1960
2. Cruet, 984, 5", 1960
3. Cook 'N' Serve Ware Ice Lip Pitcher, No. 22, 7¾"
4. Bowl, "webbed" treatment, 29, 8", 1955
5. Bowl, "webbed" treatment, 29, 6", 1955

Row 3: 1. Cook 'N' Serve Ware Shaker, No. 14, 4"
2. Just Right Vegetable Cookie Jar, 28, 8¾"
3. Just Right Vegetable Salt Shaker, USA, 25, 3½"
4. Just Right Vegetable Pepper Shaker, USA, 25, 3½"
5. Just Right Vegetable Bowl, 20-5"

Row 4: 1. Cookie Jar, unmarked, 10¾". decal decorated, 1940
2. Duck Cookie Jar, 966, 11½", decorated over the glaze, 1940
3. Cookie Jar, 9½"-30, 10¾", decorated underglaze, 1940

PLATE 121

266

PLATE 122

Crescent: 1952-1954
Debonair: 1952-1955
Plaidware: 1950

COMPANY'S USUAL MODE OF MARKING:

These kitchenware lines most commonly carried the incised script form, Hull, USA, along with mold number and size identification. Crescent was numbered in a "B" series formula, while Debonair was headed by an "O" in its mold identification plan. Plaidware did not carry the Hull trademark and was incised with mold numbers and size identification only. A foil label, "A. E. Hull Pottery Co., Hull Ware, Crooksville, Ohio," in three lines was used on the Plaid kitchenware. The label had a light blue background with silver lettering.

DESCRIPTIONS:

CRESCENT: This kitchenware line was named for the crescent-shaped lids and handles, a crescent moon being part of the company's advertising. This ovenproof line was decorated in solid high gloss color combinations of chartreuse with dark green trim, or high gloss strawberry with maroon trim. Twelve shapes were available in the Cresent line.

DEBONAIR: Fifteen-piece ovenproof kitchenware line offered in high gloss wine and chartreuse or high gloss duo-tone lavender and pink with black center banding.

PLAIDWARE: An eleven-piece ovenproof kitchenware in high gloss white background decorated with a horizontal striped yellow application over white background, followed by either red or green crisscross design.

PLATE 123
Row 1: 1. Plaidware Shaker, 64, 3¼"
      2. Plaidware Shaker, 64, 3¼"
      3. Plaidware Range Jar, 63, 5½"
      4. Plaidware Covered Sugar, 68, 4"
Row 2: 1. Crescent Creamer, B-15, 4¼"
      2. Crescent Teapot, B-13, 7½"
      3. Crescent Sugar, minus lid, B-14, 4¼"
      4. Crescent Individual Casserole, B-7, 5"
Row 3: 1. Crescent Covered Casserole, B-2, 10"
      2. Crescent Mug, B-16, 4¼"
      3. Crescent Shaker, B-4, 3½"
      4. Crescent Shaker, B-4, 3½"
Row 4: 1. Crescent Bowl, B-1-5½"
      2. Crescent Bowl, B-1-7½"
      3. Crescent Bowl, B-1-9½"
Row 5: 1. Crescent Cookie Jar, B-8-9½"
      2. Spatter Ware Bowl, green over yellow, yellow interior, No. 10-9", 1951
      3. Debonair Cookie Jar 0-8, 8¾"

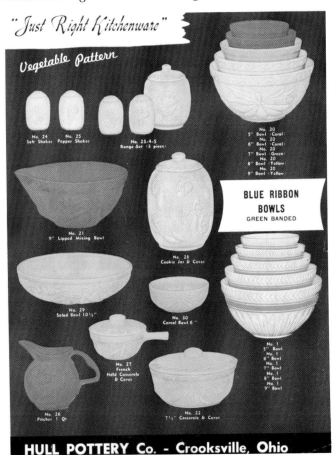

268

PLATE 123

Debonair

PRODUCTION DATES:

Wine and Chartreuse: 1952-1954

Pink and Lavender with Black Banding: 1955

COMPANY'S USUAL MODE OF MARKING:

Incised script Hull, USA, followed by "O," mold number, and size identification.

DESCRIPTION:

Classic ovenproof kitchenware in high gloss wine and chartreuse or high gloss duo-tone lavender, (referred to as grey in company information,) and pink with black center banding. Fifteen items were catalogued. The Spatter Ware bowls are a spin-off of the Just Right Kitchenware Floral and Vegetable lines, and may be experimental. They were attained from the collection of Byron Hull.

PLATE 124

Row 1: 1. Debonair Covered Casserole, 0-17, 8½"

Row 2: 1. Debonair Shaker, 04-5, 3½"

2. Debonair Shaker, 04-5, 3½"

3. Debonair Teapot, 013, 8"

4. Debonair Mug, 016, 3¾"

Row 3: 1. Debonair Bowl, 0-1-5"

2. Debonair Cookie Jar, 0-8, 9"

3. Debonair Pitcher, 06, 5"

4. Debonair Creamer, 014, 3½"

Row 4: 1. Charcoal Spatter Ware Bowl, No. 40, 7", 1951

2. Charcoal Spatter Ware Batter Bowl, No. 41-9", 1951

3. Debonair Bowl, 0-1-9"

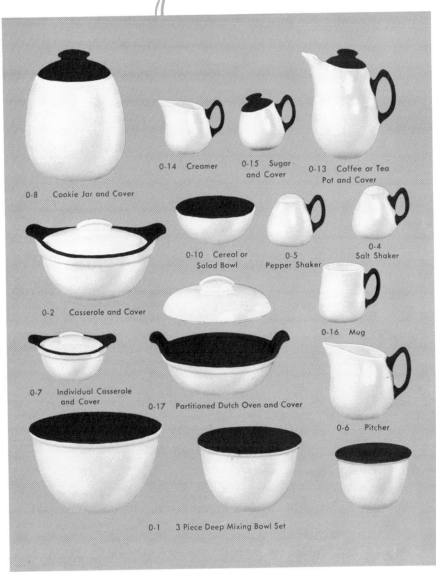

Debonair · Oven-Proof Kitchenware

0-8 Cookie Jar and Cover
0-14 Creamer
0-15 Sugar and Cover
0-13 Coffee or Tea Pot and Cover
0-2 Casserole and Cover
0-10 Cereal or Salad Bowl
0-5 Pepper Shaker
0-4 Salt Shaker
0-16 Mug
0-7 Individual Casserole and Cover
0-17 Partitioned Dutch Oven and Cover
0-6 Pitcher
0-1 3 Piece Deep Mixing Bowl Set

Hull Pottery Co. CROOKSVILLE, OHIO

PLATE 124

271

Heritageware: 1958
Marcrest: 1958
Sun Valley Pastels: 1956-1957

COMPANY'S USUAL MODE OF MARKING:

HERITAGEWARE: Incised script Hull, U.S.A., © 58, with an "A" series mold identification number.

MARCREST: The "Marcrest Quality, Oven Proof" logo was incised into the mold and appeared on many Marcrest items. These items were used for premiums and grocers' giveaways. The Marcrest ashtrays were marked in raised block, Marcrest, USA.

Marcrest, was a trade name used by Marshall Burns, a distributor of the Chicago area and was the name used on nearly all pottery and dinnerware items marketed by this firm. What is important to note is that Hull was not the only producer of Marcrest items, however, Hull appears to be the only producer of the pastel colored dinnerware for Marshall Burns. Brown Marcrest dinnerware was produced by Western Stoneware of Monmouth, Illinois.

SUN VALLEY PASTELS: Marked with an incised script Hull, mold number and USA.

DESCRIPTIONS:

Although Marcrest and Heritageware kitchenware shared several of the same molds, they were two distinctively different lines in their application of color glaze and treatment.

MARCREST: High gloss oven proof kitchenware items used for grocery store giveaways, high glazed in pastel colors mint green, pink, yellow, coral and white. Marcrest items were not trimmed with foam, while Heritageware items were given the contrasting decoration. The Marcrest trademark in raised block form was used on the ashtrays which were also sales premiums. They were glazed in both solid high gloss and satin finishes.

HERITAGEWARE: An ovenproof kitchenware line the company described as high gloss mint green or azure blue with a light touch of foam edge. An additional treatment was the textured or semi-matte finished glaze with contrasting white lids or companion pieces, i.e., shakers, cruets. Company information illustrated fifteen shapes.

SUN VALLEY PASTELS: A seventeen piece assortment for chain store sales in which eleven items were offered in satin finish of pink exterior with high gloss gray interior, or satin finish of turquoise exterior with high gloss yellow interior. The additional seven items were offered in satin exterior finishes of pink, willow green and white with gloss interiors.

PLATE 125
Row 1: 1. Marcrest Ashtray, 7½"
      2. Sun Valley Pastel Leaf Tray, 31, 8¾"
      3. Marcrest Ashtray, 7½"
Row 2: 1. Heritageware Shaker, 3½"
      2. Heritageware Shaker, 3½"
      3. Heritageware Pitcher, A-7, 4½"
      4. Marcrest Mug, 3¼"
      5. Heritageware Mug, 3¼"
      6. Heritageware Oil Cruet, 6¼"
      7. Heritageware Vinegar Cruet, 6¼"
Row 3: 1. Marcrest Pitcher, 7½"
      2. Marcrest Pitcher, 7½"
      3. Marcrest Pitcher, 7½"
Row 4: 1. Heritageware Grease Jar, A-3-5¾"
      2. Heritageware Cookie Jar, 0-18-9½"
      3. Heritageware Pitcher, A-6-7"
      4. Heritageware Cookie Jar, 0-18-9½"

PLATE 125

273

Mirror Brown
House 'N Garden: 1960-1985

COMPANY'S USUAL MODE OF MARKING:

Incised lower case hull, Ovenproof, USA, and incised script Hull, USA. Many later molds (1982-1985), carried place of origin, incised Crooksville, Ohio. Incised HP CO and/or Ovenproof, USA, were also commonly used trademarks for House 'n Garden dinnerware items. It is not uncommon to find Mirror Brown items marked Crestone, as molds were shared. Some of the Crestone molds used for Mirror Brown were later reworked to bear the Hull Ovenproof mark.

DESCRIPTION:

Dark brown high gloss dinnerware and accessories with ivory foam became mainstays of the company's business from 1960, through the company's closing in 1985. Popularity remained strong in the United States and Canada for twenty-five years, and from 1980 to 1984, Hull's Mirror Brown House 'n Garden line was sold in great quantities in Australia at in-home dinnerware parties.

PLATE 126
Row 1: 1. Jug/Creamer, 4¼"
       2. Salt Shaker, 3½"
       3. Pepper Shaker, 3½"
       4. Continental Mug, 6"
       5. Coffee Mug, 3½"
       6. Coffee Mug, 3"
Row 2: 1. Divided Baker, 11"
       2. Teapot, 6"
       3. Oval Baker, 10"
Row 3: 1. Duck Covered Casserole, 8", 1972-1985
       2. Imperial Vase, lion's heads, unmarked, 6¾"
       3. Chicken Covered Casserole, 9½", 1968-1985
Row 4: 1. Open Baker with Rooster decor, 13½", 1969-1972
       2. Butter Dish, 7½"
       3. Cylindrical Vase, 4"
       4. Cylindrical Vase, 9"
       5. Cylindrical Vase, 6"

274

PLATE 126

275

Figural Casseroles: 1968-1985
Mirror Almond: 1981-1983
Mirror Brown: 1960-1985
Ridge: 1982-1984

COMPANY'S USUAL MODE OF MARKING:

Incised lower case "hull", Ovenproof, USA and incised script Hull, USA. Ridge dinnerware's newly molded or remolded items had the incised origin, "Crooksville, Ohio," added to the trademark.

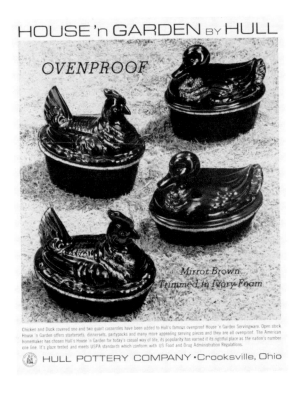

PLATE 127

PLATE 127
Row 1: 1. 16-piece Almond with Caramel House 'n Garden boxed set dinnerware, 1981-1983.
Row 2: 1. Flint Ridge 6-piece boxed set, Continental Mugs, 1982-1984
2. Flint Ridge boxed Duck Covered Casserole, 1982-1984
Row 3: 1. 16-Piece Mirror Brown boxed set dinnerware, 1978
2. 8-Piece Mirror Brown House 'n Garden boxed Canisters, 1978

PLATE 128
Row 1: 1. Chicken Covered Casserole, 8½", Green Agate, 1968-1970
Row 2: 1. Duck Covered Casserole, 8", Flint Ridge, 1984
2. Chicken Covered Casserole, 8½", Mirror Brown, 1968-1985
Row 3: 1. Duck Covered Casserole, 9", Mirror Brown, 1972-1985
2. Chicken Covered Casserole, 11½" X 13½", Mirror Brown, 1969-1972. The baker base has an incised rooster decor.
Row 4: 1. Chicken Covered Casserole, 8", Mirror Brown, 1968-1980
2. Covered Casserole, 7½" X 12", Mirror Brown, 1968-1972
3. Chicken Covered Casserole, 8" semi-matte experimental glaze, 1975

PLATE 128

Mirror Brown: 1960-1985

COMPANY'S USUAL MODE OF MARKING:

Incised lower case hull, Ovenproof, USA, many later molds (1982-1985,) carried place of origin, incised Crooksville, O. Incised HPCO and/or Ovenproof, USA were also common trademarks for House 'n Garden dinnerware items. It is not uncommon to find Mirror Brown items marked Crestone, as molds were shared. Some of the Crestone molds used for Mirror Brown were later reworked to bear the Hull Ovenproof mark.

DESCRIPTION:

The dinnerware items shown are from both older and updated molds, but all are dark brown high gloss with ivory foam which became mainstays of the company's business from 1960 through the company's closing in 1985. Earlier House 'n Garden was characteristically darker in shade and had a deeper, more apparent contrasting foam edge. The experimental glasses in House 'n Garden glazes can double as juice glasses if you are fortunate enough to garner a set. It is desirable to gather a few Imperial vases or planters to include with your table settings.

PLATE 129

PLATE 129

Row 1: 1. Hull mold section for House 'n Garden Mushroom Pepper Shakers.

Row 2: 1. Hull mold section for House 'n Garden stein.
  2. Hull mold section for House 'n Garden Bean Pot.

PLATE 130

Row 1: 1. Experimental glass, solid Mirror Brown, incised 48, 175, 173, 3½"
  2. Experimental glass, Mirror Brown with drip, incised 9-2, 5-8, 3½"
  3. Imperial Planter, unmarked, 5"
  4. Soup and Sandwich, mug 5", tray, 9½"
  5. Handled Server, 11½"

Row 2: 1. Individual French Handled Casserole, 5"
  2. Vinegar Cruet, 6½"
  3. Oil Cruet, 6½"
  4. Bowl, 6¾"
  5. Bowl, 5¼"

Row 3: 1. Ice-Lip Pitcher, 7½"
  2. Cheese Shaker, 6½"
  3. Plate, (Crestone shape without the Crestone mark,) 9½"
  4. Leaf Dish, 7½"

Row 4: 1. Leaf Chip 'n Dip, 15"
  2. Bean Pot, 6½"
  3. Dinner Plate, 10½"

PLATE 130

279

Mirror Brown: 1960-1985

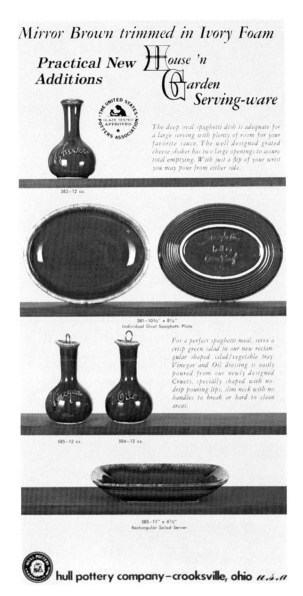

PLATE 131
Row 1: 1. Pepper Shaker, 3¾", 1978-1983
     2. Oval Salad, incised rooster, 6½", 1968-1972
     3. Salt Shaker, 3¾", 1978-1983
Row 2: 1.*Individual French Handled Casserole in Basket, 5", 1975
     2. Jumbo Stein, University logo in gold, 1976
     3. Spoon Rest, 6½", 1978-1983
     4. Cup and Deep-Well Saucer; Cup, 3½", 1963-1985, Saucer, 5¾", 1963-1969
Row 3: 1. Egg Plate, 9¼", 1978-1983
     2. Cookie Jar, 8", 1960-1985
     3. Fish Tray, 11", 1978-1983
Row 4: 1. Canister, 9", "Flour", 1978-1981
     2. Canister, 8", "Sugar," 1978-1981
     3. Canister, 7", "Coffee', 1978-1981
     4. Canister, 6", "Tea", 1978-1981

*A set of six casseroles with lids in these wicker basket holders were given this author by Byron Hull. The set was originally shipped to Mrs. Richard Watts in Connecticut, but was returned to the company more than once due to incomplete address. This set remains in its original shipping box.

PLATE 131

Mirror Brown: 1960-1985

COMPANY'S USUAL MODE OF MARKING:

Incised lower case hull, Ovenproof, USA, and incised script Hull, USA. Many later molds (1982-1985,) carried place of origin, incised Crooksville, Ohio. Incised HPCO and/or Ovenproof, USA were also used as trademarks for House 'N Garden dinnerware items.

The Mirror Brown proved so popular, that items in demand went far beyond table accessories. The drawer pulls illustrated were produced by way of a contractual agreement between Hull and Amerock Corporation of Rockford, Illinois. The drawer pulls were shipped to the plant from Wisconsin Porcelain in greenware state. Hull was responsible only for the glazing and firing of these drawer pulls, which were then returned to Amerock for assembly and marketing.

PLATE 132

Row 1: 1. Duck Planter, F69, 10"
       2. Imperial Window Box, F10, 12"
Row 2: 1. Bowl, marked Crestone, 6"
       2. Rectangular Salad Server, 11"
       3. Individual French Handled Casserole, 5"
Row 3: 1. Gingerbread Boy Coaster/Spoon Rest, 5"
       2. Tab Handled Baker, 6¾"
       3. Square Baker, 9½"
       4. Experimental Low Flower Bowl, 9¼"
Row 4: 1. Experimental Imperial Frog Planter, unmarked, 6"
       2. French Handled Casserole, 11¾"
       3. Pie Plate, 9¼"
Row 5: 1. Cylindrical Vase, 9"
       2. Bread and Butter, 6¾"
       3. Oval Steak Plate 12"
       4. Coffee Server, 11", (later redesigned with lock lid)

PLATE 132

Mirror Brown: 1960-1985

PLATE 133
Experimental Gingerbread Train Canister Set

Row 1: 1. Caboose, 7½"
       2. Kiddie Car, 8"
       3. Express Car, 7"
       4. Engine, 9"

PLATE 134
Row 1: 1. Ashtray, 18, 7"
       2. Shaker, 3¼", discontinued in early 1970
       3. Shaker, 3¼", discontinued in early 1970
       4. Carafe, 6¾", discontinued by late 1970
       5. Drawer Pulls, 1¾" diameter, contractual
          item, 1981
Row 2: 1. Batter Bowl, unmarked, 10½"
       2. Mixing Bowl, unmarked, 9"
       3. Mixing Bowl, unmarked, 8"

This mixing bowl set is usually marked, however, this nested set was a gift to this author from Byron Hull. He had taken the set from the plant before the molds were in full production, therefore, the bowls carry no trademark.
Row 3: 1. Cassserole with Warmer, 8" overall, 1963-1978
       2. Gingerbread Man Cookie Jar, 12", 1984

Avocado: 1968-1971
Country Squire: 1963-1967
Rainbow: 1961-1967

COMPANY'S USUAL MODE OF MARKING:

Incised lower case hull, Ovenproof, USA, and incised script Hull USA.

DESCRIPTION:

AVOCADO: Ovenproof dinnerware in high gloss or satin avocado color with or without an ivory foam edge. This line was created at the time avocado kitchen appliances emerged on the market and was intended to produce a desire for coordinated dinnerware sets.

Hull's Rainbow consisted of oven proof casual serving ware in solid high gloss colors of Mirror Brown, Tangerine, Green Agate and Butterscotch, all with contrasting foam edge. This ware was an assortment created to mix and match. Only the joint combination of colors was referred to as Rainbow, for what the company advertised as a "rainbow" table setting. Rainbow's Tangerine became a spin-off dinnerware line formed from Rainbow's popular colors. Hull also created a Green Agate line, which was referred to as Country Squire.

Hull intended for Rainbow to be a mix-and-match dinnerware line, so let's not forget to have fun when collecting and putting dinnerware sets together. Hull produced many shapes other than kitchenware that can be used as accessories to their dinnerware lines. Be sure and add an item or two, whether it be a florist vase, an ashtray, a duck planter, or even a set of experimental glasses for juice, to your dinner table.

PLATE 135

Row 1: 1. Rainbow Luncheon Plate, 8½"
2. Rainbow Soup & Sandwich; Tray, 9¾", Mug, 5"
3. Rainbow Luncheon Plate, 8½"

Row 2: 1. Rainbow Dinner Plate, 10½"
2. Rainbow Soup & Sandwich: Tray, 9¾", Mug, 5"
3. Rainbow Dinner Plate, 10½"

Row 3: 1. Avocado Pepper Shaker, 4"
2. Avocado Salt Shaker, 4"
3. Avocado Mug, 3½"
4. Avocado Teapot, 6½"
5. Avocado Butter Dish, 7½"

Row 4: 1. Rainbow Bud Vase, F90, 6½"
2. Rainbow Pitcher, 9"
3. Avocado Baker, 10"
4. Avocado Dinner Plate, 10½"

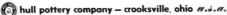

PLATE 135

Tangerine: 1963-1967

COMPANY'S USUAL MODE OF MARKING:

Incised lower case hull, Ovenproof, USA, and incised script Hull, USA.

DESCRIPTION:

The kitchenware illustrated is a line which evolved from Hull's Rainbow dinnerware. The initial orange line was referred to as Hull's "900 Series," Tangerine House 'n Garden. A short time later, Golden Anniversary dinnerware entered the market. Both were one and the same glaze, although different assortments were available. This same glaze was also referred to as Burnt Orange when offered exclusively for J. C. Penney Co.

Tri City Grocery Company advertised its upcoming gala 50th "Golden Anniversary," which included use of Hull's House 'n Garden line in tangerine as an incentive to buy groceries while the customer earned dinnerware coupons redeemable for the ware. Fifteen pieces were coupon-earned during this event. Hull's Tangerine dinnerware line included at least forty shapes in this great glaze.

PLATE 136
Row 1: 1. Experimental Coffee Mug, 3½"
        2. Toast 'n Cereal Tray, 9¾", Bowl, 6½"
        3. Experimental Coffee Mug, panel design, unmarked, 3½"
        4. Deep-Well Saucer, 5¾"
        5. Coffee Mug, 3"

PLATE 137
Row 1: 1. Creamer, 4½"
        2. Salt Shaker, 4"
        3. Pepper Shaker, 4"
        4. Covered Sugar, 4"
        5. Butter Dish, 7½"

Row 2: 1. Teapot, 6½"
        2. Ashtray, 8"
        3. Pitcher, 6½"
        4. Gravy Boat/Syrup, 6"
Row 3: 1. Leaf Dish, 7"
        2. Leaf Chip 'n Dip, 15"
        3. Luncheon Plate, 8½"
        4. Bud Vase, 9"
Row 4: 1. Bean Pot with Warmer, 9"
        2. Tidbit Server, 10"
        3. Leaf Dish, 12"

PLATE 136

PLATE 137

Country Squire: 1963-1967

COMPANY'S USUAL MODE OF MARKING:

Incised lower case hull, Ovenproof, USA, and incised script Hull, USA.

DESCRIPTION:

The kitchenware line illustrated is a line known to have evolved from Hull's Rainbow dinnerware. The separate line of Green Agate was named Country Squire and included at least forty items. Again, you'll want to add a few "fun" items to your dinner table, such as a duck planter, flower bowl, or vase.

PLATE 138

Row 1:
1. Imperial Jardiniere, F470, 4"
2. Experimental Glass in green agate, 3½"
3. Imperial Duck Planter, unmarked 10"
4. Imperial Planter, unmarked, 3"
5. Country Squire Cup, 3¼"

Row 2:
1. Country Squire Jug/Creamer, 4¼"
2. Country Squire Salt Shaker, 3½"
3. Country Squire Pepper Shaker, 3½"
4. Country Squire Soup 'n Sandwich; Mug 5", Tray, 9½"
5. Country Squire Deep-Well Saucer, 5¾"

Row 3:
1. Imperial Planter, unmarked, 3¾"
2. Imperial Planter, F27, 4"
3. Country Squire Syrup/Gravy Boat, marked Crestone, recessed lid and handle, 5"
4. Country Squire Mug, 5"
5. Imperial Planter, F476, 4¾"

Row 4:
1. Imperial Chickadee Planter, F474, 5"
2. Imperial Vase, lion's heads, unmarked, 6¾"
3. Country Squire Covered Baker, 10"
4. Country Squire Ice-Lip Pitcher, 7½"

Row 5:
1. Experimental Cylindrical Vase, unmarked, 6"
2. Experimental Cylindrical Vase, unmarked, 9"
3. Experimental Cylindrical Vase, unmarked, 4"
4. Experimental Low Flower Bowl, unmarked, 9¼"
5. Country Squire Dinner Plate, 10½"

Country Squire **SERVING-WARE**

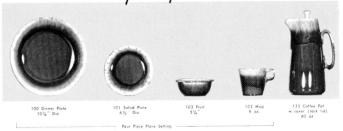

100 Dinner Plate 10¼" Dia. — 101 Salad Plate 6½" Dia. — 103 Fruit 5¼" — 102 Mug 9 oz. — 172 Coffee Pot w/cover (lock lid) 60 oz.

Four Piece Place Setting

105 Mixing Bowl 5¼" — 106 Mixing Bowl 6¾" — 107 Mixing Bowl 8¼" — 109 Water Jug 5 pint — 125 Jug 2 pt. — 118 Jug ½ pt.

110 Bean Pot w/cover 2 qt. — 124 Individual Bean Pot w/cover 12 oz. — 119 Sugar Bowl w/cork — 118 Creamer 8 oz. — 111 Bake Dish 3 pt. / 112 Casserole w/cover 3 pt. — 113 French Handled Casserole 5¼" / 127 French Handled Casserole w/cover — 126 Beer Stein 16 oz.

114 Ice Jug 2 qt. — 115 Salt Shaker w/cork 3½" Hi. — 116 Pepper Shaker w/cork 3½" Hi. — 121 Leaf Shaped Chip 'n Dip 13"x10½" — 123 Cookie Jar w/cover 94 oz.

C. M. S. ATTACH TO FILE T-145-A

styled in a beautiful blend of turquoise and green agate

OVEN AND DETERGENT PROOF

141 Individual Oval Steak Plate 11¾" x 9" — 142 Divided Vegetable 10¾" x 7¼" — 143 Open Oval Baker 10" x 7¼"

146—Three piece Salad Set consisting of: 1 only #145—Salad Bowl, 1 only #147—Fork & Spoon Set

144 Oval Casserole & Cover 10" x 7¼" (3 pt.) — 145 Salad or Spaghetti Bowl 10¼" — 147 Fork and Spoon Set

148 Oval Casserole & Cover 2 qt.—10" x 7¼" — 149 Tea Pot & Cover 5 cup — 151 Jam or Mustard Jar & Cover Set with Spoon

#155—8 pc. Set Consisting of: 4 only #153 Soup Mugs 11 oz., 4 only #154 Trays — #156—8 pc. Set Consisting of: 4 only #102 Coffee Mugs 9 oz., 4 only #154 Trays — #157—8 pc. Set Consisting of: 4 only #103 Cereal 12 oz., 4 only #154 Trays

Hull Pottery Company, Crooksville, Ohio

PLATE 138

289

Crestone: 1965-1967

COMPANY'S USUAL MODE OF MARKING:

Crestone was marked with an incised lower case hull, USA, along with its incised script "Crestone" signature, © 65.

DESCRIPTION:

Original company advertising describes Crestone as, "Ovenproof casual serving ware in high gloss turquoise with white foam edge." Thirty items were available.

The company advertised the ware's prominent features, "extra deep, form fitting well in saucers of items like standard cups and the gravy boat; casserole covers have large deep rings as knobs to serve as glazed over trivets when inverted; platform type chimes prove far superior to ordinary handles; gravy boat is separate from saucer and is ideal as syrup pitcher, carafe holds 2 cups to start of neck - no need to burn fingers; same cover fits 9 oz. French handled casserole and soup-salad, duplication unnecessary." "Designed specifically for present day living habits in the breakfast nook, on the patio, at the T. V. or barbecue, as well as normal table service, only Crestone offers these features at prices all can afford."

PLATE 139

Row 1: 1. Covered Sugar, 4¼"
      2. Teapot, 7"
      3. Creamer, 4¼"

Row 2: 1. Fruit Bowl, 6"
      2. Shaker, 3¾"
      3. Shaker, 3¾"
      4. Carafe with Cup, 8"
      5. Cup, 3½"

Row 3: 1. Chip 'n Dip Leaf, 14½"
      2. Vegetable/Salad Bowl, 10"

Row 4: 1. Salad Plate, 7½"
      2. Dinner Plate, 10½"
      3. Coffee Server, 11"

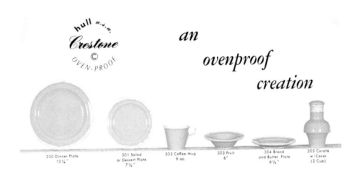

PLATE 139

Crestone: 1965-1967
Rainbow: 1961-1967
Ridge: 1982-1984

COMPANY'S USUAL MODE OF MARKING:

Crestone was marked with an incised lower case hull, USA, along with its incised script "Crestone" signature, © 65. Ridge and Rainbow wares were marked with an incised lower case hull, Ovenproof, USA, and incised script Hull, USA. Newly molded, or remolded items had the incised origin, "Crooksville, Ohio," added to the trademark.

PLATE 140

Row 1: 1. Tawny Ridge Salt Shaker, 3"
2. Tawny Ridge Pepper Shaker, 3"
3. Experimental glass in tawny, inscribed 120, 3½"
4. Experimental glass in flint, 3½"
5. Flint Ridge Continental Mug, 6"
6. Flint Ridge Ramekin, 1½"
7. Rainbow Cup, butterscotch, 3½"
8. Experimental glass in butterscotch, inscribed 30, 3½"
9. Leaf Dish, 7½"

Row 2: 1. Crestone Butter Dish, 7½"
2. Crestone Bread and Butter Plate, 6¾"
3. Experimental glass in Crestone turquoise, inscribed 54, 3½"
4. Crestone Cup, 2¾"
5. Crestone Carafe, 6½"
6. Crestone Stein, 5"

Row 3: 1. Flint Ridge Gingerbread Boy Coaster/Spoon Rest, 5", embossed, "Crooksville Bank 80th Year, 1982."
2. Tawny Ridge Gingerbread Boy Coaster/Spoon Rest, 5", embossed, "Crooksville Bank 80th Year, 1982."
3. Experimental Tawny Ridge low flower bowl, unmarked, 9¼".
4. Tawny Ridge Gingerbread Boy Coaster/Spoon Rest, 5".
5. Rainbow Divided Baker, 11"
6. Experimental glass in tangerine, inscribed 16, 117, 114, 3½".

Row 4: 1. Tawny Ridge Cookie Jar, 9"
2. Coronet Ashtray, unmarked, factory drilled for metal accessory, 11¼".
3. Tawny Ridge Duck Covered Casserole, 8".

PLATE 140

293

Gingerbread Man Server: 1978-1985
Gingerbread Man Cookie Jar: 1982-1984
Ridge: 1982-1984

COMPANY'S USUAL MODE OF MARKING:

Incised lower case hull, Ovenproof, USA. Newly molded or remolded items had the incised origin, "Crooksville, Ohio," added to the trademark. Gingerbread Man items proudly carry the Gingerbread name in incised script form. The handled server bears an incised "Server" trademark.

DESCRIPTIONS:

GINGERBREAD MAN: The adorable Gingerbread Man character was the animated design used for serving pieces which accompanied House 'n Garden dinnerware. Designed by Louise Bauer, and first produced in 1978, the Gingerbread Man Cookie Jar was later expanded to include a mug, bowl, and coaster/spoon rest. A four-piece train canister set was trialed in 1985, but never placed on the retail market.

RIDGE DINNERWARE: Ridge was created from previously used molds, updated molds and entirely new molds. In the early 1980's Hull's "Collection" was glazed in gray, tan and brown. These same color glazes were advertised shortly thereafter as Flint Ridge, Tawny Ridge and Walnut Ridge. These items are dated by color glazes and not molds.

The Gingerbread Boy Coaster/Spoon Rests with the Crooksville Bank logo were made in all three colors glazes. This special order commemorated the bank's 80th year. Hull President, Larry Taylor's wife is an employee of the bank.

PLATE 141

Row 1: 1. Butter Dish, 7½"
     2. House 'n Garden Shaker, 3", limited production, 1965
     3. Continental Mug, 6", "3rd Annual American Art Pottery Association Convention, Zanesville, Ohio 1982" logo
     4. House 'n Garden Shaker, 3", limited production, 1965
     5. Butter Dish, 7½"

Row 2: 1. Handled Server, 11½"
     2. Individual Covered Casserole, 5"
     3. Handled Server, 11½"

Row 3: 1. Gingerbread Man Server, 10"
     2. Gingerbread Boy Coaster/Spoon Rest, 5", inscribed, "Crooksville Bank 80th Year, 1982"
     3. Gingerbread Man Server, 10"
     4. Gingerbread Boy Coaster/Spoon Rest, 5"
     5. Gingerbread Man Server, 10"

Row 4: 1. Cookie Jar, 9"
     2. Gingerbread Man Cookie Jar, 12"
     3. Teapot, 6½"

PLATE 141

Mirror Almond: 1981-1983

COMPANY'S USUAL MODE OF MARKING:

Incised lower case hull. Ovenproof, USA. Newly molded or remolded items had the incised origin, ''Crooksville, Ohio,'' added to the trademark.

DESCRIPTION:

The kitchenware line illustrated was high gloss Almond with Caramel trim. It included newly designed mold items along with carry-overs from the long-lived House 'n Garden Mirror Brown line.

Items illustrated in allover almond with no contrasting color decoration were those Byron Hull used in his home. Mr. Hull ordered his set without the caramel trim, as the solid almond better suited his taste. Many Almond items, which did not have benefit of the caramel trim, were sold through area pottery outlet stores, such as the cruets, a rectangular baker and a round divided server.

PLATE 142

Row 1: 1. Vinegar Cruet, 5¾"
2. Divided Bowl, 11"
3. Jug/Creamer, 4½"

Row 2: 1. Mug, 3¼"
2. Saucer, 6¾"
3. Bowl, 5¼"
4. Individual French Handled Casserole, 5½"

Row 3: 1. Oval Steak Plate, 12"
2. Salad Plate, 6½"
3. Oval Steak Plate, 12"

Row 4: 1. Dinner Plate, 10"
2. Gingerbread Man Server, 10"
3. Dinner Plate, 10"

327 AMERINE STREET
CROOKSVILLE, OHIO 43731

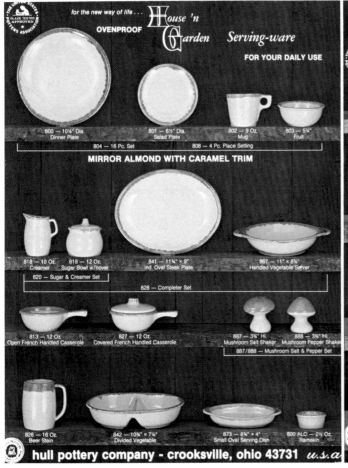

296

PLATE 142

Heartland: 1982-1985

COMPANY'S USUAL MODE OF MARKING:

Incised lower case hull, Ovenproof, USA, and area of origin, "Crooksville, Ohio."

DESCRIPTION:

Described by Company advertisement as "handmade by American craftsmen," this ware was "satin creamy glaze with hand applied brown decoration and gold shading on rims." This is a satin ware closely resembling Pfaltzgraff wares, and it's no surprise that it was designed by the same free-lance designer, Maury Mountain.

In the early 1980's, The Hull Pottery was taking a very serious pride in its work. The pottery was genuine in its desire to regain the dinnerware market lost to stagnate designs, continuous labor strikes and poor management decisions. So intense was this dedication, that costly dinnerware lines with newly designed molds and color glazes which included hand decorations such as this country heart stamp were executed.

PLATE 143

Row 1: 1. Salt Shaker, 6"
      2. Pepper Shaker, 6"
      3. Pie Plate, 11"
      4. Covered Jar, "Chowder," 8"

Row 2: 1. Duck Covered Casserole, 8½"
      2. Experimental Handled Server, 11½", note the "3-flower stamp"
      3. Mug, 5"
      4. Pitcher, 4"

Row 3: 1. Mixing Bowl, 6"
      2. Mixing Bowl, 8"
      3. Mixing Bowl, 10"
      4. Experimental Pitcher, 9", note the "3-flower stamp"

Row 4: 1. Canister, "Flour", 9"
      2. Canister, "Sugar", 8"
      3. Canister, "Coffee", 6"
      4. Canister, "Tea", 6"

The Heartland Collection

298

PLATE 143

Heartland: 1982-1985
Mirror Almond: 1981-1983

COMPANY'S USUAL MODE OF MARKING:
Incised lower case hull, Ovenproof, USA, and area of origin, "Crooksville, Ohio."

DESCRIPTIONS:
HEARTLAND: One of Hull's "Collection" dinnerwares which was offered in shaded satin cream with hand applied brown heart and flower stamp.

MIRROR ALMOND: Kitchenware line glazed in Almond with contrasting Caramel trim. Gingerbread Man items were also available in Almond glaze with Caramel trim.

PLATE 144

Row 1: 1. Experimental Glass, Heartland glaze, 3½"
2. Almond Bowl, no trim 5¼"
3. Almond with Caramel Trim, Individual French Handled Casserole, 5"
4. Almond Sugar, no trim, 3"

Row 2: 1. Heartland Soup/Salad Bowl, 8"
2. Heartland Plate, 7¼"
3. Heartland Sugar, 4¾"
4. Heartland Creamer, 4¾"

Row 3: 1. Heartland Pitcher, 9"
2. Heartland Covered Jar, "Chili", 8"
3. Heartland, Luncheon Plate, 8½"

Row 4: 1. Almond Rectangular Baker, no trim, 12"
2. Heartland Souffle, 8¾"
3. Almond Divided Server, no trim, 11"

PLATE 144

301

Blue-Belle: 1985

COMPANY'S USUAL MODE OF MARKING: Incised lower case hull. Ovenproof, USA, and area of origin, ''Crooksville, Ohio.''

DESCRIPTION:

High gloss winter-white background with hand-stamped blue decoration of trailing bluebell florals, also designed by Maury Mountain of Pfaltzgraff fame, this dinnerware boasted a glaze that Hull stated was identical to the glaze of Lenox China. In original advertising, Hull illustrated the No. 71 swan as a centerpiece for this line. This swan, originally from the Medley line, was first introduced in 1962.

PLATE 145

Row 1: 1. Pitcher, 3½"
2. Cheese Shaker, 6½"
3. Swan, unmarked, 8"
4. Mug, clear glaze, no stamp, 5"
5. Mug, 4¼"

Row 2: 1. Pie Plate, 11"
2. Luncheon Plate, 8½"
3. Oval Platter, 12"

Row 3: 1. Canister, 5"
2. Canister, 5"
3. Canister, 6¼"
4. Canister, 7¼"

Row 4: 1. Bowl, 12"
2. Rectangular Baker, 14"

302

PLATE 145

303

Blue-Belle: 1985

COMPANY'S USUAL MODE OF MARKING:

Incised lower case hull, Ovenproof, USA, and area of origin, "Crooksville, Ohio."

DESCRIPTION:

High gloss winter-white background with hand-stamped blue decoration of trailing bluebell florals.

PLATE 146

Row 1: 1. Covered Sprout Casserole, 7½" has a satin finish, similar to Heartland, but is not part of Heartland design.

Row 2: 1. Salt Shaker, 6"
2. Pepper Shaker, 6"
3. Soup/Cereal Bowl, 6¾"

Row 3: 1. Beverage Pitcher, 7½"
2. Handled Server, 11½"

Row 4: 1. Mixing Bowl, 8"
2. Dinner Plate, 10"
3. Teapot/Coffee Server, 9"

PLATE 146

305

Experimentals

The next several pages illustrate Hull Experimentals and Specials, Trials and Sample wares, each an entirely different category. Please make note of the explanation given for each category.

EXPERIMENTALS:

The experimentals in the following pages, illustrate items which were not available on the retail market but did make their way outside the plant: in some cases these items having been sold to area pot shops as seconds or leftover lots; taken from the plant by workers; having been shelved by the ceramic engineer in his workroom or another section of the Hull plant for reference at a later date; or even thrown in the trash pile by employees during quality control checks. These items having significant historical value, are in fact, the company's undocumented testimonials of individual craftsmanship.

Experimentals included several levels of variation. The mold itself may have been experimental in nature, a new design or shape; more often than this, the experimentation was in the color or glaze treatment. In some cases the color and glaze was what the company intended for a certain design, and this type of ware usually included an incised code that related to the color and glaze formulation. This incised alphanumeric code was most often a quality-control measure, and many of these items fall into the trial glaze category. However, if the glaze was entirely new or different than expected, and related to a newly devised glaze compound, it is considered experimental.

In summary, Experimentals are characterized by molded wares not in production, or by extreme variation in color and glaze treatment of a specific line, or a combination of the two. The categories of experimentals included, unmarketed molds with unmarketed glaze treatments, unmarketed molds with marketed glaze treatments, and marketed molds with unmarketed glaze treatments. Most wares from experimental molds were unmarked due to the fact that the ware was in an experimental stage, not near enough to the company's inclusion as a marketable line to bear the trademark in the mold itself. Marketed or production molds with experimental glaze treatments were usually trademarked.

Production "trials," are the wares in marketed molds and marketed colors characteristic of the particular design, with bases being both marked and unmarked, but which most often additionally contained the incised configurations of test glaze formulas. Great are the numbers of Experimental Trials in Hull's last twenty-five years of production with the magnitude of styles offered in Imperial and House 'n Garden dinnerwares.

The experimental category may often be confused with label-marked sample wares. Sample items were marked on the ware itself or with a foil or paper label indicating "sample," while experimentals were in most cases left unmarked. Sample wares were in fact, production molds in the color and glaze treatment expected, actually no different than marketed specimens, except for the sample seal.

PLATE 147:
Row 1: 1. Experimental Parchment and Pine Teapot, unmarked, 6", 1954.
2. Experimental Fantasy Vase, 72, incised decor on mirror black, 8½", 1959.
3. Experimental Vase, "webbed" decor, unmarked, 8½", 1960.

PLATE 148
ROW 1: 1. Experimental Tokay/Tuscany Pedestaled Vase, 10"

PLATE 147

306

PLATE 149

Row 1: 1. Baby Shoe, 2½", 1925
2. Baby Shoe, 2½", 1925
3. Stein, elusive cobalt decor, 492, 6½", 1920
4. Bear Figural, 1½", 1925
5. Owl Bank, 3¾", 1925
6. Kitten Figural, 1½", 1925
7. Frog Bank, Rosella clay, 3¾", 1945
8. Kitten Figural, 1½", 1925
9. Rabbit Figural, 2¾", 1925
10. Rabbit Figural, 2¾", 1925
11. Rabbit Figural, 2¾", 1925
12. Rabbit Figural, 2¾", 1925

Row 2: 1. Stoneware Vase, 7", heavy metallic copper
luster, 1920
2. Stoneware Teapot, inscribed script "Mrs. Mary
Stewart" at base and inscribed initials "M. S."
at lid, 6¼", buff body, matte glaze, 1925

3. "Roscoe" Corky Pig Bank, "Frazeysburg
Alumni" under glaze, "Hopewell, S. Zanesville,
Conesville, Rosecrans, Deaver Town, Union,
Glendford", 1960, 5"

Row 3: 1. Blossom Flite Basket, unmarked, 10", 1954
2. Calla Lily Ewer with gorgeous Stoneware glaze,
508-10", 1935
3. Basket, 72, Sponged black and white exterior
with sponged gold and white interior, 12½",
1952

Row 4: 1. Vase, unmarked, 11", heavy "webbing," black
and silver Granada Pottery foil label, 1958
2. Stoneware Pretzel Jar, underglaze decorated by
Sylvanus Burdette "Mose" Wilson, 9½", 1925
3. Tidbit Server, black with white edged
"webbing," 10½", 1960

307

Experimentals
Specials
Samples

Experimentals and Specials are two entirely different categories, Experimentals having been previously explained. Specials refer to wares which have been additionally or specially decorated outside the Hull company and are not considered experimental. The surrounding pottery villages had many talented craftsmen who purchased bulk lots of pottery, decorated and fired in Hull's usual fashion. These items were then taken to studios or homes with kilns, where not only gold decor was added, but also complete redecoration.

Gold decorators were plentiful in the Ohio pottery region, some recolored and redecorated the entire pottery item before refiring, while others added gold decor only. Many of these items had specialty foil labels, such as, "Hand Painted Fired Ceramic Colors," This label further indicated gold content.

For nearly fifty years, Granville, "Grany," Shafer, of the Shafer Pottery Company of Zanesville, Ohio, designed and molded his own lines of pottery and additionally decorated many local pottery items, including Hull, Shawnee, McCoy and Ungemach, to name a few. Shafer, who was responsible for many of Hull's gold decorated items, began his decorating business in 1932. With very limited capital, Shafer purchased bulk lots of pottery which he redecorated and refired in his own kilns. From that meager beginning, Shafer Pottery Company soon had outlets in major cities such as Chicago and Denver for the gold decorated wares.

Community-minded, Shafer offered his talents to the clay region's annual pottery festivals. A festival announcement of mid-1960 states:

BELIEVE IT OR NOT; THIS YOU WILL HAVE TO SEE!

"Zanesville, Ohio, being one of the oldest pottery towns in the U.S.A. now has very few potteries in existence. Next to the oldest pottery now in operation in that city is the G. C. Shafer Pottery Company at 542 Merrick Ave., Zanesville, Ohio. A craftsman in his kind of work. Hand decoration in 23 karat gold, beautiful lusters, over-glaze colors, decal work, and specialties. He has worked in his back yard for the past 32 years! Shafer Pottery ships to florists and gift shops all over the U.S.A.

For the Roseville and Crooksville Pottery Show, he will keep his shop open Friday and Saturday till 9:00 P.M. Sunday - 12:00 Noon till 6:00 P.M.

EXTRA SPECIAL FOR VISITORS! Shafer will have two girls working on four hour shifts starting at 1:00 P.M. Friday, July 16th. The girl you will see is not a hobbiest, but a trained artist decorating beautiful pieces of pottery for a nation. Expect to see many other surprises come out of this small factory."

Other known Ohio gold and specialty decorators who operated between 1930 and 1960, included Bob Young, Roseville; Arthur Wagner of the Zanesville's Chic Pottery; Art Richards of the Crooksville China Company; Roseville's Arthur Pemberton and Zanesville's George Earl, known as Pemberton-Earl or P&E Decorators; and John and Edith Hilaman, Zanesville, known as J&E Decorators. Additional area artists decorated multitudes of Hull wares which were sold as souvenirs during the local pottery festivals. Many of these wares were decorated on-the-spot in cold-color application.

PLATE 150
Row 1: 1. Special Wild Flower No. Series Vase, 52-6¼", 1942-1943
2. Special House 'n Garden Teapot, luster decorated by Edna Mae Kettlewell, a local artist for more than twenty-five years. Kettlewell, taught by Arthur Wagner, was dared to put three lusters to fire, this being her outcome. This particular item was decorated in a marvelous metallic luster which combines the most delicate floral effects, executed within the same metallic coloring. Decorator's signature is included in the luster decoration on the base and handle, 7", 1968
3. Special Camellia Vase, 123-6½", 1943-1944
4. Special Water Lily Ewer, L-3-5½", interior also lined in gold, 1948-1949

PLATE 150

PLATE 151

PLATE 151
Row 1: 1. Experimental Candle Holder, unmarked,
          3½", 1930
       2. Experimental Console Bowl, unmarked,
          6½" X 9", 1930
       3. Experimental Candle Holder, unmarked,
          3½", 1930
Row 2: 1. *Woodland blank Wall Pocket, W13-7½", 1952
       2. *Woodland blank Basket, W9-8¾", 1952
       3. **Experimental Woodland Vase, W1-5½",
          test glaze incised 500-B, 1951
       4. **Experimental Woodland Vase, W1-5½",
          test glaze incised 500-B, 1951
Row 3: 1. Sample Rosella Vase, R-15-8''', misspelled
          "Sampel" inscribed into clay on base, 1946
       2. Experimental Serving Dish, unmarked,
          13", 1950
       3. Special Wild Flower No. Series Vase, 61-6¼",
          1942-1943

Row 4: 1. Special Magnolia Vase, 8-10½", 1946-1947
       2. Experimental Ashtray, made from base of
          Magnolia Vase, "Burt" inscribed into clay,
          5½", 1946-1947
       3. Experimental Magnolia Basket, 10-10½",
          1946-1947
       4. Special Wild Flower No. Series Vase,
          71-12", 1946-1947

*There is great likelihood that this was a separate line pro-
duced for a chain-store package since it is most commonly
found with the Hull trademark and color and glaze treatment is consistent.

**The experimental Woodland glazes are consistent with
the green with brown flow glaze formula used for Cook 'N'
Serve Ware during the same production period. However,
the Cook 'N' Serve treatment was high gloss, while this is
satin finished.

Experimentals

PLATE 152
Row 1: 1. Basket, unmarked, 13" X 15", 1950.

Colorful Overglazes, and Genuine 23 K. Gold Decorated by

Mr. G. C. Shafer

ZANESVILLE, OHIO

Over 40 years of handcrafted pottery. Now over 70 years and semi-retired.

Granny Shafer included the above advertising copy with many of his decorated wares of the 1960's and 1970's.

PLATE 153
Row 1: 1. Tokay/Tuscany Basket, inscribed test glaze E747A, 7" 1965
2. Swan, 69, 8", 1954
3. Sun Valley Pastel Pedestaled Planter, 156, gold veiling, 5", 1956
Row 2: 1. *Woodland blank Wall Pocket, W13-7½", 1954
2. Woodland Wall Pocket, W13-7½", 1953
3. Woodland Wall Pocket, W13-7½", bisque fired, 1952
4. Woodland blank Wall Pocket, W13-7½", 1954
Row 3: 1. Vase, inscribed test glaze CG 52-B, 9", 1951
2. Leaf Dish, unmarked, 12", 1955
3. Fiesta Pitcher, 48, 8¾", dark green high gloss, 1956. Trial rather than experimental, inscribed test glaze code.
Row 4: 1. Woodland Ewer, W24-13½", inscribed test glaze 75-A 75-C, 1951
2. *Woodland blank Vase, W18-10½", 1954
3. Woodland Ewer, W24-13½", inscribed test glaze 77-C, XXG, 1951

*There is great likelihood that pastel satin glazed Woodland blanks comprised a separate line produced for chain store sales, since these items are most commonly found with the Hull trademark, color and glaze treatment being consistent.

PLATE 153

311

Experimentals

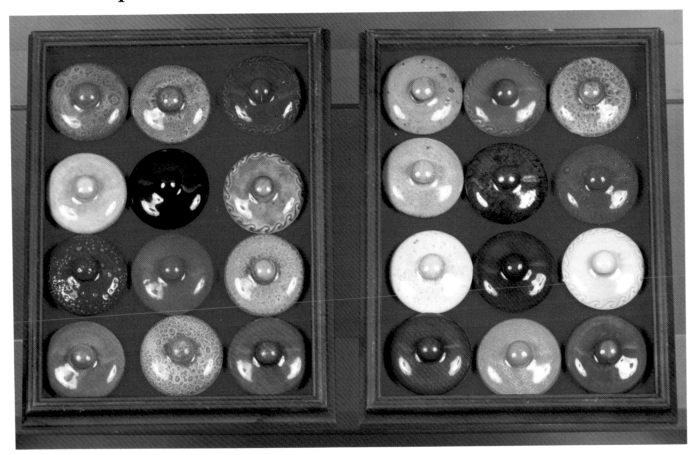

PLATE 154
Experimental test glaze lids, 3½" diameter, alphanumeric codes relating to Ceramic Engineer's glaze formulas are on the underside. Hundreds of these lids once hung in the Ceramic Engineer's workroom at the Hull plant.

PLATE 155
1. Experimental Picture Frame Wall Pocket, unmarked, 6½" X 8", 1960

PLATE 156
Row 1: 1. Dancing Lady in bright yellow, 955, 7", 1940
       2. Pinecone Vase, unmarked, 5", 1936
       3. Wishing Well Planter, hand decorated under the glaze, unmarked. Top area is lacier than the redesigned version that was placed on the market, in 1951, 7½"
Row 2: 1. Madonna Planter, beautifully tooled, front and back, unmarked, 10½", 1960
       2. Supreme Basket, unmarked, 9", 1960
       3. Lady Head Planter, unmarked, company seal "Style F482," 8½" X 8½", 1960
Row 3: 1. Woodland Teapot, gray and bright yellow, W26, 6½" 1952
       2. Vase, unnamed line, unmarked, 8¾", 1940
       3. Ewer, unmarked, 9½", 1930
       4. Iris Vase, blue and bright yellow, unmarked mold, 8¾", 1940
Row 4: 1. Gold-Medal Flowerware Egyptian Vase, unglazed base, incised test glaze 999, 12", 1959.
       2. Supreme Vase, olive with red, unmarked, 6", 1960
       3. Mardi Gras/Granada Vase, matte magenta over high gloss turquoise, 219-8", 1940
       4. Supreme Vase, satin ebony with white, unmarked, 6", 1960
       5. Pinecone Ewer, embossed pine cone and floral design, (Butterfly mold with Serenade back ground color and texture,) script Hull, USA, 13½", 1956

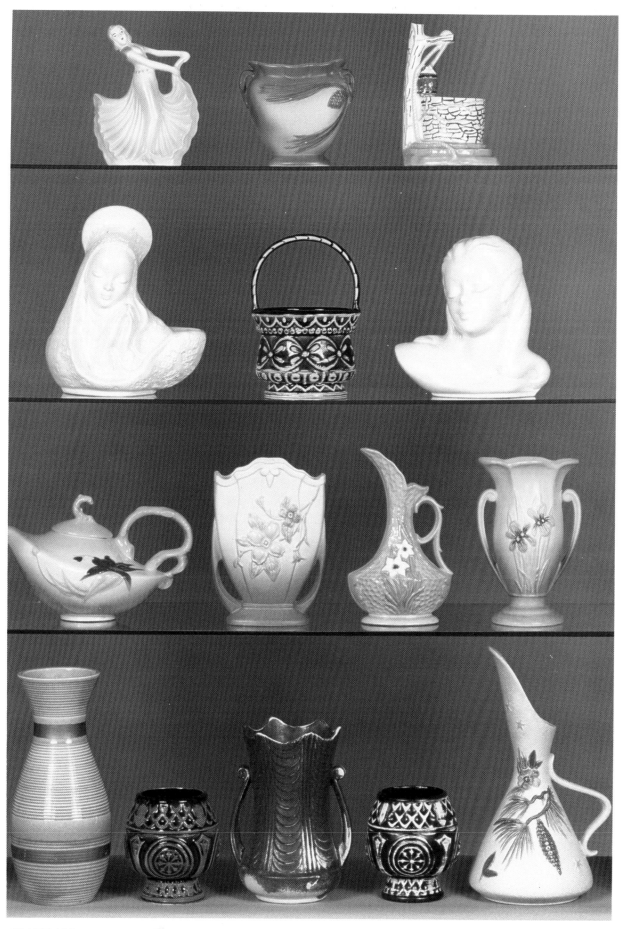

PLATE 156

Experimentals

There is no set pattern for determining values of Experimentals, Trials, Specials and Samples, as many, many variables apply. First of all, determine the value of the item if it were not experimental, etc., then decide exactly the category or categories in which the item falls. Probably the most important factor is determining the level of experimentation based upon what is normal production for the particular line. Add to this the period and term of production, its availability, collector interest, condition, your locale, and of course, our own good judgment.

While some lines have surfaced in greater numbers of experimentation, experimentals were certainly not limited to any particular production years, but comprised all eras of Hull manufacture.

PLATE 157
Row 1: 1. Parchment and Pine Cornucopia, S-2-L, 7¾", wine interior, 1951
Row 2: 1. Blossom Flite Cornucopia, green with tan interior, unmarked, 10½", Hull later restyled mold, 1955
     2. Blossom Flite Jardiniere, T4, 6", 1955
     3. Blossom Flite Cornucopia, pink with yellow and brown, unmarked, 10½", Hull later restyled mold, 1955
Row 3: 1. Continental Vase/Candle Holder, test glaze incised 169B, 10½", 1959
     2. Turn-About Cat Bank, 198, 11", 1968
     3. Continental Vase/Candle Holder, test glaze incised 169C, 10½", 1959
Row 4: 1. Turn-About Cat Door Stop, unmarked, 11", 1968
     2. Parchment and Pine Ewer, unmarked, gray interior, 14", 1951
     3. Turn-About Cat Bank, unmarked, 11", 1968

Brochure Information for Hull's Bicentennial Ware which was never placed on the retail market.

PLATE 157

315

Experimentals

The sculptured designs of Supreme were referred to as ''tooled wares'' by company personnel. The ware was dipped in glaze, but before firing, was run through a series of brushes that scraped the ware to reveal inner layers to which additional color glaze was applied. Some supreme experimentals never touched those brushes. Although there was a full production run with brochure pages and advertising ready to follow, the line was never placed on the retail market. Take a close look at the colors and glazes Hull contemplated for this design. The company finally settled on the color combinations of Agate with Chartreuse and Ripe Olive with Orange. Any piece of Supreme is considered experimental since it was never placed on the market, however, look for the alternate color combinations. As illustrated, the tooled effect can be from absolute base to top of the ware, with some pieces being additionally decorated with contrasting foam edge. Overall high glosses, to semi-high gloss finishes to satin finishes were available, with color combinations not necessarily limited to two colors. Interiors many times were glazed in contrasting colors.

PLATE 158
Row 1: 1. Supreme Candy Dish, F27, 7", 1960
       2. Supreme Footed Bowl, 4¾", 1960
       3. Supreme Urn, unmarked, 6", 1960
       4. Supreme Jardiniere, unmarked, 4¾", 1960
Row 2: 1. Supreme Urn, black with gold, unmarked, 6", 1960
       2. Supreme Urn, blue with olive, unmarked, 6", 1960
       3. Supreme Urn, brown with yellow, unmarked, 6", 1960
       4. Supreme Urn, olive with green and gold, unmarked, 6" 1960
Row 3: 1. Supreme Pedestaled Vase, unmarked, 10", 1960
       2. Supreme Vase, unmarked, 12½", 1960.
       3. Supreme Jug, unmarked, 9¼", 1960

PLATE 158

316

PLATE 159

PLATE 159

Row 1: 1. Alligator Planter, unmarked, 7½", 1951
2. Trivet/Coaster, satin finished, unmarked, 3", 1951
3. Trivet/Coaster, satin finished, script Hull, USA, 3", 1951
4. Trivet/Coaster, satin finished, script Hull, USA, 3", 1951
5. Poodle Planter, pink and green, unmarked, 8", 1951

Row 2: 1. Sun-Glow Pitcher, 5½"-90, 1948
2. Colt Figurine, black with pink veiling, unmarked, 5½", 1953
3. Sun-Glow Vase, 6½"-93, 1948
4. Supreme Urn, high gloss brown with red and yellow, unmarked, 6", 1960

Row 3: 1. Supreme Urn, olive green with blue, incised "7328C," unmarked, 6", 1960
2. Pitcher, embossed orchid decoration, unmarked, 8", 1960
3. Supreme Jardiniere, olive with blue, unmarked, 4¾", 1960

Row 4: 1. Supreme Pedestaled Vase, hull F30 USA, 10", 1960
2. Supreme Vase, unmarked, 12¼", 1960
3. Supreme Jug, unmarked, 9½", 1960
4. Supreme Pedestaled Vase, hull F30, USA, 10", 1960

Experimentals

PLATE 160

Row 1: 1. Fantasy Planter, unmarked olive with drip,
4½" 1958

2. Swan, unmarked, 8", heavy greens and blacks,
1953

3. Supreme Bud Vase, unmarked 8", 1960

Row 2: 1. Supreme Jardiniere, unmarked, 4¾", 1960

2. Supreme Candy dish, F27, 7", 1960

3. Supreme Footed Bowl, unmarked, 4¾", 1960

Row 3: 1. Bicentennial Shaker, unmarked, 3", 1976

2. Bicentennial Shaker, unmarked, 3", 1976

3. Baby Shoes, unmarked, 3½", 1960

4. Bicentennial Bean Pot, unmarked, 7", 1976

5. Bicentennial Covered Sugar, unmarked,
3½", 1976

6. Bicentennial Creamer, unmarked, 4", 1976

Row 4: 1. Plate, 10¼", 1967

2. Plate, 10¼", 1965

3. Plate, 10¼", 1967

318

PLATE 160

319

Greenware

DESCRIPTION:

Greenware is molded ware which is either in a fired or unfired state. Illustrated are items which made their way out of the plant and may give you an idea of the way in which items could be construed as experimental when in fact others may be "playing" at in-home kilns.

Up to 1985, most items of the described differentiation can in fact be considered experimental, showing characteristics of Hull's style and quality of work. Unclaimed molds which left the pottery account for many of the impending experimental types of wares we can expect to see on the market. Since the plant's closing, it is a known fact that hundreds of molds have been, and may continue to be in use. Not only molds, but actual Hull greenware was available to the public during the dispersal of the company. This puts an end to most items that could have been considered experimental from production years 1980 to 1985.

Some of Hull's most popular molds have been the financial gain of many a ceramic artist, but pieces typically are smaller due to the shrinkage which cannot be controlled when items are remolded from original wares. Use of Hull's actual molds would not account for this difference, and identification must be determined from clay content and weight, along with color glaze and treatment.

PLATE 161

Row 1: 1. Shaker, 3" eagle decor, mold made for Bicentennial, 1976, few were glazed and none were sold on the retail market
2. Shaker, same as above, 3", 1976
3. Planter, 7" embossed birds, unmarked, mid-1950's

Row 2: 1. Pig Bank, 3½", embossed florals, 1958
2. Mayfair Planter, 87, 10¼", 1958
3. Pig Bank, 3½", embossed florals, 1958

Row 3: 1. Pheasant Planter, 8", 1951
2. Bank, "The Little Texan", 9½", 1972, a premium made for Graham Chevrolet, Mansfield, Ohio
3. Parrot Planter, 60, 9½", 1951

Row 4: 1. Jigger bowl mold, Vegetable Pattern, No. 20-5", 1951
2. Swan, 7"
3. Jigger bowl mold, Blue Ribbon Pattern No. 1-5", 1951

Row 5: 1. "70" Swan 2-Piece Mold

PLATE 161

320

Experimentals

PLATE 162

PLATE 162
Row 1: 1. Covered Casserole, unmarked, 8½", 1945
       2. Mug, test glaze incised 6914C, 3", 1968
       3. Teapot/Jug, incised floral decor, 5", 1968
Row 2: 1. Luncheon Plate, cobalt, 8½", 1960 (Note the
          concentric ring pattern which is characteristic
          to reverse sides of many House 'n Garden
          items.)
       2. Ice Lip Pitcher, 7½", 1960
Row 3: 1. Pineapple Teapot, unmarked, 7", 1948
       2. Pineapple Cookie Jar, unmarked, 11", 1948
       3. Pineapple Pitcher, unmarked, 6½", 1948
Row 4: 1. Cinderella Blossom Plate, unmarked, 9½", 1948
       2. Cookie Jar, unmarked, 8½", 1945
       3. Cinderella Blossom Divided Plate, unmarked,
          11", 1948

Experimentals

PLATE 163

PLATE 164

Hull House 'n Garden Dinner plates were often the targets of experimentation. Company employees found it difficult to resist the squiggles they could make from the squeeze bottles of "Run down" glazes.

The incised grape decor dinnerware was trialed in 1960, at the same time The Hull Pottery was producing both Tokay and Tuscany artware lines. This experimental dinnerware, glazed in Milk White and Forest Green, was strikingly sophisticated, but was never placed on the retail market.

PLATE 163
Row 1: 1. Experimental Plate, incised grape decor, unmarked, 10½", 1960
2. Experimental Pitcher, incised grape decor, Ovenproof, USA, 8½", 1960
Row 2: 1. Experimental Coffee Mug, incised grape decor, unmarked, 3¼", 1960
2. Experimental Bowl, incised grape decor, unmarked, 5¼", 1960
3. Experimental Saucer, incised grape decor, unmarked, 6", 1960

PLATE 165
Row 1: 1. Experimental Heritageware Bowl, satin finished copper, A-1-7½", 1958
2. Experimental Glass, underglazed hand painted floral, "Jean, 1951," on reverse
3. Experimental Coffee Server, Hull Ovenproof, USA, 11", in trial turquoise, 1956
4. Experimental Glass in cobalt blue, 1980
5. Experimental Heritageware Bowl, unmarked, satin yellow, 8½", 1958
Row 2: 1. Experimental Creamer, Cinderella blank, underglazed hand decorated, 28-4½", 1948
2. Experimental Baker, Cinderella blank under glazed hand decorated, 21-8½", 1948
3. Experimental Glass in fired bisque, personally inscribed to this author, "Best of Luck Brenda, Paul Sharkey, 5-31-78." "S" incised on base
4. Experimental Plaidware Sugar, yellow with brown banding, unmarked, 3¼". 1950
5. Experimental Plaidware Creamer, yellow with brown banding, unmarked, 3". The handle was later redesigned on this piece before it was marketed, 1950
Row 3: 1. Experimental Cinderella Blossom Bowl, script Hull brown ink stamp, 6¾", 1948
2. Experimental Cinderella Blossom Creamer, 28-4½", glaze numbers, 1948
3. Experimental Cinderella Blossom Teapot, 26-42 oz, glaze numbers, 1948
4. Experimental Cinderella Blossom Covered Sugar, 27-4½", glaze numbers, 1948
5. Experimental Cinderella Blossom Bowl, script Hull brown ink stamp, 6¾", 1948

PLATE 165

Experimentals

With Hull's production of House 'n Garden casual serv-ingware spanning twenty-five years, there are no doubt several variations as far as experimentals and trials are concerned. Enough variation, at least, to make the search interesting.

The swirl dinnerware was one of the most attractive din-nerwares produced by Hull. While this grouping proves it was made in a somewhat complete set, little of it was produced, and less has survived. The raised twisted swirl pattern seems to have caught and drizzled the "run down" glaze quite effectively, and makes this color treatment even more attractive on this ware than on the plain House 'n Garden servingware pieces. The servingware shown was further accented by gold trim decor.

The cobalt blue House 'n Garden dinnerware, produced in 1960, with the use of Continental's Mountain Blue glaze, is quite attractive also. It is not known to what extent this ware was produced, however, it appears to be so few in number that it is classified as experimental.

Provincial House 'n Garden servingware was manufactured in 1961. The line itself was not experimental, but was in production not more than one year. At least twenty-three items were available, including a cookie jar. The Provincial experimentals shown on the following page have glaze number designations, and dinner plates have been found glazed in colors other than white.

PLATE 166

Row 1: 1. Corn Serving Dish, unmarked, 9½", this item is a trial piece which was later marketed in the early 1970's
2. Cobalt Saucer, Ovenproof, USA 5¾", 1960
3. Cobalt Coffee Mug, Ovenproof, USA, 3¼", 1960
4. Cobalt Luncheon Plate, Ovenproof, USA, 8½", 1960
5. Covered Sugar, unmarked, 3½", 1970
6. Creamer, styled from the coffee mug design, unmarked, 3", 1970

Row 2: 1. Bright Butterscotch Coffee Mug, hull Ovenproof, 3½" 1964
2. Bright Butterscotch Plate, hull Ovenproof, 10¼", 1964
3. Bright Butterscotch Bowl, hull Ovenproof, 5½", 1964
4. Satin Avocado with Blue Drip Coffee Mug, hull Crestone, Ovenproof, 2¾", 1968
5. Satin Avocado with Blue Drip Plate, hull Ovenproof, 10¼", 1968
6. Satin Avocado with Blue Drip Bowl, hull Ovenproof, 5¾", 1968
7. Provincial Plate, hull Ovenproof, 10¼", glaze numbers, 1961
8. Provincial Coffee Mug, Ovenproof USA, 3½", glaze numbers, 1961
9. Provincial Saucer, hull Crestone Ovenproof, 5¾", glaze numbers, 1961

Row 3: 1. Swirl Coffee Mug, unmarked, 3½", 1963
2. Swirl Bread and Butter, unmarked, 6½", 1963
3. Swirl Bowl, unmarked, 6½", 1963
4. Swirl Bowl, unmarked, 5¼", 1963
5. Swirl Plate, unmarked, 10¼", 1963
6. Swirl Mug, unmarked, 5", 1963
7. Swirl French Handled Casserole, unmarked, 7½". 1963

OVENPROOF *Provincial* SERVING WARE

Hull Pottery Company -- Crooksville, Ohio

PLATE 166

Experimentals

While Mirror Brown Bicentennial wares were never placed on the retail market, the consistency of the avocado glazed items which bear the Hull trademark leads one to believe it may have also been scheduled for marketing. The company was unable to produce this ware timely for the Nation's Bicentennial, due to the fact there were staggering numbers of back orders of House 'n Garden Mirror Brown during this same period. A brochure was designed for advertisement of the brown glazed Bicentennial ware, however, the line was shelved after a period of trial production.

The teflon-lined House 'n Garden items were not marketed. These few kitchenware items were lined, and returned to the company without further experimentation or production.

PLATE 167
Row 1: 1. Dinner Plate, incised star decoration, unmarked, 10¼"
2. Mug, incised flowers, tea kettle, bean pot, unmarked, 3¾"
3. Dinner Plate, incised rooster and weather vane decor, Ovenproof. 10¼"

PLATE 168
Row 1: 1. Square French Handled Casserole, unmarked, 7½", 1963. The square casserole was never placed on the retail market. It was molded with a deeply recessed thumb-hold for ease in handling.
2. Bud Vase, unmarked, 8¼", this trialed vase was later retailed in volume, 1970
3. Square French Handled Casserole, unmarked and unmarketed, 7½", 1963
Row 2: 1. Bicentennial Stein, hull USA, 6¼", 1976
2. Bicentennial Bowl, unmarked, 5¾", 1976
3. Bicentennial Bean Pot, hull USA, 9½", 1976
4. Bicentennial Mug, unmarked, 4", 1976
5. Bicentennial Pitcher, unmarked, 8", 1976
Row 3: 1. Teflon-line House 'n Garden French Handled Casserole, unmarked, 12", 1962
2. Teflon-lined House 'n Garden Baker, hull Ovenproof, USA, 9¾", 1962
3. Teflon-lined House 'n Garden French Handled Casserole, unmarked, 12", 1962
Row 4: 1. Bicentennial Stein, unmarked, 6¼", 1976 ·
2. Bicentennial Casserole, unmarked, 11", 1976
3. Bicentennial Pitcher, unmarked, 8", 1976
4. Stein, unmarked, 6¼", 1968
Row 5: 1. Platter, hull Ovenproof, USA, 12", 1982
2. Teflon-lined House 'n Garden pie plate, hull Ovenproof, USA, 9¼", 1962
3. Platter, hull Ovenproof, USA, 12", 1982

PLATE 167

PLATE 168

Experimentals

PLATE 169

Row 1: 1. Ashtray, unmarked, brown, red and yellow,
10¼", 1960

2. Ashtray, unmarked, red textured finish, 10¼",
1960

3. Ashtray, unmarked, green agate with turquoise,
10¼", 1960

Row 2: 1. Leaf Ashtray, unmarked, olive with red, 12½",
1960

2. Free Form Ashtray, unmarked, olive with red,
13", 1960

PLATE 170

Row 1: 1. Ashtray, white gloss textured, unmarked, 8",
1958

2. Free Form Ashtray, unmarked, 10½", 1959

Row 2: 1. Ashtray, unmarked, 8", green and blue, 1960

2. Ashtray, Woodland Jardiniere Base, W11, 5¼",
1952

3. Ashtray, incised test glaze 6636A, 8", 1960

Row 3: 1. Ashtray, unmarked, olive with blue and green,
10¼", 1959

2. Ashtray, unmarked, 12", cobalt textured finish,
1958

Row 4: 1. Ashtray, unmarked, 8", 1962

2. Ashtray/Server, unmarked, 13", 1960

3. Ashtray, unmarked, 8, 1962

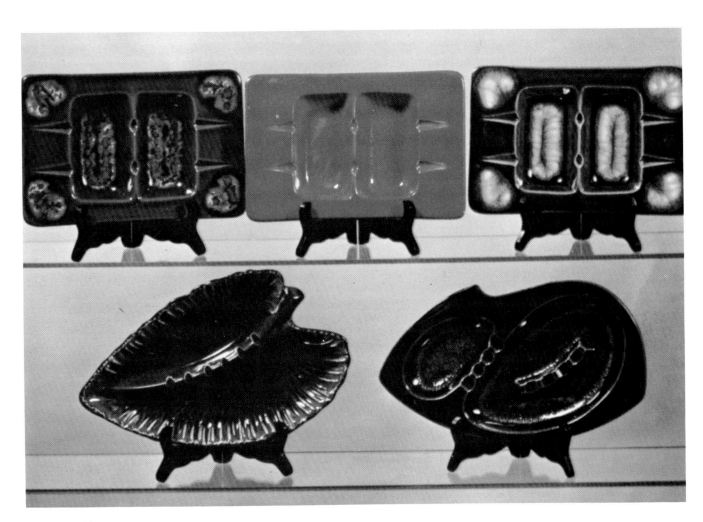

PLATE 169

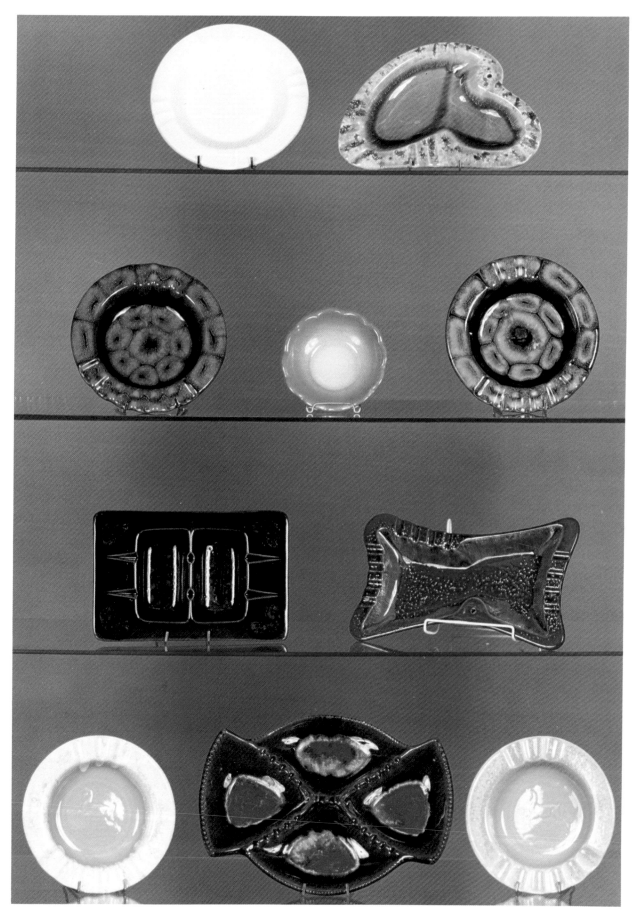

PLATE 170

329

Bibliography

Better Homes and Gardens, Hull Advertisements: February, May, October, November and December, 1946; February, April, May, August, October, and November, 1947; April, June, October, November and December, 1948; April, June, August and October, 1949; and April, 1950.

Ceramic Industry, June, 1956.

China and Pottery, 1940, St. Louis: Blackwell Wielandy Company, reprinted edition, Antiques Research Publications, Mentone, Alabama, 1968.

Columbus Evening Dispatch, "Damage Hits Millions in Wake of Cloudburst," Columbus, Ohio, June 16, 1950.

Columbus Evening Dispatch, "Crooksville Battered By Flash Flood: Woman Drowns, Fire Levels Pottery," Columbus, Ohio, June 17, 1950.

Crooks, Guy E., "*Brief History of the Pottery Industry of Crooksville 1868-1932,*" printed in booklet form, The Crooksville Messenger, Crooksville, Ohio.

Crooksville Advance, The., "The Stoneware Story," Crooksville, Ohio, 1902.

Crooksville Exempted Village Schools, "*J. Brannon Hull Scholarship Fund,*" First Edition, Crooksville, Ohio, January, 1987.

Crooksville-Roseville Area Pottery Festival, "*Crooksville Bicentennial Community,*" Official Souvenir Program, Advance Printing Co., Crooksville, Ohio, 1975, p. 24.

Crooksville-Roseville Area Pottery Festival, "*Youngest Potter to Start in Roseville,*" Official Souvenir Program, Advance Printing Co., Crooksvile, Ohio, 1971, p. 10.

Dougherty, John Wolfe, "*Pottery Made Easy,*" The Bruce Publishing Company, New York, 1939.

Encore Magazine, Ridge Collection advertisement, 1982.

Filkins, C. C., "*The China Painters, A B C,*" The Courier Company of Buffalo, New York, 1915.

Hammer, Michael L., "*History of The Hull Pottery Company,*" Crooksville-Roseville Pottery Festival, Second Annual Souvenir Program, July, 1967.

Hommel, O., company correspondence directed to W. K. McClellan, regarding crystaline glazes, Pittsburgh, PA, April 21, 1927.

Hommel, O., company correspondence directed to W. K. McClellan, regarding overglazes, Pittsburgh, PA, March 29, 1934.

House and Garden, Hull Advertisement, May, 1950.

House Beautiful, Hull Advertisements, April and May, 1947; May, 1948, and October, 1949.

Hull Pottery Company, Seniority Lists dated 1968, August 10, 1977, 1985, and others which are undated.

Huxford, Sharon and Bob, "*The Collectors Encyclopedia of Roseville Pottery,*" Collector Books, Paducah, KY, 1976.

Huxford, Sharon and Bob, "*The Collectors Encyclopedia of Weller Pottery,*" Collector Books, Paducah, KY, 1979.

Knittle, Rhea Mansfield, "*Antiques, Ohio Pottery Jars and Jugs,*" The Ohio Historical Society, Vol. XXIV, No. I, Columbus, Ohio, July, 1933.

Krause, George H., "*The Growth of Our Pottery and Tile Industry,*" Zanesville Sesquicentennial, 1797-1947, Zanesville Chamber of Commerce, October, 1947, pp. 21-25.

Lehner, Lois, "*Complete Book of American Kitchen and Dinner Wares,*" Wallace-Homestead, Des Moines, Iowa, 1980.

Lewis, Thomas W., "*A History of Southeastern Ohio and the Muskingum Valley,*" Vol. III, S. J. Clarke Publishers, Chicago, 1928.

Lewis, Thomas W., "*Zanesville and Muskingum County Ohio History,*" Volumes I and II, S. J. Clarke Publishers, Chicago, Illinois.

Lewis, Thomas W., "*Zanesville - For the Manufacturer, Merchant and Home Seeker,*" Zanesville Chamber of Commerce, Zanesville, Ohio, 1923.

Martzolff, Clement L., "*History of Perry County Ohio,*" Ward and Weiland, New Lexington, Ohio, 1902.

McCall's, Hull Shulton Old Spice Advertisement, December, 1942.

Modern Packaging Magazine, "Shulton's Old Spice," New York, September, 1953.

Muskingum County Directories, Southwestern Ohio Publishing Company, Springfield, Ohio, 1936, 1937, 1938.

Ohio Historical Society, "*Echoes, A Publication of the Ohio Historical Society,*" Vol. I, No. 11, November, 1962.

Peaslee-Gaulbert Co., General Catalog, C. T. Dearing Printing Co., Louisville, KY, 1927.

Phillips, David R., "*Finding Treasures in Your Attic,*" Lady's Circle, September, 1981, pp. 40-41, 63.

Pottery, Glass, and Brass Salesman, "A. E. Hull Cereal Sets," May 31, 1917, p. 16.

Rickett, Beth, "*A. E. Hull Started Pottery in 1907,*" The Times Recorder, Zanesville, Ohio, February 9, 1991.

Roberts, Brenda, "*Family Tradition Ends ... Hull Pottery Closes,*" American Clay Exchange, El Cajon, CA, August 30, 1986.

Roberts, Brenda, "*Hull Art Pottery: Rosella,*" The Collector, Heyworth, Illinois, March, 1981.

Roberts, Brenda, "*Hull Headlines: Banking Your Investment,*" The Glaze, Springfield, MO, May and June, 1980.

Roberts, Brenda, "*Hull Headlines: House 'n Garden,*" The Glaze, Springfield, MO, July, 1980.

Roberts, Brenda, "*Hull Headlines: Jarring Update,*" The Glaze, Springfield, MO, October, 1980.

Roberts, Brenda, "*Hull Headlines: Nuline Bak-Serve,*" The Glaze, Springfield, MO, December, 1980.

Roberts, Brenda, "*Hull Headlines: Old Spice Product Containers,*" The Glaze, Springfield, MO, August, 1980.

Roberts, Brenda, "*Hull Headlines: Rainbow and Crestone Dinnerwares,*" The Glaze, Springfield, MO, November,

1980.

Roberts, Brenda, "*Hull Headlines: Rosella,*" The Glaze, Springfield, MO, September, 1980.

Roberts, Brenda, "*Hull Pottery: Behind the Lines,*" The Antique Trader Weekly, Dubuque, Iowa, March 4, 1981.

Roberts, Brenda, "*Hull Pottery Closes,*" The Antique Trader Weekly, August, 1986.

Roberts, Brenda, "*Hull Pottery Closes, An End to a Family Tradition,*" The Collector, Heyworth, Illinois, September, 1986.

Roberts, Brenda, "*Hull Pottery: Closing Doused Family Tradition,*" Antique Week, Knightstown, IN, September 22, 1986.

Roberts, Brenda, "*Hull Pottery: Cookie Collecting,*" American Clay Exchange, El Cajon, CA, March 1981.

Roberts, Brenda, "*Hull Pottery Old Spice Product Containers,*" The Collector, Heyworth, Illinois, December, 1980.

Roberts, Brenda, Personal Collection of Hull Company Brochures, Price Lists, Original Company Correspondence, Photographs of Employees and Plant Operations.

Roberts, Brenda, Personal Collection of notebooks encompassing glaze and body formulas of Ceramic Engineers, William K. McClellen and Edgar McClellan.

Roberts, Brenda, Personal Interviews and/or Correspondence: J. B. Hull, Robert W. Hull, Byron Hull, Louise Bauer, William Callihan, Larry Taylor, Marlin King, Jack Frame, Harold Showers, Douglas Young, Gene Whitlatch, Edgar McClellan, Granville Shafer, Daine Neff, Esta Marshall, Gladys Showers, Helen Aichele, Marie Bradshaw, Hattie Sturgill, Bernice Walpole, Lois Lee, Russell Lee, Elsie Robinson, Isabella Dusenberry, Gene Dusenberry and Paul Sharkey.

Roberts, Brenda, "*The Collector's Encyclopedia of Hull Pottery,*" Collector Books, Paducah, KY, 1980.

Schneider, Norris F., "*Clay Industry,*" Zanesville Times Signal, Zanesville, Ohio, November 3, 1957.

Schneider, Norris F., "*Decorative Tile,*" Zanesville Times Recorder, Zanesville, Ohio, May 21, 1972.

Schneider, Norris F., "*Hull Pottery,*" Zanesville Times Recorder, Zanesville, Ohio, April 25, 1965.

Schneider, Norris F., "*Potter's Alley,*" Zanesville Times Signal, Zanesville, Ohio, November 16, 1958.

Schneider, Norris F., "*Roseville Grew Rapidly During 1890 Boom,*" Sunday Times Signal, Zanesville, Ohio, August 2, 1959.

Schneider, Norris F., "*Shawnee Pottery,*" Zanesville Times Recorder, Zanesville, Ohio, October 16, 1960.

Schneider, Norris F., "*Zanesville Art Pottery,*" published by author, Zanesville, Ohio, 1963.

Shawnee Pottery Company, "*Shawnee Pottery Company Prospectus,*" Zanesville, Ohio, May 6, 1937.

Shulton Company Catalogues, "*Early American Toiletries, Old Spice,*" Shulton, New Jersey, 1938, 1939, 1940 and 1942.

Smith, Marvin E., "*Cue Sheet, National Association of Variety Stores,*" Inc., Chicago, Illinois, April, 1972.

Supnick, Mark E., "*Collecting Hull Pottery's Little Red Riding Hood,*" L-W Book Sales, Gas City, IN, 1989.

Taylor, Robert Hull, "*Hulls in 1850, A Directory of Persons Surnamed Hull in the U. S. in 1850,*" Gateway Press, Inc., Baltimore, MD, 1983.

United States Patent and Trademark Office, "Little Red Riding Hood," Washington, D. C., 1943.

Zanesville, Ohio, Bell Telephone Company Directory, 1922.

Zanesville Times Recorder, "Perry County Towns Flooded," Zanesville, Ohio, June 17, 1950.

Zanesville Times Recorder, "Morale Mounting in Flooded Areas," Zanesville, Ohio, June 20, 1965.

Zanesville Times Recorder, "Ship Pottery From Crooksville," Zanesville, Ohio, June 23, 1950.

Zanesville Times Recorder, "Stricken Villages Clean Up Flood Debris," Zanesville, Ohio, June 19, 1950.

Index

Notes

Notes